The Power Game

About the first edition
'This book is a fascinating account of the dramatic aspects of
Fianna Fáil politics in the past 40 years'
Ryle Dwyer THE IRISH EXAMINER

'There is plenty of new material, incisive comment and
considered judgement to make this a book to be read'
Brian Farrell THE SUNDAY TRIBUNE

'An invaluable primer to the period which not only sums up all
we know but provides an important new evidential framework
which helps to explain many of the connections'
John Horgan THE IRISH TIMES

'Stephen Collins writes in a lively, readable style ...
an excellent and at times entertaining read'
Bruce Arnold IRISH INDEPENDENT

'Bertie Ahern is brilliantly captured in Stephen Collins's
superb book about Fianna Fáil since Lemass'
Fergus Finlay, THE IRISH EXAMINER

Stephen Collins is the Political Editor of the *Sunday Tribune*. He was educated at Oatlands College, Mount Merrion, and University College Dublin, where he graduated with an MA in Politics. His career in journalism began with the Irish Press Group and he has been covering Irish politics for nearly two decades. A frequent contributor to radio and television programmes, he is also the author of *The Haughey File*, *Spring and the Labour Story* and *The Cosgrave Legacy*. He is married, with three children, and lives in Dublin.

THE POWER GAME

Ireland under Fianna Fáil

Stephen Collins

THE O'BRIEN PRESS
DUBLIN

This updated edition first published 2001
by The O'Brien Press Ltd,
20 Victoria Road, Dublin 6, Ireland.
Tel. +353 1 4923333; Fax. +353 1 4922777
E-mail books@obrien.ie
Website www.obrien.ie
First published in hardback 2000.

ISBN: 0-86278-720-3

British Library Cataloguing-in-Publication Data
Collins, Stephen, 1951 June 22-
The party of power
1.Fianna Fail 2.Ireland - Politics and government -
1949-
I.Title
324.2'417'03

2   3   4   5   6   7   8   9   10
01   02   03   04   05   06   07

The O'Brien Press receives
assistance from
The Arts Council
An Chomhairle Ealaíon

PHOTOGRAPHS
The author and publisher thank the *Irish Indpendent*
and the *Sunday Tribune* for permission to use
photographs.

Editing, typesetting, layout, design: The O'Brien Press
Colour separations: C&A Print Services Ltd.
Printing: Leinster Leader

CONTENTS

DEDICATION
For Eoin, Niamh and Catherine

ACKNOWLEDGEMENTS

I would like to thank all the people who helped me in the preparation of this book, particularly the politicians and journalists, some currently working others retired, who generously gave up their time to talk to me about the period. I would also like to thank the staff of the Oireachtas Library, the National Library and UCD Archive Department for their unfailing courtesy; Bea McMunn of the *Sunday Tribune* and Lorraine Curran, librarian at the *Irish Independent,* for their help in assembling a wonderful collection of photographs and Paul Dunne, chief news editor, for permission to use the *Independent* archive.

A special word of thanks is due to Des Fisher, who read the book in draft stage and made many valuable suggestions as well as editing the text with meticulous attention to detail. Others, including my wife Jean, also read the draft, gave helpful advice and corrected errors. The mistakes that remain are entirely my own responsibility. I would also like to thank Michael O'Brien and Íde ní Laoghaire of O'Brien Press for prodding me into attempting this project.

INTRODUCTION

THE SERIES OF SCANDALS WHICH CONVULSED FIANNA FÁIL at the turn of the millennium had its genesis in the leadership struggle which followed the decision of Seán Lemass to step down as party leader in November 1966. With Lemass's departure, the generation which had taken part in the 1916 Rising and which had established Fianna Fáil after defeat in the Civil War finally relinquished control of the party.

Since its foundation Fianna Fáil had been a stable, monolithic institution which came to dominate Irish politics. Its first leader, Eamon de Valera, remained at the helm for more than 30 years and while Lemass led for just seven there was a seamless transition from one to the other. After Lemass the unity of purpose which had characterised the party for its first 40 years disappeared.

In the process, Fianna Fáil – ironically itself the product of a split in the old Sinn Féin party – was itself to divide. But while the 1926 split which created Fianna Fáil founded a strong, modern party whose early leaders had an enviable record of electoral success, the 1985 departure of Desmond O'Malley and the foundation of the Progressive Democrats provided dramatic evidence of a sickness at the heart of the organisation – though it did not cure it.

One reason for the loss of Fianna Fáil's original unity of purpose was a growing sense of frustration that, after almost half a century of partition and the failure of all attempts to undo it, the reunification of the country was, if anything, further away than ever from realisation. Lemass had tried to break the confrontational pattern of de Valera's northern policy but his 'hands across the Border' approach had only hardened Unionist hostility and inflamed the republican sympathies of a minority in his own party. The outbreak of the troubles in 1968 would precipitate a major rift among its members as moderates and militants pursued very different ends.

Another factor was even more significant. Because they had not shared the experiences of the founding fathers, the younger members of the parliamentary party, most of whom had come into the Dáil from 1957 onwards, had not been inculcated with the same values and sense of commitment that animated their elders. On the positive side, some of this new generation brought no civil war baggage with them and were content to follow the Lemass policy of a peaceful approach to the Northern problem and all that it entailed for politics in the south. Nevertheless, some younger TDs did not possess the same sense of selfless service to the state, the frugal lifestyle and the high ideals of the Free State's early leaders for whom politics was a way to serve others. For them, politics offered a way to power, privilege and wealth. By the end of the century, their pursuit of mercenary ends was to bring themselves, their party and Irish politics as a whole into disrepute.

The combination of these factors left the party open to divisive and corrupting influences from within. Had it been able to maintain the strong leadership and unity of purpose which marked its first 40 years, it would have been able to defeat the dangers quickly and easily. As it was, Lemass's resignation precipitated the first leadership challenge in the history of the party. For the rest of the twentieth century, the party was riven by factionalism and bitter personal rivalries that saw one leader after another overthrown by his successor.

Lemass himself had long been regarded as de Valera's natural successor and he took over without missing a step. When his own turn came to go, there was no agreed replacement, mainly because the two or three Ministers he had encouraged to put their names forward were unwilling to stand. In the end, Jack Lynch, the most diffident of the leading figures, was persuaded to take the job and turned out to be a leader in the honourable tradition of his two predecessors.

It was in Lynch's term of office that the destructive elements in the party began to combine into an explosive mixture. The spark that touched off the explosion which almost wrecked the party and the stability of the state was the plot to import arms to help the Provisional IRA in Northern Ireland. In his finest hour, Jack Lynch managed to hold the centre against the forces of anarchy. Ironically, he was to be succeeded as party leader in office by Charles Haughey, the very man who had precipitated the crisis and who was to become Taoiseach and lead four governments in the years ahead.

Although there have been four Fianna Fáil Taoisigh since Lemass – Lynch, Haughey, Albert Reynolds and Bertie Ahern – the figure who dominated the party for the entire period, down to the opening of the new millennium, was Haughey. The nationalist credentials he earned in the course of the arms crisis cost him his position in 1970 but they were later to commend him to the party's grassroots and lead to his taking it over in 1979. Other leaders like Lynch and Reynolds had, arguably, greater achievements to their credit but Haughey's grip on the party's imagination was far greater than theirs. He was the central figure in a process that saw the party gradually permeated by a culture of venality and lies. It is only in the recent years that the full extent of the corruption he engendered has been exposed in the various judicial tribunals set up in the 1990s.

Despite the internal dissension of the past three decades and the corrupt practices which were being brought to light at the turn of the century, Fianna Fáil has remained the dominant political force in the country, a position it first obtained in 1932, six years after its foundation. At the beginning of the new millennium, despite all the revelations about the vast amounts of money that Haughey took from wealthy businessmen and the similar behaviour of some of his leading ministers, Fianna Fáil remains the largest political party in the country. The party's resilience is the most extraordinary feature of Irish political history since independence.

The secret of its success has been that, from an early stage, it created an image of itself as being a national movement and not just a political party. De Valera famously remarked: 'Whenever I wanted to know what the Irish people wanted, I had only to examine my own heart.' His followers also came to regard themselves as the only true representatives of the Irish people. Everyone else was suspect. The lingering effects of that belief have sustained the party through all the crises of the past 30 years and still appear to have some potency in the new millennium.

This book aims to describe the vicissitudes of the party from Lemass's resignation in 1966 to the present day and to throw light on the events which marked these turbulent years. It traces the struggle for power between rival individuals and rival factions within Fianna Fáil and the process by which the values and ideals of the party's founders were made subservient to the ambitions of one man, Charles J. Haughey. For background on the earlier period I interviewed a number of politicians who played a part in the events of the 1960s and 1970s and consulted the available government archives to trace the origins and development of the arms crisis. The incidents described in the last two decades are based on personal experiences reporting on politics firstly for the *Irish Press* group and then the *Sunday Tribune*. I have used my own diary entries and newspaper reports as source material along with the published accounts of some of the key participants.

The half-century which this book covers has seen some of the most momentous events in the country's history – the arms crisis of 1970, the accession of Haughey to power in 1979, the year of GUBU in 1982, the formation of the Progressive Democrats in 1985, the conversion of Fianna Fáil to fiscal rectitude in 1987, the presidential election campaign of 1990, the development of the peace process throughout the 1990s. The most extraordinary development of all, however, has been the work of the judicial tribunals which have lifted the lid on the seamy connections between Irish politics and business. They have exposed a network of corruption, which developed during the Haughey era, that was far deeper and more extensive than even his most bitter opponents had ever believed.

I
EARLY DAYS

1. THE FOUNDING FATHERS

FIANNA FÁIL WAS BORN ON 16 MAY 1926 in the La Scala Theatre (now Penney's) in the centre of Dublin when Eamon de Valera and the trusted band of comrades who had left Sinn Féin with him two months earlier launched a new political movement. The party, formed from one faction of the defeated side in the Civil War which had ended only three years earlier, managed in just a few years to become the dominant political force in Ireland, a position it was to retain for the rest of the twentieth century.

Some of the key reasons for its success can be traced back to that first meeting. For a start there was the party's name. Fianna Fáil had all sorts of mythic and mystical connotations which clearly struck a chord with a significant section of the Irish people. Seán Lemass, ever the pragmatist, wanted to call the new organisation simply The Republican Party, but de Valera would have none of it. For him the name had other, more important, attractions: it echoed the golden age of Finn Mac Cumhail and the Fianna and, as Dev himself wryly observed, it was nearly impossible to translate. Forging links with a mythical past was a crucial element in the success of a party founded in the bitter years when the hangover of the civil war still cast a pall over the country. De Valera also saw initial merit in the name Fianna Fáil because it was a title used by the Irish Volunteers after the split with Redmond in 1913 and he liked the suggestion of continuity. The Republican Party was tagged on as a subsidiary title to cover all the bases.[1]

De Valera was lucky that the group of young men who left Sinn Féin with him in March 1926, in frustration with the majority's policy of abstentionism, contained some of the most dynamic figures from the struggle for independence. In addition to himself and Lemass, the founding fathers were Frank Aiken, Seán MacEntee, Gerry Boland, James Ryan, Seán T. O'Kelly and P.J. Ruttledge who would form the core of successive Fianna Fáil governments for almost 30 years. De Valera at 44 was the elder statesman in the group, with the majority being young men in their late twenties. Despite their youth (Lemass was 26 and Aiken 28), most were battle-hardened veterans who had come through the furnace of the War of Independence and the Civil War. Lemass was de Valera's right-hand man from the beginning and after the split with Sinn Féin played a decisive role in persuading 'the Chief' (de Valera) not to retire from politics. Aiken, the former chief of staff of the IRA who had ended the Civil War with his order to dump arms, was another strong personality who would play a senior role in politics for the next four decades and more. MacEntee, a formidable political debater with a fine intellect, had been a poet in his younger days while Boland came from an old Fenian family and his brother Harry was one of the republican martyrs of the Civil War.

With other prominent figures like Ryan, O'Kelly and Ruttledge, these men wasted no time putting an organisation in place. 'In a Baby Austin car, on bicycles and on foot, they travelled the country both before and after the inaugural meeting, constantly arguing the case for their New Departure, this time to be the final push for Ireland's freedom.'[2] The first wave of recruits on whom they depended was made up of former comrades from the IRA. Many of these men and women had abandoned Sinn Féin after the Civil War and were motivated to get involved in Fianna Fáil by the prospect of practical political progress rather than floundering in endless political theorising. To retain the loyalty of his old supporters, however, de Valera continued to speak in the language the IRA understood. 'I have never said, and I am not going to say now, that force is not a legitimate weapon for a nation to use in striving to win its freedom,' he proclaimed.[3] In Tim Pat Coogan's words, de Valera 'brought to a fine art the process of acting constitutionally while cloaking his actions in revolutionary rhetoric.'[4] Lemass famously summed up the situation by saying that Fianna Fáil was 'a slightly constitutional party'.

The timing of Fianna Fáil's launch was ideal, as it came shortly after widespread disillusionment with the Cosgrave Government because of the Boundary Commission report which effectively copper-fastened partition. Before the La Scala meeting de Valera outlined five principles on which the party would be based; they formed the core values of Fianna Fáil and the inspiration for its members for more than half a century. Those five aims were:

1 Securing the political independence of a united Ireland as a republic

2 The restoration of the Irish language and the development of a native Irish culture

3 The development of a social system in which, as far as possible, equal opportunity would be afforded to every Irish citizen to live a noble and useful Christian life

4 The distribution of the land of Ireland so as to get the greatest possible number of Irish families rooted in the soil of Ireland

5 The making of Ireland an economic unit, as self-contained and

self-sufficient as possible, with a proper balance between agriculture and other essential industries.'[5]

This mixture of lofty aspirations and practical policies proved to be a very potent political formula. Ironically, the two central principles – a united Ireland and the restoration of the Irish language – have so far proved to be unattainable, while the more prosaic elements of the party's programme were substantially implemented. Yet in a curious way it was precisely the apparently unattainable nature of the twin national aims, as they came to be called, that made them so potent. Over the succeeding decades the party was able to present itself as a movement constantly striving to implement these ideals. In the eyes of its supporters Fianna Fáil became not simply a political party but a national movement. This enabled it to harness their idealism and give a great many people a new pride in their identity. Many joined the party and served it through thick and thin from a sense of duty to their country.

On the negative side, this led to an arrogant dismissal of political opponents as being less than truly Irish. Fine Gael was scorned as the party of the 'West Brits' and Labour denounced as a socialist menace. This approach was articulated by the *Irish Press*, the newspaper founded by de Valera, in a blunt fashion. 'Free speech was governed by certain conditions, one of which was that no party advocating foreign domination was entitled in any country to misguide the people.'[6]

At the first meeting in the La Scala theatre, de Valera gave a hostage to fortune on one issue – the oath of allegiance that Dáil deputies had to take to the British monarch – which threatened to strangle the new party at birth. Despite the best efforts of the negotiators to dilute it the oath had been included in the Treaty settlement and it was the principal reason for the Civil War. It had later figured in de Valera's decision to leave Sinn Féin, the issue on which he split the party being whether it would abandon its policy of abstentionism and take seats in the Dáil if the oath were removed.[7] The nature of the oath itself remained a problem for the new party. De Valera declared: 'The question is raised whether this oath is really an oath at all in the theological sense ... For me it is enough that it is called an oath officially and that it begins with "I do solemnly swear" and that, whenever it suits, it will be held to be an oath by those who impose it and will be so understood by the world.'[8]

A little over a year later, de Valera swallowed his words and took the hated oath. The occasion came in the aftermath of the 1927 general election in which Fianna Fáil, just over a year after its foundation, did unexpectedly well, winning 44 seats, only three less than W.T. Cosgrave's Cumann na nGaedheal. De Valera tried to lead his party into the Dáil without taking the oath but the doors were shut in their faces. He then attempted to organise a petition calling for a referendum on removing the oath from the Free State Constitution. The tactic might or might not have succeeded but it was swept away in the backlash from the assassination of the dynamic Minister for Justice, Kevin O'Higgins, by IRA men acting on their own initiative. Cosgrave seized the opportunity to introduce new security measures and an Electoral Amendment Act requiring all candidates for the Dáil to give an advance pledge to take their seats if elected. Essentially he gave de Valera a choice – take the oath and enter democratic politics fully or stay outside on the margins as Sinn Féin had done. Pragmatism won the day. Describing the oath as an 'empty formula', de Valera led his followers into the Dáil, put the bible aside but signed his name under the oath.

Inevitably, their action was criticised by both their former Sinn Féin comrades and by their Cumann na nGaedheal opponents as hypocritical double-speak. It did, however, serve a good purpose in that it brought Fianna Fáil into the democratic system. By entering the Dáil in 1927 Fianna Fáil managed to harness the enthusiasm and idealism of the radicals and of many republicans while convincing the suspicious middle-ground voters that they were a safe democratic party. On the negative side, the verbal gymnastics involved meant that, if political circumstances required, meanings could be turned on their head to suit the exigencies of the situation.

Following its entry into the Dáil, Fianna Fáil's march towards power continued. In the second election of 1927 it still did not succeed in getting into Government but its number of seats increased significantly to 57 and for the next five years it became an increasingly confident Opposition in the Dáil. In the run up to the 1932 election Fianna Fáil leaders placed at least as much emphasis on the need for social and economic change as they did on the twin national aims. 'Political freedom is regarded by me simply as a means and purpose to a greater end beyond it,' said de Valera. 'It is the primary duty of any government in any civilised country to see that men and women will not starve, that little children will not starve, through opportunity for work being deprived to the breadwinner.'[9] Over the next few years a range of policies was developed which stressed the party's commitment to increased employment and a fairer distribution of wealth. Economic protectionism was offered as the panacea which would bring these socially desirable goals into existence.

A related issue, which proved important in winning support from farmers, was a commitment not to pay the land annuities to the British Government. These were repayments which farmers were obliged to make for land purchased with British Government loans under the various Land Acts. Abolition of these mortgage payments was naturally an attractive proposition for farmers who did not bother to look at the small print of de Valera's argument. In fact, he proposed not that the annuities be abolished but that the money should be paid into the Irish exchequer rather than into the British one.

As well as popular policies de Valera was keenly aware of another necessary ingredient for political success – good propaganda. As early as 1924 he identified effective publicity as the key to electoral success. Commenting on the Cosgrave Government's lack of skills in this regard he said, 'They have no publicity department worth talking of. Any Government that desires to hold power in Ireland should put publicity before all.'[10] Feeling that he was not getting fair treatment in the pro-government newspapers de Valera founded his own, the *Irish Press*, in 1931. Whether it represented 'the truth in the news' as its masthead proclaimed or was an Irish *Pravda* as its opponents claimed, the *Irish Press* provided a powerful battering ram for Fianna Fáil and helped to sour the political atmosphere for an already beleaguered government.

The general election of 1932 marked one of the political turning points of twentieth-century Ireland. Six years after its foundation Fianna Fáil was ready for office. Cumann na nGaedheal had been in power for ten difficult years and, while by any standards Cosgrave and his government had done a remarkable job in laying the foundations of a democratic state, the voters wanted change. Fianna Fáil put forward a series of policies which matched the public mood and contrasted with the austerity promised by the government. The party also developed a superb organisation and had the open support of the IRA which added a bit of muscle to intimidate opponents.

By contrast Cumann na nGaedheal had a poor organisation and relied on the support of local notables rather than a strong local organisation. It did come up with some inspired negative propaganda but that was not enough to make up for the deficiencies in organisation and policies. 'The Shadow of a Gunman – Keep it from your Door,' read one anti-Fianna Fáil election poster while a newspaper advertisement read: 'The gunmen are voting Fianna Fáil, the Communists are voting Fianna Fáil.' The most famous Cumann na nGaedheal poster of all read: 'Devvy's Circus, absolutely the greatest road show in Ireland today – Señor de Valera, world famous illusionist, oath swallower and escapologist. See his renowned act: Escaping from the straitjacket of the republic. Frank F. Aiken, fearsome fire-eater. Shaunty O'Kelly, the man in dress clothes. Monsieur Lemass, famous tight rope performer, see him cross from the Treaty to the Republic every night. Performing frogs, champion croakers, marvellous trained sheep.'[11]

The insults did nothing to halt the Fianna Fáil bandwagon. Even the

Catholic Church, which had excommunicated de Valera and his followers during the Civil War, quickly established good relations with Fianna Fáil. Some of the bishops and many parish priests continued to support Cosgrave but the curates tended to support Fianna Fáil. De Valera even had backers among the hierarchy and at senior levels in Rome. Seán MacEntee boasted after the election that Fianna Fáil had won the Catholic vote.[12] In the event the party increased its number of seats to 72 and was by far the biggest party in the Dáil. De Valera was elected Taoiseach with the support of the Labour Party and he was to govern without interruption for the next 16 years. On taking office he gratified his supporters by cutting the salaries of TDs and ministers. Along with his ministers he also refused to wear the top hat and frock coat which were regarded as the appropriate garb for formal occasions. Such populist touches endeared him to ordinary voters frustrated that independence had made no real difference to their lives.

At the first party Árd Fheis after the election de Valera encapsulated his party's appeal. Summoning up the dead generations and focusing on the near mystical aspiration of a united Irish republic, as well as on the practical programme of government, he said: 'It may not be given to us in our time to see the end, but the young faces that I see here are pledged to the day when the work so many died to accomplish will pass into good hands if we fail.'[13] The emphasis on the unattainable national ideal gave Dev a powerful weapon to motivate his party over the decades that followed.

On the political front, de Valera moved immediately after his election to implement his political programme by abolishing the oath, introducing tariffs and refusing to pay the land annuities to the British exchequer. The result was the economic war with Britain which had a devastating effect on the Irish economy but which was politically beneficial for Fianna Fáil. The wave of nationalist fervour that followed the beginning of this war and Britain's imposition of tariffs on Irish exports encouraged de Valera to go to the country again in January 1933. During the campaign he promised to halve the land annuities. The outcome was a clear victory for Fianna Fáil, giving it an overall majority and enabling it to dispense with the support of the Labour Party.

During the 1930s, Fianna Fáil pursued protectionist policies and tried, with limited success, to develop a native manufacturing base behind tariff walls. The Economic War benefited the party, even if it damaged the country. One stern critic of Fianna Fáil from a later period, the Fine Gael politician John Kelly, believed that the economic war showed de Valera at his best. 'His truculence and his profession of Irish interests, even though perhaps wrong, did embody a certain sense of pride and self-respect and I admired him for that.'[14] The electorate clearly admired him for it as well because in these years Fianna Fáil became entrenched as the dominant political force in the country. The old ruling Cumann na nGaedheal party and its conservative allies fractured under the strain in opposition, later coming together again as Fine Gael – but the party was never able to match the appeal of Fianna Fáil.

Fianna Fáil's strength was based on the combination of nationalist rhetoric and policies aimed at improving the lot of working people and, while the policies did not always succeed, they reinforced Fianna Fáil's image as the people's party. The new industrial jobs which emerged behind the shelter of protectionism, big slum clearance projects and the building of new local authority housing schemes, the establishment of semi-state companies like Bord na Móna all combined to reinforce the party's power base. In 1932 the party's heartland was the west of Ireland with its small farms, but during the decade it managed to expand that base into all the big urban centres including Dublin.

De Valera's appeal to a significant portion of the Irish electorate is captured in the vision he expounded during a St Patrick's Day radio broadcast in 1943. 'That Ireland which we have dreamed of would be the home of a people who valued material wealth only as the basis of right living, of a people who were satisfied with the frugal comforts and devoted their leisure to the things of the spirit – a land whose countryside would be bright with cosy homesteads, whose fields and villages would be joyous with the sounds of industry, with the romping of sturdy children, the contests of athletic youth and the laughter of comely maidens, whose firesides would be the forums for the wisdom of serene old age. It would, in a word, be the home of a people living the life that God desires that a man should live.'[15]

In later years it became fashionable to sneer at this vision of the good life. While it is certainly true that tens of thousands of people voted with their feet and left for England rather than live in frugal comfort in Ireland, Dev's vision has to be considered in the context of the times. What is almost invariably overlooked by those who sneer at it is that at the time de Valera made his remarks most democracies had fallen under the yoke of fascism or communism. De Valera's vision may seem quaint today but it was a benign one, particularly when compared to the political madness of right and left that engulfed most of Europe in the 1930s and 1940s. De Valera, like W.T. Cosgrave before him, presided over a democratic state and did what had to be done, including executing old republican comrades, to ensure that liberal democratic values were preserved. Because he succeeded, that achievement is taken for granted, but it should never be underestimated.

De Valera was confident enough to write his own constitution in 1937 and to pursue a policy of neutrality during the Second World War. He was also confident enough to confront the threat to the state posed by Sinn Féin and the IRA who allied themselves with the Nazi war effort. The Minister for Justice, Gerry Boland, spearheaded the drive against the IRA and proved every bit as ruthless as Kevin O'Higgins in the 1920s. 'By 1944 the crushing of the IRA was almost complete. At least 16 active republicans had been hanged, shot or executed by this time in the 26-county area,' according to an informed republican source.[16] The way the republican threat to democracy was defeated proved once and for all that Fianna Fáil had become a totally constitutional party. There was still considerable residual sympathy for the ultimate aim of the republican movement – a united Ireland – but not if that involved a confrontation with the Irish Government. By the early 1940s republicans were left in no doubt at all that if they challenged the institutions of the 26-county state, Fianna Fáil under de Valera would use the apparatus of the state to defend the rule of law. The Offences Against the State Act of 1939 gave the government sweeping powers to deal with subversives and it used those powers, including internment without trial, military tribunals and the death penalty to defeat the IRA.

De Valera governed without interruption from 1932 until 1948 when virtually all the Opposition forces in the Dáil combined to form the first Inter-Party Government. Dev bounced back in 1951 and, while he lost again in 1954, he returned to office in 1957. It was the beginning of another 16 years of uninterrupted power for Fianna Fáil. De Valera maintained an extraordinary grip on power even though the economic policies pursued by his governments led to a slow but steady erosion of economic well-being. The Irish standard of living dropped significantly by comparison with every other West European country between 1922 and 1970.[17] While the rest of the western world enjoyed an unprecedented economic boom in the 1950s, Ireland continued to stagnate. De Valera's major failure was undoubtedly his government's inability to deal with the economic problems which gripped the country, particularly after 1945, and triggered another wave of mass emigration. By the late 1950s emigration was threatening to undermine the confidence of the people in the notion of Irish independence.

It was not until de Valera relinquished the Taoiseach's office in 1959 and went for the Presidency that things began to change. Seán Lemass, who succeeded to the leadership, immediately set about dismantling the protectionist system he himself had created as Dev's long-serving Minister for Industry and Commerce. Lemass was lucky that when he took over the reins of power the most remarkable Irish public servant of the twentieth century, T.K. Whitaker, had been installed in the top job at the Department of Finance. Whitaker was one of the truly great figures of independent Ireland. Promoted as Secretary of the Department of Finance in 1956 at the very young age of 39 by a Fine Gael-Labour government, he saw the crying need for a reversal of economic policy. Ironically, his initial battle was trying to persuade Lemass at the Department of Industry and Commerce to begin dismantling protection. The minister and his officials resisted the erosion of their power base far more furiously than Irish manufacturers objected to the break-up of the protective barriers that sustained them. Once Lemass took over as Taoiseach his attitude underwent a sea change under the influence of Whitaker. 'The historic task of this generation is to ensure the economic foundations of independence,' Lemass proclaimed in 1959 as he proceeded to dismantle protectionism and open up free trade. The combination of Lemass and Whitaker changed the face of Ireland in a few short years. The first *Programme for Economic Expansion* was published and the country began belatedly to participate in the world economic boom. Tax incentives were introduced to encourage foreign investment and, even more crucially, the importance of education was identified as the key to the future. Later, the swashbuckling Minister for Education, Donogh O'Malley, introduced free secondary schooling and the numbers participating in second-level education increased dramatically.

Fianna Fáil reinforced its hold on power as it became identified as the party which had finally brought economic success to the country. To the twin virtues of nationalism and social concern it had added another – the perception of the party as the one best fitted to run the economy. This combination of factors gave Fianna Fáil another 16-year unbroken spell in government from 1957 to 1973.

Lemass was a much more prosaic and practical figure than de Valera. He did not indulge in flamboyant gestures but he commanded the total loyalty of his supporters. He was known as 'The Boss' rather than 'The Chief' and it was altogether more appropriate to his style. Yet there was a strong emphasis on personality. 'Let Lemass Lead On' was the Fianna Fáil election slogan in 1965 with the stress on the personality of the leader. By comparison, the other parties had slogans which reflected a theme rather than an individual.

It is currently fashionable to dismiss the first 40 years of Irish independence as a complete failure while regarding the second 40 years, beginning with Lemass, as a resounding success. Just as it is far too simplistic to underestimate the achievements of the first four decades, it is equally wrong to paint too rosy a picture of what came afterwards. One feature of Fianna Fáil that came hand-in-hand with the modernisation of the party was the gradual flowering of a culture of corruption whose extent is still being revealed. From the beginning of the 1960s boom, unhealthily close links were forged between the party and Ireland's business elite. This was not entirely new, of course. From the beginning the party did not hesitate to seek financial support from businessmen who might benefit from its policies and in 1926 wrote to 200 or so 'wealthy friends' asking them for money. Gerry Boland bemoaned the influx of big contributions from business as early as the 1930s. When a subscription of £500 came from Joe McGrath, a former Cumann na nGaedheal TD and minister in 1931, Boland wanted to send it back. However, he was over-ruled by the Fianna Fáil national executive on the advice of Lemass.[18] By the early 1960s the links between the party and business had become a bit too close for comfort, even in the eyes of many of its own supporters. The establishment of an organisation called Taca institutionalised the links between Fianna Fáil and business, particularly the building industry. Another by-product of the commitment to business was a proudly philis-tine attitude towards the destruction of Ireland's urban heritage. Many of Dublin's Georgian architectural treasures were demolished with the con-nivance of the authorities in the 1960s.

These negative features of the party would later become spectacu-larly intertwined in the character of one man who would come to domi-nate Fianna Fáil, just as de Valera had done. However, in the party in the early 1960s, they were counterbalanced by the values of loyalty and ideal-ism which continued to inspire leading figures and ordinary members alike. The trouble was that the party's values always had the potential for perversion in the wrong hands. Loyalty was a natural product of the par-ty's history but in time it could lead to jobbery. The motto 'all things being equal, the Fianna Fáil man gets the job,' is attributed to a number of lead-ing figures including Seán Moylan and Donogh O'Malley, and it undoubt-edly reflected a cast of mind which had become established at certain levels in the party. There might have been some justification for it in the circumstances of the 1930s, when the party represented the have-nots, but increasingly in the 1960s it became a cloak for something else.

Another important change during the Lemass era was the redefini-tion of the first national aim. Just as he did in economic matters, Lemass abandoned a political policy that was patently not working. De Valera had denounced partition for 40 years, but far from doing any good all his vari-ous anti-partition campaigns did was to reinforce the border and drive North and South farther apart. Lemass challenged Dev's simplistic anti-partitionism, which was so attractive to many members of the party, by travelling to Northern Ireland to meet the premier of the six-county state, Terence O'Neill. It took political courage to embark on this new departure because many members of Fianna Fáil regarded the Unionist-controlled North as virtually an enemy state. There was considerable sympathy in the Republic for the IRA border campaign of the 1950s, as long as the IRA restricted its violence to the North. The funerals of IRA men killed in raids across the border attracted enormous crowds, the most spectacular being that of Seán South in Limerick. Many members of Fianna Fáil saw no contradiction between the policy of interning republicans in the South and supporting their activities in the North.

The decision by Lemass to travel to Belfast to meet O'Neill, who was cautiously attempting to develop a more moderate and accommodating form of unionism, opened up the prospect of an historic compromise between North and South. Lemass made his historic visit to Stormont in 1965 and followed it up with another meeting two years later. O'Neill paid a return visit to Dublin in January 1968. At a dinner in Iveagh House hosted by Lemass's successor, Jack Lynch, and attended by all the key members of the cabinet, including Haughey, the Northern leader made the point that the Lemass visit had amounted to 'a kind of recognition' of partition.[19] Reflecting the new conciliatory approach in the Republic, an all-party Oireachtas Committee on the Constitution proposed in December 1967 that the territorial claim to the North enshrined in Article 2 of the Constitution should be replaced by an aspiration to unity 'in harmony and brotherly affection between all Irishmen'. For his part, O'Neill began a tentative process of attempting to reform the sectarian nature of the Northern state. T.K. Whitaker played a crucial role in shaping the changed policy on the North, just as he had in modernising Fianna Fáil on economic issues.

There was considerable unease within Fianna Fáil at the Lemass initiative because there was no getting away from the fact that it amounted to recognition of sorts of the legitimacy of the Northern state. Unfortunately the pressure of events never gave the initiative a chance to flourish. The ending of the deep freeze in North-South relations caused the Unionist monolith to crack, but it also exposed deep fissures within Fianna Fáil.

II
THE LYNCH YEARS

2. LYNCH TAKES OVER

IN OCTOBER 1966 LEMASS ANNOUNCED HIS RETIREMENT. The decision itself did not come as a surprise to some of his cabinet colleagues with whom he had, somewhat vaguely, discussed his plans in advance. But the timing of it was unexpected and most of the ministers were convinced that Lemass had behaved precipitately. There was no external pressure on him to go; he had been Taoiseach for only seven years. But he was 67 and his health was beginning to fail, although he had not been diagnosed as having a terminal illness as many assumed. Patrick Hillery recalled his astonishment when Lemass told him he was going to resign. 'No one speaks badly about you; they criticise some of your Ministers but nobody speaks badly of you,' Hillery told the Taoiseach. Lemass responded cryptically, 'You should go before that happens.'[1]

The two most likely candidates to the succession, Charles Haughey and George Colley, were out of the country when the news broke and had to rush home to throw their hats in the ring. Both men were just 41 and were regarded as having equally good prospects. Colley, who flew back from an industrial promotion in the US to stake his claim, had the backing of senior figures like Aiken and also expected the support of Jack Lynch. Haughey returned from London and received a raucous welcome from supporters at Dublin Airport who carried banners proclaiming 'Charlie is our darling.' In a pattern which was to be repeated for the next quarter of a century, Haughey used the Fianna Fáil rank and file to buttress his title to the leadership.

Many members of the party were unhappy that the only choice they were being offered was Haughey or Colley. 'People in the party didn't think much of what was offering,' recalled Hillery, though he and other more experienced ministers like Jack Lynch stood back with what now looks like a strange sense of diffidence. Later, Neil Blaney, the Minister for Local Government, was to enter the race, with the strong backing of the republican rump of the party. Ultimately, however, after a short period of uncertainty, the leadership was thrust on Lynch but not before the party had been split into warring factions – centred on the original two unsuccessful candidates – which thereafter never went away.

The two main contenders were as different as chalk and cheese. Haughey was widely regarded as the representative of the brash new Ireland, his hands in various financial pies, impatient to escape from the stuffiness of de Valera's vision. In contrast, Colley, the son of a party elder, was seen as the clean-cut representative of old-time values repackaged for the modern age. His lifestyle was sober and correct. He spoke fluent Irish and was the standard bearer for the traditional wing of the party which was deeply suspicious of Haughey's extravagant lifestyle, his unexplained wealth and his links with business.[2] The power struggle was not just a battle for supremacy between two men but a struggle for the soul of Fianna Fáil. In the event, that battle was put on hold because it threatened to wreck the party.

When the contest for the succession began, Haughey, who had been in the Dáil for just nine years, was a controversial Minister for Agriculture. He had married Lemass's daughter in 1951 but he didn't settle down to a life of quiet domesticity. He socialised with younger cabinet colleagues like Donogh O'Malley and Brian Lenihan and enjoyed the good life. He became, in Tim Pat Coogan's oft-quoted phrase, 'the epitome of the men in the mohair suits'.

When first elected to the Dáil in 1957 he was in the process of acquiring a fortune. He had qualified as an accountant and set up the firm of Haughey, Boland and Company in 1951 with his old school friend, Harry Boland. He worked hard and by 1960 was a wealthy man by the standards of the day. During the 1960s as he climbed the political ladder, he mysteriously amassed further wealth, buying a farm in Co. Meath, racehorses, a chicken hatchery and Innishvickillaun, one of the Blasket Islands off the Kerry coast. In 1969 he bought Abbeville in Kinsealy, an eighteenth-century mansion which once served as a summer home for the Lords Lieutenant of Ireland. The house, a portion of which was designed by James Gandon, stands on 250 acres of land, and it symbolised the Haughey style. How he could manage to live like a lord on the modest salary paid to a government minister was a source of endless speculation. Over the years Haughey stoutly maintained that his private affairs were nobody else's business and he dealt brusquely with journalists who tried to probe him on the issue.

His political style also rubbed some people the wrong way. Nonetheless, his father-in-law promoted him, first in 1960 as a Parliamentary Secretary to the Minister for Justice and the following year as a full cabinet minister. Haughey grabbed the opportunity with open arms and began to make his mark. Important new legislation like the Succession Act, which protected the inheritance rights of wives, and the Extradition Act were piloted through the Dáil. In his first month in office he drew up a ten-point programme that pinpointed the crushing of the IRA as a primary objective. The Special Criminal Court was reactivated and in less than a year the IRA called off its campaign. 'While he was in Justice, Mr Haughey was a dynamic Minister. He was a joy to work with and the longer he stayed the better he got,' recalled Peter Berry, the powerful Secretary of the Department of Justice.

Berry also recalled another aspect of Haughey's personality that manifested itself in arrogant bullying of his officials. At one stage when Berry objected to a blatantly political promotion in the immigration service, Haughey literally flung the departmental file at him and the papers were strewn about the floor of the minister's office.[3] While he made a success of Justice, Haughey's next portfolio in Agriculture proved more difficult. He became involved in a succession of controversies with the powerful farmers' lobby. Nonetheless, he continued to receive enormous publicity, as much for his flamboyantly wealthy lifestyle as for his contribution to politics.

Conor Cruise O'Brien, who was later to become an inveterate political opponent, wrote a perceptive description of him at this time: 'Mr Haughey's general style of living was remote from the traditional republican and de Valera austerities. He had made a great deal of money, and he obviously enjoyed spending it, in a dashing eighteenth-century style, of which horses were conspicuous symbols. He was a small man and, when dismounted, he strutted rather. His admirers thought he resembled the Emperor Napoleon, some of whose better known mannerisms he cultivated. He patronised, and that is the right word, the arts. He was an aristocrat in the proper sense of the word: not a nobleman or even a gentleman, but one who believed in the right of the best people to rule, and that he himself was the best of the best people. He was at any rate better, or at least more intelligent and interesting, than most of his colleagues. He was considered a competent Minister, and spoke in parliament with bored but conclusive authority. There were enough rumours about him to form a legend of sorts.'[4]

George Colley was a very different person, one who was respected by the ageing founding fathers of the party like Aiken and MacEntee. Aiken, in particular, tried to pilot Colley towards the leadership and was annoyed that Lemass had stepped down before his protégé had time to build up significant support in the parliamentary party. One of the reasons that some of the older party figures respected Colley was that his father, Harry, had been a founder member of Fianna Fáil and had served as a TD. Colley attended the same school, St Joseph's, Marino, as Haughey and, ironically, encouraged Haughey to join Fianna Fáil in 1951. More ironically still, Haughey ousted Colley's father from the Dáil in the 1957 general election. That put some strain on their relationship but things really soured when Colley ran for the Dáil in the same constituency of Dublin north-east in 1961. The bitterness of constituency rivalry was intensified by Colley's rapid progress through the ranks of Fianna Fáil. He was appointed Minister for Education in 1965 and after just five years in the Dáil had established a power base and was prepared to challenge for the leadership.

According to Hillery, some party members opposed to Haughey blamed Colley for showing too much early ambition: 'George came into the Dáil and was soon made a Parliamentary Secretary. He immediately showed he wanted to be Taoiseach. Talleyrand famously said, "Don't exhibit zeal" but George exhibited great zeal.' However, Hillery believed that Colley decided to run for the leadership only because neither Lynch nor he himself was prepared to go. 'That is why Colley put himself forward as the runner on that side of the party. He never explained it like that but I think that it was a justification for having such ambitions.'

Bobby Molloy, who was a TD for little over a year at the time, is quite emphatic that Colley was forced into the position of being a contender because more experienced colleagues, particularly Lynch, refused to go forward. 'I wasn't very long in the Dáil but the leadership was a subject that came up a lot in discussions among the TDs, certainly among the group I was meeting most, because it was obvious Seán Lemass wasn't in the best of health. On every occasion we discussed it, Jack Lynch's name didn't run because he made it clear he wasn't going to stand and that he didn't have any interest in standing. I would have been automatically voting for Lynch but he just wasn't in contention then. Haughey was obviously interested and so was Blaney. I wasn't happy with either of them and my clear preference was for George Colley.'5

Molloy believed Colley represented all that was best in the Fianna Fáil tradition. 'He was the ideal Fianna Fáil person. He believed in all the aims of the party, the peaceful reunification of the country and had a genuine commitment to the language. He had all the good qualities; he was in the Jack Lynch mould but more so. He came from the Fianna Fáil tradition; his father had helped to found the party and had been a member of the Dáil. You didn't ever doubt where he stood in regard to the basic principles of the party. But I suppose he wasn't devious enough to survive in that milieu.'6

Yet, although he appeared to represent traditional values in the 1960s, Colley was in many ways a more modern man than Haughey. Colley's wife, Mary, who was a powerful influence on his life, had strong views on political issues. The hard-drinking macho Fianna Fáilers like Haughey and his cronies derided Colley for treating his wife as an equal. They were astonished that a man in a powerful political position would take his wife's views seriously.

Colley was not the only one who was the butt of jokes because of his relationship with his wife. Jack Lynch, who was Minister for Finance at the time, had a similar relationship with his wife Máirín. The principal reason for his reluctance to throw his hat into the ring for the leadership was her strong opposition to the idea.

Lynch was an obvious candidate for the leadership from the beginning but his claims were obscured by media speculation about the Haughey-Colley rivalry and by his own reluctance to seek the position. Not only did Lynch occupy the most important Ministry in the cabinet but he was also a national sporting hero because of his exploits as a hurler and footballer in the 1940s when he won six All-Ireland medals in a row. It is a record that has never been equalled in the history of the GAA.

Lynch was born in Shandon in Cork City in 1917, the fifth of seven children of a quiet hardworking tailor, Dan Lynch, and his wife Norah. He was christened John Mary, but as he grew up was commonly known as Jack. Lynch went to the local Christian Brothers school, the North Monastery, where he proved a diligent student and a magnificent sportsman. His mother died when Jack was still in his early teens and his father took the children to live with his sister, who had six children of her own. His father was a shy man who spoke little unless he had a few drinks taken, and Jack inherited some of his father's quietness and reserve. 'My father was not political and very seldom was politics ever mentioned in our house. I remember when Dev came to Cork in 1932, during the general election campaign of that year, going to the city boundary. I carried a banner for that rally and there was great feeling for Dev at the time. I was conscious of him as a marvellous, romantic figure,' recalled Lynch.[7]

When Lynch finished school he got a job in the Department of Justice where he served for a time as private secretary to the Secretary of the Department, Stephen Roche. He also began to study for the bar and qualified in 1945. He took a big gamble and retired from his secure civil service post to practise as a barrister.

In 1946 Lynch was approached by the Fianna Fáil organisation in Cork to stand in a by-election, but he declined because he knew Pa McGrath who was in line for the nomination. In later years, Lynch was fond of pointing out that the War of Independence hero Tom Barry, who ran in the 1946 by-election, polled fewer votes than the Communist Party candidate, Michael O'Riordan. It was Lynch's oblique reply to critics of his in Fianna Fáil who decried the fact that his family did not have an IRA record in the War of Independence.[8] In 1948, Lynch agreed to run in the general election and was the leading Fianna Fáil candidate on his first attempt. He met de Valera for the first time during that campaign when the Taoiseach came to Cork for the final rally. He recalled: 'I met Dev a couple of hours before the meeting. He was usually keen to find out at such meetings what the local issues were. He then went back outside the town to make a processional entry. I had a reverential awe for him but at that meeting I found him very human.'[9]

Fianna Fáil lost office for the first time in 16 years in that election and the party decided to appoint a researcher and a secretary to the parliamentary party. The new TD for Cork was asked to take on both jobs, along with his duties as a TD, and his attempts to build up a practice at the bar. He had to draft speeches for de Valera as well as prepare briefs for front-bench members and index Dáil debates and newspapers for his colleagues. Lynch did the job for a year, but eventually he told de Valera that he would have to take more time to concentrate on his legal practice and he scaled back his work. He clearly made an impression on 'The Chief' because when Fianna Fáil was returned to power in 1951 the relatively inexperienced Lynch was surprised to find that he had been appointed Parliamentary Secretary to the Taoiseach. 'I got the first hint that I was to be promoted to Government office when I went to my pigeon hole in Leinster House to collect my mail on the day the Dáil resumed. The Fine Gael TD for North Kerry, also called Jack Lynch, handed me a letter, which he had mistakenly opened. He said something to the effect that the news would please me. It was a letter from Dev informing me of my appointment and asking me to come to see him. I did so and he informed me in Irish that he was appointing me to a new position, Parliamentary Secretary to the Government, with roving responsibilities for the Gaeltacht and the congested districts.'[10]

After the 1957 election, de Valera offered Lynch a cabinet position as Minister for Education. Lynch initially refused the offer and, in a pattern that was to repeat itself again and again, relented only after intense pressure from Dev. 'My wife would very much have preferred me to stay at the Bar but I felt I had an obligation to accept the offer once it was made,' he said. 'I was, of course, flattered to be offered a Ministry at all.' Lynch did not find his chief remote. 'I got on very well with Dev and liked him a lot. One of his traits I noticed particularly was his meticulous attention to the words he used in public speeches. I used to help him on his speeches from 1948 to 1949 and I learned a lot of the need for precision in speech from Dev.'[11]

Being at cabinet meetings was not a new experience for Lynch because he had attended them as Parliamentary Secretary, but he was now able to participate fully in decision-making. 'When I was in Education I had very little difficulty in getting things through cabinet. Dev, who had been Minister for Education at one time for a few months, was sympathetic to the demands I made. He used to ring up every now and again to enquire how things were going.' Lynch was impressed by the older members of the cabinet. 'Seán MacEntee, precise on every subject, especially his own, was very forceful then. So too was Paddy Smith in an earthy way. He brought subjects down to bedrock pretty quickly and didn't confine himself to Agriculture. Frank Aiken too was very strong. Seán Moylan used to scribble very good verse about some of the topics we discussed at Government meetings.'

When Seán Lemass took over from de Valera in 1959 Lynch was made Minister for Industry and Commerce. 'I was none too keen on the change,' he recalled later, but Lemass called him up to his old office in Kildare Street and snapped at him, 'I want you to sit at this desk.' Jack did as he was told and served for six years at the department which Lemass himself had built up into one of the most powerful in the government.

Writing in November 1979, as he entered his own last few weeks in office, Lynch contrasted his style of government with that of de Valera and Lemass. 'Dev ran the cabinet more the way I do. I like to engage everybody around the table like Dev did. I don't count heads. Nowadays we argue it out and eventually I interpret a decision if it has not already become clear-cut. I usually have an idea myself in advance what decision I think is the right one, and this is usually the one that we make, though not always.'

Lemass's style at cabinet was quite different. 'Lemass was more direct in handling government meetings. Under Dev, government meetings went on very long and invariably there were two meetings a week. It was fairly unusual to have two meetings a week under Lemass.' Lynch recalled that Whitaker's brainchild, the *First Programme for Economic Expansion*, which was brought to cabinet by Jim Ryan, took just one meeting to win approval. 'We very quickly appreciated its worth and of course Lemass supported it vigorously.'[12]

In his new portfolio Lynch presided over enormous changes in industrial life as the high walls of protection gave way to free trade. He was involved in Ireland's first application to join the EEC, as the European Union was then known, an application which foundered when President de Gaulle of France vetoed the British application. As 95 per cent of Ireland's trade was with Britain, Ireland could not proceed into Europe on its own. However, moves were made to change the nature of the trading relationship between Ireland and Britain, and Lynch was involved with Lemass in the negotiations which led to the Anglo-Irish Free Trade Agreement, which was signed in 1965. Lynch found the demands of Industry and Commerce, which at that time included labour relations, quite severe. 'Constant demands were being made on ministerial time, at public functions and engagements throughout and outside the country. There were a number of occasions during which I was called back from holiday because of strikes and my wife and I lost a few holiday deposits during that period.' It was to guard against this that the couple bought a holiday home in West Cork at this time.[13]

After the general election of 1965 Lemass promoted Lynch to Finance and speculation began that the reluctant Corkman might one day succeed to the Taoiseach's office. This was something that did not appeal to him. 'Quite early on, as the speculation mounted, my wife and I discussed the prospect and we concluded definitively that I should make it clear from the outset that I would not be a contender for the position. We had found that our family life had already been greatly disturbed by the demands of public office and we were both anxious to minimise this as much as possible. We both enjoy our own company in the privacy of our home, listening to music, watching television, reading or just chatting. Ministerial life didn't leave much time for private life and we knew that being Taoiseach would leave even less time.'[14]

While the media generally took his reluctance at face value, his reputation continued to grow. In August 1965 *Business and Finance* magazine remarked of Lynch: 'Of one Irish politician it is often said that he is too straight and honest for his calling. Yet this man's years in the Dáil have been highly successful. To date he has filled three cabinet posts and now holds the all- important portfolio of Finance.'[15]

About eight weeks before he eventually retired, Lemass called Lynch into his office and enquired if he was interested in succeeding him and was told emphatically that he was not. 'Some weeks later, however, he called me into his office again, this time in the company of Charlie Haughey and George Colley and again he told us that we should be thinking about the future leadership of the party,' Lynch recalled later. 'I reminded him of my previous interview with him when I said I was not interested. I cannot precisely recall the response from the other two but they seemed to indicate that they were interested.'[16]

The other possible contender who ruled himself out of contention to succeed Lemass was Patrick Hillery, who had been a TD since 1951 and was appointed to the cabinet by Lemass in 1959. He was considerably more experienced than Haughey or Colley and was seen by many people in the party as a potential leader. Well before Lemass stepped down, Hillery was asked by senior people like Jim Ryan if he was interested, but he said he was not. 'I didn't have an ambition that time to be Taoiseach,' he said. 'I just didn't feel I wanted the office. It is hard to explain it.' Lemass himself asked Hillery if he would let his name go forward but again he ruled it out. He regularly had lunch with Lemass and one day the Tao-iseach told him he was going to resign. Lemass then looked at Hillery and said, 'You can do it,' but the minister's response was to say no again. 'My thinking that time was that Lemass must not resign. I wasn't going to show any ambition because I was trying to say to Lemass you mustn't go,' he said.[17]

With Lynch and Hillery apparently out of contention and before a two-horse race could develop between Colley and Haughey, a third candidate threw his hat into the ring. Neil Blaney was an experienced, dour, tough-talking Donegal man who had more ministerial experience than either Haughey or Colley. His father before him was a Fianna Fáil TD and Blaney had earned a reputation during the 1960s as a superb organiser. 'Blaney was driving the party; he took over the organisation,' said Molloy. 'He ran by-elections and drove people very, very hard. He was a bit over-enthusiastic, we all thought.'[18]

Blaney had the strong support of his cabinet colleague, Kevin Boland, whose Fianna Fáil pedigree was even better. His father Gerry was a minister in all de Valera's cabinets until 1957, while his uncle was the famed Harry Boland who was killed fighting for the republican side in the Civil War. Blaney and Boland represented the hard, nationalist wing of Fianna Fáil; arrogant in their belief about the party's divine right to rule, they despised some of their colleagues whom they regarded as going soft in the liberal 1960s.

Blaney's entry into the race changed its complexion overnight, although there are different interpretations about what happened next. According to the conventional account, a group of Fianna Fáil TDs from Cork began a 'draft Jack' campaign and deputies from all over the country began to support it. 'Boland pushed Blaney forward because he didn't want either of the other two. It became a bit of a show; they all seemed to be going for it but the majority of those who wanted anyone wanted Jack Lynch,' said Hillery. 'Lemass asked him again. Jack had phoned me to say he wouldn't go but he rang again to say he would. Jack was convinced by Lemass.'[19]

Lemass finally intervened to ask Lynch once again to let his name go forward and he encouraged the three declared candidates to with-draw. Lynch came under pressure from many quarters and finally agreed to discuss the matter with his wife. 'Lemass again invited me to his room, informed me that several backbenchers wanted me to run and that the party generally favoured me as his successor. He pointed out that I owed the party a duty to serve, even as leader. He gave me to understand that the other contenders, to whom he had already spoken, were prepared to withdraw in my favour. I told him I would reconsider my position and would discuss it with my wife. We decided after a long and agonising discussion that I would let my name go before the party.'[20]

Colley too wanted to discuss with his wife the proposition that he withdraw from the contest. This allegedly prompted Lemass to remark: 'What kind of people have I got when one man has to get his wife's permission to run and the other has to get his wife's permission to withdraw?' Haughey told of how he was called in by Lemass who informed him Lynch was now in the race. The Taoiseach asked his son-in-law to withdraw and Haughey agreed. 'I'm glad someone can give me a straight answer around here,' Haughey quoted Lemass as saying.[21] To the surprise of Haughey and Blaney, however, Colley did not withdraw but pressed the issue to a vote, even though he must have known that he didn't have a chance against Lynch who had the support of the other runners behind him.

Molloy does not accept the view that Lynch was drafted in as a compromise to prevent a split in the party. 'As it happened, I think that the Haughey/Blaney side saw that Colley was getting more support than they had expected. With the three of them running it could end up that Colley might actually succeed and, from their point of view, that would have been a disaster because they were not prepared to tolerate Colley's level of integrity. They then got into a huddle and decided that they had better postpone this contest between themselves. So they decided to get Jack Lynch to come in as a *via media*. They got some of the senior members of the party to approach Jack on the basis that the party was going to split down the middle and would be permanently damaged. He was persuaded that he owed it to the party to take on the mantle of leadership and throw his hat into the ring and that if he did all the other candidates would withdraw. But it was a Haughey/Blaney ploy.'

Molloy, who heard the news of Lynch's intervention on his car radio on the way home from the Dáil to Galway, maintained that Colley was not consulted until the decision was a *fait accompli*. When he arrived home he got a phone call from Eoin Ryan, Colley's campaign manager, asking him if he had heard the news. 'I want you to know that George is not pulling out and never said he was pulling out,' said Ryan. Molloy replied, 'I hope he is not pulling out. As far as I am concerned this is just another ploy to hold this thing open for another day. These fellows have no respect for Lynch. I am sticking with George.' Ryan's response was: 'I am glad to hear that. I am ringing you to let you know he is leaving his hat in the ring.'[22]

When Molloy arrived back in Dublin the following Tuesday he received a message to see Colley in the Department of Industry and Commerce. 'Thank you. I understand you are supporting me. I would like to ask you would you mind seconding my nomination. Frank Aiken is going to propose me,' said Colley to a surprised Molloy. 'Hold on a second,' responded Molloy. 'I am only in here a short while. I am still wet behind the ears. Why would I be getting up at the parliamentary party seconding the next leader of the party?'

'Well, Frank Aiken is from the old tradition, one of the party's founders. He is going to nominate me and I would like one of the younger generation to second me,' replied Colley. Molloy then agreed: 'I am greatly honoured. If you want me to do it, certainly I will.'[23]

When the parliamentary party gathered on 9 November 1966, to choose the new leader, Molloy was taken aback at the bad-tempered nature of the meeting. 'When Frank Aiken got up to nominate Colley he suffered a barrage of abuse from Kevin Boland. It astonished me. I had never seen this side of things in Fianna Fáil up to then. It was cussedness on his part that the man he was supporting was being opposed. He verbally abused Aiken, but Aiken was a tough man and it didn't distract him from his task. He proposed George anyway and I seconded him.'

TDs were also stunned to hear MacEntee launch into a ferocious attack on Lemass for stepping down at this time. 'The devious course which he has pursued, not only in relation to his leadership and on the succession, but to other questions as well, have confounded the members of our organisation so that none of them knows where we stand on any issue,' he said.[24] In the event, Lynch, who was proposed by Kerry TD Tom McEllistrim, easily beat Colley by 59 votes to 19.

Ironically, the people who opposed Lynch in 1966 showed themselves to be his most loyal supporters, while those most active in getting him the top job proved later to be his mortal enemies. After he became leader, the pro-Colley camp, including party elders like Aiken, MacEntee and Paddy Smith, gave Lynch their total backing as did rising young TDs like the Minister for Lands and the Gaeltacht, Pádraig Faulkner, and parliamentary secretaries Jim Gibbons and Paddy Lalor. Bobby Molloy said later that the Colley people considered themselves 'just good Fianna Fáil people who had to make a choice. We weren't personally attached to any individual; we were concerned about the best interests of the party as we saw it.' Meanwhile, the group which had been most vociferous in supporting Lynch for the leadership of the party turned out to be his most bitter enemies.

3. Lynch Battles for Control

THOUGH JACK LYNCH ENTERED THE TAOISEACH'S OFFICE in November 1966 as the choice of the great majority of his Dáil colleagues, he moved with a caution and diffidence that appeared to many people as weakness. One problem was that he had been put in the top job by the Haughey and Blaney factions within the party and until he won his own mandate in 1969 he felt beholden to them. He was also daunted in the initial stages by the fact that he had succeeded such giants as de Valera and Lemass.

For his cabinet he retained all the ministers Lemass had appointed in 1965 and merely reshuffled them. 'There was inevitably no radical change in the composition of the Government once I took over. Seán Lemass had already effected the transition from one generation to another and I had merely to endorse the changes he had made,' recalled Lynch in 1979. 'While superficially this made life easier for me it did cause problems for I was thereby deprived of one major strength every Prime Minister usually enjoys: the power of cabinet appointment. Of course I had that power formally but in effect most Ministers knew that they owed their position to Seán Lemass, not to me.' He also discovered that because people knew of his reluctance to stand for the leadership it was widely assumed he was not committed to the job. He confessed he was irritated by people who told him: 'Don't worry, you won't need to be there long – there is always the Park.'[1]

In reshuffling his ministers, Lynch paid due regard to Charles Haughey's role in settling the leadership issue by appointing him Minister for Finance, the most important post in his cabinet. Blaney was moved from Local Government to Agriculture to sort out the farmers' problems while George Colley remained at Industry and Commerce. Erskine Childers was given Posts and Telegraphs to add to his Transport and Power portfolio. While Lynch felt obliged to reward the Haughey-Blaney faction which had backed him, he was never completely in thrall to them. He firmly resisted pressure from them to drop Colley supporters like Pádraig Faulkner from the cabinet.[2] His decision to retain Colley in a key department prevented any split with the losing faction in the leadership contest. Over time, Lynch and Colley gradually became closer and came to trust each other completely.

The promotion of Haughey to Finance also worked for a time. With his accountancy background, his interest in economic matters and his driving personality, the job suited him ideally. He also occupied the post at a time of unprecedented economic boom, which was not repeated until the late 1990s. This gave Haughey the opportunity to bring in imaginative reforms in his four budgets from 1967 to 1970. He introduced free travel and subsidised electricity for old age pensioners, brought in special tax concessions for the disabled, made various provisions for the arts, including the abolition of income tax for artistic work, and expanded public spending each year.

Even though his government operated smoothly, Lynch's position as party leader was clearly weaker than that of his predecessors. The free rein Lynch gave his ministers in the early years encouraged the view that he was a stopgap leader. Lynch himself maintained that his style simply marked a move back towards the de Valera method of cabinet government in which individual ministers were allowed to get on with the job of running their own departments.

Lynch was wounded by the jibes that he was only holding the fort as Taoiseach until one of the strong men of the cabinet emerged to take over. The journalist Desmond Fisher recalled meeting Lynch at the Irish Embassy in London after he had written a piece in the English magazine, *The Statist*, using the term 'interim Taoiseach'. Lynch came over to him and whispered: 'Interim Taoiseach, indeed! I'll show you.'[3] Fisher can be forgiven for his judgement because, apart from Lynch's later handling of the 1970 arms crisis, it quickly became obvious after he took office that he was a much more reactive personality than Lemass. Even before he became Taoiseach, civil servants had observed how difficult it was to get him to make decisions. This personality trait encouraged the leading members of his cabinet to grow more daring in the way they flouted his authority, but it also fooled them into seriously underestimating his steeliness in a crisis. During his sporting career Lynch had been noted both for his hurling style but also for his bouts of laziness. In fact, anecdote had it that one of his own players was often deputed by the team trainer to hit him in the course of a match in order to rouse him into top form.[4]

One of the problems faced by Lynch in the late 1960s was the rampant development of a culture in Fianna Fáil involving close links between business and politics, a culture which was already well established when he became Taoiseach. It was epitomised by an organisation called Taca, which attracted enormous publicity in the 1960s. Taca was a fund-raising organisation of 500 businessmen who attended monthly dinners in the

Gresham Hotel and were given special access to ministers in return for contributions to the party. Haughey and his group, including Donogh O'Malley and Brian Lenihan, were prominent attenders of Taca dinners, but so were traditionalists like Blaney and Boland who saw nothing wrong with the organisation.

Haughey was the politician most associated with Taca in the public mind as he organised the first dinner, a lavish affair attended by the whole cabinet. 'We were all organised by Haughey and sent to different tables around the room,' Kevin Boland recalled. 'The extraordinary thing about my table was that everybody at it was in some way or other connected with the construction industry.'[5] Opposition TDs questioned the whole ethos of the organisation and, in particular, the links between ministers and property developers. There were suggestions about the selection of property being rented by government departments and state agencies, which was mushrooming at a time of unprecedented economic growth. In particular there were persistent rumours about a link between Haughey and John Byrne, one of the first property developers on the scene, who built O'Connell Bridge House, which was promptly leased by the government.

Opposition TDs questioned the propriety of the cosy relationship between Fianna Fáil and the building industry. 'Our people will get the Government they voted for,' lamented James Dillon, leader of Fine Gael from 1959 to 1965. 'If it is Animal Farm they want they should vote for Fianna Fáil but if it is democracy and decency they want I suggest they will have to look elsewhere. I think the acceptance of corruption as the norm in public life is shocking.' Dillon was also quick to spot the threat to Lynch – whom he described as a young man of integrity – from some of his own cabinet ministers. 'There is not an hour, or a day, or a week until they break his [Lynch's] heart, that the clash of knives will not be heard in the corridors of Fianna Fáil.'[6]

It was not only Opposition TDs who were concerned about the trend in public life. In May 1967 George Colley, speaking at an Ógra Fianna Fáil conference in Galway, urged those in attendance not to be dispirited 'if some people in high places appear to have low standards'. This was widely regarded as a reference to Haughey and, even though Colley denied that it was meant to be taken as such, it further deepened the rift between the two men. Lynch eventually moved to wind up Taca and appointed a rising young party activist and businessman, Des Hanafin, to take charge of fundraising. Hanafin stopped the dinners and the unseemly public interaction between ministers and business but he continued to tap the business community for party funds.

The media treated Haughey and Taca with indulgence. Haughey was very aware of the power of the media and even as a new backbench

TD in the 1950s he hired his own public relations consultant. He first approached Terry O'Sullivan of the *Evening Press* and when O'Sullivan turned down the job he hired Tony Grey of the *Irish Times*. The strategy paid off and Haughey became the subject of a great deal of press attention, most of it flattering, in the early stages of his career. As he progressed he found a hugely influential media ally in John Healy who wrote the groundbreaking 'Backbencher' column in the *Irish Times*. Healy regarded the young Haughey as something special and he did a lot to encourage the rising star, not only praising him in print but, more insidiously, denigrating those politicians inside and outside Fianna Fáil who stood in Haughey's way. Healy was bitterly disappointed that Haughey did not get the leadership in 1966 and afterwards regularly wrote in a sneering fashion about Lynch. He dubbed the Taoiseach 'Honest Jack', which was intended not as a term of endearment but as a snide put-down.

With the country booming and his powerful ministers working hard, Lynch's quieter hands-off approach worked for a while. The dynamism generated by the Lemass era carried through and, although there was criticism of the government over growing social problems like the housing crisis in Dublin, the political situation remained stable. Fianna Fáil easily won six by-elections over the following two years and lost only one, in Wicklow. One of those by-election victories brought the young Des O'Malley into the Dáil, following the untimely death of his uncle Donogh at the age of 47. Those electoral successes were an early tribute to Lynch's popularity but many commentators instead gave the credit to Neil Blaney and his 'Donegal mafia' who ran the campaigns with military precision.

One way or another the myth of the invincible Fianna Fáil machine gained new currency and encouraged Lynch to push his luck. In 1968 he gave in to cabinet pressure and agreed to a referendum on changing the voting system. In 1959 Fianna Fáil had tried and failed to get the people to vote to abolish proportional representation and opt for the straight vote. Less than a decade later Lynch and his ministers again failed to persuade the electorate to change. This was a boost for a demoralised Opposition and it began to cause doubts about whether Lynch was capable of winning a general election.

The outbreak of the Troubles in Northern Ireland had a dramatic effect within Fianna Fáil. 'It was very quiet at first,' recalled Hillery. 'Jack seemed very contented. It was very peaceful. When the marches began in the North of Ireland there was a sudden testing of the Fianna Fáil policy.' Looking back in later years he remembered that de Valera and his front bench had responded decisively to the IRA campaign in the 1950s. 'I often think of it, the wisdom of that group. They called a party meeting for the whole day to reassert the Fianna Fáil policy. They made it very clear that they would not recognise any army other than the army under the government. They also made it clear they would not accept the use of force in the North at that time. It was very timely just before an election.'[7]

The civil rights campaign against the systematic discrimination which had been endured by the Catholic people of the North since partition posed a terrible challenge for the Irish Government. Lynch quickly came to understand that the simplistic demand for Irish unity would do nothing to help the campaign for equality and social justice for Northern Catholics. But that was not the way a group of his senior ministers viewed it. The attack by the RUC on a small civil rights march in Derry on 5 October 1968 marked the start of the violence. A few weeks later Blaney made a strong speech which was aimed as much at changing the direction of Fianna Fáil as it was at the Northern Unionists. Blaney maintained that the Lemass-O'Neill meetings had been futile and he called for a reassertion of the territorial claim on the North. He appeared concerned that the civil rights movement in the North, with its emphasis on equality within the United Kingdom, might dilute the anti-partition united front of traditional nationalism North and South.[8]

Kevin Boland, writing after his departure from politics, recalled that within the government a minority of ministers tried at this stage to establish an approach based on 'the fundamental reason for the existence of the political party to which we all belonged,' i.e. the ending of partition. In this group were Boland himself, Blaney and Haughey, with some support from the Minister for Justice, Micheál Ó Móráin, a gruff Mayo solicitor whose heavy drinking reduced his effectiveness. Lynch refused to adopt the hard line advocated by this group and was supported by Colley as well as experienced ministers like Hillery and Childers. Crucially, he also had the backing of the veteran founder member of Fianna Fáil Frank Aiken, who was Minister for External Affairs. The other cabinet members did not take sides but were prepared to bend with the prevailing wind. 'This group was typified by Lenihan who cheerfully and appropriately described himself as the X in OXO, with one leg on each side of the fence,' recorded Boland.[9]

It was something of a surprise that Haughey was a member of this hard-line clique. Unlike Boland and Blaney, he had not come from a family of Fianna Fáil aristocrats. His father had been a Free State Army officer, something that did not go unnoticed by many in the party. There was also his obvious wealth and his lavish lifestyle which ran directly counter to the traditional Fianna Fáil value of austerity. What many in Fianna Fáil and outside did not realise at the time was that the Haughey family background had a huge influence on his views about the North. His father and mother came from Swatragh in Co. Derry and the plight of Northern nationalists was probably the most talked about political issue in the household while he was growing up.[10]

A clue to Haughey's character was provided by an escapade in which he became involved as a student at University College, Dublin. On VE day in 1945, Trinity College, which along with the *Irish Times* at that time represented one of the last vestiges of the Anglo-Irish mind-cast, flew the Union Jack and other Allied flags over the entrance to the college. When some passers-by objected, Trinity students took down the Irish tricolour, which was also flying over the college, and burned it. Word quickly travelled to UCD, then located at nearby Earlsfort Terrace. A group of UCD students marched down to Trinity and Haughey produced a Union Jack that was burned at College Green. A riot developed and the Gardaí had to disperse the crowd with batons.[11]

As the Northern troubles unfolded the group opposed to Lynch at cabinet became increasingly strident and they had support from those in the know within the party organisation. In the eyes of the republican purists Lynch was not a real Fianna Fáil man at all. His father had not participated in the War of Independence or the Civil War and this lack of a republican pedigree was regarded with suspicion. Jack Lynch did not say much about it at the time but he was always aware that his political background was quite different from that of other prominent Fianna Fáilers. In an interview in the *Irish Press* in 1986, after he had retired as a public representative, Lynch told me that his father had introduced him to political debate and that the elder Lynch's political allegiance was not to either of the civil war factions of the early 1920s but to William O'Brien, who dominated Cork politics before 1918. Jack Lynch was keenly aware of his family's political allegiance and it is hardly a coincidence that when the crisis in the North developed he followed the O'Brienite policy of 'conciliation and consent' rather than the militaristic republicanism of his opponents at cabinet.[12] 'Both Jack and I were outsiders,' recalled Hillery. 'It was strange; the two who didn't know anything about politics were the ones who talked about policy.'[13]

Lynch found a powerful ally outside the cabinet for his moderate views in T.K. Whitaker, who at the beginning of the Troubles was Secretary of the Department of Finance but who moved in the spring of 1969 to the position of Governor of the Central Bank. Whitaker's influence on policy went much wider than economic affairs. As noted earlier, he had played a crucial part in the Lemass-O'Neill meetings, travelling with Lemass to the first meeting at Stormont Castle. A native of Rostrevor in Co. Down, he brought personal experience as well as a keen intellect to consideration of the Northern problem. In 1968 Haughey was his minister in the Department of Finance but he had also served with Lynch in the same department and knew both men well.

In November 1968, Whitaker wrote a note to Lynch on North-South relations which established the framework of Irish Government policy on the issue for the rest of the twentieth century. He opened by saying that force had rightly long since been abandoned as a means of undoing partition because it would accentuate rather than remove basic differences and was not militarily feasible in any event. He pointed out that partition had actually been strengthened, rather than weakened, by the IRA campaign of the late 1950s when the people of North and South almost ceased visiting one another. The only choice was to seek unity in Ireland by agreement between Irishmen. 'Of its nature this is a long-term policy, requiring patience, understanding and forbearance and resolute resistance to emotionalism and opportunism. It is none the less patriotic for that.'[14] That, unfortunately, was not the way some of the most senior ministers in the government saw it.

In the spring of 1969, as the violence worsened in the North, Whitaker, who had just moved to the Central Bank, wrote to Haughey suggesting a policy of moderation. He said the Irish Government should do nothing to inflame the situation further by reacting negatively to the use of British troops. 'Avoid playing into the hands of extremists who are manipulating the civil rights movement and who wish to stir up trouble and disorder. Civil war, or anything like it, would make real North-South unity impossible by destroying goodwill and causing fierce new enmities and divisions.' He suggested that pressure should be applied on the Northern administration and the British to remedy the social and other grievances against which the civil rights movement was campaigning and which he saw as the immediate cause of the then disturbed situation.

It later became evident that Whitaker's advice to Haughey had fallen on deaf ears. But the developing tensions within the government in early 1969 were held in check because a general election was expected that year. Having prepared the ground carefully, Lynch called the election for June and sought his own mandate from the people. After the setback of the referendum he was taking nothing for granted. Before the election, Kevin Boland carried out a revision of constituency boundaries which was a blatant gerrymander, designed to maximise the number of Fianna Fáil seats. The party platform was essentially a continuation of the policies that had served Fianna Fáil for a decade and the director of elections for the campaign was Charles Haughey.

By the time of the election, Haughey had barely recovered his full health after being seriously injured the previous September in a mysterious car crash in Co. Wicklow on his way back to Dublin from Courtown in Co. Wexford. For some reason, Haughey himself was driving the state car and it was widely believed that he had been drinking. After the crash, Garda drivers were ordered never to allow anybody, even ministers, to drive state cars. Some people who knew him well believe that Haughey underwent a personality change as a result of his injuries. 'It exacerbated his dark side and, while he recovered his old drive over time, he lost some vital quality which changed him as a man.'[15]

Lynch proved himself to be a great campaigner and his quiet, reassuring style attracted many voters who would not have been traditionally Fianna Fáil. He was helped by the fact that the Opposition was also deeply divided. Fine Gael under Liam Cosgrave was troubled by internal dissent, with a younger group known as the 'Young Tigers' trying to pull the party to the left against strong resistance from the old conservative element. More significantly, the Labour Party had adopted the trappings of international socialism and was adamantly opposed to coalition with either of the bigger parties. Campaigning on the platform that the 'seventies will be socialist', the party had high hopes of overtaking Fine Gael as the second party in the state. A number of leading intellectuals like Conor Cruise O'Brien, David Thornley and Justin Keating joined the party, earning it massive media coverage in the campaign. In the event, while the new Dublin high-flyers made it to the Dáil, many of the old rural Labour seats were lost and overall the party's tally of seats dropped from 22 to 18.

Fianna Fáil used the old 'red scare' tactic to good effect outside Dublin and Lynch's quiet-spoken style and his habit of calling in to convents up and down the country during the campaign proved reassuring to older voters. Fine Gael more than held its ground and gained three seats to end up with 50, but the absence of any transfer arrangement and the clear unwillingness of Labour to participate in coalition gave victory to Lynch with 75 Fianna Fáil seats in the 144-member Dáil. It was the first time Fianna Fáil had won an overall majority since de Valera's victory of 1957 and it put Lynch in a much more commanding position within the party.

Interestingly, one of the big issues in the campaign was Charles Haughey's wealth. In the middle of the election campaign the *Evening Herald* revealed that he had sold his home at Grangemore in Raheny to the well-known property developer and builder, Matt Gallagher, for over £200,000 and that he had bought the Abbeville estate and its 250 acres for £140,000. 'I object to my private affairs being used in this way. It is a private matter between myself and the purchaser,' Haughey maintained.[16] It was a line he was to maintain for the next 30 years when anybody broached the subject of his extraordinary wealth.

Gerald Sweetman of Fine Gael made a serious political issue of the sale by claiming that Haughey had benefited from legislation he had introduced himself, amending part of the 1965 Finance Act, that ensured he did not have to pay tax on the profits. Haughey then publicly announced that he would refer the matter to the Revenue Commissioners, who duly reported that 'no liability to income tax or surtax would have arisen' under the 1965 Act even if it had not been amended. This appeared to leave Haughey in the clear but, looked at in the light of the privileged treatment accorded to him by the Revenue over more than three decades, it may simply have been another case of the institutions of the state acting under duress to protect him. Conor Cruise O'Brien, a Labour candidate in Haughey's Dublin north-east constituency, did not let the issue go and hammered away at what he described as 'the Fianna Fáil speculator-orientated mentality' throughout the campaign. Haughey replied by accusing his opponent of indulging in personal vilification while Boland dubbed the new Labour candidate 'Dr Conor Cruise God Bless Cuba and Albania O'Brien'.

The election victory gave Lynch authority in his own right for the first time. The media gave him the major share of the credit for the result and suddenly he was no longer regarded as a stop-gap leader. 'It is a personal triumph for the Taoiseach, Jack Lynch, whose meet-the-people tour must have contributed a great deal to the result,' commented *Irish Press* political correspondent Michael Mills.[17] Lynch demonstrated his authority by promoting allies like Paddy Hillery to External Affairs and Pádraig Faulkner to Education while he made Erskine Childers Tánaiste in place of Frank Aiken. He also promoted parliamentary secretaries Jim Gibbons and Paddy Lalor, who had been in the Colley camp, to the cabinet and he made Des O'Malley his chief whip.

O'Malley was in every way a different politician to his late uncle. Donogh had been a devil-may-care character who acted on impulse and who became the subject of innumerable colourful anecdotes. Des shared his uncle's intelligence but he was a much more sober and diligent character who could be tetchy when ruffled. Lynch took an immediate shine to the young O'Malley and found in his protégé his most able lieutenant when the going got really rough. Lynch was still far from being in complete control of the party, however, and there were reports that he had attempted and failed to demote both Blaney and Boland to less powerful cabinet positions. With the North reaching a crisis point, a life-and-death struggle for control of Fianna Fáil got underway. This struggle was to have incalculable effects on Ireland, North and South, for the next 30 years.

4. THE PLOT AGAINST LYNCH

JACK LYNCH'S AUTHORITY AS TAOISEACH was given an enormous boost as a result of his election victory but it was not long before he faced a fundamental challenge to that new-found status. The crisis arose directly from the eruption of widespread violence in Northern Ireland. Deep divisions emerged at cabinet table, not simply because of a clash of powerful personalities; they came down to fundamental questions about the reasons for Fianna Fail's existence and the legitimacy of the 26-county state. Some ministers viewed the chaos in the North as the opportunity for a final solution to the partition problem, regardless of the consequences in terms of loss of life and political stability. Lynch and his allies at cabinet held the line in defence of the rule of law and democratic principles. The resumption of the IRA campaign of violence in the middle of the political crisis added the final dangerous element to the cocktail.

The government in Dublin watched helplessly as the violence in the North worsened steadily throughout July 1969. Then the annual Apprentice Boys march in Derry on 12 August led to a complete breakdown of law and order. As dramatic pictures of rioting in Derry filled television screens in the Republic and abroad, Lynch summoned an emergency cabinet meeting for the following day. It was to be the first of nine bruising meetings in eight days as ministers divided not just over tactics but over basic principles.

Public opinion in the Republic was affected powerfully by the nationalist uprising in Derry and the failed attempt of the RUC to quell it, and there was enormous pressure on the government to come up with a quick response. According to one informant of the author, who claims to have been a friend of Neil Blaney at the time, the Chief of Staff of the Army, Lt Gen. Séan MacEoin, attempted to contact the Taoiseach the night the Battle of the Bogside erupted. He was unable to do so, as Lynch was on holidays in West Cork. 'He got on to Blaney in his own house on the Howth Road and Gerry Jones was one of the two persons present. The Chief of Staff reported riots in Derry and how he had moved Army ambulance and medical personnel to Buncrana to provide assistance. Blaney got very angry and said our troops should go into West Derry to protect "our people". The Chief did not respond and Blaney ordered him to do it. The Chief saluted, asked for the instructions of the Government in writing and walked out.'[1]

This is an uncorroborated story but it has the ring of truth, as Blaney took a central role in all that happened subsequently. For instance, the cabinet files show that Blaney rang the Secretary of the Department of External Affairs, Hugh McCann, in the middle of the following night demanding that Irish diplomats should make contact with the British Home Secretary, James Callaghan, to have the police action in Derry halted. McCann acted on Blaney's instructions and got the Irish ambassador in London out of bed to make contact with the Foreign Office.[2]

At the cabinet's emergency meeting on 13 August, Lynch produced a proposed statement on the crisis, drafted by civil servants in External Affairs. He was immediately challenged by Blaney, Boland and Haughey.[3] They demanded a much tougher statement in response to the worsening security situation, followed by action to back it up. The Taoiseach's instinct was to proceed cautiously, recognising that there was little the Irish Government could do in the short term without inflaming the situation.[4] But other ministers rowed in with the hawks and he had to bow to the pressure for a strong statement. Lynch effectively lost control of his cabinet on that first day of the crisis and his statement was redrafted a number of times until it was strong enough to meet the requirements of the hard men in the government.

Whether the cabinet seriously considered an invasion of the North is a matter for dispute. Blaney was widely believed to have pressed for Army intervention in Derry as a tactic designed to force the intervention of the United Nations. Boland, Haughey, Ó Móráin and Seán Flanagan backed Blaney in varying degrees while Brian Lenihan adopted an ambiguous attitude. The hardliners did not argue that an immediate intervention was necessary but wanted a contingency plan to protect Northern nationalists in a doomsday situation. Lynch counselled calm and was supported in his rearguard action by Hillery, Colley and the Tánaiste, Erskine Childers.

Lynch's stance was bolstered by a report from the Minister for Defence, Jim Gibbons, which pointed out that the Army was utterly unprepared for invasion in terms of manpower or equipment.[5] This enabled Lynch to agree a compromise whereby the Army would establish field hospitals along the border and the FCA reservists would be called up for duty. It was a policy that gave the impression but not the substance of dramatic action. The combination of emotional relief and practical help appeased the republican element in the cabinet for the moment.

Despite his misgivings, the Taoiseach agreed to deliver a tough statement to the nation on television that night, as demanded by his more hawkish ministers. Haughey and Blaney participated in drafting the speech and included a call for UN intervention and a demand that the British should immediately begin negotiations about the constitutional position of the North. It was inevitable that the statement would exacerbate an already tense situation, but in the circumstances it was the minimum that Lynch's more strident colleagues in government would accept.

A whole folklore subsequently developed about the background to Lynch's television address that night, particularly in relation to one passage where he said, 'The Government of Ireland can no longer stand by and see innocent people injured and perhaps worse.' Some newspapers reported the following day that he said the Government could no longer 'stand idly by' and that phrase went into the folklore of the period. According to rumour at the time, Lynch changed the wording at the last minute, believing it was unnecessarily provocative. A story that went the rounds in RTÉ was that a secretary deputed to type the speech left out the word 'idly' by mistake. What actually happened was that the phrase 'will not stand idly by' was included in the early, more moderate, drafts of the speech that came before the cabinet from External Affairs.[6] The final draft that Lynch brought with him to RTÉ was riddled with insertions and deletions all over the typed text. Desmond Fisher, the Deputy Head of News at RTÉ, provided Lynch with a room to work in and also fetched the Taoiseach a bottle of his favourite drink, Paddy whiskey. 'I could not help noticing that his script was badly typed, with corrections in ink scrawled all over it,' Fisher recalled. 'I told him he could not possibly go on air with a script in that state and immediately arranged to have it typed out in a large typeface with double spacing between the lines. He asked for a private telephone and I overheard him telephoning his wife, Máirín, to consult her on changes he proposed to make.' Fisher's account shows how vulnerable Lynch was at the time. Isolated and browbeaten by the hardliners at cabinet, the only trusted adviser he could rely on absolutely was his wife. Between them they produced the final draft of what was probably the most fateful statement a Taoiseach has ever made on television.

Another indication of just how isolated Lynch was emerged in a discussion before the broadcast with Fisher. 'At one point he asked me what I thought would happen if he were to order the Army into the North, as some of his advisers counselled. I said that I thought they would get about 20 miles into Down or Derry before they would be massacred in a fight with the British. He smiled wanly at my answer and said he had come to the same conclusion himself.'[7]

Despite the final revisions, the statement was very tough and it indicated how far Lynch was prepared to go to placate his hard men. 'It is obvious that the RUC is no longer accepted as an impartial police force,' he declared. 'Neither would the employment of British troops be acceptable nor would they be likely to restore peaceful conditions – certainly not in the long term. The Irish Government have therefore requested the British Government to apply immediately to the United Nations for the urgent despatch of a peacekeeping force to the Six Counties ... Recognising, however, that the re-unification of the national territory can provide the only permanent solution for the problem, it is our intention to request the British Government to enter into early negotiations with the Irish Government to review the present constitutional position of the Six Counties of Northern Ireland.' Lynch went on to say that, as many of the injured did not wish to be treated in Northern hospitals, 'we have ... directed the Irish Army authorities to have field hospitals established in County Donegal adjacent to Derry and other points along the border where they may be necessary.'[8]

Inevitably, the statement gave the impression that a major confrontation between Ireland and Britain was beginning. Most of the media focus was on the movement of the Irish Army and there were immediate rumours of an invasion which inflamed the situation in the North, just as Lynch had feared.[9] Rumours swept Derry that the Irish Army was on the way and the rioting intensified. The following night the notorious B Specials were mobilised and much more serious violence erupted in Belfast where, over the next few weeks, thousands of Catholics were burned out of their homes and five people were murdered by Protestant mobs backed by the B Specials, the official state militia. During the cabinet meeting on 13 August a decision had been taken to instruct the Irish ambassador to London to request the British Government to halt 'the police attacks on the people of Derry'. The ambassador was also instructed to request the British to apply immediately to the United Nations for the 'urgent despatch of a peacekeeping force' to Northern Ireland and to inform the UN Secretary General of the request. This decision and those authorising the Army to establish field hospitals along the border and to move troops to the border areas concerned, though referred to in Lynch's televised address, were not recorded in the cabinet minutes.[10]

They were not the only decisions taken by the government during these desperate days that were unrecorded in the minutes; in fact, three full cabinet meetings pass entirely unrecorded. The cabinet met again on 14 August and at this meeting it was formally decided that Hillery should seek a meeting with the British Foreign Secretary or Home Secretary and that the Minister for Defence should send troops to the border to protect the field hospitals. The government also decided that the Garda intelligence network in the North should be expanded and a committee of key departmental secretaries from Justice, Defence, External Affairs and

Local Government was established to keep the situation under review and to advise the Taoiseach. This decision crucially provided the Secretary of Justice, Peter Berry, with direct access to the Taoiseach. Hillery was dispatched to London to ask the British to agree to a United Nations peacekeeping force, or even an Anglo-Irish force for the North. The minister suffered the indignity of being fobbed off with a junior minister at the Foreign Office, Lord Chalfont, rather than the Foreign Secretary or the Home Secretary.

'The British tested the belief that you could achieve things by peaceful means because they gave no possible help to maintaining the peaceful policy,' recalled Hillery. 'When the Government decided that I had to go to London, they made it clear that they didn't want to talk to me, but I went over anyway and waited in the Irish embassy to see if a meeting could be arranged.' While waiting in the embassy Hillery watched television and he remembers being impressed by Conor Cruise O'Brien who popped up on various channels to explain the complicated situation to a British audience. 'The simple truth is that the British didn't want me. They regarded it as an intrusion in their internal affairs. In the end Harold Wilson sent Chalfont to see me.' At the time Hillery regarded Lord Chalfont as a minor character but he subsequently learned that he was a confidant of Wilson's.[11]

Chalfont gave Hillery 'a courteous brush off', according to the Irish media, but Irish cabinet papers show that the brush off was far from courteous. A transcript of their conversation shows that Chalfont disputed Hillery's right to express any view about what was happening in the North and he accused the Irish Government of interference in the domestic affairs of the United Kingdom. Hillery gave as good as he got, blaming partition as the root cause of the problem and accusing the British of being directly responsible for the abuses of power, which they had tolerated in the North.[12]

After the bruising encounter, Hillery told reporters he would have liked to meet the Prime Minister. He remembers coming out from the meeting and being approached by a young RTÉ reporter with a microphone who asked him if he was satisfied with the meeting. 'I am not and I am going to do something about it,' responded Hillery who immediately began preparations for a visit to the United Nations in New York to highlight the Irish Government's concern.[13] Meanwhile Wilson, far from acceding to the Irish demand for UN intervention or a British-Irish force, ordered the British Army on to the streets to take control of the deteriorating situation. It was a fateful decision which even at the time caused some foreboding. Lynch had publicly opposed the notion of a direct intervention by the British Army and Hillery told Chalfont in no uncertain terms that it would turn out to be a disaster. Even some people in the British Government realised the potentially dire long-term consequences of the intervention. The Belfast Catholic, socialist politician, Gerry Fitt, recalled congratulating Home Secretary Jim Callaghan on the decision, only to be told: 'It was easy to send them in but it will be a damn sight more difficult to get them out.'

Ironically, the initial response of Northern Catholics to the British Army intervention was entirely positive. The soldiers were seen as protecting the nationalist community from the repressive security apparatus of the Unionist state in the wake of the pogrom against Catholics in Belfast and the police attacks in Derry. At the height of the pogrom nationalist politicians in the North wanted intervention from the Republic. Politicians like Paddy Devlin, Paddy Kennedy and Paddy O'Hanlon even came to Dublin pleading with the Secretary of External Affairs, Hugh McCann, to get Lynch to send in the Irish Army or, failing that, to provide guns for nationalists.[14] The hysteria among nationalists afraid of a wholesale massacre abated following the intervention of the British Army and calm was temporarily restored to the streets of the North.

The Irish Government was not very happy with the development, however. The cabinet met for a third day in a row while Hillery was in London. They decided that, in anticipation of British agreement to a UN peacekeeping force or failing that a joint British-Irish peacekeeping force, the front line of the reserve Army should be mobilised. The reason for this was 'to ensure that they will be in readiness at the earliest practicable date', before the British decision to send in the Army was announced.

By this time the atmosphere around the cabinet table had become very fraught. Lynch, confronted with the biggest crisis of his political life, consulted the wisest man he knew, Ken Whitaker, by now the governor of the Central Bank. Whitaker was on holiday in a house in Carna, Co. Galway, at the time but the Taoiseach contacted him through the Gardaí. A Garda arrived at the house early on the morning of 15 August to tell Whitaker that the Taoiseach wished to speak to him urgently. Whitaker went back into Carna with the Garda and phoned Lynch from the barracks. The two men had a long discussion about the political situation and the options facing the government. Returning to the holiday home, Whitaker put his advice in writing and posted it to the Taoiseach that afternoon. In the notes which formed the basis of that letter, Whitaker expressed his horror at the 'teenage hooliganism and anarchy' evident in the rioting which 'no Government can benefit from appearing to support'. He warned against the 'terrible temptation to be opportunist – to cash in on political emotionalism – at a time like this'. He went on: 'It should never be forgotten that a genuinely united Ireland must be based on a free union of those living in Ireland, on mutual tolerance and on the belief that the ultimate governmental authority will be equitable and unprejudiced. Every effort should be made in any government statements from Dublin to avoid identifying the government solely with the Catholics or nationalists of NI and to make it clear that the aim of a united Ireland would be a fair deal for all – indeed that the position of NI Protestants would be particularly respected. A special effort is needed to reassure the many moderate Protestants who otherwise may be driven to side with the extremists, under threat, as they see it, of losing their freedom, religion and laws.' Finally Whitaker warned Lynch against allowing his government to appear as if it were 'driven before the emotional winds fanned by utterly unrepresentative organisations such as Sinn Féin,' and he criticised the 'quite disproportionate publicity' they were getting on RTÉ.[15]

These views reinforced Lynch's instinctive response to the crisis but they ran completely counter to the demands for action being voiced by wilder elements of the cabinet. There is no record of what was said at cabinet but Lynch, probably emboldened by his conversation with Whitaker that morning, infuriated Boland so much that the Minister for Local Government decided to resign that day. 'After a few days of interminable wrangling it became apparent to me that the policy of "to preserve what we have down here" and "to restore normality up there" had prevailed,' Boland said. 'Having watched the unbelievably cynical rejection by my colleagues of all that we had professed over the years, I resigned at a Government meeting on 15 August, gathered my personal belongings and went home.'[16] Haughey and Blaney pressurised Boland to withdraw his resignation and he was surprised to note that no announcement was made by the government that night. Boland's resignation was not all that surprising to his colleagues as he had frequently resigned before when he did not get his way. On one earlier occasion, after a row over a social welfare measure, he announced his resignation and went home to his Co. Dublin farm to make hay. This time around, though, he signed a resignation note, something he had never done before.[17]

Boland's resignation was not recorded in the cabinet minutes or the files. Nor is there any record in the cabinet minutes of an emergency meeting of the government that night, presumably to discuss the resignation and the decision of the British to send in the Army. The only indication of this meeting and of two subsequent ones that took place in the following days are the attendance sheets which have been left in the archives.[18]

The cabinet met again the following morning in formal session, without Boland, and Hillery reported back on his rebuff by the British. It was arranged that he should travel immediately to New York to bring the question of the violence in the North before the UN Security Council and also to have the matter included on the agenda of the next session of the General Assembly. Even before he left, Hillery knew that there was no chance of getting the Security Council to agree to a peacekeeping force, because the British would veto it. He had also been told that the Americans would back the British veto. 'People have a funny notion about America but they were on the side of the British so that the optimum I could get out of it was being allowed to address the Council,' he said later. In the circumstances he followed the advice of Ireland's vastly experienced ambassador to the UN, Con Cremin, who, in his own words, steered him through 'the least worst option' available. That option was to travel to New York, get as much publicity as he could for the Irish position, raise the matter with the Security Council, but under no circumstances push for a vote, as Ireland would be humiliated.[19]

This was a course which Hillery remembered had been recommended to him by Lemass years before. He had asked Lemass why Ireland did not go to the United Nations about the North of Ireland. 'He had this cryptic way of speaking and he said to me: "If you are willing to accept the result." I began to think of this when I was over there. If you went as far as a vote, then partition was copper-fastened forever. So you had to get out without a vote and at the same time make a big fuss about it. It worked out like that. It was an achievement.'[20] He was to find out that not all the cabinet would agree with his assessment.

Some inkling of the difficulty Lynch faced in attempting to bring his more truculent cabinet ministers around to his way of thinking is illustrated by the recollections of the most junior member of the Government, Paddy Lalor, the Minister for Posts and Telegraphs. Lalor was steadfast in his support for the Taoiseach but he later recalled how the crisis challenged his deepest beliefs about the meaning of nationalism and republicanism. 'I grew up firmly believing that the island of Ireland would never be truly independent until all unionists were expelled – or at least driven into the North Channel on the way. My difficulties in 1969 and 1970, when then a member of the Government, will therefore be appreciated. I had, at Government meetings, to hear and absorb lessons on the undoubted need for all Irishmen and women at that troubled time to accommodate and make proper provision to embrace the two traditions which must be merged on this island, or at least be enabled to live peacefully together.'[21]

5. AID FOR THE NORTH

HILLERY'S BELIEF THAT HE HAD SECURED AN 'ACHIEVEMENT' at the UN Security Council by creating 'a big fuss' over the Northern Ireland crisis did not impress the militants at home. At a cabinet meeting on 16 August, they succeeded in getting a decision to give Haughey, as Minister for Finance, control of a fund to provide aid for victims of violence in the North. Not only that but 'the amount and the channel of disbursement' were left completely to Haughey. Finally the cabinet on that fateful day decided that machinery should be established with the object 'of maintaining permanent liaison with opinion in the Six Counties'. This decision was subsequently expanded on at a meeting on 21 August when it was arranged that Haughey, Blaney and two other ministers from border constituencies, Pádraig Faulkner from Louth and Joe Brennan from Donegal, would 'consult together with a view to selecting one or more persons to endeavour to promote a united, cohesive force of anti-Unionist and anti-partition opinion in the Six Counties.' Haughey and Blaney later used these decisions as cover for activities which contributed to the creation of the Provisional IRA and which led to the Arms crisis of 1970.

However, other ministers who were present at that cabinet meeting, including Faulkner and Lalor, maintained that the government decisions were not nearly as far-reaching as Haughey and Blaney portrayed them. 'As far as we were concerned, aid for "the victims of violence" meant exactly that. It did not mean the supply of guns or tanks to the North,' said Faulkner. While accepting that it could be argued there was a certain amount of ambiguity involved, he pointed out that the decision had to be read in conjunction with a statement issued on the same day (16 August) by the Government Information Bureau in order to establish the true intentions of the government. This read: 'The Minister for Finance will make funds available from the Exchequer for the relief of victims of the disturbances in the Six Counties and will have an early consultation with the chairman of the Irish Red Cross.' The following day's *Sunday Independent* reported that Haughey would have immediate talks with the chairman of the Red Cross as to the administration of the aid fund.[1] Whatever the intentions of the government as a whole, however, the decisions were used by Haughey and Blaney as a cover for their own purposes.

Meanwhile Boland stayed away from the cabinet over that crucial weekend even though he was put under huge pressure to return by Haughey and Blaney. Lynch also wanted Boland to come back, fearing that a resignation at this stage could split his government apart. The rebellious minister was summoned to Áras an Uachtaráin by the President, Eamon de Valera, and asked not to go through with it. 'The President talked of the constitutional crisis that would be caused by my resignation – particularly on this issue. He foresaw a change to a Fine Gael-controlled government and pointed out the seriousness of this in the circumstances that existed,' Boland was to say later.[2]

Boland eventually capitulated to Dev's argument but with hindsight he came to believe that he returned to his post on the basis of a false premise. 'A Fine Gael Government would probably have been as bad but it certainly couldn't have been worse. At least it would have been recognised for what it was.'[3] Hillery recalled the fraught atmosphere of the time, even though he missed many of the contentious cabinet meetings because he was abroad trying to get international recognition of the issue. 'Boland resigned a couple of times. I remember saying at one of them when I came back, "Can't ye behave when I am away?"'[4]

Boland returned to an informal cabinet meeting on 18 August 1970, which was formally recorded. He was now back in the fold. There was another unrecorded meeting two days later and then on 21 August a full formal meeting. A number of decisions were taken at this meeting, including the formal establishment of the sub-committee. It was also decided that Lynch should make a statement in response to the British rebuff over the UN peacekeeping force. This was the last meeting in the series of nine to deal with the Northern crisis. The cabinet did not meet again for eight days and there was no reference to the North for some time in any of the formal decisions. It was back to business as usual.

In later years Boland, and others, claimed that the cabinet had made a decision on a contingency plan to provide arms to defend nationalists in the North in a doomsday situation. There is no reference in cabinet minutes to any such decision but going on all the evidence it appears that there was a discussion of the options facing the government in such a last resort. This discussion was also used as a blind by those who favoured stronger action than Lynch was prepared to contemplate.

The story of Boland's resignation and the pressure on Lynch in the cabinet did not appear in any of the Irish newspapers but there was a stunningly accurate report in London's *Sunday Times*. 'The startling pugnacity of Dublin's reaction to the violence in Ulster was an attempt by the Prime

Minister, Jack Lynch, to head off dangerous splits in his own country – specifically those threatened by an upsurge in IRA strength and by disunity within his own government,' wrote one of the paper's reporters, Eric Jacobs, who had been sent to Dublin. Jacobs then went on to elaborate on the disunity in the cabinet. 'This has not so far broken the surface at all. There is a tight clamp on news in Dublin ... Nevertheless there are persistent reports of a crisis a few days ago within the government during one of its numerous cabinet meetings. Cabinet business, it is said, broke down in confusion when Mr Kevin Boland, the Local Government Minister and former Minister for Defence, demanded that the Free State Army troops should be put across the border; if not he would resign. It took several hours, according to reliable sources, to persuade him to toe the Government line.'[5] The Irish newspapers on the following day carried denials of the story by a government spokesman and it did not emerge in public until Boland himself wrote about it a few years later.

At this stage, the more devious hawks at cabinet were not nearly as unhappy as Boland. They believed that with the decision to put Haughey in charge of the aid fund and the establishment of the sub-committee, they had scored a crucial victory over Lynch. The sub-committee never actually functioned. It had one formal meeting in late August at which there was a general discussion about the North. Blaney told the others about plans to appoint a journalist friend, Seamus Brady, to assist with publicity about the plight of Northern nationalists. Lynch was not happy with this and later vetoed payments to Brady. A second meeting of the sub-committee was scheduled but only Faulkner and Brennan, both Lynch supporters, turned up. They waited for some time but Haughey and Blaney did not show up and did not send a message to give a reason for their non-appearance. Brennan told Faulkner that he was busy in his department and could not afford to wait around indefinitely. The two ministers called it a day and returned to their departments. The sub-committee never met again.[6]

After that Haughey and Blaney acted on their own initiative without any reference to the other two members who were kept completely ignorant about what was going on. Although the sub-committee had effectively ceased to exist it proved a very effective device for Blaney and Haughey to develop their own strategy while keeping Lynch in the dark. It provided the appearance of official government sanction for their actions, while Haughey's control of the £100,000 aid fund provided wide scope for their plans. Over the next six months Haughey and Blaney went far beyond any reasonable interpretation of the cabinet decisions made at the height of the August 1969 crisis.

Subsequent events were shaped by a remarkable cast of characters.

Chief among them was Peter Berry, an extraordinary public servant who was Secretary of the Department of Justice. Berry was a man of great ability and vast experience who had joined the department in January 1927 and served 14 Ministers for Justice, beginning with Kevin O'Higgins, the very first minister in the department, and ending with Des O'Malley. His enemies in the republican movement and in the liberal media liked to present Berry as a sinister snoop who kept tabs on everybody, *à la* J. Edgar Hoover. Certainly he was in touch with everything that was going on and was regarded with awe and even fear by some senior ministers. But most regarded him as a patriotic civil servant with an unrivalled insight into the subversive republican forces which threatened the security of the state.

Berry had had a prominent role in dealing with IRA subversion from 1940 onwards and when he became head of the department he continued to keep all the threads of security matters in his own hands. His main informant on security matters was another remarkable public servant, the former head of the special branch, Phil McMahon. Tim Pat Coogan described McMahon as the nemesis of the IRA in the 1950s and, as Berry recorded in his diary: 'So he was.' When McMahon came to retirement age in 1966, a special Act was passed by the Dáil to keep him on in his post for a further two years. Even after his formal retirement he was retained as a paid adviser on subversive matters to Garda headquarters and was paid out of the Secret Service vote. He had a top-level informer within the IRA who dealt only with him and whose information was crucial in the unfolding drama.

McMahon and Berry became alarmed in the aftermath of the 1969 crisis as persistent reports filtered through from Garda intelligence sources about highly unusual contacts between subversives and certain cabinet ministers. Involved in much of this activity linking ministers and the IRA was an Army intelligence officer, Captain James Kelly. A native of Bailieboro, Co. Cavan, Kelly was an experienced officer who had seen duty with the United Nations in the Middle East. He held strong republican views which were typical enough for someone who grew up in a border county and he had a natural sympathy with the more militant elements among Northern nationalists. He was sent to Derry on an intelligence-gathering mission during the Battle of the Bogside and he reported back to his superiors about developments there. He became a pivotal go-between in the autumn of 1969. The available evidence is that he was acting with the full authority of his superior, Colonel Michael Hefferon, and that the Minister for Defence, Jim Gibbons, was kept informed, at least to some degree, about Kelly's activities. How much Gibbons knew, and when, are still matters of dispute. Kelly has always claimed that Gibbons was fully briefed about what went on, but that is disputed by associates of Gibbons. It appears that Kelly regularly reported directly to Blaney in Agriculture, as well as to Gibbons. For a period Kelly had a base in the Department of Agriculture which allowed him direct access to Blaney.[7]

A complicating factor in the subsequent events was that Ó Móráin, the Minister for Justice, was at this stage of his career going to pieces and drinking heavily. His communications with Lynch and his top civil servants were totally confused and he did not pass on to them the detailed reports from Justice being provided by Berry. A solicitor from Castlebar in Co. Mayo, he enjoyed the rough and tumble of politics. He nicknamed a rival politician in his constituency 'The Maggot Durkan' while he dubbed the new Labour Party intellectuals as 'left wing political queers from Trinity College and Telefís Éireann.'

It was against this background of ambiguous lines of authority and communication within the government that contact was opened between the Haughey-Blaney axis and the IRA. Blaney was the driving force behind the strategy but Haughey was also actively involved. There are divergent views as to whether this was from conviction or because he wanted to make sure Blaney did not steal a march on him in the leadership stakes, but the two men were certainly in it together. The IRA had formally announced a resumed military campaign after the violence of August but the organisation was in a weak and demoralised state and desperately seeking to be re-armed. Contacts were even opened up between Blaney and the more militant socialist-republican group, Saor Éire.[8]

The atmosphere of the time was quite extraordinary. Captain Kelly has recorded how respected Northern politicians like Gerry Fitt and Paddy Devlin pleaded with him for arms for citizens' defence committees during the height of the troubles in August, and government files in the National Archives bear this out. Subsequently, various groups of Northern nationalists came down to Dublin demanding guns so that the nationalist community could defend itself. Within the republican movement those who believed in street politics and social action struggled for control with those who wanted a return to the simple philosophy of the 'armed struggle'. Haughey and Blaney plunged into this maelstrom, with money no object. Not only had Haughey control of government funds for 'relief' but, according to some republican sources, substantial sums from the private sector also began to flow into a general purposes fund. 'From the very beginning, official Government action mingled with private party action and official funds with private funds.[9] It was also common knowledge that a number of Fianna Fáil TDs handed over their own guns to the IRA, through intermediaries, at this time.

Lynch and most of his ministers had nothing to do with this strategy and were unaware about what was going on. The problem was that some of the people looking for guns naturally believed that Haughey and Blaney were speaking for the government as a whole. Hillery remembers that at a cabinet meeting around this time Lynch clearly told his ministers that they were not to get involved with the IRA. 'One day at a meeting, quite unexpectedly as far as I was concerned and I am sure a lot of the others, Jack said that he had heard something about Ministers being involved – I don't remember the exact words now – in this kind of activity. He said he didn't want any Minister involved.'[10]

When the IRA announced on 18 August that it was resuming its military campaign, Lynch responded firmly. In a statement the following day he warned that he would not tolerate any further action by the IRA. 'No group has any authority whatever to speak or act for the Irish people except the lawful Government of Ireland freely elected by the people. The Government will not tolerate the usurpation of their powers by any group whatsoever.'[11] It was a classic restatement of the Irish Government position which echoed W.T. Cosgrave during the Civil War and Eamon de Valera during the 1930s and 1940s. It came as a severe shock to republicans because they had been led to believe, by Blaney and his friends, that the old principles had been abandoned and that aid and succour would be provided by the government.

Lynch was quite clear about his determination to ensure that the rule of law was upheld and his cabinet colleagues can have been under no illusions about that. The limited evidence available in the cabinet papers for 1969 shows that Lynch moved firmly and quickly in response to the IRA announcement. He contacted McCann at External Affairs and not only asked him to bring his statement on the IRA to the attention of the British but also to pass on to them private information about the extent of IRA activity which he had decided to exclude from his statement. McCann asked the British ambassador, Sir Andrew Gilchrist, to come to see him at his home during lunchtime and he duly arrived at 1.45 p.m. 'The ambassador had already learned from the RTÉ 1.30 p.m. news of the Taoiseach's public statement. He expressed appreciation of this. When I gave him the additional private information he said that it was important that this should be conveyed to the British cabinet as soon as possible and he undertook to do so.' Gilchrist complained to McCann at the publicity being given to the IRA by RTÉ and he followed that up the next day by meeting McCann to express his government's concern at the activities of the IRA. He also expressed appreciation at the discreet manner in which he had been given information about the IRA and he offered to convey messages directly from Lynch to Harold Wilson.[12]

Just as good lines of communication were being developed between the Taoiseach's office and Downing Street, Phil McMahon and the head of the Special Branch, Supt John Fleming, arrived at Peter Berry's home in Rathgar with a disquieting report. 'In the previous week a cabinet Minister had had a meeting with the Chief of Staff of the IRA, [Cathal Goulding], at which a deal had been made that the IRA would call off their campaign of violence in the 26 counties in return for a free hand in operating a cross-border campaign in the North.'[13] McMahon told Berry the IRA obviously did not understand the Taoiseach's statement, as it had been accepted by them that the cabinet Minister was speaking to their Chief of Staff with the authority of the government.

Berry was not given the name of the minister involved but he made a detailed report to Ó Móráin the following day. Ó Móráin was curious about the identity of the unnamed minister and speculated that it might be Blaney or Boland. He went to the cabinet meeting and read out Berry's report to his government colleagues. Haughey piped up, ' That could have been me. I was asked to see someone casually and it transpired to be this person. There was nothing to it. It was entirely casual.'[14] This should have sent alarm bells ringing in Lynch's head but, as happened so often throughout Haughey's career, his easy lie was accepted. Even Berry himself was reassured in view of Haughey's uncompromising attitude towards the IRA when, as Minister for Justice, he had effectively rolled up the last border campaign. Berry told McMahon and Fleming that there seemed to be no truth in the story but the two policemen were not reassured and told Berry firmly that their sources were good. Despite the high-grade intelligence, Berry was simply not prepared to believe at this stage that Haughey was involved in plotting with republicans.

It is an indication of how things were spinning out of control that, just as Lynch was denouncing the IRA, two of his most powerful Ministers were embarked on a policy of supporting and re-arming the organisation, on condition that it dropped its left-wing agitation in the Republic and concentrated its efforts on destabilising the North. Army intelligence was in the thick of the operation while the Garda Special Branch looked on in surprise and reported back to Berry who found it difficult to believe what was happening. The result was not just the creation of political instability and the near collapse of the government of the Irish Republic. Events at this period also led directly to the creation of the Provisional IRA and fuelled the long war in which more than 3,000 people died and tens of thousands were maimed and wounded.

6. ARMING THE IRA

THROUGHOUT THE AUTUMN OF 1969 the plot, orchestrated by Haughey and Blaney, to create a new and well-armed IRA, free of Marxist ideology, took firm shape. The carrot being offered to republicans was money, guns and a free run at the North as long as there was no military activity against the Southern state. Lynch and most of his ministers appear to have been blissfully unaware of the developments, although there were rumours in circulation. The brazen ability of Haughey and Blaney to lie, which did not become apparent until years later, lulled the moderates in the cabinet into a false sense of security. The conspirators were also helped by the high tide of public emotion in the South in favour of strong action to help Northern nationalists in the wake of the August pogrom.

As well as the Exchequer funds allocated for 'relief' in the North, private business interests donated considerable sums for similarly undefined purposes. The New Ireland Assurance Company donated a house in Kildare Street for the use of the Citizens Defence Committee. This was secretly used as a cover for contacts between Blaney not only with leading IRA figures but also with the group known as Saor Éire, an extreme republican organisation noted for its Marxist ideology and criminal methods. One good, if admittedly biased, source claimed that a whole range of contacts developed in September-October 1969 with a single objective – to obtain a substantial supply of arms through illegal channels and distribute them in the North.[1]

The first moves which led to the split in the republican movement in the North came after the violence of August. In Belfast a small group of active and former members of the IRA, outraged by the organisation's inability to protect nationalist areas during the rioting, talked over their options. They met on 24 August at the social club in Casement Park without the knowledge of the IRA leadership. Among this group were some legendary republican figures who had not been active for a long time, including Joe Cahill who had been sentenced to death with Tom Williams in the 1940s. Others present included John Kelly, who was later to become a linkman with Capt. Kelly and a key figure in the Arms crisis, David O'Connell and Jimmy Drumm. Also at the meeting was a young man from a staunchly republican family who was destined to become one of the greatest republican legends of all. His name was Gerry Adams.

In essence the meeting marked the conception of the Provisional IRA. One of the main topics for discussion was the offer of money and arms from Dublin. 'They decided to overthrow the leadership of the Belfast IRA, to take control themselves and to accept Fianna Fáil's offer of money and arms, for use in the city, of which they had now heard from Capt. James Kelly.'[2]

As well as encouraging the embryonic provisional faction, Haughey and Blaney opened contacts with the official republican movement. In August, Haughey's brother, Jock, met Cathal Goulding, the IRA Chief of Staff, in London to discuss what the Irish Government could do to help. In early September a leading mainstream Belfast IRA man was part of a group, including Paddy Devlin, which travelled to Dublin to meet Blaney in his office in the Department of Agriculture. Two weeks later they met Haughey at his home in Kinsealy. According to an account published later by sources close to the Official IRA, Haughey raised the issue with the Belfast IRA man of whether arms could be obtained if the money was forthcoming. 'The IRA man said that obtaining arms was easy enough provided a sum of not less than £50,000 was available and Haughey stated that such a sum would be no problem to provide.' In fact nothing came of the venture. The source continued: 'It was becoming clear to members of the cabinet in Dublin that the IRA was not going to be so easy to take over and that perhaps the creation of a new IRA would be a quicker, cheaper and more rewarding process.'[3]

In late August or early September, Capt. Kelly learned through a contact in Belfast that Haughey had promised £50,000 to a three-man Belfast delegation. 'This promise of money from the Dublin Government was announced at a gathering of Defence Committee people in Belfast in a matter of days. It was also stated at the meeting that the money was for the purchase of arms.'[4] Capt. Kelly told Haughey of the development and the minister was very annoyed at the indiscreet way the matter was being talked about. He instructed the Captain to inform the Central Defence Committee that money would not be forthcoming from his department until a proper and reliable finance committee was formed in Belfast. This was duly arranged and Haughey was mollified. Capt. Kelly recalled that money from the fund for relief of distress was paid into a bank account initially located in Clones, Co. Monaghan, and later transferred to the Munster and Leinster Bank in Baggot Street in Dublin.[5]

As these contacts were going on, Berry at the Department of Justice received a number of verbal reports about the activity of Irish Army intelligence officers along the border. Capt. Kelly's name cropped up again and again in Garda reports as consorting with known members of the IRA. According to Berry, 'It was alleged that he was so forthcoming in advocating the use of arms that doubts were entertained by his listeners as to whether he was, in fact, an intelligence officer.'[6] In the same month Kelly and his superior officer, Col. Hefferon, twice visited Kinsealy to meet Haughey. The minister asked for their advice on the composition of a committee to oversee the distribution of financial relief in the North.

Haughey was running what looked like an alternative government from his home. Besides the leaders of the IRA and Army intelligence officers, the British ambassador Gilchrist was invited out to Abbeville to discuss the future of the North. At a meeting during the first days of October, Haughey told the ambassador there was no constitutional position he would not sacrifice, including the position of the Catholic church and Irish neutrality, if the British would give a secret commitment to move towards Irish unity. He offered NATO bases on Irish soil as part of the deal.[7] Gilchrist politely declined the offer on the basis that he was not sure what the Irish Government wanted. 'I doubt if they did,' he added in his report to the Foreign Office. All the available evidence suggests that Haughey was now wholeheartedly pursuing his own Northern strategy and flouting the authority of the Taoiseach on all fronts. He did submit a memorandum to Lynch at the end of September seeking a co-ordinated policy from all government departments designed to explore and eliminate all obstacles to the end of partition. Haughey wanted Lynch to circulate this memorandum to all his ministers but it appears that the Taoiseach did not comply.[8] It is not as if Haughey and Blaney could have been under any illusion about official government policy by this stage. Both in public and in private, Lynch had expounded the clear view that the use of force had been ruled out by the Irish Government, but that did nothing to deter Haughey and Blaney.

Paddy Hillery is adamant that Lynch did not know what was going on at this time. 'There was no winking or anything like that. Jack wouldn't do that. Jack was so straight he was kind of innocent. I remember one time someone said the farmers would water the milk going into the creameries if it wasn't tested. Jack couldn't believe that people would do that. He was straight up all the time. I am quite clear about that.' Hillery, though, could understand how Capt. Kelly believed he was acting on behalf of the government at that time. 'If you were an Army captain and you had the Minister for Finance and the Minister for Agriculture authorising your actions you would believe it was sanctioned by the Government.'[9] Faulkner took a similar view. 'If a junior officer in the Army was given access to a Minister or Ministers and told it was Government policy, of course he would think that it was Government policy.'[10]

On 4 October, the same day that the British ambassador reported to his superiors, Capt. Kelly organised a conference in the Commercial Hotel in Bailieboro, Co. Cavan, owned by his brother. The people invited to attend this meeting were members of the Defence Committees which had been set up in the Catholic areas of the North after the August pogrom. The stated objective of the meeting was to set up a controlling body for all Defence Committees and to discuss the purchase of arms. In fact, many of those who attended were leading IRA figures from the North who favoured breaking with the Sinn Féin leadership in Dublin and going it alone. Questions were asked about whether money and guns could be organised and, to their delight, Capt. Kelly was able to inform them that £50,000 could be obtained for the purpose.

Back in Dublin, Berry, who was in hospital for a serious operation, was given the alarming information that the meeting with known IRA activists was about to take place. 'It looked as if an officer group in the Army were collaborating with members of an organisation which had been proclaimed by government order to be unlawful and who were engaging in violence contrary to the declared views of government,' he wrote in his diary.[11] Berry phoned his own minister and then the Taoiseach and, ironically, when he could get no reply from either, he phoned Haughey who promised to be with him within the hour.

When he arrived at Mount Carmel hospital, Haughey caused more excitement among the nurses than any of Berry's other visitors, including President de Valera. The powerful charisma and the deep duplicity of the man combined to lull Berry into making a rare error of judgement. 'I told him of Capt. Kelly's goings on and of the visit planned for Bailieboro. He did not seem unduly perturbed about Capt. Kelly but was quite inquisitive about what I know of Goulding. I felt reassured. I was not to know … that Haughey had seen Capt. Kelly with Col. Hefferon at his home in the last week of September, and on 3 October – the day before he visited me – he had given a cheque for £500 for Capt. Kelly's expenses for the Bailieboro meeting.' Kelly later described the Bailieboro meeting as 'the genesis of the plan to import arms'.[12]

Berry would have been even more alarmed if he had known that within days of the meeting Haughey phoned the Red Cross in Dublin. He asked that £5,000 of the funds allocated to the organisation from the government's relief fund be transferred to an account in the Bank of Ireland in Clones. The account holders included Paddy Kennedy and Paddy Devlin, both MPs at Stormont and at that stage deeply involved with the Defence Committees. The money was distributed according to the arrangements made at Bailieboro and went 'to pay full-time men on vigilante and defence organisation.' At the time the IRA was beginning to fracture into the two wings which ultimately became the Officials and Provisionals. Initially the money was carefully divided between the two sides but over time the bulk of it went to the Provisionals. Capt. Kelly impressed almost all of the IRA men he met with his sincerity, even those from the Official wing who were gradually frozen out; their view was that 'his brief seems to have been to create the conditions inside the North which would allow for a complete breakdown in law and order in the area and so justify the incursion of the Irish Army.'[13]

Meanwhile on 16 October Berry, who was still in hospital undergoing a battery of tests, received a fuller report on the meeting which so alarmed him that he rang the Taoiseach. Lynch called to the hospital to see him and, although he felt a 'bit muzzy' at the time, Berry is certain he told Lynch about Capt. Kelly's activities. 'I told him of Capt. Kelly's prominent part in the Bailieboro meeting with known members of the IRA, of his possession of a wad of money, of his standing drinks and of the sum of money – £50,000 – that would be available for the purchase of arms.' Lynch later denied that Berry had told him in such detail about what was happening. He did remember that the meeting took place but recalled it only in general terms as there were frequent interruptions by medical staff treating Berry. The medical attachments to the civil servant's nose and throat made communications difficult and eventually Lynch left, telling Berry to deal with the matter himself. However, Lynch did raise the matter of the Army's behaviour with Gibbons. The minister asked Hefferon for an explanation but Hefferon rejected Berry's complaint and there the matter rested. Berry was adamant that he had made Lynch aware of the plot and was disappointed the Taoiseach made no more than a cursory enquiry. According to one well-placed source Lynch at this stage was not sure how seriously to treat Berry's claims. 'He was told by some colleagues that Berry was far too conspiratorial and had an obsession about republicans and "reds under the bed" so he was not totally convinced.'[14]

The Irish media appeared blissfully unaware that all this was going on but accurate information continued to appear in the British media, probably informed by Embassy sources in Dublin. As early as 12 September the satirical magazine *Private Eye* carried a lengthy report on Ireland which referred to the deep split in the cabinet between Haughey, Blaney and Boland on the one hand and Lynch, Hillery and Colley on the other. More to the point, the magazine suggested that if republican views were popular with some members of the cabinet they were even more popular in the Army. 'The generals may support Lynch but the colonels, majors and NCOs are in the main keen for action. The considerable troop movements in the Republic have served to increase these demands ... the

Army Intelligence corps has not been inactive in the Catholic-dominated border towns of Northern Ireland. The civil rights headquarters recently established at Monaghan, south of the border, is paid for by the Government out of secret service funds.'[15]

Ambassador Gilchrist was also interested in what was going on in Monaghan. 'I have been trying to probe for some time reports linking Mr Haughey with an organisation in Monaghan devoted to trans-border activities,' he reported to London on 10 November. He concluded that Haughey set up the organisation from party funds when in fact exchequer funds were used, but he did confirm that Irish Army intelligence was involved. Gilchrist believed that there were plans afoot to supply weapons across the border but said he could not be sure whether this had already happened.[16]

The only clue available to the Irish public about the developing tensions in government came through a series of political speeches. On 20 September Lynch, in a major statement of policy in Tralee, was emphatic that the Irish Government had no intention of using force to end partition. 'The unity we seek is not something forced but a free and genuine union of those living in Ireland based on mutual respect and tolerance and guaranteed by a form or forms of government authority in Ireland providing for progressive improvement of social, economic and cultural life in a just and peaceful environment. Of its nature this policy – of seeking unity through agreement in Ireland between Irishmen – is a long-term one. It is no less, indeed it is even more, patriotic for that.'[17] Whitaker drafted the speech for Lynch, restating in clear and unambiguous terms the fundamental doctrine that underpinned Irish Government policy. It was delivered more than two weeks before Haughey provided Capt. Kelly with the money for the Bailieboro meeting.

The impact of the Tralee speech was crystal clear as far as Hillery was concerned. 'I was away at the United Nations when Jack made the speech in Tralee. That was the most important speech during the whole period. After it we knew where we were going and the Fianna Fáil policy of peaceful means was clearly set out.' Hillery was aware of Whitaker's influence on Lynch's thinking and also recalled the input by the Central Bank governor into the speech he himself had made to the United Nations general assembly at that time. 'Whitaker was very good all through. He would be quieter than I was. I remember meeting him before I spoke in the UN. The Department of Foreign Affairs would be more my way, you know. But Whitaker was very sound. He was always trying to subdue what I would say at the UN. It was very important. I think he was a great man.'[18]

Lynch followed up his speech by moving at government level to lay down clear lines of policy. He endorsed a detailed memorandum from the Department of Foreign Affairs on the approach to the North. This memorandum fleshed out the Whitaker thesis and formed the basis of the policy pursued by Lynch and his successors for the next 20 years. It stressed the need for co-operation with the British Government to ensure that there were fundamental reforms in the North to benefit the nationalist community. It suggested that the long-term objective of a federal Ireland should be pursued through diplomatic channels but that fundamental changes in the Republic on issues like divorce and contraception were required to push this policy forward. The memo also proposed the establishment of an Anglo-Irish division in the Department of External Affairs, which would work in tandem with the Taoiseach's department. A key part of this division's role would be to liaise with nationalist political and community leaders in the North. One of the brightest officials in the department, Eamon Gallagher, was given this role. Ironically, just as Haughey and Blaney were busily working on a secret strategy which helped in the creation of the Provisional IRA, Lynch and Hillery set in train an officially sanctioned government strategy which led to the formation of the SDLP. This became official government policy in November 1969.[19]

With the support of a majority in the cabinet, Lynch had laid down the government's Northern policy in clear and unambiguous terms by the autumn of 1969 but the hawks continued to go their own way by word and deed. Blaney used the occasion of a function in Letterkenny in early December celebrating his 21 years in the Dáil to nail his colours to the mast. 'I believe, as do the vast majority, that the ideal way of ending partition is by peaceful means. But no one has the right to assert that force is irrevocably out. The Fianna Fáil party has never taken a decision to rule out the use of force if the circumstances in the Six Counties so demand.'[20] This was a straightforward defiance of Lynch's policy which earned newspaper headlines and Dáil jibes from the Opposition about a split in Fianna Fáil.

As early as September 1969, Lynch had demonstrated his disapproval of collusion with Northern republicans. A number of men from Derry had been inducted into the FCA for weapons training by the Irish Army with the approval of Gibbons, but the training was immediately cancelled when the Taoiseach found out about it. Then at the end of December there was confusion when a number of armed Derry men were arrested in Donegal. When Lynch was informed he wanted to 'throw the book at them', indicating to Peter Berry that he was making a public stand to show that the government was not prepared to collude with those involved in violence. The following day Haughey rang Berry in a fury, inquiring who had given the Gardaí 'the stupid decision' to arrest the men.

Berry told him the decision came from the top and he repeated the instructions from Lynch. Haughey was livid. 'His language was not of the kind usually heard in church,' recorded Berry.[21]

Against this background the split in the republican movement moved towards its conclusion. In December, an IRA army convention backed a decision by its Dublin leadership to end the policy of abstaining from participation in any political institutions. The traditionalists were appalled and prepared to leave if a Sinn Féin Árd Fheis ratified the decision. On 29 December, the first statement from the Provisional IRA Army Council appeared in the newspapers and the battle began for control of the Árd Fheis in January. 'In the interval between the IRA convention and the Sinn Féin Árd Fheis, the scramble for delegates was only equalled by the scramble for dumps.'[22] On 10 January, the biggest Sinn Féin Árd Fheis since the 1920s was held in the Intercontinental Hotel (now Jury's) in Dublin. The highlight of the conference was a walkout led by Seán Mac Stíofáin and Ruairí Ó Brádaigh. The Provisionals were now a separate political and military force.

A showdown between Lynch and his enemies was predicted at the Fianna Fáil Árd Fheis of 17 January but in the event the Taoiseach sidestepped a row. Kevin Boland made a trenchant contribution in which he echoed Blaney's Letterkenny speech without spelling it out quite as clearly. 'The Taoiseach knew exactly what I was doing,' maintained Boland later. 'He knew it was mainly to him I was talking in my speech and that I was castigating him in public.'[23]

If Lynch knew it he gave no indication in his Árd Fheis contribution. Instead, after a hurried consultation with Seán MacEntee, he contented himself with reaffirming in general terms his adherence to Fianna Fáil policy. The following day in a radio interview with Mike Burns on RTÉ's 'This Week' programme, Lynch claimed there was no contradiction between his views and those of Blaney and Boland and that he had been concerned only about misleading newspaper headlines.

The Fianna Fáil faithful were very relieved to hear their leaders dismissing reports of disunity but those in the know took different and contradictory views of what the Árd Fheis speeches meant. 'Lynch was still the prisoner of his cabinet colleagues,' was the view in the IRA and ironically this view also came to be shared by the top echelons of the Gardaí.[24] By contrast, Boland's assessment was very different. 'He [Lynch] was already laying his plans to change to the old Cumann na nGaedheal policy but this was not to be done in a straight-forward way by confrontation with those who adhered to the old principles. It was to be done in his own distinctive style by stealth, treachery and subterfuge.'[25] But, Lynch's loyal ministers, like Hillery and Faulkner, had no doubt that the Taoiseach was sticking to a policy they understood clearly and which they believed in.

However, some of the participants in the unfolding drama were still not sure whether Lynch knew what was going on but was turning a blind eye or was genuinely ignorant about the full extent of the activities of Haughey and Blaney. Capt. Kelly and many Northern republicans were convinced that he was in the know. Berry and senior Gardaí thought he might be but, in the end, Berry concluded that Lynch had been kept in the dark. In November 1969, the official organ of the republican movement, *The United Irishman*, published a very well-informed story written by its editor, Séamus Ó Tuathail. He claimed there was a conspiracy afoot involving senior government ministers attempting to gain control of the civil rights movement in the North. 'The finance for the take-over job involves large injections of Fianna Fáil money channelled from Messrs Blaney and Haughey,' Ó Tuathail wrote. Photographs of the ministers appeared with the captions 'He knows' and a photograph of Lynch was captioned 'Can he not know?'[26]

It was in this 'Through the Looking Glass' world, where some ministers knew and others did not, that the plot to import arms for the IRA with taxpayers' money began to take definite shape. Boland claimed that everybody in government had heard rumours of a decision to import arms from the continent and he assumed this related to discussions at cabinet about a contingency plan if the worst was to happen in the North. 'It is only fair to say that I felt sure this importation would not be agreed to by the Taoiseach if it came up for specific Government decision but, while I myself did not approve of the idea of acting in a way that would almost certainly be contrary to his wishes, I was aware that it was being done under lawfully delegated authority. I could also see that the project could be related to the contingency plan which was Government policy.'[27]

The existence of a contingency plan to send the Irish army across the border in a doomsday situation was used as a cover by the plotters in 1970 and an excuse for their actions in the years since then. It was not until the release of official documents to the National Archives in 2001 that the nature and scope of the contingency plan became somewhat clearer.

What happened was that on the afternoon of 6 February 1970 the Minister for Defence, Jim Gibbons, contacted the Army Chief of Staff, Lt. Gen. MacEoin, to say that he had been instructed by the cabinet earlier that day to order the Army to prepare and train for 'incursions into Northern Ireland if and when such a course of action becomes necessary.' He instructed MacEoin to have 'respirators and arms and ammunition made ready in the event that it would be necessary for the minority to protect themselves.' Gibbons went on to say that the Taoiseach and other ministers had met delegations from the North at which urgent demands were made for items such as respirators, weapons and ammunition, the provision of which the Government agreed 'as and when necessary'.[28]

Strangely, the cabinet minutes for 6 February 1970 contain no reference to any decision by the Government on a contingency plan and there have even been suggestions that Gibbons issued the instruction to the Army at the behest of Blaney alone, but this seems unlikely. Despite the absence of any formal Government decision, the indications are that the issue was discussed at cabinet before the Minister issued his directive and Boland makes reference to such discussions in his memoirs.

A week after the instruction was issued, MacEoin met the Minister to clarify its precise meaning. The Chief of Staff put it to the Minister that: 'The military assume that incursions would only be mounted in circumstances where there would be a complete break-down of law and order in Northern Ireland and where the security forces were unable or unwilling to protect the minority.' Gibbons confirmed that such an interpretation was correct. MacEoin then went on to say: 'The military assume that the sole object of incursions would be the protection of the lives and property of the minority.' Again Gibbons confirmed the Chief's interpretation.

A series of further probing questions from MacEoin established that Gibbons had not thought through the implications of the instruction to the army. MacEoin asked if diplomatic representations to the British would be made before an incursion but the Minister said such representations would not be made. When MacEoin asked a crucial question about the quantity of arms, ammunition and respirators that were to be made available and to whom and in what circumstances they were to be handed over, the Minister said he had no idea, but he agreed that stockpiles were to be held in Dublin and Dundalk.[29] In a later memo, MacEoin spelled out that what the Army was being asked to undertake was not an invasion but a humanitarian intervention and that the Irish Army would withdraw from the North once its job in protecting the Catholic minority from attack had been achieved.

The critical question is whether the instruction to the army to prepare a contingency plan meant that the Government had agreed to import arms to give to nationalists in Northern Ireland. The weight of evidence is that the contingency plan meant no such thing, but its existence was used in 1970, and in the years since then, by the Haughey-Blaney faction of Fianna Fáil as justification for the attempted importation of guns and ammunition. It is clear from MacEoin's clarification of the plan that any incursion would take place only in a doomsday scenario and that the Irish army would withdraw from the North as quickly as possible. By contrast, Blaney and his followers wanted army intervention as a means of ending partition for good.

Boland later made it clear he did not believe Lynch would agree to the importation of arms to send to the North if the issue was raised at cabinet. There is also supporting evidence for the view that the Haughey-Blaney faction of the cabinet knew, contingency plan or no contingency plan, that the Taoiseach and his supporters at cabinet would not agree to sending arms to the North.

A vivid picture of how republicans and the Fianna Fáil hard men regarded Lynch was painted in a memoir by Derry nationalist Paddy Doherty. He recalled a trip to Dublin at Blaney's invitation in February, 1970, along with senior IRA figure, Sean Keenan. They met Blaney at his ministerial office, went to lunch with him in the Shelbourne Hotel, and were then joined by Haughey in the afternoon. The Northerners told the ministers that they needed guns to protect the nationalist community from a massacre. Haughey turned to Blaney and said, 'You'd better get Jim Gibbons down here immediately.' Blaney made the phone call and Gibbons arrived a few minutes later. 'The names of two other members of the cabinet came up. Kevin Boland was not available and Ó Móráin, "the man from Mayo" as they called him, was ill. Blaney and Haughey agreed that both would be sympathetic.' Doherty recalls Haughey as saying, during the discussion: 'Let's take the North. We should not apologise for what is our right.' Gibbons quickly intervened to say: 'We couldn't. The Army is 3,500 under establishment figures.' Gibbons went on to say that he was preparing for a doomsday situation in the North and that if the fears expressed by the Northern delegation became a reality the Government would have to become involved.

Blaney then said, 'These men should meet Lynch. It's time he did something,' but he was reluctant to make the arrangement, asking Haughey to do it instead. 'You'd better ring him. I can't stand the man,' Blaney told Haughey. A meeting was duly arranged for the following morning between the Northern delegation and the Taoiseach, but Doherty was to be disappointed. In response to loud demands for guns, Lynch looked uneasy. 'Gas masks I can give you, even for humanitarian reasons, but guns I will have to think about,' Doherty recalls him as saying. After the meeting Doherty was convinced that Lynch had no intention of getting involved in Northern Ireland, at least not in the way the Northerners wanted. While it may be doubted if Doherty's quotes can be exact after a lapse of 30 years, his vignette provides an illuminating picture of the mood and attitude among the key figures in the arms crisis in February of 1970. He did not have confidence in Lynch precisely because he formed the clear impression that the Taoiseach was not willing to provide guns for Northern nationalists.[30]

Two months later Gibbons issued another controversial order to the

Army. This time the instruction was clearly made at Blaney's insistence. On 2 April Gibbons was on his way home to Kilkenny from a cabinet meeting in Dublin when, on Blaney's instructions, he was intercepted by the Gardaí at Naas. The Minister went into the Garda station in Naas to take a telephone call from Blaney who told him that an all-out assault was about to be launched on the Catholic community in the North. Blaney claimed the British security forces would be withdrawn to facilitate the attack on a defenceless minority. He told Gibbons that arms and ammunition should be moved to the border so that they could be made available to northern nationalists who wanted to protect themselves against the imminent attack. Gibbons, in turn, rang the Chief of Staff and told him of Blaney's request, and orders were immediately issued for the movement of 500 rifles and 80,000 rounds of ammunition from Dublin to the army barracks in Dundalk.[31]

There was consternation among the Army officers in Dundalk barracks when the consignment arrived on the night of 2 April. Some of them feared that the operation was a set-up, designed to facilitate the handing over of the weapons to the IRA. The officer in charge at Dundalk made his views known to his superiors and early on 4 April the bulk of the consignment, 350 rifles, were sent back to Dublin. The night after the weapons were sent back a group of men from Belfast arrived at the barracks demanding arms and ammunition which they said had been promised to them. They were turned away amid much recrimination. A few weeks later military intelligence reported there was a possibility of an IRA raid on the barracks and the remaining 150 rifles and the 80,000 rounds of ammunition were also sent back to Dublin. Military intelligence also reported that the information given to Gibbons by Blaney about the planned attack on the minority and the withdrawal of British security forces was 'without foundation'. Gibbons later maintained that he only agreed to the movement of the rifles and ammunition to Dundalk 'in order to placate Mr Blaney and thus prevent Mr Blaney doing something rash.'[32]

Gibbons also said later that around this time he had a conversation with Blaney on the subject of gun-running. 'Although he [Blaney] spoke somewhat obliquely I clearly understood that what he was conveying was whether I knew that the Minister for Defence could authorise the customs-free importation of arms and if there were any circumstances in which I would consider issuing this authority irregularly. I told him I would not consider it under any circumstances. He said, "You would not?" and I replied, "No." He seemed angry and disappointed.'[33]

The plan to import arms went full steam ahead in the early months of 1970. Capt. Kelly organised the purchase of arms on the continent and in

March the consignment was due to be shipped from Antwerp to Dublin on *The City of Dublin.* In his capacity as Minister for Finance, Haughey instructed customs to clear the cargo without inspecting it but, unfortunately for the plotters, it was never loaded because the paperwork was not in order due to the activities of British intelligence. Capt. Kelly went to the continent to have the cargo transferred to Trieste for shipment to Ireland, but he changed plans again and had the guns offloaded in Vienna so that they could be flown direct to Dublin on a chartered plane.

As Kelly chased around Europe trying to organise the shipment, events at home took a sinister turn which dramatically changed the indulgent public atmosphere towards those prepared to use violence for political ends. In late 1969 Saor Éire carried out a spate of armed bank robberies. Gardaí regarded the group as psychopaths who could not be contained without internment.[34] In January 1970 two leading members of the gang, Seán Doyle and Tom O'Neill, were charged with illegal possession of arms and shooting with intent to commit murder. Legal bungling led to the charges being dropped and the two were not re-arrested outside the court as they should have been. A third member of the group, Joseph Dillon, had been allowed out of jail two years earlier when Mr Justice Seamus Henchy decided that a mistake in a ministerial order moving him from Mountjoy to Portlaoise warranted his release. The Supreme Court ruled in 1969 that it was wrong to release Dillon but the Gardaí were not able to recapture him.[35]

On 20 February the gang took over the Co. Wicklow town of Rathdrum for a few hours, cutting all communications and firing over the head of a Garda while robbing a bank in the town. Public disquiet at the lack of action by the authorities began to grow, particularly when the political rumour mill suggested that Ó Móráin had earlier intervened with the Gardaí on behalf of one of the Saor Éire gang because of local Mayo ties. Blaney also had direct contacts with Saor Éire elements in the quest for arms but very few people knew this at the time.[36]

Then on the morning of Friday, 3 April 1970, the gang robbed the Royal Bank on Arran Quay in Dublin, triggering the alarm. Gardaí rushed to the scene and arrived just as the robbers were leaving. One of the heavily armed gang shot and killed the unarmed Garda Richard Fallon. The murder stunned the country but despite a huge security operation the gang escaped. There was fury within senior ranks of the Gardaí at what they believed were indiscriminate contacts between key ministers and subversives who may have been involved in the robbery. A rumour, which was widely believed within the Gardaí, suggested that in the aftermath of the robbery members of the gang were driven to the border in a state car and told to make themselves scarce in the North. No evidence ever emerged to substantiate this rumour and Blaney vehe-mently denied it in the Dáil the following month. However, it is indicative of the way trust in the institutions of state was breaking down that senior Gardaí believed the rumours about Blaney's involvement. They were also highly critical of Ó Móráin for what they regarded as a lack of zeal in pur-suing the killers. Some Gardaí believed that the Minister for Justice was trying to protect members of the Saor Éire gang.

Speaking in the Dáil in July 2001 Des O'Malley referred back to this incident. 'There is some reason to believe Garda Fallon may have been murdered in April 1970 with a weapon which had been part of earlier illegal shipments into this state. There is also reason to suppose that some senior Gardaí suspected that a prominent politician was fully aware of this earlier importation and had turned a blind eye to it. These same Gardaí became aware through intelligence reports that by December 1969 certain politicians were funding illegal organisations.'[37]

In the days following Garda Fallon's funeral there was outrage among the Gardaí when stories of indiscriminate ministerial contacts with subversives, including Saor Éire, gained wide currency. It was against this climate that John Fleming, the head of the Special Branch, and Phil McMahon came to Berry with reports about the murder and outlined the connections they believed existed between Blaney and Saor Éire. They also provided Berry with a full report on the progress of the plan to import arms. By this stage Berry was becoming increasingly worried that the secu-rity of the state was being undermined by senior ministers. He was not sure what his own minister, Ó Móráin, was up to and there were suspicions that he was tipping off colleagues about the Garda intelligence coming into Berry's hands.

The Taoiseach then finally got involved. He phoned Berry on 13 April and asked him to call into Government Buildings that evening to give him a briefing on the IRA situation and the North. When Berry gave Lynch the up-to-date background, including the Garda information about the participation of ministers in supplying arms to the IRA, the Taoiseach appeared genuinely surprised.[38] Lynch decided that he would have to take action but did not know what to do. One decision he made was to put all other issues to one side and concentrate his energies on trying to sort out the mess. Lynch approached Trinity economics lecturer, Martin O'Donoghue, during this period and asked him to become his special adviser. He told O'Donoghue that he wanted him to oversee his depart-ment's handling of Ireland's entry application to the EEC and the main lines of economic policy as he had other matters to attend to. O'Donoghue agreed to become the first non-civil service adviser to the Taoiseach.

The meeting in the Taoiseach's office at which O'Donoghue was offered the job was interrupted by a civil servant who told Lynch that two customs officers from Dublin Airport were waiting to see him. O'Donoghue only realised the significance of this a few weeks later.[39] On 17 April Berry learned of the plan to bring 6.8 tons of arms and ammunition into Dublin Airport four days later. In consultation with senior Gardaí action was taken immediately and the airport was staked out by detectives who had instructions to seize the cargo. Berry told Ó Móráin what was happening.

The following day Berry was at home when he received a phone call from Haughey at 6.30 p.m. in the evening.

'You know about the cargo that is coming into Dublin Airport on Sunday?' asked Haughey.

'Yes, Minister,' replied Berry.

'Can it be let through on a guarantee that it will go direct to the North?'

'No.'

'I think that is a bad decision,' said Haughey, who asked if Ó Móráin knew.

'Yes.'

'What will happen to it when it arrives?'

'It will be grabbed.'

'I had better have it called off,' said Haughey and the conversation ended.

The conversation with Haughey clarified a key issue for Berry. 'I had some lingering doubts that all this could not have gone on for several months without the knowledge of the Taoiseach unless he was wilfully turning a blind eye. But it now seemed evident that, at most, a caucus was involved and that Government qua Government were not behind the arms conspiracy.'

Berry then took an extraordinary step. Convinced that his drunken minister was not keeping Lynch properly informed, he decided to consult President de Valera about what he should do. In a telephone conversation with the President he said: 'I have come into knowledge of matters of national concern. I am afraid that if I follow the normal course the information may not reach the Government. Does my duty end with informing my Minister or am I responsible to the Government by whom I was appointed?' Asked by de Valera if he was sure of his facts, Berry said he was and the President then said: 'You have a clear duty to Government. You should speak to the Taoiseach.'

Berry did not tell de Valera about the nature of the information nor did the President ask, but Berry now knew what he must do. He saw Lynch at the first possible opportunity, which was on 20 April, and handed him

the Garda report on the situation and an account of what had been happening over the previous few days. Lynch was angry at a comment from
Berry which indicated his belief that the whole government might be
secretly involved. 'I saw red: I was not able to speak to you I was so furious,' the Taoiseach later told Berry. The next day Berry and Lynch met
again and the civil servant told the Taoiseach of his conversation with the
President. Lynch made no comment but decided that he would have to
confront Haughey and Blaney about the plot.[40]

7. THE ARMS CRISIS

LYNCH'S DETERMINATION TO CONFRONT HIS REBELLIOUS MINISTERS was thwarted by an extraordinary turn of events. Haughey, who was due to deliver his Budget speech to the Dáil on 22 April 1970, did not turn up; he had been taken to hospital early in the morning following an alleged fall from his horse. Lynch made the announcement to an astonished Dáil: 'Before leaving his home this morning the Minister for Finance met with an accident which has resulted in concussion. He is now in hospital and has been ordered to remain under medical observation for some days.' Haughey's accident has gone down in folklore with rumour putting it down to a variety of causes, the most popular one being the anger of a wronged husband. One way or another, Lynch had to deliver the Budget speech himself and his plan to confront Haughey and Blaney was put on the backburner. The plot to import arms, though, had been quashed due to the action of Berry.

A week later Lynch sent for Berry and told him he was about to confront Blaney and Haughey about their role in the arms conspiracy. The Taoiseach paced up and down the room muttering to himself, 'What will I do, what will I do?' Thinking Lynch was asking for his advice, Berry interjected: 'Well, if I were you I'd sack the pair of them and I would tell the British immediately, making a virtue of necessity, as the British are bound to know anyway all that is going on.' Lynch rounded on his civil servant, abused him for giving unsolicited advice and shortly thereafter left the room.[1]

Later in the day Lynch summoned Blaney, told him what he knew of the plot to import arms and asked for his resignation. Blaney simply refused to resign, believing that as no guns had been imported no prosecutions were possible. Lynch then went to the Mater Hospital and confronted Haughey with the facts and asked him too to resign. Haughey asked for time to consider his position. Lynch was then left with the stark option of leaving his ministers *in situ* or firing them. He had to weigh his options very carefully for political and even for legal reasons.

According to Berry, Lynch sent for him again the next day, told him he had seen Haughey and Blaney and that the matter was closed; there would be no repetition. Berry was stunned. 'Does this mean that Mr Haughey remains Minister for Finance?' asked Berry 'What will my position be? He knows that I have told you of his conversation with me on 18 April and of the earlier police information,'.

'I will protect you,' Lynch responded, but Berry felt shattered after returning to his department, where he told the tale to some senior colleagues. Later that evening Lynch phoned Berry asking him to have the head of the Special Branch, Supt Fleming, sent to his house that evening at 8 p.m. Berry himself was not invited to the meeting at the Taoiseach's home on Garville Avenue, Rathgar. When Fleming arrived at the house, he found the Attorney General, Colm Condon, the Minister for Defence, Jim Gibbons, and the new head of Military Intelligence, Col. Delaney, there. At this stage Ó Móráin had been hospitalised and was not expected back in action for a considerable time. The Taoiseach and the Attorney General did most of the talking but no clear decisions were taken. Fleming called to Berry's house on his way home and spoke of his bewilderment about what was going on.[2]

Faced with the dilemma about how to act, Lynch turned to one of Fianna Fáil's patriarchs, the 75-year-old Louth TD, Frank Aiken, who had been his Minister for External Affairs up to the previous June. Aiken had helped de Valera found the party in 1926 and had been a minister in every Fianna Fáil government until he asked not to be considered for reasons of age after the 1969 election. Pertinently, Aiken had also been the Chief of Staff of the IRA at the end of the Civil War and had issued the order to dump arms which had brought that conflict to an end in 1923. When Lynch briefed him about the activities of Haughey and Blaney, he responded indignantly. 'You are the leader of the Irish people – not just the Fianna Fáil party. The Irish people come first, the party second and individuals third. If you are asking me what I would do, the whip would be off these men as from now.' However, Lynch still prevaricated.[3]

When the cabinet next met on 1 May, the Taoiseach told his colleagues about the plot to import arms and that allegations had been made that two ministers were involved. He added that the ministers had denied their involvement and that the matter was, for the present, closed. Blaney was not sure if he was off the hook but Boland at this stage believed the plotters were in the clear and wanted to go to the Mater Hospital immediately to talk to Haughey and bring him up to date. On the same day, Capt. Kelly was arrested and questioned in the Bridewell. He asked to see Berry and also his political boss, the Minister for Defence. Gibbons came to see the Captain, told him to make a full statement and was then told by Fleming to leave.

The visit of a government minister to see a person being questioned in the Bridewell was highly unusual, but even stranger things were to follow. Chief Supt. Fleming asked Kelly if he would speak to the Taoiseach and when the Captain agreed, a meeting was quickly arranged. Kelly was brought from the Bridewell to the Taoiseach's office in Government Buildings where he had a long conversation with Lynch that evening. Fleming left the two of them together in the presence of a civil servant but, as it turned out, they were completely at cross-purposes. Lynch understood that Kelly was prepared to name names, including cabinet ministers, and outline precisely what he knew. But Kelly simply wanted to convince the Taoiseach that he had acted under legitimate orders at all times and should be allowed to go free. According to Kelly's account, the Taoiseach wanted to bring Blaney into the room but when the Captain made it clear that he was not prepared to act as accuser the meeting quickly came to an end. Fleming then brought Kelly back from the Taoiseach's office in Merrion Street to the Bridewell, where he was locked up and held for further questioning.[14] Meanwhile President de Valera phoned Berry to ask about the arrest of Capt. Kelly and the rumours about the plot to import arms. The President asked about the dependability of the Gardaí and of the army.

Three days later Lynch asked Berry to go with him to Mount Carmel Hospital to persuade Ó Móráin to resign. Ó Móráin's heavy drinking had already begun to catch up with him. On the evening of the Budget he attended a legal dinner in the Gresham Hotel at which a Canadian lawyer spoke about the famous barrister Sergeant Sullivan, who had defended Roger Casement. Ó Móráin heckled the speaker and then collapsed. He was later taken to Mount Carmel nursing home where Berry had been a patient only a few months earlier. 'He will go quietly,' Lynch told Berry after meeting his minister alone at the hospital.[5]

No hint of these astonishing developments had escaped to the public but the dam was about to burst because the Fine Gael leader, Liam Cosgrave, was by now aware of the facts. He received two tip-offs about the plot to import arms in the days before the news broke on an unsuspecting public. The first came directly from the retired detective Phil McMahon, who played a central role in foiling the arms plot. He was perturbed that Lynch appeared to be taking no action and decided to intervene himself by informing Cosgrave.[6] The second tip-off to the Fine Gael leader came by way of an anonymous note written on Garda headed notepaper. It read: 'A plot to bring arms from Germany worth £80,000 for the North under the guise of the Department of Defence has been discovered. Those involved are Captain James Kelly, I.O., Col. Hefferon, Director of Intelligence (both held over the weekend in the Bridewell), Gibbons, Haughey, Blaney and the Jones Brothers of Rathmines Road and

Rosapenna Hotel, Donegal. See that the scandal is not hushed up.'

Cosgrave was stunned by the information and he talked about it to a journalist and trusted friend, Ned Murphy, political correspondent of the *Sunday Independent*. Murphy wrote down the details and went to his editor, Hector Legge. After some consideration a decision was taken not to run with the story because of the obvious difficulties in confirming the information and because Legge decided it would not be in the national interest. When the Dáil next met on Tuesday, 5 May, neither Lynch nor the ministers involved had any idea that Cosgrave was in possession of the crucial information. The Taoiseach took TDs by surprise when he announced at the beginning of the day's business that Ó Móráin had resigned. Cosgrave was on his feet immediately to ask: 'Can the Taoiseach say if this is the only Ministerial resignation we can expect?'

'I do not know what the deputy is referring to,' replied Lynch, to which Cosgrave responded: 'Is it only the tip of the iceberg?'[7] Cosgrave went on to make the cryptic comment that the Taoiseach could deal with the situation and he added that smiles were very noticeable by their absence on the government benches. Most TDs and journalists had no idea what Cosgrave was talking about and Lynch still did not get the message that the Fine Gael leader knew what was going on. When nothing further had happened by that night Cosgrave was puzzled and he began to wonder whether the tip-offs he had received were designed as a trap. He gathered a few of his closest colleagues together that evening to ask their advice. Those present were Tom O'Higgins, Michael O'Higgins, Mark Clinton, Denis Jones and Jim Dooge. Cosgrave began by saying there was something important he wanted to tell them and proceeded to let them know about the a tip-off regarding a plot to import arms. 'I want your advice. What should I do? Is this a plant? Is someone trying to plant this on me to make me go over the top?' he asked.

One of those present said: 'We argued first of all as to whether he could take it as being something he could act on, because he feared the danger of just being hoist on a petard. And we came to the conclusion that yes, on balance, we had to act.'[8] Having agreed on this Cosgrave said he had a second question about the form of action he should take. 'What do I do? Do I bring it up in the Dáil? Do I go to the newspapers? Do I go to the Taoiseach?'

Mark Clinton was the first to advise. 'I think this is of such national importance the only thing is go to the Taoiseach and go to him tonight.' The others present agreed. 'And Liam went off and rang Jack Lynch's office and established that Jack was still in Leinster House. The Dáil had risen and Liam went off for a while and we all sat around wondering what was happening. He came back, looked at us and said: "It's all true." I will always remember that. And then he called a front bench meeting for the following morning,' said one of the people present that night. In fact Lynch did not tell Cosgrave it was all true. He confirmed the substance of the letter but said that two of the names on the list, Jim Gibbons and Col. Hefferon, were not involved in the plot. 'The first thing Lynch said to Cosgrave when the Garda note was drawn to his attention was that Gibbons and Hefferon were not involved,' recalled Michael Mills. He added that if they had been involved the entire affair would have been legitimised. Mills believed, though, that while neither of them played any role in the clandestine operation, they knew it was in progress and did not try to stop it.[9]

There has always been a mystery about the precise role played by Gibbons in the whole affair. One confidant of Lynch believed that Gibbons was sucked into the conspiracy in the early stages, assuming, because of the seniority of Haughey and Blaney, that it was officially authorised. However, in the Spring of 1970 he began to have doubts and went to Lynch. The Taoiseach, believing that there was not sufficient proof to tackle the conspirators, instructed Gibbons to do nothing but to report back to him on developments.[10]

Following Cosgrave's visit Lynch spoke personally to Blaney and phoned Haughey. He again asked both men to resign but they refused. He then went home to consult his wife and at 2 a.m. he instructed the head of the Government Information Service, Eoin Neeson, to issue a statement that Haughey and Blaney had been fired. There is little doubt that Lynch took action that night as a direct response to Cosgrave's intervention.[11]

The country woke up on 6 May to the astounding news that two top ministers had been sacked. A third, Kevin Boland, resigned, as did junior minister Paudge Brennan. It was the most amazing turn of events since Fianna Fáil entered the Dáil in 1927 and there was widespread public anxiety not only about the stability of the government but about whether the institutions of the state could cope. Paddy Hillery had flown over to London late the night before for a meeting with British minister George Thompson, that morning. 'The ambassador came to me at 7 in the morning making a great fuss. He told me I was wanted back in Dublin as Jack had fired two Ministers. It was a big shock.'[12]

When the Dáil met at 11.30 a.m. that morning Lynch proposed to a stunned chamber that the day's sitting be postponed until 10 p.m. that night to give his parliamentary party an opportunity to discuss the issue. Cosgrave reluctantly agreed while making the point that a Fianna Fáil party meeting should not take precedence over the business of the country. Dáil deputies of all parties were shell-shocked and few believed that Lynch could carry the party with him against Haughey, Blaney and Boland. 'The atmosphere in Leinster House for those few days was incredible, the most incredible of my life,' said Brendan Halligan, the then general secretary of the Labour Party. 'Nobody went to bed. For the first time, RTÉ put an outside broadcast unit at the Dáil and was running a commentary non-stop. There were all sorts of rumours sweeping the place and people, as you saw with the fall of the government in 1994, were prepared to believe anything. In this case, however, the issues were very serious: they were talking about the Gardaí, they were talking about the army, they were talking about the role of parliament itself.'[13]

To general surprise, the crisis had transformed the Taoiseach. After almost a year of hesitation and prevarication he followed up his early morning sackings by a display of political toughness and cunning which confounded his enemies within Fianna Fáil, kept the Opposition at bay and kept his government in office. His first priority was to survive the parliamentary party meeting and after that to win the confidence of the Dáil. His handling of the party meeting was masterly. Contrary to the expectation of most of his excited deputies, he did not open up a debate on Northern policy and whether or not the use of force was legitimate. Instead he proposed a motion confined to the narrow ground which confirmed a Taoiseach's constitutional right to hire and fire ministers. 'When I got back from London that morning the Government, what was left of it, was in a fairly continuous session,' recalled Hillery. 'How we were to deal with the party was the first thing. Going into a meeting like that you didn't want a vote of confidence. A vote of confidence is a sure sign you are in trouble.'[14]

Boland worked hard before the meeting to get a common front with Blaney and Haughey to force Lynch into a debate on the wider issues. The strategy failed because Haughey, still in hospital, could not make up his mind how to respond. So, despite the strength of forces arrayed against him within Fianna Fáil, Lynch not only carried the parliamentary party but got unanimous support, even from those he had sacked and those who had resigned. Blaney, Boland and Brennan all expressed unreserved loyalty to Lynch at the meeting while Haughey sent in a statement of loyalty from his hospital bed. It was, in the words of the renowned political writer Dick Walsh, 'probably the most remarkable example of an Irish party's instinct for self-preservation overcoming its internal divisions, an example of pragmatism without parallel in the history of constitutional nationalism in Ireland.'[15] Lynch's deft political footwork showed that it is well nigh impossible to shift a Fianna Fáil leader against his will, a lesson which Charles Haughey would learn well.

With a somewhat bemused party now behind him, Lynch was prepared for the Dáil debate at 10 p.m. on the night of 6 May. Again his tactics were superb. The motion he put before the Dáil related solely to the appointment of Des O'Malley as Minister for Justice in place of Micheál Ó Móráin. 'At the party meeting Jack said he proposed to have a debate on the nomination of Des O'Malley,' recalled Hillery. 'I remember sitting beside Blaney and he said "It's all right" to himself. So that took the steam out of it. That was the clever way to do it so that Jack himself wasn't on the line. That got the party relaxed because they knew what the strategy was. Still, it was an awful time, a sad time.'[16]

Although he confined the Dáil motion to O'Malley's appointment, Lynch made it clear that he was prepared later in the week to debate all the issues involved in the arms crisis and to nominate other new ministers in the course of the debate. In a speech which, extraordinarily, lasted for less than five minutes, he outlined to the Dáil the fact that he had been made aware by the security forces of 'an alleged attempt to import arms from the continent' and that these reports involved two members of the government. He quickly went through the sequence of events that had led him to ask Haughey and Blaney to resign a week earlier and to repeat the request the previous evening. 'I did so on the basis that I was convinced that not even the slightest suspicion should attach to any member of the government in a matter of this nature.' He also referred to the fact that he had been approached by Cosgrave the previous evening.[17]

Cosgrave then rose to speak. 'Last night at approximately 8 p.m., I considered it my duty in the national interest to inform the Taoiseach of information I had received and which indicates a situation of such gravity for the nation that it is without parallel in this country since the foundation of the state. By approximately 10 p.m. two Ministers had been dismissed and a third had resigned ... There is an inescapable obligation on the Taoiseach and his colleagues to resign and to give this country an opportunity of electing a Government of integrity, of honesty, of patriotism, in whom the people and the world can have confidence.'[18]

In a short and emotional debate, which lasted until almost 3 a.m. on the morning of 7 May, Conor Cruise O'Brien warned of the impending national tragedy which was building. 'Now the people have heard that the Taoiseach, who at Tralee last year made a very sensible statement, expelled from his Government people who were playing with violence only when those people were exposed by the leader of the Opposition, Deputy Cosgrave. They would not have been exposed had not Deputy Cosgrave done it. I do not think that in all matters I would agree with Deputy Cosgrave but he has rendered a public service.'[19] When the vote was taken on the appointment of Des O'Malley the government won by 72 votes to 65. Blaney and Boland walked through the lobbies in support of the government.

Haughey then issued a statement from hospital committing himself to a strategy which was ultimately to lead to a parting of the ways with Blaney and Boland. 'The Taoiseach informed the Dáil that he requested my resignation on the grounds that he was convinced that not even the slightest suspicion should attach to any members of the Government. I fully subscribe to that view. So far as I have been able to gather, the Taoiseach received information of a nature which in his opinion cast some suspicion on me. I have not had the opportunity to examine or test such information or the quality of its sources. In the meantime, however, I now categorically state that at no time have I taken part in any illegal importation or attempted importation of arms into this country. At present I do not propose to say anything further except that I have fully accepted the Taoiseach's decision as I believe the unity of the Fianna Fáil party is of greater importance to the welfare of the nation than my political career.'

When the Dáil met again at 10.30 a.m. on Friday, 8 May, the country was still in a state of frenzy, but Lynch was in complete control of the Fianna Fáil party and the Dáil. The issue now was the appointment of three new ministers to replace Haughey, Blaney and Boland. The new appointees were Gerry Collins, Bobby Molloy and Gerry Cronin. This time the debate continued for 36-and-a-half hours until 11 p.m. on Saturday night. There was a great deal of drunkenness in the corridors and wild talk in the Dáil chamber during the marathon debate. In total, 69 deputies spoke but only 16 of the speakers were from Fianna Fáil.

Lynch opened the debate with a speech which lasted for less than a minute, simply naming the new ministers and the portfolios to which they were assigned. He then sat back and listened to the debate. One Opposition speaker after another flayed him and the government, but he was more concerned with the speeches from his own side. Boland spoke early and took a hard line on the North saying, 'Arms importation into this part of our country by any agency other than the state is illegal and should not be permitted, but arms importation into the part of the country in which the writ of this Government does not run is not illegal, so far as I am concerned.' Nonetheless he supported the right of the Taoiseach to select his ministers and said that the three deputies whose nomination they were being asked to approve were 'suitable in every way for the positions for which they have been proposed'.[20]

Blaney began by denying any link with Saor Éire and particularly the suggestions of a tie-up between that organisation and certain ministers who were said to have used their influence to allow the killers of Garda Fallon to escape. Referring to Saor Éire as 'this lousy outfit', Blaney said that he had nothing but contempt for them and that any association would be repugnant to him. On the political issue before them, Blaney announced that he was speaking for Charles Haughey as well as himself. 'I say that there is no question about our allegiance to the leadership of Fianna Fáil, to the members of the Government and past colleagues and to new members who are coming into the Government. So long as there is a Fianna Fáil party standing on their constitution, so long will they have the support of myself, Kevin Boland and I am sure, Charlie Haughey and, I hope, those who come after us bearing the same names.'[21]

At this stage Lynch knew that he had won and when the division was finally called his ministerial appointments were approved by 73 votes to 66. The Opposition continued to express outrage and tabled a motion of no confidence in the government the following week. Again Lynch came through with his troops intact and his administration secure. It was difficult for the Opposition parties to comprehend which was the more incredible – the attempt to import arms or the survival of the government despite the uncovering of the plot and the dismissal of the ministers involved. The crisis did have one long-term effect which was ultimately to do real damage to the government. It brought Fine Gael and Labour together in the realisation that they would have to co-operate if they wanted to remove Fianna Fáil from office; both parties felt it was imperative after the arms crisis that Fianna Fáil should not win the next election.

Having secured his political position, Lynch then moved on to the next phase of the struggle with his internal enemies. The papers dealing with the attempted arms importation were handed to the Attorney General and, by the end of May, Haughey and Blaney were arrested and charged with conspiracy to import arms. His arrest by detectives who called to his Kinsealy mansion was something Haughey never forgot or forgave, particularly as the noted Supreme Court judge, Brian Walsh, was a guest at Kinsealy that evening. Capt. Kelly, the Belfast republican John Kelly, and the Belgian-born businessman Albert Luykx, were also charged with gun-running.

Unfortunately for Lynch this phase of the struggle for power within Fianna Fáil did not go nearly as well for him and in the long term it paved the way for his enemies to re-group and ultimately destroy him. The charging of the two Kellys and Luykx was also morally dubious and reflected little credit on the government. Capt. Kelly was acting under orders; John Kelly had good reason to believe that he had the tacit support of the Irish Government and Luykx was simply sucked into the affair through his association with Blaney. The people with the political and moral responsibility for the plot were Blaney and Haughey and they are the only ones who should have been charged. In the event the two ex-ministers behaved disgracefully by issuing flat denials to protect themselves. They left their unfortunate co-accused in the lurch; these men could easily have gone to jail while the two politicians walked away from the consequences of their actions.

In July the charges against Blaney were dismissed in the District Court because he denied all knowledge of the plot. As there was no evidence linking him to the escapade he was allowed to walk free, but Haughey and the other defendants were returned for trial. Boland was outraged at this turn of events and accused Lynch of 'felon setting'. Boland was expelled from the parliamentary party for his dissent although 11 TDs voted for him, including Haughey and Blaney. The trial of Haughey and the other defendants began in the Central Criminal Court on 22 September. They were charged with conspiring to illegally import 500 guns and 180,000 rounds of ammunition. The trial collapsed sensationally after six days when the judge, Andreas O'Keeffe, took grave exception to being accused of bias by counsel for Luykx. The judge discharged the jury and ordered a new trial.

The second trial, presided over by Mr Justice Seamus Henchy, opened on 6 October and continued for 14 days. In line with his statement from his hospital bed in May, Haughey denied all knowledge and any involvement in the attempt to import arms. This put him at odds with the other defendants who all admitted their role in the affair but maintained that everything they had done was legal as it was sanctioned by the Minister for Defence, Jim Gibbons. This made Gibbons the crucial state witness and placed him in direct opposition to Haughey. There was one major conflict of evidence between the two men. This related to a specific conversation between them on either 17 or 20 April 1970. Gibbons said he made it clear to Haughey in this conversation that the Departments of Defence, Justice and Transport and Power were aware of the plan to import arms through Dublin airport. He recalled Haughey saying 'the dogs in the street are barking it' and that Haughey had promised to stop the process 'for a month'. Gibbons had then replied: 'For God's sake stop it altogether.'[22]

In his evidence, Haughey accepted that the meeting had taken place in his office but he totally denied that the conversation, as described by Gibbons, had ever taken place. He did accept that importation of 'a certain consignment' had been called off but he maintained that he did not know what was in the consignment or why it was of such concern to other government departments, ministers and senior civil servants. In his summing up, Mr Justice Henchy said the only conclusion about this fundamental conflict of evidence was that either Gibbons or Haughey was guilty of perjury. The evidence of other witnesses was damaging to both Gibbons and Haughey because it indicated that there was official approval for the attempted arms importation and that Capt. Kelly was properly acting under orders. The judge also said there was a direct conflict of evidence between Haughey and Berry and that one of them too must be lying.

However, on 23 October the jury found Haughey and his co-defendants, Capt. Kelly, John Kelly and Albert Luykx, not guilty. That night Haughey threw a party to celebrate and among the revellers was at least one member of the jury. The whole affair had a Sicilian whiff about it but naturally Haughey was jubilant and he immediately threw down the gauntlet to Lynch who was in New York to address the United Nations. Haughey was carried shoulder high from the Four Courts and immediately he challenged Lynch. 'Those responsible for the debacle have no option but to take the honourable course open to them,' he declared. 'I think there is some dissatisfaction about the leadership at the moment. The Taoiseach's position is something that will be decided by the parliamentary party.' Then he headed off to a celebration party. In response Lynch issued a statement in New York saying he was confident he would win any leadership challenge. He gave a press conference the following day saying that the attempted importation had not been disproved and that he was sure an effort to bring in arms had been made.[23]

If there was any doubt about the strength of Lynch's position it was dispelled when he returned from New York after the weekend. In an extraordinary show of solidarity he was met at the airport by the entire cabinet – apart from two ministers who were out of the country – 50 TDs, 27 senators and the two leading party elders, MacEntee and Aiken. Nothing like it had been seen outside the Soviet bloc and it gave Lynch the confidence to give an up-beat press conference during which he announced that the source of the funds for the attempted gun-running would be tracked down. When the Fianna Fáil party met the following day Haughey's challenge collapsed; he had the support of only five people, including himself and Blaney.

As if that wasn't bad enough for Haughey the Opposition moved to capitalise on the conflict of evidence during the arms trial between himself and Gibbons by putting down a Dáil motion of no confidence in Gibbons. Lynch responded by putting down an amendment turning it into a vote of confidence in himself and his ministers. There was a wide expectation among the Opposition parties that, given the total conflict of evidence between himself and Gibbons, Haughey would have to vote against the government or at the very minimum abstain. Lynch knew Haughey better because, clearly anticipating the outcome, he issued a warning to a meeting of the Fianna Fáil parliamentary party in advance of the motion. 'I do not want any deputy to go into the lobby with me to buy time, because I am not in the market for buying or selling time.'[24] That, however, is precisely what Haughey did. He swallowed his pride and marched through the lobbies to vote confidence in a Taoiseach he despised and a minister whose evidence under oath had run directly counter to his. It was an act of self-abasement which most people could not even have contemplated, but Haughey did it in order to live to fight another day. Blaney did the same but Kevin Boland could not stomach it any longer. Some of the positions he took during his political career may have been pig-headed and mis-guided but his parting words to the Dáil, as he announced his intention to resign his seat rather than vote confidence in people he deeply opposed, did have integrity. 'As I look around me I can see quite clearly that there is nothing left to me but my own personal honour, such as it is – and I pro-pose to retain that,' he declared.[25]

Since 1970 a whole mythology has grown up around the arms crisis. The lies told by Haughey and Blaney gained such credence that it came to be widely accepted that Lynch was aware of the plot all along and did nothing to stop it until Cosgrave came to him with the evidence. Capt. Kelly, who had every reason to believe this was actually the case, repeat-edly voiced this view and it gained wide acceptance. However, apart from Berry's confused recollection of one conversation in October 1969, there is no evidence to suggest that Lynch knew about the plot until Berry came to him in April 1970. The fact that Haughey and Blaney did so much to hide their actions from him tells its own story. Even Boland is quite clear that Lynch would have vetoed any attempt to import arms if the issue had been raised at cabinet.

It is true to say that Lynch did not move decisively when Berry informed him of the plot at the end of April and that he was only pushed into action by the Gardaí and Cosgrave a week later. However, that is a far cry from turning a blind eye to the plot. Michael Mills, who was active as a political correspondent at the time, had no doubt that Lynch was not aware of what was going on. In a retrospective analysis written in 1998, fol-lowing a television programme on BBC Northern Ireland which sug-gested that Lynch knew all along about the plot to import arms, Mills said: 'There may well be a growing perception but there is no positive evidence to support this viewpoint. Anybody with the slightest knowledge of Jack Lynch's character would know that the assertion does not stand up to seri-ous consideration. There are things he should have known, and he should have exercised more authority over individual members of the govern-ment, but he exercised a hands-off approach to his ministers in the knowl-edge that many of them had more experience than himself and he believed that they would act at all times in the interests of the state.'

Mills recalled that Lynch was greatly shocked at the reports and would have preferred to have kept the whole affair quiet while privately rebuking Haughey and Blaney. The matter was taken out of his hands when Liam Cosgrave made him aware of the Garda note and when, more significantly, the Gardaí, fearing the whole thing would be hushed up, arrested Capt. Kelly. Shortly after the crisis Lynch told Mills that he lost all trust in people. 'How can you expect me to trust anybody after what happened?' he asked.[26]

Still, there will always be questions about why Lynch left it so late in the day to act decisively. The obvious answer is that he did not feel himself politically strong enough to move earlier. From the beginning of the crisis in August 1969 Lynch knew that he did not have the unanimous support of his cabinet for the moderate approach which he favoured. He fought a rearguard action in August 1969 to blunt the demands of the hawks for direct intervention. He succeeded in diverting them by a series of measures, including the establishment of the sub-committee and by allowing Haughey to preside over the fund for relief. He must have known that it was a risky strategy but the alternative of direct confrontation with the hard men at cabinet could have plunged the Republic into chaos and led to conflagration in the North and the destruction of the Republic's efforts to become a modern industrialised country. 'At this time I was in charge of the negotiations about entry to the EEC which were in retrospect very important, but at the time it was difficult to get the party interested,' recalled Hillery. 'God, if it had gone wrong there would have been death all over the place and we would never have got into Europe.'[27]

Presented with an awful dilemma, Lynch successfully played for time and managed to get control first of his cabinet, and then of his party, and ultimately to bring the country with him. Lynch's tactics did allow the arms crisis to develop but only because he had not reckoned on how far his opponents at cabinet were prepared to go in pursuit of their own strategy. They escaped the consequences of their actions because nobody in government wanted the full unvarnished and embarrassing truth to come out at the time, in view of the damage it might do to the party. That allowed the waters to be muddied in the aftermath of the arms crisis to such an extent that the whole affair is frequently attributed to 'the culture of the times', just like the corruption scandals of subsequent decades. Haughey and Blaney even found plenty of sympathisers who used the existence of the cabinet sub-committee for relief to turn the responsibility for the whole crisis on its head. Yet Pádraig Faulkner, who was at the crucial cabinet meetings and was a member of the sub-committee, is quite sure that whatever Haughey and Blaney did they did not have the sanction of the government for their activities. 'The references to the Irish Red Cross make clear the type of relief we as a Government intended providing for those who had suffered as a result of violence in the North, and to suggest that the provision of arms of any kind was involved, would be to stretch the facts beyond credulity,' Faulkner declared. He also pointed to the fact that the sub-committee met only once.[28]

Yet despite the weight of evidence there is a tendency among historians, as well as journalists, to shift the responsibility for what happened from the plotters and on to the shoulders of Lynch. He has been widely criticised down the years for not stopping the plotters sooner and then for prevaricating when he found out. It has even been accepted in some quarters that Lynch knew about the plot to import arms all along and only disowned Haughey and Blaney when Cosgrave came to him with the details. Within Fianna Fáil, in any case, a significant number of people never had any problem about Haughey's role in the arms crisis, just as they did not want to know about the source of his dubious wealth.

For instance, the influential senior Fianna Fáil figure Martin Mansergh gave the following analysis of the arms crisis in 1996. 'The covert but authorised importation of small arms from the continent, which was the cause of the arms crisis, was stopped by the zeal of a senior civil servant in the Department of Justice against a background of armed action by radical republicans within the state, possible British intelligence penetration, as well as the danger of misappropriation. The leader of the Opposition, who was tipped off by someone, precipitated the political crisis, which would otherwise probably not have happened. Whatever about some dabbling in troubled water at the edge by marginal figures, Official IRA and later Workers' Party inspired allegations that Fianna Fáil caused the split in December 1969 in the republican movement and spawned the Provisional IRA have not been substantiated by any serious historian who has written about this period.'[29]

The interpretation of the arms crisis advanced by the supporters of Haughey and Blaney in 1970 was given a whole new lease of life by RTE's flagship current affairs programme 'Prime Time' in the spring of 2001. On the basis of Capt. Kelly's interpretation of a statement made to Gardaí in May 1970 by Col. Michael Hefferon, which was released in the National Archives, the programme purported to show that key evidence had been suppressed in the arms trial of 1970. The clear implication of the programme was that this had happened at the instigation of Des O'Malley or Peter Berry. A raging controversy blew up over the events of 30 years earlier, with Sinn Féin, some members of Fianna Fáil and a range of media commentators claiming that the document proved a conspiracy on the part of the state to jail an innocent man in 1970. A second 'Prime Time' programme built on this thesis and aired the theory that Gibbons had perjured himself during the arms trial and that Jack Lynch was somehow complicit in the importation.

Only a few of those who commented loudly in the aftermath of the programmes took the trouble to read the original documents in the National Archives, which help to explain the complex picture of what really did happen in 1970. Des O'Malley and a researcher working for him carefully combed through the document at the centre of the controversy. They demolished the thesis that marks made on the Hefferon statement in the Department of Justice corresponded to deletions made to the statement before it was incorporated in the book of evidence for the arms trial. O'Malley showed that there was only a 20% correlation between the marks and the deletions. On top of that, he demonstrated that the changes were made by the lawyers for the prosecution, acting on the basis of legal practice current at that time, and stated that they had nothing whatever to do with the Department of Justice.

Inquiries conducted by the Minister for Justice, John O'Donoghue, and the Attorney General, Michael McDowell, backed up O'Malley's conclusions, but they took three months to prepare and did not generate anything like the same amount of publicity as the initial claims when they were published. Addressing the central question raised by 'Prime Time' as to whether O'Malley and Berry were involved in editing Hefferon's statement, the Attorney General's investigation concluded: 'None of the documents available to this office indicate or hint at any such involvement in the process of editing Colonel Hefferon's statement.' The report went on: 'It is apparent that the Department of Justice markings do not correspond closely with the deletions in the statement by the time it reached the book of evidence.'[30]

The reports naturally had less to say about the wider claims regarding who was ultimately responsible for the arms crisis, but they did address the oft-repeated assertion, aired on 'Prime Time', that Gibbons had been involved in the arms plot and had perjured himself during the trial. Addressing the question of what Gibbons knew about the attempted illegal arms importation, the report from the Minister of Justice said: 'It cannot be determined on the basis of an examination of any of the materials now to hand, or on any basis known to the Department, that what Gibbons had to say on this issue was untrue and it would clearly be wrong therefore to suggest otherwise.'[31]

In a short Dáil debate about the reports, O'Malley, having welcomed his own vindication and that of Peter Berry, broadened out the debate to the fundamental issues at the heart of the arms crisis. He pointed out that by definition the arms importation had to be illegal since neither the Minister for Defence nor the Minister for Justice had authority to licence the importation of arms for use by any organisations in Northern Ireland. 'Beyond the issue of mere legality it is also clear that the plotters must have known that what they were doing had not been sanctioned by the Government. Why else would they have taken such elaborate steps to cover their tracks? Why, for example, was the cost of Captain Kelly's trips to the continent paid out of the funds of the Northern Ireland Defence committees if it had been duly authorised? Why was there a departure from all known arms procurement procedures if the Department of Defence had sanctioned this purchase? Why would Captain Kelly not co-operate with the investigating Gardaí or the Taoiseach if the operation had, in fact, been duly sanctioned? Why, indeed, was Captain Kelly, on his own admission, reporting to the Minister for Agriculture rather than to the Minister for Defence regarding his activities?'

O'Malley was adamant that the Government in 1969–1970 never authorised the importation of arms. 'There is no record whatever of the Government ever having purported to take a decision to import arms for this purpose and the evidence refutes that contention. I know. I was there. I sat at the table from July 1969 onwards.'[32] The available evidence in the National Archives supports O'Malley's contention. The cabinet minutes for 1969 and 1970 contain no record of a Government decision to author-ise the importation of arms.

We have the word of Lynch, Hillery, Faulkner, Lalor and O'Malley that no such decision was taken and Kevin Boland, who was very unhappy at Lynch's policy, makes no such claim either. Even Haughey and Blaney never stated openly that there was a government decision to import arms. In fact, they denied all knowledge of the whole matter when their skins were at stake. Given what we know about the integrity of the cabinet members involved, there is no reason to believe the Haughey line but every compelling reason to accept Lynch's integrity in the matter.

As to the question of whether Fianna Fáil was involved in the estab-lishment of the Provisional IRA it is certainly true that neither the party as a whole nor the government as an entity connived at its creation. How-ever, there is overwhelming evidence that Haughey and Blaney were involved in encouraging the republican split and that arms were promised in return for a commitment by republicans to confine their campaign to the North. On this score there is the detailed diary of a dedicated public servant, Peter Berry, the intelligence reports of the Gardaí, the testimony of leading members of the Official IRA, some of whom met Haughey, and the fact of the plot to import arms. At the end of the day, all anybody – politician, journalist or historian – can rely on to make a judgement is the trustworthiness of the witnesses.

8. LYNCH IN CONTROL

LYNCH MAY HAVE ESTABLISHED his control of the party in November 1970 but Haughey and Blaney were still there, lurking in the long grass. The Taoiseach moved to consolidate his position by establishing a Dáil committee of inquiry into what had happened to the money voted for relief of distress in the North.

When the Public Accounts Committee began its hearings in December 1970, some of the evidence was almost as sensational as the events of the previous May because it allowed information to be provided without the legal constraints which applied to the arms trial. Chief Supt. Fleming of the Special Branch told the committee that he knew from confidential sources that Haughey had a meeting with one of the leading members of the IRA and had promised him £50,000 for IRA activities in the North.

Haughey, in an indignant letter to the committee chairman, issued a flat denial. 'No such meeting ever took place and no such promise was ever made by me.' The formula of 'no such meeting' was to be a recurring theme in Haughey denials of various allegations, major and minor, for the next quarter of a century. Although they had to wait until the McCracken tribunal report of 1997 to confirm their beliefs, it was clear to those in the know that such assertions often cloaked untruths. 'No such' was a formula, borrowed from civil service speak, designed to provide a figleaf of deniability in every circumstance. If an allegation did not describe the precise circumstances and mention the exact minute of the day an alleged meeting or event had taken place, he could deny it with apparent conviction.

The Dáil committee interviewed a number of key witnesses but was denied access to others, including Lynch. Berry was told by Lynch and O'Malley not to give evidence but he did provide information for the committee in a private session. Haughey continued to deny knowledge of the purchase of arms by Capt. Kelly and told the committee that the fund for relief of distress in the North, for which he was responsible, would have been totally inappropriate for such a purpose. The committee ran into a serious problem when Haughey's brother, Jock, was called to give evidence about his role as an intermediary in negotiations to buy arms in

London. Jock refused to answer questions put to him by the committee and was cited for contempt and sentenced to six months in prison. However, on appeal to the Supreme Court, the sentence was quashed on the grounds that his constitutional rights to natural justice had been infringed. The judgement destroyed the capacity of the committee to follow the money trail in the arms crisis and frustrated further Dáil inquiries until 1999 when Jim Mitchell began his inquiry into the DIRT tax evasion scandal. Only in 1997 and 1999 was legislation on the compellability of witnesses passed to get over the effects of the Jock Haughey judgement.

The committee was also hamstrung by the invocation of the Official Secrets Act. Among other things, this prevented the publication of a memo that had been sent by Berry to the Secretary of the Department of Finance shortly after the crisis of early May. The memo identified the sub-heading in the Finance estimate identifying the area from which over £100,000 had come. Nonetheless, the committee continued in its work for 18 months without the power to compel witnesses. It ultimately issued a report in July 1972, which clarified to some extent the process by which exchequer funds were used by Haughey to finance the attempt to import arms. It found that of the £105,000 in the fund for the relief of distress in the North, £29,000 had been spent for that purpose, over £34,000 had been spent in Belfast for 'undetermined purposes' and more than £41,000 was missing. A rider to the report stated that the committee was not satisfied that Haughey's decision to use the money in that way was justified.[1]

The committee's report had curiously little impact, largely because by the time it reported politics had moved on. Just after it was established, Lynch had to face the challenge of getting through the Fianna Fáil Árd Fheis of January 1971. It was a tense and dramatic occasion at which Lynch's enemies made a last stand. Patrick Hillery made a powerful speech in favour of Lynch in the teeth of howls from the pro-Blaney and Boland elements of the party. As members of the audience punched and kicked each other just below the platform, Hillery shouted above the din: 'You can have Boland but you can't have Fianna Fáil.' It was a memorable moment in Fianna Fáil's history, immortalised by the television cameras. The anti-Lynch faction created a rumpus but they were outnumbered on the floor and routed by Hillery from the platform. Haughey kept his head down and said nothing.

The Árd Fheis cemented Lynch's authority and for the time being put to rest doubts about his continued leadership. The party, though, was still in a state of barely concealed disarray after all the turmoil. Lynch gave Gerry Collins the task of trying to get control of the organisation and of isolating the Haughey and Blaney supporters. Lynch had to undertake a similar exercise in the Gardaí and Army, moving people whose loyalty could be questioned out of key positions. 'I never remember anybody smiling or being in a happy mood from the time of the arms crisis until we won the 1977 election,' said one key figure.[2]

As Lynch increased his grip on the party, Boland resigned from Fianna Fáil and founded a new party, Aontacht Éireann. A young Dublin deputy, Seán Sherwin, was the only Fianna Fáil TD to join the new party. Boland had little political clout by this time because, following his decision to resign from the cabinet, he honourably resigned his Dáil seat as well. Lynch's position was further strengthened because his various critics on the party's republican wing failed to co-operate against him. Boland had his new party; Blaney continued to snipe from inside Fianna Fáil until his later expulsion, but would not join Boland, while Haughey kept his mouth shut and toed the party line. Another well-known TD, Des Foley, who had been a Dublin football and hurling star in the 1960s, also attacked Lynch's policy but he resigned and opted out of politics.

The Opposition also set a trap designed to flush out the remaining tensions within the government rather than with any hope of bringing it down. In November 1971, it tabled a vote of no confidence in Jim Gibbons, the Minister for Agriculture, who had been the target of a great deal of abuse since the arms trial, where the judge had said either he or Haughey was lying. Since Haughey was later acquitted, many of Gibbons's Fianna Fáil colleagues had treated him as a perjurer. He was also attacked on another front by Capt. Kelly who maintained that the minister knew what he was doing during the arms crisis. A sensitive man, known for his cartoon sketches of his ministerial colleagues around the cabinet table, Gibbons never recovered personally from the trauma, even if he progressed politically. 'He found it every difficult to accept that his honour had been questioned in this way and that people regarded him as having committed perjury. I believe it contributed towards the deterioration of his health,' said his son, Senator Jim Gibbons, years later.[3]

Fine Gael and Labour, the Opposition parties, believed that Haughey and Blaney would not support the vote of confidence. The vote did prove to be the last straw for Blaney. He abstained and was expelled from the parliamentary party and ultimately from Fianna Fáil. Haughey, though, was again prepared to abase himself to keep within the party fold. 'I intend to honour my party pledge and vote in favour of the Government motion of confidence,' he said before the debate. 'In Fianna Fáil we have serious differences over policies and personalities. I believe these can only be solved through the ordinary democratic party process and that this must be done ... My aim, therefore, will be to do everything I can to restore its unity and reaffirm its purpose so that it may successfully carry on its work for the nation. Fianna Fáil is too much a part of my life for me to take any other course.' It was Haughey's excuse for voting confidence in a man he hated and despised. Though deeply humiliating, the move paved the way for his eventual rise to the leadership of Fianna Fáil.[4]

With Lynch now well in control of the party, Haughey set off on a long course of rehabilitation, travelling up and down the country and addressing any unit of the organisation prepared to issue him an invitation. He was accompanied on these trips by P.J. Mara, a young businessman who was to become one of his closest political confidants in the years that followed. There was just one constituency in the country which Haughey was effectively barred by the sitting TD from visiting. That was Limerick West where Gerry Collins ruled the roost, and it was something that rankled with Haughey for the rest of his political career. Eating chicken and chips at endless *comhairle ceanntair* and *cumainn* functions was a far cry from the *haute cuisine* and fine claret Haughey relished at top Dublin hotels and restaurants. Yet the tour of the country gave Haughey a unique insight into the Fianna Fáil organisation and enabled him to make invaluable contacts for the years ahead.[5]

The strategy of cultivating the grass roots was effective as he quickly rebuilt a base in the party. At this time Lynch had the support of the country but within the Fianna Fáil organisation there was a huge reservoir of support for Haughey's actions during the arms crisis. His decision to provide money to buy guns, even though he denied it himself, appealed to many rank-and-file party members who longed for the simplicities of old-fashioned anti-partitionism. By contrast, Lynch's more mature and subtle approach appealed to the wider electorate. Most Fine Gael and Labour TDs instinctively shared Lynch's views and he had the formal backing of his parliamentary party. His feat in routing Haughey, Blaney and Boland was remarkable because a large swathe of the Fianna Fáil organisation was emotionally on the side of the rebels and only reluctantly went along with the tradition of supporting the leader.

As early as the Árd Fheis of 1972, Haughey was re-elected one of the five honorary vice-presidents of the party. His supporters went wild with excitement when he mounted the platform. Some of his most steadfast opponents like George Colley felt bound to applaud and to shake hands with him, if only in a perfunctory fashion. An exception was Erskine Childers, who not only refused to applaud or shake hands but sat ostentatiously reading his newspaper while the commotion went on all around him. It was becoming increasingly clear that Haughey was still a force to be reckoned with in Fianna Fáil.

Although he generally kept his views to himself, Haughey did make the odd foray into controversy. Following the introduction of internment in the North in the summer of 1971, he attacked partition as the root of all evil and again called on the UN Security Council to send a peacekeeping force to the North. 'A policy of looking to the British Government to ensure reform and an end to injustice while the British Army kept the peace has failed,' he declared in flat contravention of his government's position.[6] Lynch ignored Haughey's intervention. In the mood of emotion following internment he thought it better to let the hare sit. In the future, Haughey would use moments of high emotion generated by the violence in the North to reiterate his old position. It was a vital ingredient in his appeal to the Fianna Fáil faithful and it helped him to salvage some dignity during his exile.

Amazingly Fianna Fáil, both as a government and as a party, recovered quickly from the trauma of the arms crisis and managed to govern well for three years. 'The party's survival bewildered its opponents and amazed its friends,' wrote Dick Walsh of this period. 'Not only did Lynch's beleaguered government hold out for two and a half years after the arms crisis, it managed to negotiate Irish membership of the EEC and to bring Anglo-Irish relations to the point where, albeit nine months after its departure, agreement on a power-sharing executive in the North proved possible.'[7]

Yet the crisis of 1970 did ultimately cost Fianna Fáil power, because it prompted an unexpected unity on the Opposition benches. Both Liam Cosgrave and Brendan Corish became convinced of the necessity to defeat Fianna Fáil and put an alternative government in place. The Labour party leadership, in advance of the vote of confidence in Jim Gibbons at the end of 1971, tackled the coalition issue head on. A special delegate conference was convened in Cork and, despite the bitter opposition of Noel Browne who led a walk-out after the decision was taken, decided to reverse the party's policy and leave the door to coalition open.

Under Lynch's leadership and with Hillery directing the negotiations, Ireland became a member of the European Economic Community on the last day of 1972. A referendum, supported by Fine Gael but opposed by Labour, had been carried massively, with 83 per cent of the electorate voting for entry. It was a momentous decision which was to have an enormously positive effect on the country.

Lynch's men now dominated Fianna Fáil. George Colley, who had firmly backed Lynch during and after the arms crisis, was clearly the number two in the government, even if he did not have the formal title of Tánaiste. He took over the Department of Finance from Haughey. Patrick Hillery, another key Lynch supporter at cabinet, wielded considerable clout in the party. His Fianna Fáil credentials were impeccable and, although shy and reserved, he proved at the Árd Fheis of 1971 that his quiet manner belied a political toughness. He was ultimately rewarded by being made Ireland's first European Commissioner. Erskine Childers, another strong Lynch supporter, did not carry as much weight in the Fianna Fáil organisation, but was popular with the public. The mixture of his republican pedigree and posh accent, the product of an English public-school education, proved a potent political asset. Pádraig Faulkner and Paddy Lalor were always dependable in their support for Lynch, while Brian Lenihan knew which way the wind was blowing. New ministers like Gerry Collins and Bobby Molloy were also rock solid.

The leadership was strengthened by the addition of the young Des O'Malley, who took over from Ó Móráin at Justice. O'Malley was easily the brightest of the younger generation of Fianna Fáil ministers. In addition to his ability he brought a much-needed steely quality to cabinet deliberations, even if this quality sometimes spilled over into irascibility. As Minister for Justice he had the courage to take on the IRA and Sinn Féin in the teeth of fierce opposition from the more extreme elements in Fianna Fáil and threats to his life from republicans. He and his family had round-the-clock protection and this early experience of the extreme side of politics left a permanent mark. O'Malley did make one significant blunder during the arms crisis. After Haughey had been charged with plotting to import arms but before the trial, he bumped into O'Malley at the races and asked for a meeting. The two met shortly afterwards in Leinster House and, while their discussion never became public, Peter Berry believed that it concerned the evidence Haughey might give at the trial. Given his position and the sensitivities involved, O'Malley later regretted the bad lapse of judgement.[8]

As Minister for Justice, O'Malley courageously faced up to the threat posed by republicans. He wanted to introduce internment without trial for IRA suspects but was forced to back off because of nervous ministerial colleagues who were intimidated by a well-orchestrated republican campaign in the streets and in the media. In the face of growing IRA violence he did introduce the Offences Against the State Bill in November 1972. This instituted non-jury courts for people accused of terrorist offences and provided for conviction of IRA membership on the word of a Chief Superintendent. The bill had the added political advantage of causing mayhem on the Opposition benches. Labour and liberal Fine Gaelers were strongly opposed to the measure but Liam Cosgrave was for it and indicated that he was prepared to vote with the government. Cosgrave was actually voted down by his own party and was on the point of being deposed as leader when loyalist bombs went off in Dublin and changed the political atmosphere in an instant. Cosgrave's party swung behind him and the controversial Bill was passed with a massive majority.[9] With the Opposition still licking its wounds, Lynch decided to pounce. On 5

February 1973, the day before TDs were due back in Leinster House after the Christmas recess, he dissolved the Dáil and called a general election for 28 February. The timing caused consternation in the Opposition ranks. The Fine Gael and Labour parties had expected Lynch to go for an election if he had been defeated in the Dáil two months earlier but they were totally unprepared for a February campaign. Their coalition talks, which had been going on for 15 months or more, had not yet come to a positive decision to form a coalition and appeared deadlocked. One senior Fine Gael figure recalls that, shortly before Lynch dropped his bombshell, Liam Cosgrave had come to a Fine Gael party meeting to review the progress of the talks and said in exasperation, 'These talks are getting nowhere. We might as well end them.' Just days later, Lynch dissolved the Dáil. 'Liam's comment leaked to him and he decided to do it. He thought he would catch us on the hop,' was the Fine Gael man's comment.

The announcement of an election jolted Cosgrave and Corish into action. Next day, accompanied by their seconds-in-command and general secretaries, the two leaders met in Cosgrave's office and agreed within minutes to offer the electorate an alternative government by fighting the campaign on a common platform. 'The plan was agreed without any problem. The smell of power, you see. Power is the aphrodisiac, recalled Peter Barry.'[10] The strongest card the Opposition parties had was that Fianna Fáil had been in power for 16 years and the mood was strongly in favour of change.

As the Opposition parties were putting their 14-point programme together, Lynch was presented with a political dilemma which, if he had handled it differently, might have changed the subsequent history of Fianna Fáil. The day after the election was called, a dinner was held in Leinster House to commemorate the Taoiseach's 25 years in the Dáil. The party's two longest-serving TDs and founder members were seated beside the leader – Frank Aiken on Lynch's right and Paddy Smith on his left. During the meal Aiken told Lynch that if Haughey was nominated by his local constituency organisation and subsequently ratified by the Fianna Fáil national executive, he (Aiken) would refuse to stand as a Fianna Fáil candidate and would notify the media that he was retiring in protest against Haughey's nomination.[11]

Two days later Aiken wrote to the Fianna Fáil director of elections saying he was willing to stand again as a party candidate in Louth but he added, 'In view of the shortness of time before Nomination Day, I wish to give you due warning, as quickly as possible, that after much consideration I formally decided this morning that if I am selected as a candidate and that Charles Haughey is selected and ratified by the National Executive I shall withdraw my agreement to stand as a Fianna Fáil candidate.'[12]

There was consternation at the highest levels in the party when both Aiken and Haughey were nominated. Lynch persuaded President de Valera to send for Aiken to talk him out of his planned course of action. The two men were old friends who met regularly and the President tried to persuade Aiken not to go public even if he felt he must step down. De Valera wanted Aiken to run for the presidency to succeed him and he emphasised that publishing the letter outlining his reasons for stepping down would damage this prospect. The conversation with de Valera did not change matters and anyway Aiken had no intention of running for the presidency.

When Haughey was duly selected and formally ratified by the party national executive, Aiken honoured his promise and withdrew his nomination, again informing Lynch that he intended giving his reasons to the press. He suggested that Fianna Fáil should approach John Hume or Austin Currie and offer to back whichever of them would agree to run as an Independent candidate in Louth.

Huge pressure was immediately brought to bear on Aiken not to go public. He wrote to his old friend and former cabinet colleague, Paddy Smith from Cavan, who had resigned from the cabinet in 1964 on a point of principle. Aiken expected support from his principled old colleague but he received a gruff rejoinder. 'I understand now what is in your mind. It is at least two years too late in my view,' wrote Smith. 'This man for better or worse has been functioning in the party ever since he made that speech after the Trial. He has voted and worked with the party and is chairman of one of its committees. At the last Árd Fheis of the party while I was in the chair he was proposed as one of our vice-presidents and he was approved with acclaim by all the delegates. I did not arrange all this but neither of us tried to stop it. He has attended party meetings; he has attended the Dáil and voted with us on all issues.'

Smith went on to say that he did not see how the issue of Haughey's nomination could be sidestepped. 'I have no brief for the man. I am not trying to be his case-maker but I know I have no course open to me but to do the only logical thing left to me and you are just as guilty as I am and every other member of the party is. The time to take action or propose the taking of such action was before this history I have so crudely outlined here. It is the truth, Frank, and it does not change the story to attempt to slip away from it. I think this is worth trying to read before taking such a foolish course. The proposal for a Curry [sic] or Hume walk-over I regard as far too childish.'[13]

There was furious activity behind the scenes involving Lynch, Colley, Seán MacEntee and the President's secretary, Máire ní Cheallaigh, in an effort to dissuade Aiken from going public. With little time left, Lynch approached Aiken's constituency right-hand man, Joe Farrell, who had worked unselfishly for the party for decades. 'Joe, I don't know what I am going to do. Frank Aiken has pulled out. He thinks that I should not have ratified Charlie Haughey. He is going to write to the press and tell the people why,' said Lynch. He then asked Farrell to make a final appeal to Aiken in order to avoid a split in the party but he did not hold out much hope, remarking: 'When he wouldn't do it for Mr de Valera, I don't believe that anybody can stop him now.'

Farrell went to Aiken and told him of the fears of a party split. Aiken replied that he did not want to split the party; on the contrary he wanted to help Fianna Fáil. 'The reason I didn't do it sooner is that I thought I would not have to do it, that somebody else would. But when nobody else did it I believe that I owe it to the men who went before me in this party. I'm convinced of that.'

Farrell continued to plead and told Aiken that if he went to the press with the letter he would be remembered as the man who split Fianna Fáil. 'Look, Joe, I have a conscience to live with,' replied Aiken. Farrell then made a final appeal. 'You did say to me many years ago that you always believed you had your life's work done when the Fianna Fáil party was founded. The work you did when Fianna Fáil came into government, the setting up of Bord na Móna and in particular the work in Foreign Affairs, all of that will be forgotten if you go to the press. I'm going to ask you for something, Frank.'

'You never asked me for anything before,' said Aiken.

'It is not for myself. I am asking your permission that when I go back up to Mr Lynch I can tell him to say that you are standing down on doctor's orders.'

After a long pause Aiken said: 'All right. Go ahead.'[14]

The following day, 13 February, Lynch came to a meeting in the Town Hall in Dundalk on the occasion of Aiken's seventy-fifth birthday and announced that he had learned with regret that the former Tánaiste and Minister for External Affairs was retiring from politics 'on doctor's orders'. Aiken himself issued a statement to the electors of Louth saying that the two Fianna Fáil candidates, Joe Farrell and Pádraig Faulkner, 'have been also in the forefront in helping the Taoiseach to maintain the national and international policy based on peace, democracy, justice and co-operation which was laid down by the leader of Fianna Fáil'.[15]

After the events of 1973 Aiken never attended another Árd Fheis or took any part in party affairs. He died in 1983 at the age of 85 having witnessed some of the turmoil which resulted from Haughey's leadership but long before the final disgrace which he had anticipated.

The Aiken saga does not reflect any great credit on Lynch. His concern to maintain the appearance of party unity in order to win the 1973 election clearly outweighed the damage he knew Haughey was capable of doing to the party and the country in the long term. He was certainly in an invidious position and could not have tried to prevent the national executive from ratifying Haughey without causing a huge rift in the party at the beginning of the campaign. However, Lynch would have done Fianna Fáil and his country some service if he had allowed an old and respected figure like Aiken to put his views about Haughey on the record. Haughey's long-term ambitions might well have been dealt a severe and possibly even fatal blow if someone of Aiken's stature had denounced him. Yet for short-term political gain Lynch did everything he could to suppress the honourable instincts of an old political war-horse who knew in his heart that he should perform his public duty and tell the truth, regardless of the consequences for the party.

Another indication of the tensions which were rife at the beginning of the 1973 election campaign is that Fine Gael and Labour had a secret weapon – a spy within Fianna Fáil. Brendan Halligan, then general secretary of the Labour Party, confirmed in 1996 that the coalition parties knew in advance of major Fianna Fáil announcements and were in a position to take counter measures, but he refused to disclose the identity of the mole, apart from saying it was not a member of the cabinet. The Fianna Fáil *volte face* on rates was one key issue where the coalition leaders were forewarned and in a position to react calmly.[16]

The rates proposal emerged after a lot of internal wrangling among government ministers about their response to the coalition campaign. The feedback from Fianna Fáil canvassers left the party leadership in no doubt that things were not going well and morale began to slip. Martin O'Donoghue then came up with a plan for the spending of over £30 million a year which would be saved on agricultural subsidies by Ireland's accession to the EEC. Initially the package was rejected on the advice of Minister for Finance George Colley, but in the light of the poor campaign Lynch decided to go ahead with it anyway. The coalition parties were alerted in advance by their Fianna Fáil informant that the package was coming and a pre-emptive speech was prepared for Cosgrave to be delivered in Rathmines on 21 February. His address, outlining how the coalition would spend the £30 million saved through EEC membership, threw the Fianna Fáil leaders into some confusion but they decided to go ahead by emphasising a small number of items from what had originally been a detailed package. The item they picked on to highlight was the complete abolition of rates on domestic dwellings. The announcement by Lynch of the plan to abolish rates on the morning of 22 February, less than a week before polling, clearly posed a major challenge to the coalition parties. 'The defining moment of the campaign was when Lynch capitulated on the question of rates and he called a press conference that morning at which he changed the party policy,' recalled Halligan.

While his opponents may have regarded it as capitulation, the pledge on rates helped to revive the Fianna Fáil campaign though the party lost power by an extremely narrow margin, polling a very creditable 46.2 per cent of the vote, which actually represented an increase on 1969. However, vastly improved Fine Gael-Labour transfers helped to swing it for the coalition and Fianna Fáil went into opposition for the first time since 1957. Considering everything that had happened since 1969, the party's performance in 1973 was amazing. Lynch came within a whisker of retaining power, an astounding achievement considering not only the events of 1970 but also the fact that the party had by then been in power for 16 uninterrupted years.

9. The Exile Returns

THE PRESIDENTIAL ELECTION OF MAY 1973 showed that, despite the narrow defeat in the general election three months earlier, Lynch's electoral appeal and that of Fianna Fáil remained undimmed. Erskine Childers was nominated as the party's candidate for the presidency and he comfortably beat Fine Gael's Tom O'Higgins, who had the support of both coalition parties. O'Higgins had come within 10,000 votes of beating de Valera in 1966 and Fine Gael and Labour had high hopes of taking the presidency off Fianna Fáil for the first time. Instead, Childers won comfortably. The victory should have strengthened Lynch's hand in dealing with the continuous pressure from some of his own backbenchers to bring Haughey back onto the front bench, despite pleas from Childers and others against such a move. To the dismay of many of the party's senior figures, Lynch continued to show a strange diffidence about taking on his deadly enemy.

A major reason for this was that, six months after his general election defeat, Lynch's authority suffered a serious setback as a result of the curious Littlejohn affair. Just before the election, two English brothers, Keith and Kenneth Littlejohn, who were wanted by the Gardaí on bank robbery charges, had fled back to England where they were arrested and brought to court for extradition proceedings. In court, they claimed to have been working for British Intelligence and to have carried out the robberies in Ireland as part of a plan to provoke internment in the Republic. Although the British Government denied the claim, it admitted to the Irish ambassador in London that the Littlejohns had been in touch with the Intelligence Service. Papers on the subject were shown to Jack Lynch when he was Taoiseach and were ultimately filed in the Department of Foreign Affairs.

In August, the issue became a matter of public controversy when the brothers went on trial in Dublin after their extradition. Jack Lynch denied that he had been made aware of papers on the subject and Colm Condon, who had been his Attorney General, very vocally supported him in his contention. The Fine Gael Minister for Foreign Affairs, Garret FitzGerald, asked the Secretary of the Department, Hugh McCann, to contact

Lynch and point out that he had in fact seen the papers on the matter in January. The former Taoiseach immediately accepted this as true, apologised for a serious lapse of memory and said he would have to consider whether he should continue as leader of the Opposition. Ironically, FitzGerald was prompted by the controversy to ask McCann at Foreign Affairs if he could see the documents for himself. 'Oh, Minister, don't you remember? I showed them to you in May,' replied the department chief. 'My sympathy for Jack Lynch went up immeasurably,' recalled FitzGerald.[1]

The incident did nothing to undermine Lynch's popularity with the voters but it temporarily weakened his political authority. After the Littlejohn affair he stood back and allowed an irresistible momentum to develop behind Haughey who continued his tour of the organisation to build up support. Dick Walsh has described Haughey at this period as being engaged in a 'half pilgrimage and half recruitment drive, motoring alone or with some helpful friend to towns and villages he once would not have visited without the accompaniment of a band.'[2]

Haughey also made a rule at this time never to discuss the arms crisis with anybody, particularly journalists. All meetings with the media were undertaken on the basis that, as P.J. Mara later put it, there would be 'none of that old arms trial shite'. Haughey's charisma and republican credentials saw to it that not only was he welcomed by the Fianna Fáil party faithful but that he got relatively benign treatment from the Irish media. He was largely accepted on his own terms: no talk about the arms trial and no questions about the source of his personal wealth.

In Opposition Lynch did move to modernise Fianna Fáil and to lay the ground early for the next election. He appointed Seamus Brennan, at the tender age of 25, as general secretary of the party and another bright young man, Frank Dunlop, as the party's press officer. Dunlop would later play a major part in the scandals that would swamp the party 27 years later. A third appointment was that of barrister Esmonde Smyth as the party's researcher. All three were to make a huge impact and put Lynch in a commanding position in the run up to the 1977 election. Martin O'Donoghue, who had been Lynch's special adviser in office, continued to play an important backroom role and began work on preparing the basis of the party's election manifesto long before the election approached.

Towards the end of 1974, when Fianna Fáil had been almost two years in Opposition, there was a lot of media speculation about a front bench reshuffle, the big question being whether Haughey would be brought back onto the front bench. In the event, the reshuffle did not take place until January 1975. Lynch felt that he had to bow to the pressure and

Haughey was appointed Health spokesman. Gibbons, who had pledged that he would never serve on the front bench with Haughey, was also brought back as Agriculture spokesman.

It was the biggest political mistake Lynch ever made. What is baffling is that he did not really need to do it. There was certainly pressure from the grassroots for Haughey's return but nobody in the parliamentary party would have dared to challenge Lynch if he had stood his ground and refused. Instead, he handed Haughey the platform from which he would be able to build himself into a leadership contender again. The emotion the move generated among people who had opposed Haughey is well summed up by the reaction of Rita Childers, the widow of President Erskine Childers who had died suddenly in 1974. Shortly after Haughey's reappointment, she was invited to attend the annual Mass organised by the party. She declined to go, spelling out her reasons in blunt terms. 'The late President would not benefit from the prayers of such a party. Happily for him he is now closer to God and will be able to ask His intercession that his much loved country will never again be governed by these people.'[3]

This reaction to Haughey's return was widely regarded as bad form by the media and caused outrage in Fianna Fáil where Rita Childers was dismissed, in any case, as a natural Fine Gaeler. It is certainly true that Mrs Childers did have a personal reason for being so caustic about Fianna Fáil for the way in which her ambitions to complete her husband's presidential term were ultimately rejected. However, her strong reaction did reflect the views of her late husband and of senior Fianna Fáil people like Aiken and MacEntee who could not understand why Lynch was willing to bring Haughey back into a senior position in the party.

Haughey's position was also made more comfortable by a debacle over a Fianna Fáil policy document on the North. The document was begun in the wake of the failure of the Sunningdale Agreement, negotiated by the coalition government and supported by Lynch, which provided for power sharing in the North and all-Ireland institutions. However, the new Fianna Fáil policy, drafted by the party's Foreign Affairs spokesman, Michael O'Kennedy, reverted to old-style nationalist rhetoric, calling for a commitment from Britain to implement 'an ordered withdrawal' from Northern Ireland. It was endorsed enthusiastically by the parliamentary party, the majority of whom had clearly learned nothing from the events of the previous few years. Lynch was deeply unhappy about the policy but felt unable to do anything about it as it was so widely welcomed by the party.[4] It was another example of his lethargic style of leadership in Opposition and it provided a big morale boost for Haughey and his supporters.

O'Kennedy's policy initiative gave Haughey the opportunity he was looking for to dress up his old Northern policy and run with it again. From his new status on the front bench he now felt free to call for a British withdrawal and to put forward views that were clearly inconsistent with those of Lynch and similar to those of the Provisional IRA. The pursuit of this more aggressive policy on the North was a vital ingredient in Haughey's strategy to succeed Lynch and it strengthened his appeal to the party's grassroots.

At the top level of the party, however, things were very different. After his return to the front bench, following an absence of five years, Haughey was excluded from the party's inner councils which were dominated by Colley, now Finance spokesman, Martin O'Donoghue, economic adviser to Lynch, and Des O'Malley. They looked on suspiciously as Haughey consolidated his position in the party organisation but they mistakenly believed that as Health spokesman he was in an isolated position from which he would not be able to mount a coherent campaign for the leadership. Haughey himself never doubted his future. A diplomat on a posting to Ireland at this period invited him to lunch and was surprised at how confident Haughey was that he would be Taoiseach one day.[5] The thousands of party members he met on his interminable circuit of the organisation were also left in no doubt about Haughey's belief that he would one day come into his kingdom.

Meanwhile the Cosgrave Government struggled with major problems. These included the aftermath of the oil crisis, which led to rampant inflation, and the intensification of the IRA campaign of violence which spilled over into the South, most spectacularly in the murder of the British ambassador, Christopher Ewart Biggs. The government ultimately got on top of the economic problems and brought inflation and borrowing back to reasonable levels but the voters never forgot the price rises which occurred during its term. The debacle of President Cearbhall Ó Dálaigh's resignation following an insult from Defence Minister Paddy Donegan, who called him 'a thundering disgrace', did enormous damage to the coalition in its final year. The increasingly republican tone of Fianna Fáil's opposition also worked to build anti-government feeling.

Still, most political commentators believed that Fine Gael and Labour had done a good job and would defy political history by winning a second term. Another factor that seemed to favour them was the so-called 'Tullymander' of the constituencies. The Minister for Local Government, James Tully, redrew the boundaries of many constituencies in a manner designed to maximise the total of Fine Gael and Labour seats. In Dublin, where both parties were strong, he went for three-seat constituencies on the basis that they would deliver one seat each to the major parties. In rural areas, where Fianna Fáil was strong, he opted mainly for four-seaters on the assumption that Fianna Fáil, though it could expect to get almost 60 per cent of the vote, would still win only two of the four.

Lynch and his front bench believed that what the political commentators were saying was largely correct and they drew up a manifesto, mainly devised by the economic guru Martin O'Donoghue, which offered the electorate a string of financial inducements to vote for Fianna Fáil. The abolition of rates on houses and the abolition of car tax were two of the plums in the give-away policy that had a huge appeal to the voters. Another key part of the manifesto was a commitment to create public sector jobs to reduce the level of unemployment below 100,000. It was not all spend, spend, spend. The manifesto also contained a commitment to wage restraint, which did not get as much publicity. Charlie McCreevy famously remarked later that it was the first occasion on which a political party promised to spend its way out of a boom.

Lynch agreed to the manifesto because he felt Fianna Fáil needed something dramatic if it was to win the election. He believed that, if he won, he would be able to revert to the moderate line on the North that he had pursued between 1970 and 1973 and which had been followed by the Cosgrave Government. If he lost, he feared that Haughey would win a leadership challenge against him and the party would revert to an outright anti-partition stance that would line it up with the Provisionals.[6]

When Cosgrave dissolved the Dáil at the beginning of June 1977, the Fianna Fáil manifesto was launched on a willing electorate. Seamus Brennan orchestrated a campaign full of razzmatazz on the American model, while Lynch travelled the length and breadth of the country drawing an amazing response. His popularity was at its height and it is doubtful if any other politician, before or since, was greeted with the same warmth and enthusiasm everywhere he went. Ironically, it quickly became clear that the manifesto and all its promises were totally unnecessary. Lynch's own charm and decency were far more potent factors in attracting votes than the manifesto policies or the slick professionalism of the Fianna Fáil campaign team. Lynch was buoyed up by the campaign and on polling day was quietly confident of winning but he had no idea of the scale of victory he was to achieve.

When the ballot papers were counted, Fianna Fáil emerged with the support of just under 51 per cent of the electorate. Only Eamon de Valera had ever done better and only once in 13 elections. Lynch won 84 seats in a Dáil of 144 members and had an overall majority of 23, the biggest majority ever obtained by a single party in the history of the state. And yet, even as the results came in on election night, a dangerous trend began to manifest itself. Constituency after constituency threw up new Fianna Fáil TDs that few people outside their constituencies had ever heard of before. But

Charles Haughey had heard of them. He had met them during his years on the chicken-dinner circuit and knew he could count on the support of most of them when the moment came for him to strike.

Having served in Opposition as front-bench spokesman on Health, it was no surprise that Lynch gave Haughey the Health ministry in his new cabinet. The key economic ministries went to George Colley in Finance and Des O'Malley at Industry and Commerce. Martin O'Donoghue, who had been elected as a TD for Dún Laoghaire, was not only appointed to the cabinet but a special new Department of Economic Planning and Development designed to implement the economic policy outlined in the election manifesto was created for him. Somewhat surprisingly, given the embarrassment his Northern policy initiative had caused to Lynch and the comfort it had given to Haughey in 1975, O'Kennedy was appointed to Foreign Affairs, as the old Department of External Affairs was now called. The rest of the cabinet, including people like Gerry Collins, Pádraig Faulkner and Paddy Lalor, were regarded as Lynch loyalists. Jim Gibbons resumed his position as Minister for Agriculture and there was some public comment on the fact that he was now serving in government alongside Haughey.

The animus between Haughey and Gibbons surfaced when Haughey produced a Family Planning Bill to deal with the issue of contraception. In Opposition, Fianna Fáil had cynically opposed the 1974 attempt by the Cosgrave coalition to legislate on the issue as it was bound to do by a Supreme Court decision. Fine Gael and Labour deputies had been allowed a free vote, on the basis that it was a matter of conscience. There were no such scruples in Fianna Fáil. The party simply opposed the Bill and managed to defeat it with the help of some conservative Fine Gael TDs, including the Taoiseach, Liam Cosgrave.

Now in government, Fianna Fáil was obliged to deal with the issue and Haughey, after consultation with the Catholic bishops, produced a convoluted piece of legislation which provided that all types of contraceptive, including condoms, had to be bought from a pharmacy on prescription and then only by married persons. Haughey famously described the Bill as 'an Irish solution to an Irish problem'. More to the point, it was a Fianna Fáil solution to a Fianna Fáil problem because a substantial majority of TDs in other parties were prepared to vote for more liberal measures.

Gibbons, who was a conscientious Catholic, had problems with Haughey's Bill and the deep enmity between the two men made the problem worse. Although a member of the government, Gibbons, in a clear break with party tradition, simply failed to turn up to vote for the measure. It was the only time in the history of Fianna Fáil that a TD, let alone a minister, was allowed to flout the party whip. Lynch turned a blind eye to his action and his enemies in the party pointed out the difference in the way Gibbons was treated compared with people like Blaney and Boland. Ironically though, the episode did more damage to Lynch than to Haughey because it stirred up old passions at a time when the Taoiseach was becoming increasingly vulnerable.

10. LYNCH DEPARTS

JUST WHEN HE HAD MADE UP HIS MIND that it was time for him to quit, Jack Lynch's legendary luck ran out. Shortly after his stunning victory in 1977, he decided that he would not lead Fianna Fáil into another election. By the summer of 1979 he had decided to step down in early 1980, after the completion of Ireland's Presidency of the European Community.[1] He made no public announcement about this, though his intentions were widely known within Fianna Fáil. But Haughey was not content to allow Lynch to retire in his own time; he wanted to humiliate his old adversary beforehand. So, in the autumn of 1979, he began to turn up the heat on the party leader.

Lynch should not have been surprised. Even in the first flush of victory in June 1977, he recognised that the scale of his win would become a problem. He remarked on television on the night of the election count that he would have preferred a smaller majority. In a remarkably short time he was proved right. Very early on, discipline in the party began to break down. An open mutiny emerged in 1978 over a proposal by George Colley to impose a 2 per cent income levy on farmers. Cork backbencher Tom Meany publicly challenged the government's policy on the issue and the new Kildare TD, Charlie McCreevy, made his first foray into the headlines by joining in the attack.

After defending the levy at the party's Árd Fheis, Colley later engaged in a humiliating climbdown. His failure of nerve led to an immediate loss of authority. The tax revolt by farmers was followed by massive protests by PAYE workers, who took to the streets of Dublin in their tens of thousands to protest at the burden of income tax. The first direct elections to the European Parliament in June of 1979 provided an opportunity for this disaffection to make itself felt and the Fianna Fáil vote slumped by 15 per cent, to just under 35 per cent of the votes cast. Alarm bells began to go off in the swollen parliamentary party as TDs began to worry about their seats.

The implications were not lost on Haughey, who saw the potential for instability in these developments. The influx of first-time deputies provided him with an ideal opportunity to expand his base in the parliamentary party. Many of the new boys were keenly aware that the party could not possibly do as well at the next election and that put their seats in danger. As the tide of public opinion began to flow against the government, Haughey fanned their nervousness into open revolt.

An added problem for Fianna Fáil was that Fine Gael, in the aftermath of the 1977 election, had elected Garret FitzGerald as leader. An economics lecturer at UCD, FitzGerald had been an enormously successful Minister for Foreign Affairs and, while he always retained an academic image, he was hugely popular. A dynamic leader, he immediately revitalised the main Opposition party. Taking a lesson out of Lynch's book, he appointed a general secretary, Peter Prendergast, to shake up the party organisation. He also toured the country, visiting every constituency and injecting life back into the demoralised Fine Gael organisation.

The economy was also beginning to deteriorate. While the government did have some successes to its credit, notably the reduction of unemployment below 100,000, the achievement was based on an expansion of the public service. In turn, this added substantially to the already swollen public service pay bill. To stop the pay bill spiralling out of control, the cabinet decided to fight a pay claim by postmen and the result was a protracted and unpopular postal strike. The government also failed to respond adequately to the second oil crisis of 1979 and long queues at petrol stations provoked further hostile public reaction.

It was against this background that the plot to remove Lynch was hatched. Haughey prepared the ground carefully from his vantage point in the Department of Health. On taking office, he asked Brendan O'Donnell, a civil servant who had been an associate of his since his days in Agriculture, to come and work for him as a special adviser while making it clear that the real job was something else. A gregarious Donegal man, O'Donnell knew many Fianna Fáil TDs and his appointed task was to be Haughey's link with the parliamentary party. He based himself in Leinster House, sitting for lunch on most days at a table inside the door of the members' restaurant. This enabled him to contact all the new Fianna Fáil TDs and renew his acquaintance with the older hands. He began assembling a list of pro- and anti-Haughey deputies which was to prove invaluable to his boss.

After the European elections of June 1979, which were disappointing for Fianna Fáil, a number of different groups in the party began to agitate on behalf of Haughey. One became known as 'the gang of five'. This was composed of Albert Reynolds, Seán Doherty, Mark Killilea, Tom McEllistrim and Jackie Fahey, who met in the Coffee Dock in Jury's Hotel most nights. New and brash TDs of the 1977 intake, such as Pádraig Flynn and Charlie McCreevy, joined more experienced Haughey supporters like Brendan Daly, Michael Smith, Ber Cowan and Seán Calleary in the Haughey camp. Other more discreet groups formed, biding their time until Haughey decided the time was right for a move. Ray MacSharry, who was George Colley's junior minister at the time, was a crucial figure in the affair. A house in Harold's Cross, occupied during Dáil sessions by MacSharry, Mark Killilea and Senator Bernard McGlinchey, was where much of the plotting took place. As the plot thickened, McCreevy became the unofficial secretary for the group, summoning caucus meetings in Leinster House.[2]

The tip of the iceberg visible to the public emerged in the shape of the young and inexperienced Síle de Valera and the exuberant fiddle-playing Clare doctor, Bill Loughnane. These unlikely allies made a number of strongly republican statements, clearly hostile to Lynch, which appealed to the party grassroots. De Valera had been elected to the Dáil at the age of 23 in 1977 and she followed that up by winning election to Europe in 1979. A granddaughter of the party founder, her name gave her considerable weight with the grassroots membership and she was a real thorn in Lynch's side.

Of all the conspirators, MacSharry was perhaps the most important, particularly as he was a junior minister, while the rest were backbenchers. He had experience and ability, combined with an inflexible will. Though Lynch had made him a junior minister after the 1977 election, MacSharry was impatient for further promotion. He had also suffered severe financial losses in his own small haulage business, making him hungry for a more senior and financially rewarding position.

MacSharry's links with Haughey went back to the arms crisis. The Sligo TD had been a member of the Committee of Public Accounts which investigated the disappearance of the £100,000 voted by the Dáil for relief of distress. He was very supportive of Haughey during the public and private sessions of the Committee and an alliance developed between the two. On a personal level, the two men were like chalk and cheese. MacSharry was rigid and austere in his approach to life and to politics. A teetotaller with a blunt straightforward manner, he had none of the subtlety of Haughey, but carried great inner conviction and once he had decided on a course of action was almost impossible to shake. He was certainly a valuable ally for Haughey and a formidable opponent for Colley. His eventual reward was to become Irish Commissioner in the EU.

Three other key conspirators who, like MacSharry, linked their future inextricably with Haughey at this stage were Reynolds, Flynn and Doherty, who came from the neighbouring constituencies of Longford, Mayo and Roscommon. All three were later to achieve very rapid promotion to cabinet office, with very different results, as the award for hitching their stars to Haughey's. Reynolds was a successful businessman who had made his money in the showband boom of the 1960s and later in the manufacture of pet food. He had spent a lot of money on his first election campaign and had pulled off the difficult political feat of replacing the sitting Longford Fianna Fáil TD, Frank Carter. A popular 'hail fellow, well met' personality, he played a key role in winning friends for Haughey among the new intake of TDs.

Doherty, who was equally ambitious, had a different background. His father had been a long-time Fianna Fáil councillor in Roscommon and he himself had been a detective in Sligo before opting for a political career. Early on he acquired the name of being a 'cute' politician with a strong vein of humorous cynicism about the political process. The third member of what was to become known as the 'Country and Western gang' was Pádraig Flynn. Even then Flynn was larger than life. His lanky figure first appeared in the Dáil in 1977 wearing a black shirt and a white suit and he was not backward about making himself known around the House. Like MacSharry, he would be rewarded with an EU Commissionership.

Charlie McCreevy, the organiser of the caucus meetings where the Haughey supporters plotted their moves, also played a leading role in the political life of the next decade but in a guise that none of them could possibly have foreseen in 1979. An accountant by profession, he was outspoken in his belief in the need for tough economic policies, but also held strong republican views and shared the same sentiments as Síle de Valera.

A much quieter member of the Haughey faction was Bertie Ahern, who came from the inner Dublin suburbs. Less flamboyant than the leading rural schemers, he felt his way more slowly, attracting little media attention to himself at the time. He concentrated on building up a strong constituency base but also began to make contacts within the parliamentary party.

The common thread linking the conspirators was that they were all outsiders to one degree or another. The party establishment was firmly behind Lynch and would back Colley in the leadership struggle. Haughey's appeal was to those outside the magic circle of power and influence. Some of these outsiders saw Haughey's election as their route to the inside track while others of them believed his elevation would change the whole outlook of the party. Some of them felt that Fianna Fáil had drifted from its roots and no longer reflected the republican vision that had inspired its founders. They saw Lynch's removal and his replacement by Haughey as a way of changing the party leaders' underlying philosophy and reverting to the original Fianna Fáil ethos of vibrant nationalism.

Haughey's attraction to his party's backbenchers was remarkably similar to that of Margaret Thatcher's to British Conservative MPs four years earlier when her victory was described as the 'peasants' revolt'. In both countries the outcasts took over power to the chagrin of those who believed themselves to be the natural ruling élite.

The Haughey campaign began to develop irresistible momentum in September 1979, when Síle de Valera, then a newly-elected MEP as well as a TD, made a speech implicitly criticising government policy. At the annual commemoration for the republican Civil War leader Liam Lynch, she called on the British to make a declaration of intent to withdraw from the North. Lynch had asked her not to make such an inflammatory speech, but she went ahead regardless. What Lynch did not know was that she was already in the Haughey camp and the speech was designed to destabilise his leadership.[3]

There was a brief lull at the end of September when Pope John Paul II visited Ireland but a political crisis blew up in the wake of that visit. Wild rumours began circulating about an alleged relationship between President Hillery and an unnamed Italian woman. The President was so concerned at the rumours that he called the country's political correspondents to Áras an Uachtaráin for a briefing and denied that he was involved in any extra-marital relationship. A few years later, in an interview with the *Irish Times,* Hillery hinted that he held Haughey responsible for what had happened.[4]

One way or another the pressure was kept on Lynch. After the Presidential rumour incident had blown over, Tom McEllistrim sparked off a major controversy when he asked why British aircraft were allowed to overfly Irish airspace. Lynch was on a trip to the US at the time and, in a speech to the Washington Press Club, admitted that he had given permission for British overflights along the Irish border in order to tackle terrorism. Bill Loughnane responded by accusing the Taoiseach of lying to the Dáil about security co-operation with the British. After consulting his Foreign Minister, Michael O'Kennedy, who was on the trip, Lynch phoned Colley to devise a strategy in response. They agreed that Colley would go to a meeting of the Fianna Fáil parliamentary party and have the whip withdrawn from Loughnane.[5] Colley, however, failed to carry the meeting and Loughnane was merely asked to withdraw the charge.

While he was still in the US, Lynch suffered the cruellest blow of all when, just before meeting President Carter, he was informed that Fianna Fáil had lost two by-elections in his native county of Cork on 7 November, one of them in his own Cork City constituency. What made it really hurtful was that key members of the Fianna Fáil organisation had hardly bothered to campaign and had even refused to select his favoured candidate, Máirín Quill, to contest the seat. They were not averse to losing so that the pressure on Lynch to resign would become irresistible. 'Jack was very wounded at what was a calculated and deliberate insult,' Quill said later. 'There was a hard core of people in Cork driven by the Haughey agenda at that stage. Jack felt badly let down by elements in the organisation in Cork.'[6] Before returning from the US, Lynch's press secretary, Frank Dunlop, asked his boss about his future intentions and was given a strong indication that the Taoiseach would resign in January.[7]

When Lynch returned from the US there was an atmosphere of incredible tension in Fianna Fáil. He went to one parliamentary party meeting saying that he had heard stories of caucus meetings and asked who was involved. Only Pádraig Flynn stood up publicly to admit his role. Lynch was later to say that Flynn was the only one of the conspirators for whom he had any respect because he at least had the guts to stand up and be counted.[8]

With the pressure on Lynch mounting on a number of fronts, Colley and his supporters decided that an early contest would suit them best, as it would not give Haughey time to organise. They pressed Lynch to announce his retirement. Caught between the desire of his friends and enemies for an early decision, Lynch abandoned his plan to retire in early 1980. Instead he announced on 5 December that he was stepping down as party leader and Taoiseach, and that his successor would be chosen two days later. Lynch felt humiliated by the fact that he was not even allowed to serve out his term as EC President but felt impelled to step down at this stage to avoid embroiling himself and the party in undignified internal rows and, more crucially, because Colley and O'Donoghue convinced him that the timing would catch Haughey on the hop.

There was widespread public surprise at Lynch's resignation, as the plotting and the strength of the tensions within Fianna Fáil had not been widely known. In a tribute to his old adversary, the former Fine Gael leader, Liam Cosgrave, who had been beaten by Lynch in the 1977 general election, described him as 'the most popular Irish politician since Daniel O'Connell'. It was an assessment that reflected the great affection that existed for Lynch everywhere, apart from a significant segment of his own party. Haughey was not taken aback in the least by Lynch's sudden decision and believed that a short sharp campaign would suit him best. Dick Walsh recalled that, only hours after Lynch made the announcement, Haughey met Doherty, McEllistrim, Killilea and McCreevy and after totting up the figures he predicted he would beat Colley by 58 votes to 24. 'Do you know, you're the worst fucking judge of people I ever met,' remarked Doherty, who had a much more realistic assessment of the situation.[9]

Immediately, the Haughey faction mounted an intense and unscrupulous campaign against Colley for the leadership. Afterwards, some of the Colley supporters were convinced that Haughey agents had infiltrated their camp to find out what was going on and to establish the strength of their opponents. There were rumours of bribery and intimidation and claims that uncommitted backbenchers were subjected to a great deal of pressure. Haughey was said to have offered considerable sums to wavering TDs to cover their 'election expenses' and there was talk of votes being traded for promises of office. One political scientist described the atmosphere as 'sulphurous'.

The level of support for the two candidates was about even but there was a vital difference in its composition. Colley had virtually the entire cabinet behind him while Haughey relied on the backbenchers. After Doherty's warning about not overestimating his support, Haughey assembled a team of supporters and gave each of them a doubtful TD to 'mark'. The late Johnny Callinan from East Galway was given the task of bringing Máire Geoghegan-Quinn into the fold and others had similar individual tasks. The Haughey campaign was conducted on a number of levels and even key campaigners like MacSharry and Reynolds were not given the full picture. Only the candidate himself held all the threads.

Meanwhile, Colley deputed Martin O'Donoghue and Des O'Malley to run his campaign. Neither of them knew the backbenchers at all well. O'Malley had been in the cabinet for almost all his political career while O'Donoghue had never been a backbencher and had only been in the Dáil since 1977. Not until it was too late in the day did the Colley camp realise that they had over-estimated their level of support.

'I don't think George Colley ran any sort of campaign. We were all taken by surprise,' recalled Bobby Molloy. 'I didn't know Jack Lynch was going to resign. In fact, it was Charlie Haughey that told me and asked me for my support.' Molloy had no hesitation in telling Haughey that he would not be supporting him. 'You know where I stand,' he said, making it clear he was a Colley man. 'Haughey had been campaigning from two years before that but George didn't campaign. He was doing his job as Minister for Finance. I don't know why Jack Lynch seemed to assume George would make it so easily. Charlie was down there every day in the restaurant having tea and coffee with the lads at 4 o'clock, after question time. He cultivated them continuously whereas Colley was doing his work as a Minister.'

Haughey had his own problems in trying to find a big name to propose him for the leadership. Brian Lenihan was asked but refused, preferring to keep his options open until the last minute. Major Vivion de Valera, a senior backbencher and son of the party's founder, was then asked to propose Haughey. Though his niece was a strong Haughey supporter and the Major was presumed to be on the same side as she, he declined.[10]

Having been refused by a cabinet minister and a party elder, Haughey then turned to MacSharry. The ignorance in the Colley camp about the whole drift of the party over the previous 12 months is illustrated by the fact that there was huge surprise when MacSharry agreed. Colley had been totally unaware that his own junior minister was one of the leading members of the campaign against him. A much more severe psychological blow was soon to fall on him. Shortly before the vote it emerged that Michael O'Kennedy was also backing Haughey. It was a devastating blow to the Colley camp. Frank Dunlop recalls receiving a phone call from Lynch the night before the vote when the Taoiseach asked him how he thought it would go. Dunlop replied that it looked as though Haughey would win. 'That is not what I am being told. George and Martin tell me they will pull it off,' replied Lynch.

The following morning Haughey rang Dunlop. 'Michael O'Kennedy is voting for me; spread the word', was his succinct message. When Dunlop arrived at Government Buildings he met Des O'Malley. 'Did you see Michael O'Kennedy?' asked the minister. 'If you are looking for him you are wasting your time. He is going to vote for Haughey,' Dunlop told a stunned O'Malley.[11]

A short time later, Colley, O'Malley and O'Donoghue went to see O'Kennedy to ask for an explanation. O'Kennedy demanded to speak to Colley alone and the other two left while Colley got the bad news. One explanation for O'Kennedy's last-minute switch to Haughey was given in a rumour doing the rounds the night before the vote. This suggested that O'Malley and O'Donoghue had promised the Department of Foreign Affairs to David Andrews instead of O'Kennedy.

On Friday, 7 December, Bobby Molloy was going in the door of the party room where the voting was taking place. He bumped into Brian Lenihan who said, 'It's all over, Bobby.' 'What do you mean?' asked Molloy. 'Ah, the O'Kennedy heave has decided it,' Lenihan told his puzzled colleague. 'What O'Kennedy heave? Sure O'Kennedy is voting for George,' said Molloy, who was amazed to hear about his cabinet colleague's decision to vote for Haughey. He then passed on the news to Gerry Collins, who was equally surprised.

Molloy has no doubt that Lenihan also voted for Haughey, despite some media reports to the contrary. 'Lenihan sat down at the edge of the sofa beside Haughey and put his arm around the back of it. He knew going in the door that Haughey had it, so he sat down right beside him. There is no way Brian went into that room and voted for George, not if he thought he was going to lose. He would have been a Charlie man anyway, in my estimation. Going back to the 1960s and the mohair suit brigade, Brian would have been one of those.'[12]

When the secret ballot was taken, Haughey won by 44 votes to 38. It was closer than Haughey had expected but there was no taking from his triumph and from the shock and bewilderment of the party hierarchy who were convinced up to the end that Colley would win. The shattered Colley and his supporters didn't know what to do. Such was the depth of distrust of Haughey that over the next few days Colley had long discussions with O'Donoghue and O'Malley to consider whether he would even vote for his rival's nomination for Taoiseach. When it came to the vote on 11 December he did vote for Haughey but the palpable hostility of the different factions in Fianna Fáil prompted an extraordinary speech from Fine Gael leader Garret FitzGerald.

In his autobiography *All in a Life,* FitzGerald refers to the incredibly fraught atmosphere in Fianna Fáil at the time and says that he heard rumours of intimidation of TDs during the voting process.[13] His awareness of the bitterness in the Fianna Fáil camp coloured the speech he made on Haughey's nomination. 'I must speak not only for the Opposition but for many in Fianna Fáil who may not be free to say what they believe or to express their deep fears for the future of this country under the proposed leadership, people who are not free to reveal what they know and what led them to oppose this man with a commitment far beyond the normal,' he told the Dáil.

FitzGerald went on to refer to Haughey's 'flawed pedigree' and said his motives could ultimately only be judged by God. 'But we cannot ignore the fact that he differs from all his predecessors in that those motives have been and are widely impugned, most notably but by no means exclusively, by people within his own party, people close to him who have observed his actions for many years and who have made their human interim judgement on him ... The feet that will go through that lobby to support his election will include many that will drag; the hearts of many who will climb those stairs before turning left will be heavy. Many of those who may vote for him will be doing so in the belief and hope that they will not have to serve long under a man they do not respect, whom they have fought long and hard, but for the moment in vain, to exclude from the highest office in the land.'[14]

It was a brave and acutely perceptive speech by FitzGerald but, ironically, it did more damage to him than to Haughey. The Fine Gael leader was widely criticised in the media for speaking the unvarnished truth. Not for the first time or the last the Irish media preferred to shoot the messenger than face up to the truth of the message. Time would, of course, prove FitzGerald right. In December 1979 he not only got to the heart of the matter but also very accurately reflected the mood in the defeated faction within Fianna Fáil. A number of Haughey's most inveterate internal opponents did indeed think of voting against his nomination for Taoiseach.

A group of them met shortly after Haughey won the leadership. 'It was very traumatic because quite a large number were seriously upset at the notion that they were going to have to serve in a party led by Charlie Haughey,' recalled Molloy. 'There was a meeting held after the parliamentary party election attended by a large number of people, TDs and ministers, and a number supported the notion of voting against Haughey as Taoiseach when it came to a vote in the House. But I argued very strongly against that. I argued on the basis of party loyalty that, as democrats, we had to accept the result. Things cooled down and people reluctantly agreed to vote for him but none of them had their hearts in it.'[15]

Martin O'Donoghue did not feel himself bound by the decision of the anti-Haughey meeting because he was not shackled by a long tradition of party membership. He made up his mind either to vote against Haughey or to abstain but eventually he was persuaded, against his better judgement, to vote for Haughey's nomination. Ironically the person who swung O'Donoghue's vote for Haughey was none other than Gibbons. He argued that in the interests of the party O'Donoghue had to put his personal feelings aside and vote for Haughey. 'If I can do it after everything that man has done to me what right have you to act differently?' Gibbons asked O'Donoghue the night before the Dáil vote.[16]

III

THE HAUGHEY YEARS

11. HAUGHEY'S LIFESTYLE

THE REASON THAT HAUGHEY AROUSED SUCH ANTAGONISM among senior people in his own party as well as in the Opposition was that they genuinely feared that he would corrupt the standards of public life if he obtained power. His involvement in the plot to import arms and the duplicity he had displayed both then and in the subsequent trial added to those fears. The fact that he undoubtedly possessed an indefinable charisma as well as great leadership ability made him all the more dangerous in the eyes of his opponents.

One of the things that worried those who cared about such things was the source of Haughey's apparently vast wealth. He had an extravagant lifestyle, clearly far in excess of his income as a public representative, with no visible means of support. The prevailing wisdom was that he had probably cut more than a few corners during the 1960s and invested his ill-gotten gains wisely. Shortly before he took over as party leader he bought Innishvickillane, one of the Blasket islands off the Kerry coast, and was building a house there. It was only in the late 1990s, some years after his departure from office, that the tawdry story emerged of how he cadged millions of pounds from members of Ireland's business élite during his time at the top and had massive loans written off by Allied Irish Banks (AIB). The story of Haughey's financial affairs was still unfolding at the judicial tribunals in 2000 but enough had already been established to blow the carefully cultivated myth to pieces and to justify the fears voiced by a succession of respected political figures since the early 1960s.

One of the key individuals in Haughey's life was Des Traynor, who died shortly before the cracks began to appear in the complicated banking edifice he had erected around 'The Boss', as Haughey began to be called after his accession to the leadership. Traynor, six years younger than Haughey, was also a Dubliner, though from the south side of the city. His father owned a garage on Grand Canal Street and he went to school to the Christian Brothers in Westland Row. The paths of the two men crossed when Traynor began work as an apprentice at the accountancy firm of Haughey Boland in the early 1950s and became an articled clerk to Haughey. Haughey was Traynor's mentor and the two men forged a close personal bond, which lasted until Traynor's death. In 1961, when Haughey was appointed a junior minister and became a full-time politician, Traynor took over the management of his financial affairs. 'Throughout my public life, the late Des Traynor was my trusted friend and financial adviser. He was held in very high esteem in business circles and was widely regarded as a financial expert of exceptional ability. I never had to concern myself about my personal finances,' Haughey told the McCracken tribunal in an affidavit in July 1997. Even though he was indeed a leading figure in the Irish business world and was chairman of the Irish multinational company CRH (Cement Roadstone Holdings) in the early 1980s, Traynor was rarely, if ever, mentioned in public as being an associate of Haughey. A notable exception was in *The Destruction of Dublin* by *Irish Times* journalist Frank McDonald, published in 1985. The book not only referred to Traynor's role as Haughey's bagman but was honeycombed with references to associates of Haughey whose names would emerge at the end of the century in the various tribunals and inquiries. The evidence McDonald was able to accumulate in the early 1980s and publish, constrained as he was by the laws of libel, should have been enough to set the alarm bells ringing about Haughey's financial dealings, but nobody followed his leads.

Shortly after Traynor qualified as a chartered accountant, he began developing into a financial wizard, who was not too fussy about breaking the law. By 1965 he had established a web of companies that would become the vehicles through which he moved money offshore on behalf of Haughey and his growing list of special clients. By 1965 he was a director of 22 companies, including Amiens Investments, one of the mechanisms he used for shifting money to the Cayman Islands into what have become known as the Ansbacher accounts.[1]

One of Traynor's early clients was the very wealthy property developer John Byrne, a close friend of Haughey, for whom he established the Carlisle Trust in the Cayman Islands in the 1960s. Byrne, the eldest of a family of 12, was born on a small farm near Lixnaw in Co. Kerry. He emigrated to England after World War II, made money in the dancehall business and returned to Ireland in the late 1950s. There he branched out into property development, building most of Dublin's first modern office blocks, including O'Connell Bridge House, widely regarded as an eyesore. Government departments leased these offices even before they were built, making it a lucrative business for Byrne.

Since that time there have been rumours, strenuously denied, that Haughey was a silent partner in Byrne's business empire. So strong was this belief that in 1979 Byrne had difficulty finding a state tenant for another of his office blocks, Seán Lemass House on St Stephen's Green.

'Wherever he turned he found himself facing a brick wall. And this wall, it transpired, was the Minister for Finance, George Colley. He personally vetoed any and all proposals to lease Seán Lemass House because he was convinced that his arch-rival, Charlie Haughey, had a stake in Byrne's property empire. At the time Haughey was serving in the same cabinet as Minister for Health and Social Welfare,' wrote Frank McDonald.[2]

As well as his friendship with Traynor and Byrne, Haughey also became close to a number of other wheelers and dealers in the boomtown atmosphere of 1960s Dublin. He socialised with businessmen like the auctioneer John Finnegan, the developer Ken O'Reilly-Hyland, architect Sam Stephenson, Aer Lingus chief Michael Dargan, car dealers Denis Mahony and Brian Dennis and the builder Matt Gallagher. Haughey's neighbour, friend and election agent, the solicitor Pat O'Connor, was another member of this tight group who were, in reality, far closer to Haughey than any of his political allies. Most of these people were also involved in Taca, the brash Fianna Fáil fund-raising organisation which caused embarrassment to the party when it came to public notice.

In December 1969, Traynor was appointed a director of Guinness and Mahon Bank, regarded at that time as the blue-chip merchant bank in Dublin. In 1976 he was appointed as deputy chairman, a full-time position which made him the *de facto* chief executive. He remained in that position until May 1986, when he resigned and was appointed as chairman of the building conglomerate CRH, which entitled him to an office at the headquarters of the company. He died on 11 May 1994 at the age of 63.

From the early 1960s Traynor had arranged for almost all of Haughey's bills to be paid by way of a cheque drawn on the Haughey Boland company's client account. A separate chequebook was kept solely for Haughey's affairs and when funds were needed Haughey Boland applied to Traynor who provided the funds, frequently by way of a bank draft drawn on the Guinness Mahon bank. The staff at Haughey Boland did not know the source of the funds other than that they were paid through Traynor.[3]

Haughey maintained at the McCracken tribunal that Traynor had managed his financial affairs since 1960 with complete discretion to act without reference back to him. He claimed that he had never asked Traynor how his affairs were managed or had ever discussed in detail the arrangements he was making. He went so far as to claim that he did not recollect ever signing any documents in relation to his own financial affairs. The tribunal judge, Mr Justice Brian McCracken, gave a caustic response to these claims, saying, 'It is quite unbelievable that all financial decisions over that period were taken by Mr Desmond Traynor without any reference to Mr Charles Haughey. There must have been serious financial decisions which had to be made during that period which no financial adviser would take without reference back to his principal.'[4]

McCracken's scepticism was proved to be absolutely right during the subsequent Moriarty tribunal when details of Haughey's relationship with Allied Irish Banks during the 1970s were revealed in public. It then became clear that Haughey was very directly involved in his own financial affairs. What emerged was breathtaking. Throughout the 1970s Haughey wrote cheques totalling approximately £12,000 a month on already over-drawn accounts. By the time he became Taoiseach in 1979 he owed AIB a whacking £1.14 million. This was equivalent to an eighth of the bank's profit in that year. The fact that the bank let him away with amassing such enormous debts from the time of the arms trial onwards undoubtedly helped Haughey to capture the leadership of Fianna Fáil. Without the indulgence of AIB he would not have been in a position to maintain his public pose as a man of great resources, living like a lord on the basis of money earned through his financial genius. Neither would he have been in a position to distribute largesse on a massive scale during election campaigns and the battle for the Fianna Fáil leadership. The brutal truth was that Haughey simply had no compunction about spending vast quantities of other people's money for personal and political ends and the bank facilitated him in that deceit.

Even by September 1971, at a time when Haughey was in disgrace for his involvement in the gun-running plot and his income as a politician was £7,000 a year, AIB had allowed him to run up debts of £255,000. The bank was 'appalled' at Haughey's extravagance but, despite a number of acri-monious meetings with him, the bank's officials were not able to rein him in. Haughey warned AIB in 1976 that if there was any drastic action taken against him he would prove to be 'a very troublesome adversary'. Asked to return his chequebook when the debt stood at over £300,000, he 'became quite vicious', saying he would not relinquish the chequebook as he 'had to live'. By June of 1978 the debt had risen to £580,000 and the board of the bank on a number of occasions considered the matter. But as Fianna Fáil was back in office, the manager of the Dame Street office where the debt had been run up was encouraged by his superiors to go easy. 'We accept that due to the change in the political climate in the past year it has not been possible for you to tackle the situation as you or the bank would wish,' Haughey was told. He was now Minister for Health and Social Wel-fare and let his bank manager know in no uncertain terms that 'he did not believe the bank would force a confrontation with him because of his posi-tion'. There were many meetings with his bankers in Haughey's minis-terial office but still no progress was made in curbing his expenditure.

When Haughey was elected Taoiseach in December 1979, he

Eamon de Valera (right) with Harry Boland (left) and Michael Collins, 1919

Eamon de Valera (left) and Harry Boland in the USA in 1920,
where they lobbied for recognition for an Irish republic

Delegation on its way to open negotiations with British Prime Minister Lloyd George in 1921:
(from left) Arthur Griffith, founder of Sinn Féin; Robert Barton, signatory of the Treaty; Larry O'Neill,
Lord Mayor of Dublin; Count Plunkett, first Sinn Féin MP, elected in Roscommon 1917; Eamon de Valera

Old-style politics – Eamon de Valera addresses an election meeting in the 1930s

Eamon de Valera (left) and British Prime Minister Clement Atlee in Downing Street 1947

The Fianna Fáil ministers in De Valera's last government, 1957: left to right (seated) Oscar Traynor, Frank Aiken, Seán Lemass, Eamon de Valera, Seán MacEntee, Jim Ryan, Paddy Smith; (standing) Seán Moylan, Kevin Boland, Jack Lynch, Erskine Childers, Neil Blaney, Mícheál Ó Moráin

Left: Taoiseach Seán Lemass (left), accompanied by Frank Aiken, says farewell to British Prime Minister Harold Macmillan after a meeting at Admiralty House, London, to discuss the breakdown of the Common Market talks in Brussels, 1963

Below right: Seán Lemass receives his seal of office for a second and last term as Taoiseach from President Eamon de Valera in 1965

Below: Captain Terence O'Neill, Northern Ireland Prime Minister (second from right), on his famous return 'Hands Across the Border' visit in 1965, with Taoiseach Seán Lemass, TK Whitaker (extreme left) and Jack Lynch (right)

Jack Lynch receives his seal of office as Taoiseach from
President Eamon de Valera in 1966

Neil Blaney (left) talks to Gerry Jones outside the Four Courts
during the Arms Trial in 1970

Left: Charles Haughey, Neil Blaney and John Kelly emerge from the Four Courts during the Arms Trial in 1970

Below: Neil Blaney and Kevin Boland in 1971

Left: British Prime Minister Edward Heath greets Taoiseach Jack Lynch at Downing Street for talks on Northern Ireland, 1972

Charles Haughey, cheered
by Liam Aylward (left) and
Tom McEllistrim
after his election as
Fianna Fáil leader, 1979

Political rivals George Colley (left) and Charles Haughey

Some of the Gang of 22 who opposed Haughey:
(from left) Charlie McCreevy, Des O'Malley, Mary Harney, 1982

Charles Haughey at the Fianna Fáil Árd Fheis, 1986

received a warm letter of congratulations from his bank manager, Michael Phelan. 'To say the task you have taken on is daunting is an understatement but I have every faith in your ability to succeed in restoring confidence in this great little nation.' In January 1980, the chief executive of AIB, Paddy O'Keeffe, became involved in an effort to sort out the problem once and for all. Des Traynor conducted the negotiations for Haughey and it was agreed to settle the £1,143,000 debt with a payment of £750,000. The money came from a Guinness Mahon account in the name of Traynor and the bank agreed to write off almost £400,000. Haughey was given back the title deeds of Abbeville and Innishvickillane.[5]

An inkling of AIB's real position appeared in an informed piece in the *Evening Press* in 1983. The story, by financial journalist Des Crowley, mentioned long-standing rumours in financial circles that Haughey owed £1 million to a major bank but that the bank had held its hand because of his political position. AIB, which had not even been mentioned in the story, immediately rushed out a statement saying the *Evening Press* story was 'so outlandishly inaccurate that Allied Irish Bank feels bound, as a special matter, to say so positively and authoritatively'.[6]

Another early clue about Haughey's links to the business élite emerged in the cautionary tale of the rise and fall of Patrick Gallagher. Gallagher was the heir to the fortune amassed by his father, Matt, the builder and friend of Haughey, who had died in 1974. Before moving to Abbeville, Haughey had sold Gallagher senior his 50-acre Grangemore estate for development. Patrick Gallagher pursued a dizzy career as a property developer and operated a small bank, Merchant Banking Ltd. He was also very close to Haughey and the two were often seen dining together in the Berkeley Court Hotel. When Haughey beat George Colley for the Fianna Fáil leadership in 1979, Gallagher was one of the handful of Haughey supporters from outside the world of politics present at his victory press conference in Leinster House.

After a series of spectacular deals Gallagher's empire eventually collapsed in 1982 with debts of £30 million, mainly to the major banks. Gallagher's own bank, Merchant Banking Ltd., collapsed with the rest of his property empire. The liquidator discovered that Haughey had received a 'loan' of £20,000 from the bank that was never repaid. Dick Spring, the Labour Party leader, subsequently raised the issue in the Dáil but nobody paid much attention.[7] In 1999 it emerged at the Moriarty tribunal that Gallagher had paid £300,000 to Haughey in 1979 for an option on land at Kinsealy that he had never actually exercised. The money was effectively a gift. After the collapse of Gallagher's bank the Garda Fraud Squad conducted an investigation but no prosecution ever ensued. However, in Northern Ireland, where the Gallagher bank did a minor part of its business, Patrick Gallagher was prosecuted and sent to jail for fraud.

From the moment Haughey became party leader, he began to pressurise Senator Des Hanafin, the secretary of the Fianna Fáil fund-raising committee, to resign. The committee had replaced Taca in 1969 and conducted an effective and discreet operation under Hanafin's direction from room 547 of the Burlington Hotel. While Jack Lynch was in charge there was a tradition of segregation between the leader and the fund-raising committee and the names of the donors were not revealed to Lynch. When Haughey took over he immediately set his sights on getting control of the operation. He commissioned his friend Dan McGing, a partner in the accountancy firm of Coopers and Lybrand, to report on the operation of the fund. McGing duly reported back to Haughey in March 1980 on the independent nature of Hanafin's operation and added: 'It might be considered that this situation is a less than desirable one from the point of view of Fianna Fáil because, although the Burlington Hotel fund is operating under the Fianna Fáil name, it would appear that the trustees have no control over its activities or the disposal of its monies.'[8]

Hanafin was an ally of George Colley and knew from the beginning that Haughey would try to grab control of the money. He resisted furiously and refused to hand over what was known as 'The Black Book', containing the names of the secret subscribers to Fianna Fáil. Initially Haughey was not in a strong enough position to force Hanafin to cooperate. While he had McGing's report to back his case, he did not have sufficient control of the party to risk a row. There was a stand-off for two years and then, in January 1982, Haughey's friend and election agent, Pat O'Connor, sent out fund-raising letters to subscribers on the list. When Hanafin's committee made its appeal to the names on the list, they were informed that they had already responded to O'Connor. Shortly afterwards Haughey told Hanafin he was fired, but Hanafin disputed the right of the party leader to fire him. Haughey then invited the chairman of the committee, O'Reilly-Hyland, and all the other members, apart from Hanafin, to his home in Kinsealy. There he asked them to sign a document instructing Hanafin to hand over the complete accounts of the committee to Fianna Fáil headquarters in Mount Street. Haughey then got complete control of fund-raising.

Haughey's finances were not the only part of his life hidden from the public. His private life was as extraordinary as his financial arrangements, particularly by the standards of the time. Again there were rumours which were treated indulgently by the media and the public. There was a remarkable contrast between the way the media pursued President Hillery over rumours about his private life, forcing him to issue a public denial that he was having an affair, while ignoring Haughey. It was widely known among the chattering classes in Dublin that Haughey had a long-standing affair with *Sunday Press* fashion correspondent, Terry Keane. When Keane's husband, Ronan, was made a High Court judge in late 1979 while Lynch was still Taoiseach, there were rumours, fostered by Terry Keane, that Haughey had promoted his cause at cabinet. Nonetheless, Haughey's affair remained a matter of gossip among a closed circle until Keane herself blew the gaffe in 1999 by disclosing details of the relationship on the *Late Late Show*. Her subsequent account in the *Sunday Times* newspaper was very revealing, both about Haughey as a man and about the milieu in which they moved.

She recalled her first meeting Haughey in 1964 at a function in Iveagh House. 'He was Fianna Fáil's young Turk but he had a reputation for being loud and dangerous. After the dinner and his speech I was among a crowd he invited upstairs for a drink. He was surrounded with cronies, fawning reporters and pretty girls.' Keane was not impressed at the time. 'Along with everyone else I viewed Charlie as a bit of a wild boy with a terrible reputation as a womaniser. Even then there was a whole series of Charlie stories, some true, some false and some frankly lurid; the most memorable involved him being seen running naked after a woman during a ball attended by Princess Grace in Enniskerry. He was considered so wild that no woman could even consider an affair with him.'

It was nearly a decade later, in January 1972, that Keane and Haughey began their celebrated affair. They met at Elizabeth's nightclub in Leeson Street and hit it off. According to Keane, as they were leaving the club in the early hours, Haughey said, 'Come to London tomorrow for lunch.' They travelled to London a couple of days later and stayed in a flat owned by Haughey's friend, the property tycoon John Byrne. Keane recalled another trip to London in the early 1970s when they went to lunch at 'a frightfully expensive restaurant' called the Mirabelle. Haughey asked Keane if she liked Cristal, the most expensive champagne on the menu. As the waiter brought the bottle to his table, another customer put his hand lightly on it to check the vintage. 'Who's that fucker and what is he doing with my champagne?' said Haughey to Keane. 'I couldn't stop laughing: the façade of sophistication demolished at a stroke. But that's Charlie.'[9]

By this time Haughey had also developed a taste for expensive clothes. The Moriarty tribunal heard evidence in 1999 of how he spent over £16,000 a year on shirts from the exclusive Charvet shop in Paris. It confirmed an anecdote told to the author by a Government official who recalled a visit to the shop with Haughey during an EU summit in the French capital in 1982. Haughey summoned his Foreign Minister, Brian Lenihan, his press officer, Frank Dunlop, his special adviser, Pádraig Ó hAnnracháin, and a couple of senior civil servants to accompany him on a mystery trip after breakfast on the morning of the summit. They piled into two cars and set off through Paris, eventually stopping outside the Charvet shop. Haughey got out of the car and entered the shop, followed by his bemused entourage. The manager made a fuss of Haughey, addressing him as Monsieur Prime Minister and summoning staff to start loading boxes into the car. Seeing the puzzlement of the people with him, the Taoiseach told them that the boxes contained shirts. 'Are you sure they are the right size?' asked one of the party. 'Of course. They have a bust of me here,' Haughey replied. When the manager looked quizzically at the Irish party, Haughey gravely intoned, 'My security people'. They were each presented with a tie before getting back in the cars. Ó hAnnracháin settled into the back of the second car and said good-humouredly to his companions, 'Would you credit it? The little shite from Donnycarney.'[10]

The Moriarty tribunal was also told of a series of expensive meals at the upmarket Dublin restaurant Le Coq Hardi, many of them paid from party funds. What is striking about Keane's revelations and the evidence unearthed at the tribunals is that, while Haughey was behaving with what he regarded as the height of sophistication, his actions more closely resemble those of a Third World dictator. He himself would regard criticism of this kind as boring, middle-class snobbery. He enjoyed flouting the rules.

It is also amazing that he was able to bridge such a yawning gulf between his private standards and his public position. The segment of the electorate which found him most appealing was conservative, nationalist and Catholic. They were the people most removed from his lifestyle and attitudes, but they loved him. Jack Lynch was a far more authentic representative of the Fianna Fáil heartland, a hurling legend with simple tastes who lived a modest lifestyle. On visits home to Cork as Taoiseach, Lynch liked nothing better than to go up to the clubhouse in Glen Rovers, get involved in a card game of whist or twenty-five and drink a few Paddies. Yet it was Haughey with his absurd notions of grandeur that so many of the Fianna Fáil faithful adored. This was mainly because of his simplistic nationalist and anti-British rhetoric, but also because his very unorthodoxy tapped into some deep part of the Fianna Fáil psyche. His pose as a man of destiny was a magnetic attraction. His record and his obvious character flaws were there for anybody with eyes to see but many people preferred not to look. And there were those at all levels of society and in the media who were quite prepared to ignore all the flaws and back him uncritically. They found the whiff of sulphur that wafted around him irresistible and took Haughey's inflated opinion of himself at face value. It is a commentary on Irish politics that the political journalist John Healy, a great supporter of Haughey's, coined the derisory nicknames 'Honest

Jack' for Jack Lynch and 'Garret the Good' for Garret FitzGerald. It says a lot about the politics of the period that honesty and goodness were regarded as insulting terms while Haughey was treated quite indulgently most of the time.

Many people in all walks of Irish life knew deep down that Haughey was fatally flawed as a politician but they turned a blind eye to the source of his wealth. Instead they preferred to luxuriate in the charm and danger of the man who brought a level of excitement to public life that no one else could match. His appeal rested on the deep ambivalence of many Irish people to politics and the law, coupled with the atavistic anti-English strain in Irish nationalism which is still so prevalent.

The fact is that a great many people in Ireland shared Haughey's ambivalence to the normal, everyday rules which govern a decent democratic society. Haughey never made any secret of his withering contempt for he what regarded scornfully as middle class values and he struck a receptive chord with a sizeable section of the electorate. He regarded himself as being in the mould of an Irish chieftain of old, or a medieval prince, who should not be burdened by the conventions which applied to ordinary people. His followers were prepared to take his own assessment of himself at face value while very few people in positions of power or influence were prepared to shout stop at the time. He was indulged not only by his colleagues in Fianna Fáil but by professional bankers, accountants, lawyers, civil servants and journalists who were in a position to know what was going on. Few, however, had the courage to do anything about it.

12. MISMANAGING THE ECONOMY

HAUGHEY WAS NOW IN THE TOP JOB IN THE LAND, the one he believed was his by destiny but which had slipped from his grasp nearly 14 years earlier. It was the chance to fulfil the promise he had shown as a cabinet minister in the 1960s and to prove that his sacking in 1970 had been a huge mistake for the country as well as for himself. Instead, Haughey's first term as Taoiseach was a terrible disappointment which exposed his huge flaws as a politician. The overriding feature of his first term was reckless economic mismanagement designed to ensure that he would win his first general election as party leader.

His first job was to select a new cabinet. Initially, he was conciliatory to the most powerful of his sworn enemies in the senior ranks of the party, retaining most of the cabinet in office; only three of the old ministers, Jim Gibbons, Bobby Molloy and Martin O'Donoghue, were dropped. The feud with Gibbons went back to the arms trial where they had differed under oath; they had been bitter enemies ever since. Molloy, who had voted for Colley in 1966, stoutly resisted Haughey's blandishments in the run up to the leadership election. He was not accorded the normal courtesy of being contacted by the Taoiseach to be informed that he was being dropped from cabinet. Having heard nothing he presumed the worst and seated himself on the Fianna Fáil back benches to await the arrival of the new ministers.

The sacking of O'Donoghue came as no surprise either. His close association with Lynch throughout the previous decade had made him deeply suspicious of the new leader and in a newspaper interview in 1977 said he would never serve under Haughey. The new Taoiseach took him at his word and not only was O'Donoghue dropped but his Department of Economic Planning and Development was abolished. In an incident worthy of a cheap gangster film, O'Donoghue received a special delivery at his home a couple of days after he had been axed. Haughey's Garda driver arrived at the ex-minister's home in Rathgar and handed in a strange parcel. When O'Donoghue and his wife opened the parcel they found two dead ducks inside, along with a short message from Haughey. 'Shot on my estate this morning.' O'Donoghue regarded the delivery as a combination of a bad joke and a menacing gesture on Haughey's part.[1] Jack Lynch later went to Haughey to ask that O'Donoghue be appointed as a European Commissioner, but Haughey told him that the job had already been earmarked for Michael O'Kennedy.

Haughey's chief supporters, Ray MacSharry and Albert Reynolds, were rewarded with cabinet office in his first government, MacSharry going to Agriculture while Reynolds took over Posts and Telegraphs after only two years in the Dáil. Another newcomer to the cabinet was Máire Geoghegan-Quinn, who had been the only junior minister apart from MacSharry to back Haughey. A formidable politician, she was given the Department of the Gaeltacht and became the first woman cabinet minister in the history of the Irish state.

Another new minister was Paddy Power from Kildare, who took over at Fisheries and Forestry. Michael Woods was a surprise promotion to Health and Social Welfare, in view of the fact that he had voted for Colley, but he amply repaid the good turn by an enduring and unconditional loyalty to Haughey for the rest of The Boss's political career. The key portfolio of Finance went to Michael O'Kennedy in clear recognition of his important role in declaring for Haughey at the last minute. After a year in government he was appointed to the EC Commissionership.

There was no room in the cabinet for some of the key conspirators in the *coup* against Lynch, like Seán Doherty and Pádraig Flynn, but both were appointed junior ministers. With MacSharry, Reynolds, Geoghegan-Quinn and Power in the cabinet, this meant that Haughey rewarded most of the plotters who had forced Lynch out. There was some grumbling at the limited nature of the changes at cabinet level and Charlie McCreevy, who had played such an important role in Haughey's campaign, was left out in the cold. In all, the changes were quite conservative. Haughey dropped only three of the outgoing ministers and though most of them had voted against him they retained high office. This was a severe disappointment to those who had voted for him in the expectation of wholesale change and personal advancement, but it reflected the cautious approach Haughey would bring to government appointments through all his terms as Taoiseach.

One of the reasons for his caution was that the new Taoiseach did not have absolute discretion about his choice. Amazingly, his adversary for the leadership, George Colley, was given an effective veto on two key appointments during a crucial meeting with Haughey on 10 December, the day before the Dáil elected the new Taoiseach. Colley told Haughey the minimum conditions acceptable if he were to serve in the government. The alternative was that he and his supporters would refuse to vote for Haughey's nomination as Taoiseach.[2] As there were only 24 hours to the vote, Haughey did not consider himself in a very strong position to argue. The terms were that Colley would remain as Tánaiste, that he would have a veto over the appointments to the Departments of Justice and Defence and that he would have to be satisfied with the overall structure of the government. As well as agreeing to these terms, Haughey offered Colley the Department of Foreign Affairs, but Colley, wishing to retain a domestic portfolio, refused and was given Energy. Having accepted the Colley veto on the security departments and with it the implication that he himself was a security risk, the Taoiseach appointed Gerry Collins, for whom he had very little time at that stage, to Justice, while Pádraig Faulkner, a Colley loyalist since 1966, took over at Defence. Brian Lenihan was rewarded for backing Haughey by getting Foreign Affairs after it was refused by Colley.

One other critical feature of Colley's conversation with Haughey on 10 December related to comments the new Fianna Fáil leader had made in the euphoria following his election, when he claimed Colley had pledged him loyalty and support. His defeated rival made it clear that he had never used such words and that he intended to put the record straight in the matter. Less than a month later, at a Fianna Fáil function in Baldoyle, Co. Dublin, he alerted the public to the qualified nature of his support for the new Taoiseach, saying that Haughey had been mistaken to attribute the sentiments of loyalty and support to him.

He also described as 'wrong and reprehensible' the attitude of a number of TDs and senators to Lynch. 'A majority of the parliamentary party has, it seems to me, at least for the life of the present parliamentary party, changed the traditional Fianna Fáil rule and legitimised the withholding of loyalty to, and support for, the elected leader. I very much regret this but I am a realist and I accept it,' said Colley. The statement was issued to the national media hours before the Fianna Fáil function and marked the beginning of a major public split in Fianna Fáil.[3] Haughey was furious and considered sacking Colley. He called in a number of cabinet ministers and strong supporters in the party to seek their advice. All his own supporters urged Haughey to fire Colley immediately. The Taoiseach's new personal adviser, Pádraig Ó hAnnracháin, and government press secretary Frank Dunlop, also urged him to fire the Tánaiste, but having weighed the matter very carefully Haughey's innate caution and his desire to keep unity in the party took over. He held a well-publicised meeting with Colley after which the Tánaiste qualified his remarks somewhat but certainly did not retract them.

The gulf between the two men was so great that less than a year later Colley put a proposition to Fine Gael leader Garret FitzGerald, which would have involved a split in Fianna Fáil and a Dáil defeat for Haughey.

In his autobiography, FitzGerald recalled that in November 1980, follow-ing the publication by *Magill* magazine of a series of articles on the arms crisis, Fine Gael put down a Dáil motion on the issue. Colley approached him with the suggestion that, if the wording of the Fine Gael motion were changed to refer to the conflict of evidence between Haughey and Gib-bons at the arms trial, then Colley and up to 20 other Fianna Fáil TDs would vote against their own government.[4] FitzGerald toyed with the idea, but when Colley declined to draft the proposed Fine Gael motion the plan was dropped. It does, however, give an indication of how deep was the resentment in the anti-Haughey camp within Fianna Fáil.

As Haughey settled in to the Taoiseach's office he made a number of important changes to the structure of his department. Noel Whelan, the secretary of the now defunct Department for Economic Planning and Development, was moved into the Taoiseach's office along with some of his senior economic planning officials, including one Pádraig Ó hUiginn. The department, which up to then had only a small secretariat, was rapidly expanded, with divisions to handle foreign affairs, economic and social policy, cultural and legal affairs. The centralisation of power resulted in a trebling of Haughey's own department staff by the time he finished his first stint as Taoiseach in 1981. It also led to an ongoing increase in the powers of the Taoiseach's Department, with a consequent dramatic impact on Irish politics.

The most significant appointment made by Haughey was the promo-tion of Pádraig Ó hAnnracháin. A senior career civil servant of assistant secretary status, Ó hAnnracháin was steeped in Fianna Fáil tradition. Just four years older than Haughey, he had been private secretary to Eamon de Valera through the 1950s and was appointed head of the Government Information Service in 1957. He held this post for 11 years under de Valera and Lemass and for the beginning of Jack Lynch's term of office. In 1968 Lynch moved Ó hAnnracháin out of the GIS to make way for a Corkman, Eoin Neeson. Though Ó hAnnracháin continued to hold a senior position in the Taoiseach's Department he was very unhappy at being moved. Briefly restored before Fianna Fáil lost office in 1973, he spent most of the decade in a peripheral role under Fianna Fáil and coali-tion governments, waiting for a recall to the centre of things. Haughey and Ó hAnnracháin spent the same years in the wilderness and a bond devel-oped between the two men. Between 1977 and 1979, Ó hAnnracháin kept in close touch with Haughey and, despite his status as a civil servant, he was regarded as an important member of the Haughey camp. Immedi-ately on Haughey's election he was promoted to the number two post in the Taoiseach's Department where he was the key official and the closest adviser to Haughey, who relied heavily on him during his first stint in

office. In theory, the secretary to the government was the most senior official in the department but the incumbent, Dan O'Sullivan, was very close
to retiring and did not develop a close relationship with Haughey. It was Ó
hAnnracháin who saw the Taoiseach first every morning to brief him on
the day's events and discuss government strategy.

When O'Sullivan retired, Haughey divided his functions and
appointed two people to replace him. Dermot Nally, who was next in line,
was appointed cabinet secretary while Noel Whelan was made Secretary
of the Taoiseach's Department. Nally, a bright and hard-working public
servant who was to play a pivotal role in Northern policy for over two decades, never formed a rapport with Haughey and did not get a chance to
demonstrate the full range of his abilities until Garret FitzGerald became
Taoiseach. Whelan had been secretary of the ill-fated Department of
Economic Planning and Development and a niche had to be found for
him when Haughey abolished that department. He, too, had an uneasy
relationship with the Taoiseach and never established himself in the role.
Ó hAnnracháin, who in theory was junior to both Nally and Whelan,
became the real power in the department and it was on him that Haughey
relied.

Frank Dunlop, who had been government press secretary to Lynch
and who had kept aloof from the leadership contest, was retained in his
post but, like Nally and Whelan, did not establish a satisfactory working
relationship with the new Taoiseach. The Haughey style was utterly different from what had gone before. An abrasive and domineering boss,
Haughey did not mince his words in dealings with his officials and some of
them never got used to his sudden bursts of violent temper and his regular
use of bad language. What made this all the more disconcerting was that
these moods alternated with periods when he was extremely affable and
charming and very understanding of personal problems involving any of
his staff. 'The tension was incredible,' recalls one of his officials from that
period. 'People were literally intimidated. He was so domineering that
ministers were scared of him and stultified into inaction as a result.'[5]

Haughey also expected people to dance attention on him and in his
first government this job fell mainly to Brendan O'Donnell, the career
civil servant who had been his henchman since his days in Agriculture and
who had played an important role in winning Haughey support among
backbenchers. Typical of Haughey's attitude was that he never wore a
watch or carried anything apart from cash in his pockets. If he needed to
know the time or wanted anything he asked a minion who was expected to
respond promptly.

The new Taoiseach also dominated his government. At cabinet
meetings he treated his ministers with courtesy and was regarded by most

of them as a excellent chairman. But he took a keen interest in what was going on in every department and interfered to a much greater extent than either Lynch or Cosgrave before him. 'He was an excellent chairman and cabinet meetings were about making decisions. His fault in this period was that he got too involved in other ministers' business and ended up trying to run all government departments,' said one minister who served in that first government.[6] He treated most of his ministers as subordinates, involving himself in all the key decisions in relation to finance and paying little heed to advice. This attitude became even more obvious when Gene Fitzgerald took over as Minister for Finance when O'Kennedy went to Brussels. The same was true in relation to foreign policy, particularly Northern Ireland, where it was Haughey rather than Lenihan who made the running. As he had not built up a relationship of trust with his senior civil servants he was operating virtually alone. With Colley and O'Malley he had a distant and uneasy relationship, but did not try to interfere in their departments to the extent that he did with other ministers.

With his background as an accountant and former Finance Minister, Haughey was widely regarded as the ideal person to sort out the burgeoning debt problem which was beginning to strangle the economy. His well-known reservations about Fianna Fáil's give-away manifesto in 1977 encouraged the belief that he would provide capable leadership on economic issues. This was reinforced when he made a special television broadcast in January 1980 to spell out to the nation just how serious the problem of the national debt had become.

'The figures which are just now becoming available to us show one thing very clearly. As a community we are living away beyond our means,' Haughey told the nation. 'We have been borrowing enormous amounts of money, borrowing at a rate which just cannot continue. We will just have to reorganise Government spending so that we can only undertake those things we can afford.' Given what emerged over a decade later about Haughey's personal finances at the time, the speech was a piece of brazen effrontery. But that was not known in 1980.

The diagnosis was correct, but having identified the problem Haughey proceeded to implement a policy which was precisely the opposite. Plans in his first Budget to introduce a resource tax on farmers and to spread the tax burden more evenly were dropped in the face of political pressure, as was a proposal to restrict the free bus service for rural school children. It was in the area of public pay, however, that the most disastrous decisions were made. Between special awards and national pay agreements, public pay rose by 34 per cent in 1980 alone. One startling example of Haughey's inexplicably profligate approach was a teachers' pay award in 1980. The government initially rejected the scale of a pay rise recommended by a special arbitration board, and conciliation talks began in the Labour Court. As these talks dragged on with the teachers taking a firm line, Haughey suddenly instructed his Minister for Education, John Wilson, to concede a pay rise larger than the initial arbitration award. The teachers were as stunned as everybody else by their good fortune and the arbitration board resigned in protest at being made a mockery of by the government.

The failure to curb existing government expenditure and the concession of massive pay increases to the public service undermined the policy announced in January 1980. In line with Haughey's address to the nation, the Budget for the year had targeted a reduction in the Exchequer Borrowing Requirement (EBR) from £1,009 million the previous year to £896 million. Instead it rose to £1,217 million, more than £300 million off target. Things got worse in 1981. Notional cuts were made in the spending estimates for a whole range of government departments but were not followed through in practice. Instead, government spending spiralled out of control in the first six months of the year. In the January Budget, Finance Minister Gene Fitzgerald set an EBR target of £1,296 million, a whopping 13 per cent of GNP. By the end of June spending was running so far ahead of budget that if it had continued for the full year the EBR would have ended up at £1,973, or 20 per cent of GNP, a profligate £700 million over target. To put these figures in context, the Maastricht guidelines limited the EBR in the 1990s to a maximum of 3 per cent of GNP.

Haughey's spending spree led to massive increases in taxation and borrowing to foot the bill. The total tax take as a percentage of GNP rose from 33 per cent in 1979 to 42 per cent in 1982. This represented a massive increase in the tax burden on the working population that was to have devastating consequences in the years ahead. As if this was not bad enough, borrowing, which had risen steeply under Lynch, continued to rise, from 9.2 per cent of GNP in 1977 to nearly 16 per cent of GNP in 1981 and 1982. The Taoiseach justified his policies for not reducing expenditure by the claim that the international recession would lead to unemployment and hardship. Rejecting calls to cut public spending as other governments in Europe were doing in response to the recession, he told the Dáil that such policies 'may be called courageous or responsible but in our economic and social circumstances we find them unrealistic and unacceptable'. So instead of cuts, Haughey increased both taxation and borrowing and in the process crippled the national economy for the next decade.

Writing in 1983 T.K. Whitaker pointed to the disastrous budgetary course pursued by Fianna Fáil governments, even though Haughey and his Finance Minister, O'Kennedy, were voicing an earnest commitment to reducing the external deficit and the level of government borrowing. 'The budget speeches of 1980 and subsequent years, however, reveal a lack of complete conviction; they contain expressions of self-exculpation, indeed of self-praise, for not yielding fully to the dictates of orthodoxy. Successive Ministers for Finance have appeared more as pre-conversion than post-conversion Augustines.'[7]

Garret FitzGerald's 'flawed pedigree' speech on Haughey's nomination for Taoiseach had set the tone for the relationship between the two men for the best part of the 1980s. FitzGerald courageously articulated the absolute distrust of Haughey which was shared by Colley and others within Fianna Fáil who were not in a position to express their true feelings. The Fine Gael leader believed Haughey was imperilling the country's fortunes and, despite a great deal of media hostility to his tactics, did not shirk from expressing his beliefs. Haughey and FitzGerald genuinely disliked each other. Despite the fact that they were educated together in UCD and knew each other from that time, they had virtually nothing in common. Haughey was a Dublin northsider, a Christian Brothers boy, a GAA supporter, a self-made man contemptuous of the élite who dominated the professional and business life of the Republic, although as time was to show that did not stop him from tapping them for enormous sums of money. FitzGerald, on the other hand, was a classic product of that élite. His father was a minister in the first Free State government and he was brought up in the comfortable middle-class surroundings of Dublin's southside and educated by the Jesuits. FitzGerald's biography, *All in a Life*, illustrates the web of connections open to people of his background, which eased his passage to a comfortable professional life. Garret, as he quickly became known to the voters, was elected to the Dáil only in 1969, after four years in the Seanad. He became Minister for Foreign Affairs in 1973 and leader of Fine Gael four years later. An honest, intelligent, enthusiastic and reforming politician with a slight air of academic otherworldliness, FitzGerald had a charisma entirely different to Haughey's. He managed to broaden Fine Gael's appeal and win over wider middle-class support by espousing a liberal message on social issues, a moderate one on the North and a realistic one on economic matters. He modernised Fine Gael, bringing in a range of new Dáil candidates, many of them young and a substantial proportion of them women.

One of the essential planks in the FitzGerald bid for national leadership was the identification of what became known as 'the Haughey factor'. Following the internal upheaval in Fianna Fáil and the defeat of that party's establishment, the Fine Gael strategy team, headed by party general secretary Peter Prendergast, identified Haughey as an electoral liability among middle-class voters and they played this card to the hilt during the three election campaigns of the early 1980s.

The gulf between Haughey and FitzGerald was nowhere more obvious than in relation to their attitudes to Northern Ireland. Haughey had always regarded the national issue as the key to his future fame. He reportedly told Mrs Thatcher during their first meeting in 1980 that no political leader would be remembered for reducing the balance of payments or for adjusting the scale of government borrowing, but that the one who came up with a solution to the problem of the North would go down in the history books. Given his role in the arms crisis of 1970 and his nationalist rhetoric, Haughey was regarded within Fianna Fáil during his early years of leadership as being 'sound' on the national question.

Attending his first Árd Fheis as leader in February 1980 he was given an ecstatic welcome by more than 5,000 delegates. He was piped into the RDS by the ITGWU brass band to the strains of 'A Nation Once Again'. In the front row, people expressed their devotion with an almost religious intensity, erecting little shrines to Haughey and displaying photographs and posters on tables they had pillaged from the press area. Delegates greeted his speech reflecting traditional Fianna Fáil attitudes to the North with hysteria. In it Haughey coined the phrase that Northern Ireland was 'a failed political entity' and he called on the British Government to declare its interest in encouraging the unity of Ireland. The tone of adulation for him at that first Árd Fheis lasted most of his time as leader.[8]

Haughey's emphasis on the traditional goal of a united Ireland contrasted sharply with FitzGerald's support for a devolved power-sharing arrangement in Northern Ireland itself as the first step towards any solution. From the beginning of his first term as Taoiseach, Haughey maintained that only the two governments could take decisions over the heads of the squabbling parties in the North. One of his first actions as Taoiseach was to embroil himself in a wrangle with the Department of Foreign Affairs which was to sour relations between him and Iveagh House for nearly a decade. It did not help that Garret FitzGerald was virtually adored in Foreign Affairs, having served as a very successful minister in the department from 1973 to 1977, and that most of the bright young officials had been promoted during Garret's reign. The row related to a decision to transfer the ambassador to the United States, Seán Donlon, to the United Nations. Donlon had taken a very active stance in opposing Noraid and other IRA support groups in the US and had driven a big wedge between such militants and moderate Irish-American political leaders like Tip O'Neill and Ted Kennedy. One of the people who actively encouraged Haughey to move Donlon was his old ally and now the Independent Fianna Fáil TD for Donegal North-East, Neil Blaney. The Taoiseach was persuaded that Donlon was splitting what could become a powerful anti-British lobby group and that a new ambassador was necessary. However, when news of the move leaked, O'Neill and Kennedy reacted furiously and made representations to Haughey who was forced into a humiliating climbdown. The Taoiseach was livid at having been out-manoeuvred by one of his own ambassadors and he never forgave Donlon.

On the wider front of Anglo-Irish relations, however, Haughey astounded his critics, particularly FitzGerald, by making a good stab at fulfilling his dream of launching a major political initiative. After six months in office he met the British Prime Minister, Margaret Thatcher, herself in her first year in government, for an Anglo-Irish summit meeting in London. He brought her an antique Irish silver teapot as a present and despite the jokes and the ridicule that followed about 'teapot diplomacy' the two leaders got off to a good start. The really significant follow-up summit took place in December 1980 in Dublin Castle. To emphasise the importance she attached to it, Mrs Thatcher brought with her the Foreign Secretary, Lord Carrington, who had just negotiated the Rhodesian settlement. The Chancellor of the Exchequer, Geoffrey Howe, and the Northern Secretary, Humphrey Atkins, made up the high-powered British team. Lenihan and O'Kennedy accompanied Haughey for most of the discussions though the two prime ministers had a private meeting lasting more than an hour.

The joint communiqué issued after the meeting described the talks as 'extremely constructive and significant' and went on to say that the 'totality of relationships' between the two islands would be considered in a number of joint studies. These covered a range of topics such as new institutional structures for the island, security matters, citizenship rights and economic co-operation.[9] Haughey made it clear that he was even prepared to consider a defence pact with Britain in the context of agreement on the North. 'We would, of course, have to review what would be the most appropriate defence arrangements for these islands as a whole. It would be unrealistic and improvident not to,' he told the Dáil.[10] The meeting with Mrs Thatcher heralded a genuinely important breakthrough. It paved the way for the Anglo-Irish Agreement signed by Garret FitzGerald in 1985 and for the peace process of the 1990s which was brought to fruition by Albert Reynolds.

Haughey could have brought much of this about himself in the period after the Dublin summit, but he showed crass political judgement as he proceeded to dissipate the achievement by insisting that the constitutional position of Northern Ireland as part of the United Kingdom was now in the melting-pot. Lenihan went even further and said that the partition question was on the verge of being solved and a united Ireland could become a reality in the next decade. Thatcher was extremely angry at the over-hyping of the summit and denied point blank that the British Government had any intention of altering the constitutional position of Northern Ireland.

As on the economy, Haughey squandered his opportunities in Anglo-Irish relations by taking a populist line directed towards winning an overall majority for himself in his first general election as Fianna Fáil leader. By early 1981 he had decided to call a general election in the spring of that year while he was still riding the crest of the popular wave. His plans were thwarted by tragedy, not once but twice. The initial plan was to call the election shortly after the party's Árd Fheis in February, but on the opening night of the conference, St Valentine's night, a fire in the Stardust nightclub in the Taoiseach's own constituency killed 48 young people. The main part of the Árd Fheis, including the Taoiseach's address, was postponed until April, as were his election plans. By April, the major H-Block hunger strike had got underway. The leader of the IRA protest, Bobby Sands, had been elected to the House of Commons and Haughey again deferred his election plans. With his options closing down and the spending targets of the 1981 Budget running out of control, Haughey dissolved the Dáil on 21 May with the general election to be held on 11 June. It was to be the first of five elections during the 1980s.

During the election campaign Fianna Fáil continued to promise the electorate more spending programmes to rival the attractive, if equally unrealistic, tax-cutting plans being put forward by Fine Gael. One senior Fianna Fáil figure contesting a marginal constituency recalls being contacted by the Taoiseach's Department in the early days of the campaign and being told to announce spending programmes of up to £3 million in his constituency. When he queried the request he was ordered to come up with a list of projects and to make announcements pledging government funding. Similar tactics were adopted in other constituencies. Haughey and FitzGerald ran presidential-style campaigns and dominated the media coverage. 'Charlie's Song', a version of a folk song about Bonny Prince Charlie, became the Fianna Fáil campaign anthem and it was played at all the party rallies during the campaign, encouraging voters to 'Arise and follow Charlie'. Fianna Fáil spirits soared in the early days of the campaign when an IMS opinion poll gave the party 52 per cent of the national vote and Haughey looked all set for a smashing victory. But, in a pattern that was to repeat itself, support ebbed during the rest of the campaign.

Fine Gael's tax-cutting promises and the swell of sympathy for H-Block hunger strike candidates who took votes from Fianna Fáil, all played their part in cutting Haughey's early lead. The media began to give him a tough time. Irritated by his arrogant style, many of the reporters covering his tour of the country developed an antipathy to him. The Fianna Fáil vote slipped from the opinion poll high of 52 per cent at the start of the campaign to 45.3 per cent on the day of the vote. It was Fianna Fáil's poorest showing in 20 years. The party won only 78 seats in the 166-member Dáil and was replaced in government by a Fine Gael-Labour coalition. That government had just 80 seats and depended on smaller parties and Independent TDs to retain power.

Haughey's economic mismanagement gave the new government enormous problems, but the Fianna Fáil leader refused to be embarrassed by his record. Instead he denounced the new government's corrective measures. Opposing the supplementary Budget he outlined an economic philosophy which was to guide his public attitudes for most of the decade. It was a philosophy that flew in the face of almost all accepted economic wisdom and one that was being rejected by governments of all political hues across Europe at this time. The opposition of most of the country's economists merely irritated Haughey and he refused to be influenced by them. 'At no time in the circumstances of any nation will you ever get a professional economist who will not prophecy disaster and demand deflationary measures being introduced ... Economics is a dismal science,' he told the Dáil during that debate.[11] Haughey's basic strategy was to attack as deflationary and monetarist the coalition government's attempts to get to grips with the national debt, and he rejected what he called the 'gloom and doom' being preached by the coalition. His flight from reality served to deepen the distrust in which he was held by some of the senior figures in Fianna Fáil since he had defeated Colley for the leadership in 1979. A surprising critic was Kildare TD Charlie McCreevy, who had been an important figure in the campaign to oust Lynch and put Haughey in his place. Now he became increasingly disillusioned with Haughey's attitude to the economy and made his views known in an interview with Geraldine Kennedy in the *Sunday Tribune*. For his pains McCreevy lost the Fianna Fáil whip in the Dáil and for a time became an Independent TD.

Haughey refused to be deflected by McCreevy or other doubters in his own party and he kept up a sustained criticism of the government's performance, buoyed up by the belief, a correct one as it turned out, that the government would not last long. FitzGerald's first government, which was to be reckoned by most commentators to have been a better and more imaginative one than his second, faced the central economic issues by hiking up taxes to try and reduce the spiralling national debt. This involved Fine Gael jettisoning most of its tax-cutting election promises in the face of economic reality. That government collapsed unexpectedly on the night of 27 January 1982, when John Bruton's Budget was defeated.

On the night of the Budget defeat a series of events took place which were to return to haunt Haughey almost a decade later. At the time they passed unnoticed in the welter of excitement generated by the unexpected general election. What happened was that after the minority Fine Gael-Labour government was defeated, the Fianna Fáil front bench issued a statement calling on President Hillery not to grant a dissolution of the Dáil but to look to Fianna Fáil to form a government. Immediately afterwards, phone calls were made from the Fianna Fáil rooms in Leinster House to Áras an Uachtaráin. It is still not clear who made those calls. In May 1990, in an interview with postgraduate student Jim Duffy, Brian Lenihan insisted that it was he himself, Haughey and Sylvester Barrett who had telephoned the Áras. Later on national television, when he was standing in the presidential election campaign, Lenihan denied this, claiming that his medical condition at the time of the Duffy interview was precarious and that he was on heavy medication following his liver transplant operation of the previous year. In a subsequent book on the issue, he insisted that he never phoned the Áras.[12] Garret FitzGerald says in his autobiography that he spoke to President Hillery that night and that seven phone calls were made to the President, but he did not know by whom. It emerged some years later that Haughey had threatened the Army officer on duty, Capt. Barbour, for acting on instructions and not putting him through to the President. So concerned was President Hillery at the threats to the officer's future career prospects that he insisted on placing a note on Capt. Barbour's personal file stating that he had acted properly under his instructions at all times. Haughey's bullying tactics were to come back nearly a decade later to end Fianna Fáil's grip on the Presidency.

13. THE YEAR OF GUBU

1982 WAS THE YEAR OF GUBU, one of the most incredible years in Irish politics. The government changed twice; there was open warfare within Fianna Fáil with three attempts to overthrow Haughey, and the truly sinister nature of his influence became apparent to all. The early days of the election campaign which followed the collapse of FitzGerald's government in January gave the first hint of trouble. In the first flush of excitement, Haughey rejected the central features of the Bruton Budget which had triggered the fall of the Fine Gael-Labour coalition. He was quickly forced to back down, however, when Colley, O'Malley and O'Donoghue threatened to disown him publicly. In a speech drafted by O'Donoghue, he reluctantly accepted the outgoing government's deficit targets but tried to maintain that spending cuts on the scale Bruton envisaged would not be necessary.

During the campaign O'Donoghue had insisted that Fianna Fáil adopt responsible economic policies and repeatedly refused to answer questions about whether he believed Haughey was a fit person to be Taoiseach. The 'Haughey factor' became one of the central issues in the campaign and proved a real liability for Fianna Fáil, which should have romped home. The Fianna Fáil party's director of elections, Albert Reynolds, accused Fine Gael of a smear campaign against Haughey, but it was the incipient divisions within Fianna Fáil itself which really gave impetus to the anti-Haughey mood. On 19 February when the votes were counted, it transpired that Haughey had again failed to win an overall majority for Fianna Fáil. Though the party had pushed up its share of the national vote to a very creditable 47.3 per cent and came tantalisingly close to winning extra seats in a number of constituencies, it ended up with 81, three seats short of an overall majority. It was a bitter disappointment, given the ideal circumstances of the election.

The result triggered the first of the leadership heaves against Haughey. Even as the election results were coming in, the conspirators were sending signals to each other on television. It was pointed out that known anti-Haughey candidates, like Jim Gibbons in Kilkenny and Joe Walsh in Cork, had been returned to the Dáil. On RTÉ's election count television programme, Gibbons told presenter Brian Farrell that he believed the parliamentary party would discuss the leadership issue before the Dáil resumed. Haughey was in a difficult corner. With 81 seats, Fianna Fáil was easily the largest party in the Dáil and would be in a strong position to form a government if it could do a deal with Independent TDs like Tony Gregory and Neil Blaney and possibly even the Workers' Party. However, before embarking on this tricky venture, Haughey had first to deal with the threat to his leadership. Moving quickly to get a grip on the situation, he brought forward to 25 February the meeting of the parliamentary party to ratify his nomination as the Fianna Fáil candidate for Taoiseach. The anti-Haughey faction was forced to act more quickly than they had expected. Haughey's two leading internal opponents, George Colley and Des O'Malley, met to consider their strategy. Typically, Colley agreed to drop his own claims to the succession and to throw his support behind his Limerick colleague on the basis that this represented the best chance of removing Haughey.

The chief organisers of the O'Malley campaign were Seamus Brennan, the former party general secretary who had been elected as a TD for Dublin South, and Martin O'Donoghue, who had forced Haughey to accept his budgetary strategy during the election campaign. Soundings among a wide range of party TDs increased the confidence of the anti-Haughey camp and the media began to forecast an O'Malley victory. *Magill* magazine published a list of 30 TDs who were tipped to vote against Haughey, with only 17 definitely in his favour, while Bruce Arnold went one better in the *Irish Independent* the day before the vote by naming 36 anti-Haughey TDs.[1]

The pressure was by no means as great as the media had been led to believe. A number of the TDs named as being in the anti-Haughey camp were actually on an information-gathering mission for their leader. Others ran scared after they were identified publicly, bringing pressure against them from the Haughey camp and from their local party organisations. Nonetheless, Haughey was still highly nervous at this stage, as a personal reminiscence will bear out.

Working at that time as a general news reporter for the *Irish Press* group, I was instructed by *Evening Press* news editor Dermot McIntyre to go to Leinster House, seek out Haughey and ask him if he was going to resign the leadership that day. Apparently the news editor had received information to that effect from a good source. Along with a photographer, Pat Cashman, I went to Leinster House with no expectation of getting near Haughey. However, Cashman's ingenuity was up to the challenge. Outside Leinster House we met Ned Brennan, a popular postman who had just been elected as Fianna Fáil TD for Dublin North-East. 'I would like to get a picture of yourself and The Boss,' Cashman told Brennan, and without further ado the new TD brought us straight up to Haughey's office.

Ray Burke, Fianna Fáil chief whip at the time, was in the room but left immediately when we entered. Cashman took a few pictures and Haughey stood up to leave. Sensing that I had better move quickly, I approached him and asked bluntly if he was going to resign that day. The reaction was one of instantaneous and overwhelming anger. 'Would you fuck off,' he shouted, making a run at me. I backed against the wall with Haughey shouting in my face. 'That's FUCK OFF' he roared, spelling out each letter for emphasis. Speechless with surprise, I made no response but Pat Cashman interposed himself between us, calming Haughey down and explaining that we were only doing our job. 'What was your question again?' he asked. I repeated it carefully this time, saying our newsdesk had been informed he would resign that day and asking if that was the case. 'That's complete nonsense. I have no intention of resigning,' he said calmly and walked away.[2]

That example of Haughey's volcanic temper provided me with a valuable insight into his personality and explained why so many Fianna Fáil TDs were afraid of him. I should add that later as a political journalist I met Haughey on a number of occasions and he always acted with courtesy and generally with good humour. However, there was usually a fraught atmosphere when he met journalists in a formal situation. In private he could be droll and disarming, but the brittle, bullying edge to his personality was never far away.

Shortly after that encounter I met Albert Reynolds, who told me that Haughey would easily win the leadership vote. 'Who else will be able to do a deal with Gregory and the Workers' Party?' he said. Throughout the heaves of the early 1980s Reynolds remained a Haughey supporter but he was one of the few to do so with good humour and he remained on friendly terms with all sides of the party. Reynolds's calm in contrast to Haughey's temper on that occasion left me unsure what was happening and the general media view was still that Haughey was in danger of being forced out.

At lunchtime that day, Ray MacSharry, who was another key figure in the Haughey camp, gave a radio interview during which he said darkly that the Fianna Fáil organisation would never forgive any TD who voted against the leader. That evening as I left Leinster House I met Ray Burke and I asked him if Haughey was on the way out. 'You must be joking. He's going to walk it if it comes to a vote,' he prophesied.

Of course, he was proved right. When the parliamentary party met the following morning it didn't even come to a vote, as Burke clearly suspected. At the start of the meeting, a number of speakers, including the highly respected Pádraig Faulkner, called on O'Malley not to go through with the challenge. The killer blow was when Martin O'Donoghue stood up and, to the astonishment of his fellow plotters, called on O'Malley to withdraw from the contest in the interests of party unity. O'Malley was furious, but felt there was little he could do except back down.

In the days after the abortive heave, stories emerged of threatening phone calls to anti-Haughey TDs and of more general intimidation. At the time, the claims sounded like sour grapes and not much attention was paid to them. Future events would show that the stories had a basis of truth. The failure of the heave left a sour atmosphere in the party ranks, even though Haughey sought to mend his fences by appointing both O'Malley and O'Donoghue to the cabinet. Colley was offered a cabinet post by Haughey, but declined office when told that he was not being re-appointed as Tánaiste. That post went to MacSharry, who was appointed Minister for Finance.

With his authority restored, Haughey was now able to concentrate on coming to an arrangement with the Independent Socialist TD for Dublin Central, Tony Gregory, to ensure his vote for the Taoiseach's post. 'As the Mafia say, it is a pleasure to do business with you,' remarked Haughey as he shook hands with Gregory. The deal committed Haughey to the nationalisation of a 27-acre site in Dublin port as well as the nation-alisation of Clondalkin Paper Mills; £4 million would be allocated to employ 500 extra men in the inner city and 3,746 jobs would be created in the same area over three years; state funding would be provided to build 440 new houses in the constituency and another 1,600 in the rest of Dublin. The terms fuelled suspicions about Haughey's capacity for eco-nomic profligacy. While the deal would help a disadvantaged part of Dublin, the fact that Haughey was prepared to commit so much taxpayers' money to ensure the vote of an individual Dáil deputy raised serious ques-tions about his judgement and capacity to run the country's affairs. He did another deal with the Workers' Party to ensure the support of their three TDs.

The new government was stuck with Bruton's Budget targets for 1982, but MacSharry alarmed the business community when he forecast on taking over Finance that 'gloom and doom' would be replaced by 'boom and bloom'. Once he had been thoroughly briefed by the depart-ment officials, it did not take him long to wake up to the economic reali-ties. However, the political pressure of the Dublin West by-election in June 1982 forced the Haughey Government to revert to its old form. There was a climbdown on the Budget arithmetic; concessions were made to those paying higher PRSI rates; the building societies were given spe-cial concessions to head off a mortgage rate increase and once again the financial projections began to go off the rails.

The Dublin West by-election had been precipitated by another Haughey 'stroke'. In an effort to remove an Opposition seat and win a badly needed extra one for Fianna Fáil, Haughey offered the vacant EC Commissionership to a Fine Gael TD Dick Burke. It was a disastrous miscalculation. Not only did Fianna Fáil lose the by-election, but Fine Gael's victory gave Garret FitzGerald renewed optimism that Haughey's government could be taken out. One of the more hilarious stories of the campaign concerned the instruction given by Ray Burke, then Minister for the Environment, to have young trees planted in a new housing estate in the constituency. After the election defeat, Burke ordered the local authority to dig them up again to show the voters what he thought of their ingratitude.

The defeat finally persuaded the government to heed MacSharry by coming to grips with economic reality. Spending plans were cut and public service pay rises deferred, at least temporarily. By the autumn of 1982, the cabinet had for the first time begun to look realistically at the nation's finances and was developing a strategy for controlling public expenditure. This was published in October as *The Way Forward*.

Fianna Fáil's belated acceptance of reality was completely overshadowed, however, by the 'GUBU' chain of events which overwhelmed the government in the autumn of 1982. The term GUBU was a joint invention of Haughey himself and his fiercest critic, Conor Cruise O'Brien. When the country's most wanted murder suspect, Malcolm McArthur, was arrested in the flat of the Attorney General, Patrick Connolly, in the summer of 1982, Haughey used the words 'grotesque, unbelievable, bizarre and unprecedented' in attempting to explain the situation. O'Brien coined the acronym GUBU from Haughey's adjectives and it came to signify the whole Haughey style of government in 1982. The sinister atmosphere of that period is evoked brilliantly in the political classic, *The Boss* by Joe Joyce and Peter Murtagh.

The GUBU incident encouraged Haughey's long-standing internal critics to think once more of removing him as leader. They were now joined by other discontented TDs including McCreevy, who had helped plot Haughey's accession to power but had been openly critical of Haughey's economic policies. McCreevy launched the second heave on Friday, 1 October 1982, by putting down a motion of no confidence in the leader for the party meeting the following Wednesday. O'Malley, who was holidaying in Spain, rushed home to join in the campaign though he disapproved of its timing. Both he and O'Donoghue felt they had no option but to resign from the cabinet in view of the fact that they were going to vote against Haughey.

As in the February anti-Haughey heave, the central figures on Haughey's side were MacSharry, Reynolds, Flynn, Ahern and Doherty, all now key members of his government. Doherty was in the sensitive Justice portfolio while Ahern was given the pivotal post of chief whip, as a reward for putting George Colley in his place in Central Dublin. Once again, the media overestimated the numbers in the anti-Haughey faction. The grassroots Fianna Fáil organisation rallied to the party leader and intense pressure was applied to any TD believed to be wavering in his or her support. As on the previous occasion, dissident TDs again told stories about intimidating phone calls and threats from the Haughey supporters in their local organisations.

As they went into the meeting on Wednesday, 6 October, the anti-Haughey camp was determined to push the issue to a vote this time. They had high hopes of a secret ballot as respected TDs like Pádraig Faulkner and Michael O'Kennedy had publicly demanded. However, a roll-call vote was taken on the issue and TDs voted by 53 to 27 against having a secret ballot. After a meeting, which went on all day and late into the evening, Haughey eventually won the open vote on his leadership by 58 votes to 22. In the circumstances, the scale of his victory was very impressive.

When the result was announced in Leinster House the place went wild. Haughey supporters who had been piling into the House all evening were ecstatic and some of them were drunk. As the TDs came down into the main hall there was a tremendous crush with reporters and Fianna Fáil supporters struggling to get near the participants. When Haughey's most implacable opponent, Jim Gibbons, appeared and tried to make his way towards the door he was surrounded by a crowd of angry Haughey supporters. One of them struck Gibbons and a group of Dáil ushers had to push in to protect him and escort him to his car. The unruly crowd spilled out into the car park and other anti-Haughey TDs, quickly dubbed the 'Club of 22', got rough treatment. McCreevy was chased across the car park, kicked and jostled and called a 'bastard' and a 'blueshirt'. The Gardaí helped him to get into his car but the crowd surrounded it, banging on the roof and shouting insults as he drove away through the Kildare Street gates of Leinster House.[3] 'Disgraceful scenes marred the Haughey victory last night when former minister Jim Gibbons was punched outside Leinster House and Charlie McCreevy had to leave under Garda protection,' reported the *Irish Independent* political correspondent, Chris Glennon. Gibbons denounced a 'Nazi fascist element' in Fianna Fáil.[4]

Though Haughey had seen off his internal critics for the second time in less than a year, he did not get much time to rest on his laurels. Later in October 1982, his minority government's position became precarious with the death of Bill Loughnane, followed a day later by the hospitalisation of Jim Gibbons, who suffered a severe heart attack not long after the traumatic attack on him in Leinster House. When the government committed itself to substantial cuts in public spending in line with *The Way Forward* economic programme, the left-wing TD, Tony Gregory, and the Workers' Party withdrew their support. Fine Gael moved to capitalise on the government's difficulty by tabling a motion of no confidence. When the vote was taken on 4 November the government was defeated by 82 votes to 80 and an election fixed for 24 November. This time, Fianna Fáil was defeated, winning only 75 seats with 45.2 per cent of the vote. Between them, Fine Gael and Labour had a comfortable majority and were able to form a coalition government under Garret FitzGerald which lasted until 1987.

For Haughey the loss of the election was quickly followed by another crisis which again threatened to destroy his leadership. Throughout the final months of 1982 there had been rumours and newspaper stories which raised a number of questions about the operation of the Gardaí while Seán Doherty was Minister for Justice. A former Garda detective, Doherty was an avid admirer of Haughey and he had been promoted to one of the most sensitive positions in the government after less than five years in the Dáil. He had neither the experience nor the temperament for the job and was a willing stooge of the leader, a role he later came to regret bitterly. The controversies involving Doherty at that period mounted as the year progressed. There was the Dowra affair, which involved a witness from Northern Ireland being detained by the RUC so that he was unable to give evidence in a court case against a brother-in-law of the minister. There was the Tully affair in Roscommon where a Garda Sergeant had successfully resisted an attempt, in which Doherty was involved, to have him transferred.[5] The operation of the Gardaí was one of the issues which prompted Fine Gael's motion of no confidence and it figured as an issue in the election campaign.

When Haughey lost power, the new Minister for Justice, Michael Noonan, investigated the situation and his findings were sensational. On 20 January 1983 he confirmed publicly that the phones of political journalists Geraldine Kennedy and Bruce Arnold had been tapped on Doherty's instructions and that normal procedures for authorised tapping had not been followed. Even more surprisingly, he disclosed that, in October 1982 when both men were government ministers, Ray MacSharry had borrowed Garda equipment to secretly record a conversation with Martin O'Donoghue. In the course of that conversation O'Donoghue suggested that if anyone in the parliamentary party was backing Haughey because they were compromised financially, the money could be found to sort matters out. Fianna Fáil was immediately plunged into another crisis and a special party meeting was held on Sunday, 23 January to discuss the implications of the revelations. When the Dáil resumed the following Wednesday there was widespread speculation that Haughey would resign. A number of TDs were reported to have gone to ask him to step down. That morning's *Irish Press* carried the banner headline 'Haughey on Brink of Resignation' and several inside pages carried a detailed account of his career. The extended coverage was immediately taken to be his political obituary.[6]

When TDs gathered in the Dáil on the morning of 27 January the general view was that Haughey would announce his resignation at the Fianna Fáil parliamentary party meeting later that day. Nothing, however, was further from his mind. Upstairs in his office at around 10 a.m. Haughey held a meeting with close supporters, including his nephew Seán O'Connor, his long-time friend P.J. Mara, and his co-conspirator in the arms crisis, Neil Blaney. They waited in silence while he finished reading the morning papers. Looking up at them, Haughey said, 'I think we'll fight the c...s.'[7]

He then called in the political heavyweights to devise a strategy for a counter-offensive. At the party meeting which began over an hour later, Ben Briscoe, previously a strong supporter, told Haughey it was time to go. 'I love you, Charlie,' said an emotional Briscoe. 'I love you too, Ben,' replied Haughey. 'I hope the papers don't hear about this,' groaned David Andrews at the back of the room – and the remarks were published in the following day's *Irish Press*.[8] In a crucial contribution, Ray Burke argued that Haughey should not be humiliated by being asked to step down immediately and should be allowed to choose when to do so. Haughey himself told the meeting that the media would not hound him from office and that he would make his own decision in his own time.

The impression conveyed to many wavering TDs was that Haughey was prepared to stand down within a short period but wanted to be allowed the dignity of resigning at a time of his own choosing. His enemies, charitably if naïvely, backed off to accommodate him. But Haughey did not want time to preserve his self-respect; he wanted the breathing space he needed to stage a comeback. An internal committee of inquiry was established to examine the facts of the phone-tapping and bugging scandal. It was chaired by Jim Tunney, the party chairman, and consisted of Bertie Ahern, chief whip, and barristers Michael O'Kennedy and David Andrews. In the meantime, a public controversy had developed between MacSharry and O'Donoghue over the bugged telephone conversation. MacSharry turned the tables on O'Donoghue by justifying the bugging on the basis that 'there were serious suggestions about financial arrangements which might be entered into, which I felt would affect my character and integrity.' When O'Donoghue maintained that he had simply pointed out that there would be money available to help anybody who had been compromised, MacSharry argued that O'Donoghue was telling him a bribe was available.

A key part of Haughey's strategy was to initiate a squabble between all the pretenders to his office. The race to succeed him began immediately with Des O'Malley being challenged by Gerry Collins and Michael O'Kennedy, and later by Brian Lenihan and John Wilson. With this confused leadership contest already in progress while the leader was still in office, another meeting of the parliamentary party was scheduled for the following week. Tunney stunned the meeting by adjourning it before anybody had a chance to speak, because of the death of Donegal TD Clem Coughlan in a road accident. The anti-Haughey faction was outraged at the high-handed adjournment and a petition calling for a proper meeting to discuss the leadership issue was circulated and attracted 41 signatures. This was a clear majority of the party TDs and the special meeting was rescheduled for 7 February. Once more, it seemed that the game was up for Haughey. In an interview on RTÉ radio with Gerald Barry on the day before the meeting, Haughey was in a defiant mood. 'I never contemplate defeat. I am not contemplating it now because I know I have the overwhelming support of the vast majority of our members and supporters throughout the country. They want me to stay on, they want me to fight on, and it's for them I'm staying on. And, in addition, I am staying on because I don't believe any small rump in the party, combined with friends in the media and other people outside the party, should be in a position to dictate who is the leader of Fianna Fáil.'[9]

It was a classic statement of the Haughey *credo*, neatly combining arrogance and victimhood, but it was perfectly true in one important respect. A clear majority of Fianna Fáil members and supporters did want him to stay as leader. All the scandals of the GUBU year had not dimmed their loyalty; if anything they had made him even more popular among the party faithful. Haughey capitalised on his support among the party's grassroots by circulating a statement addressed to the members of all Fianna Fáil *cumainn* throughout the country. He said it was his duty to stay on and lead the party out of its difficulties. 'Are its policies and its leader in future to be decided for it by the media, by alien influences, by political opponents or, worst of all, by business interests pursuing their own ends?'[10] A demonstration by members outside the party headquarters on Mount Street added to the drama. Placards proclaimed Haughey's 'crown of thorns'. MEP Niall Andrews addressed the crowd and accused the media of trying to execute Haughey just as the leaders of the 1916 Rising had been executed. The pressure on TDs was so great that three members of the parliamentary party collapsed and two were taken to hospital suffering from the effects of strain during the two weeks of the controversy.

The crucial party meeting began on 7 February. Crowds gathered on Kildare Street throughout the day as Fianna Fáil TDs debated the issue from 11 a.m. until midnight. The first item to be raised was the report of the Tunney committee investigation into the phone-tapping and bugging. This was read out to the meeting by Bertie Ahern. Haughey's opponents listened aghast as Ahern listed the findings of his committee which cleared Haughey and placed more blame on O'Donoghue than it did on either Doherty or MacSharry. 'Ray MacSharry's action in taping his conversation with Martin O'Donoghue is contrary to the normally accepted standards of behaviour between colleagues. It must be recorded, however, that Ray MacSharry found himself in an unenviable position. More serious, however, is the fact that any of the discussions or proposals in question should ever have been raised or pursued by Martin O'Donoghue, albeit his "honest broker" position in the affair.'[11]

When Ahern finished, Haughey announced that he intended to seek the agreement of the meeting for the removal of the party whip from Seán Doherty and Martin O'Donoghue. David Andrews refused to go along with the findings and issued his own minority report. In it he said Doherty's telephone taps had been motivated by 'internal party considerations rather than by considerations of national security'. Andrews also courageously suggested that Haughey should take ultimate responsibility for the whole affair.

As the meeting progressed, the Haughey supporters kept the focus on O'Donoghue and the allegation that money was available from mysterious sources to change the direction of the party. A lot of time was also spent attacking the media, and Charlie McCreevy, who had given a detailed interview to the *Sunday Press* the day before, was the butt of much criticism. Finally, Ben Briscoe proposed the motion requesting Haughey to resign and Colley seconded it. This time around TDs decided they wanted a secret ballot which, it was widely assumed, would spell the end for Haughey. However, the secret ballot produced the same result as the open vote a few months earlier. While the result was closer, Haughey still won by 40 votes to 33.

Journalists were corralled in the main hall of Leinster House and the first news of the vote was brought to them by Senator Donie Cassidy, who came rushing down from the party rooms to shout that Haughey had won. Pandemonium ensued as Haughey emerged triumphant through the door. Surrounded by reporters and photographers, he made his way slowly down the steps of Leinster House towards the main gate. The crowd of supporters on the street outside went mad. As snowflakes began to fall, Haughey went to the railings and shook hands with people in the street. He seemed to be in some ecstatic state, as well he might, having confounded his critics once again.

14. THE PARTING OF THE WAYS

WITH THE PARTY COMPLETELY UNDER HIS THUMB and most of his enemies having no stomach for further dissent, Haughey felt he could contemplate the future with confidence, but he reckoned without the fighting
spirit of Des O'Malley. Deserted by many of his former supporters,
O'Malley was almost isolated in Fianna Fáil but he refused to bow the
knee. Some of his strongest allies were no longer around to help. In 1983,
George Colley at the age of 57 died suddenly in Guy's Hospital in London
while undergoing tests for a heart condition. For many, his death marked
the end of an era and they feared that the values epitomised by Haughey
would prevail within Fianna Fáil.

'George Colley didn't want anything out of politics but he made a
huge contribution to political life in this country,' said Bobby Molloy. 'He
suffered enormously while he was here for the truth and the stance that he
took. He never gave out about the things that he saw going on around him;
he would just give a big sigh. He died because of a heart problem. I think
that arose because he kept everything in and didn't left fly. He was too
polite and too nice.'[1] Haughey's other main opponents, Jim Gibbons and
Martin O'Donoghue, were no longer in the Dáil, having lost their seats in
the November 1982 election, while others simply tired of the struggle and
decided to keep their heads down.

Haughey was secure enough of his position to put up fierce resistance in the Dáil to one of the first decisions made by the Fine Gael-
Labour government. On taking up office at the end of 1982, Garret
FitzGerald was concerned to discover that in the interval between the
defeat of Fianna Fáil and the appointment of his government, a number
of controversial public appointments had been made. The outgoing Minister for the Environment, Ray Burke, had appointed to An Bord
Pleanála five members with no apparent relevant qualifications or experience. Dick Spring, the new Tánaiste and Minister for the Environment,
'was gravely concerned at this, especially in view of information that suggested that some appeals were in effect being delegated to groups of
board members that might include no non-political appointees,' recalled
FitzGerald.

Spring brought the matter to the attention of the government and was authorised to prepare a Bill that would limit ministerial power to make appointments to the board. The Bill confined the choice of chairman to a person nominated by a committee consisting of six prominent people in the public and private sectors. It also limited the choice of four other members of the board to those proposed by professional, environmental, development and community interests and one member who was to be a civil servant. The reforms meant that the government had effectively decided to replace the board, giving the existing members the option of resigning or being dismissed. FitzGerald maintained that the reform was necessary to protect the planning appeals system from political influence which, given the amounts of money at stake, could be open to accusations of corrupt use.

Haughey reacted with undisguised fury to the attempt by Spring to isolate An Bord Pleanála from corrupt influence. 'We are dealing here with one of the most spiteful pieces of legislation this Dáil has ever seen,' he told the Dáil . 'It is a dirty piece of legislation. It is a mean, debasing piece of legislation. It has no motivation except party political vindictiveness.'[2] So furious was Haughey with the decision to guillotine the passage of the Bill that he withdrew Fianna Fáil co-operation in all Dáil committees for a period. 'This business of physical planning and our environment is essentially a social matter. Because it is a social matter it must be a political matter. We totally reject this idea of depoliticising the planning process,' he said in his own justification.[3]

Within Fianna Fáil the final breach with O'Malley began with the New Ireland Forum, set up on the initiative of Garret FitzGerald and designed to establish a unified position on the North for all constitutional nationalist parties on the island. There was considerable tension in the Forum between Fianna Fáil and the other parties over how the traditional aspiration towards a united Ireland would be presented in the final report, and at times this led to frayed nerves. FitzGerald recalled one dramatic episode which occurred just before Christmas 1983. Annoyed at leaks of the Forum's secret deliberations, FitzGerald complained about the stream of disclosures to the press. Haughey then spoke in similar terms, but Dick Spring tackled the Fianna Fáil leader and accused him of being the source of the leaks. Haughey was furious and demanded that Spring withdraw the allegations, but the Labour leader refused. FitzGerald recalled later: 'At this Haughey, now looking more hurt than angry, appealed to Forum members to realise that he had been entrusted by me with confidences in relation to matters of state, which he had never betrayed and that it was despicable to suggest that he would be the source of leaks from the Forum. "No one has suffered more than I have from journalists," he said – and at that broke down. Because I was sitting on the same side of the table as Haughey I could not see clearly what was happening, and my first impression was that he might be acting a part. I realised almost immediately, however, that this was not the case, for, in an undoubtedly emotional state, he had to be helped from the room by Ray MacSharry. It now became clear that he had arrived at the meeting in a very upset condition because of the recent publication of a book, *The Boss*, written about him and in particular about the GUBU events of the previous year.'[4] This was one of the rare occasions on which Haughey let his private emotions break through into the public arena. Normally in political debate he wore a mask that effectively concealed his personal feelings. He was able to wax eloquent or indignant as the occasion demanded and could divorce his inner feelings from his public persona as political necessity dictated.

At the Forum itself, Haughey eventually agreed to a form of words which acknowledged a unitary state as 'the particular structure of political unity which the Forum would wish to see established' but which also referred to the federal solution and joint authority as other options to be considered. Immediately on its publication in May 1984, he reversed positions and maintained that only a unitary state would bring peace to the North. FitzGerald, Spring and SDLP leader John Hume were horrified by Haughey's reaction which almost upstaged the Forum Report itself.

There was some disquiet in Fianna Fáil at the manner in which Haughey had effectively decided party policy without a full debate. Senator Eoin Ryan demanded a meeting of the parliamentary party to discuss the issue, but when it was held after some delay there was overwhelming support of the Haughey line. Following the three-hour meeting O'Malley publicly criticised what he termed the stifling of debate within the party. Haughey reacted immediately and demanded that the whip should be withdrawn from O'Malley. On a roll-call vote the motion to withdraw the whip was passed by 56 votes to 16. Dissent within the party was now effectively crushed. Party press officer P.J. Mara, briefing political correspondents, summed up the new mood in the party with the old Italian fascist party slogan *Uno duce, una voce*. 'There'll be no more nibbling at my leader's bum,' he added by way of explanation.[5]

Mara was a larger-than-life character who quickly established himself as one of the features of Leinster House and did incalculable work for Haughey in mending fences with the media. Born in 1941 Mara was from Drumcondra on Dublin's northside and as an ordinary member of Fianna Fáil he supported Haughey during the arms crisis. He later travelled with him on the rubber-chicken circuit during the early 1970s, often acting as Haughey's driver. He was appointed as one of the Taoiseach's 11 appointments to the Seanad in 1982 and Haughey made him party press officer in 1984 after the job had been turned down by Frank Dunlop and Seán Duignan, among others.

At the time, Mara was at something of a loose end after the failure of his carpet distribution business but he took to his new post like a duck to water. An excellent raconteur, he was a fund of witty and politically observant stories of life in Fianna Fáil. He kept the political journalists entertained with anecdotes and impersonations of the leading lights in the party, including his boss. His indiscretions soon became legendary but they were often so scabrous or libellous that they were unprintable. While they didn't do any harm to his boss, they conveyed the impression that Mara was telling all there was to know. As a result, journalists believed they were getting the inside track on what was happening in government but at the same time they never got much usable information. In an affectionate piece in the *Irish Times* during the fourth heave against Haughey in 1991, John Waters described Mara thus: 'P.J. Mara doesn't so much do a job as weave a spell. His social skills are described in terms approaching awe by even those journalists who know that his job is to pull the wool over their eyes. His *modus operandi* is inseparable from his personality. He creates a web of bonhomie and laddishness around himself which is difficult to resist. He is an apparently bottomless source of witty remarks, epigrams and he is a brilliant mimic.' While Mara made it his business to charm political journalists he didn't always take the time to impress general reporters who crossed his path only from time to time. 'The Boss rarely ventures forth without P.J. at his side. Renowned for colourful language and denials, he manages to keep reporters on side by wit, impudence and telling them to fuck off, something they love,' wrote Liam Collins of the *Sunday Independent*.

Another side to Mara was that underneath the jokes and funny impersonations lurked an intelligent and well-read man. RTÉ's Seán Duignan, during one of the periodic controversies surrounding Haughey, likened Mara to Putzi Hanfstaengl, a legendary press officer for the German Government in the 1930s who rationalised Hitler's policies to the foreign press. Mara took grievous umbrage at the comparison, but what was surprising was not his anger but the fact that he knew the reference. Apart from Duignan, none of the other media people present had ever heard of Putzi Hanfstaengl. Sometimes, though, Mara's relaxed style got him into trouble. His facetious *Uno Duce, una voce* comment was quoted by Geraldine Kennedy in the *Sunday Press* and this got him into extremely hot water with Haughey. 'You go into that room where they all hate me and you give them this,' shouted his leader at him the day after the quote was published. But relations were soon mended. It didn't take Mara long to bounce back and he was soon referring to his boss as the *Caudillo* or even *El Diablo* rather than the *Il Duce*. Mara's irresistible charm ensured that he was quickly on good terms with most political journalists. This was critically important because one of the main functions of a government press secretary is to provide a daily briefing for political correspondents, who are known in Leinster House as the Lobby. Mara had the ability to remain on good terms with the Lobby, regardless of whether individual correspondents had used his briefings in a friendly or a hostile fashion, and through all the storms that inevitably beset any government he almost invariably retained his composure and good humour.

As well as getting on well with the political correspondents, Mara also won over potentially hostile Fianna Fáil TDs and Opposition politicians. As a former senator he had access to the members' bar in Leinster House and this became another forum for his funny routines and comical stories. All this enabled him to perform the crucial function of acting as Haughey's eyes and ears around Leinster House. Very little happened without Mara being aware of it and this was a vital source of intelligence for Haughey. He was also useful in that he acted as a sounding board and could tell Haughey how the media or the Fianna Fáil parliamentary party would react to any particular development.

P.J., as he was known around Leinster House, though Haughey always called him Mara, had a meeting with his boss first thing on arriving at the office each morning, whether in Opposition or in government. They discussed the newspapers and the radio and television coverage of the major political happenings and planned how to handle that day's news. Even on Sundays, Haughey generally rang Mara for a quick run over the day's papers. For a man who always publicly dismissed the media and newspaper headlines, Haughey paid very close attention to what was being said about him.

Another key member of the Haughey kitchen cabinet was his adviser on Northern Ireland, Martin Mansergh. A son of distinguished Anglo-Irish historian Nicholas Mansergh, and educated at Kings School, Canterbury, and at Oxford, Mansergh was a somewhat incongruous figure in Fianna Fáil. He joined the Department of Foreign Affairs after university and was seconded to the Taoiseach's Department during Haughey's first term in office to act as an adviser on Anglo-Irish issues. When Haughey went into opposition, Mansergh resigned from the diplomatic service and took up a post with Fianna Fáil as adviser to the party leader. Despite his Protestant Anglo-Irish background, Mansergh took a tough republican line on the North and on a number of occasions managed to irritate the Fine Gael-Labour government, particularly Garret FitzGerald, in a manner reminiscent of the way Erskine Childers infuriated Arthur Griffith and W.T. Cosgrave.

Haughey, now totally in control of Fianna Fáil, felt secure enough to bring Seán Doherty back into the fold. Doherty had resigned the whip to save the party embarrassment during the dramatic days of early 1983 and had been agitating for some time to get back into the parliamentary party. His return at the end of 1984 showed just how strong Haughey's grip was in Fianna Fáil at that stage. Meanwhile, O'Malley was isolated as a nominal Fianna Fáil TD without the party whip. He was so marginalised that Fine Gael's John Kelly described him as being reduced to 'sleeping under political bridges'.[6] The final parting of the ways with an increasingly confident Haughey was now inevitable. The breach arose out of O'Malley's refusal to vote with parliamentary colleagues against a bill to liberalise the family planning laws in February 1985.

The legislation brought forward by the Minister for Health, Barry Desmond, was designed to end the increasingly anomalous situation whereby contraceptives, including condoms, were in theory available only to married people on prescription. As it had done on all controversial social legislation which was a matter of conscience, Fianna Fáil sought to use the issue to embarrass the government rather than debate the merits of the measure itself. In typical fashion, Haughey justified his opposition to the bill on the grounds that the legislation was badly timed. 'At a time when grave economic and social issues press with increasing severity on our people, it is irresponsible to throw the national community into the kind of acrimonious, divisive debate which is bound to follow the introduction of this legislation,' he declared.[7]

O'Malley could not stomach the sheer opportunism of the Fianna Fáil position on contraception and he refused to toe the line. He delivered an electrifying speech to the Dáil which left his Fianna Fáil colleagues squirming as he systematically dismantled their arguments. Defending the concept of a pluralist state, O'Malley stressed the effect a defeat for the bill would have on opinion in Northern Ireland and he denounced the partitionist mentality of those who opposed the government's legislation. 'The politics of this would be very easy,' he declared. 'The politics would be to be one of the lads, the safest way in Ireland. But I do not believe that the interests of this State or our Constitution and of this Republic would be served by putting politics before conscience in regard to this. There is a choice of a kind that can only be answered by saying that I stand by the Republic and accordingly, I will not oppose this Bill.'[8]

The use of the old civil war catchphrase 'I stand by the Republic' rubbed salt into the wounds of many of his Fianna Fáil colleagues but the speech was hailed by TDs of all parties as one of the best heard in the Dáil chamber for years. The former minister, who was now just an ordinary member having already lost the party whip, attempted to balance the impact of his speech by abstaining on the vote rather than crossing the floor to support the government Bill. But if he hoped still to have a future in Fianna Fáil, Haughey thought otherwise. On the night of 26 February, O'Malley was summoned to party headquarters in Mount Street to face a motion calling for his expulsion. His wife, Pat, and a crowd of supporters from Limerick waited outside on the cold winter's night as he was arraigned before the party's national executive for 'conduct unbecoming' a party member.

Haughey, who had seen off three attempts by O'Malley to remove him from the leadership, came to that meeting determined to get rid of his old adversary. 'It's him or me,' Haughey told a number of people who tried to intercede for O'Malley. For the showdown, 82 people crammed into the meeting room. O'Malley was allowed to address the gathering. He asked for a secret ballot on the expulsion motion but Haughey demanded a unanimous decision in public. On three different occasions during the meeting, Haughey intercepted to say: 'I want it to be unanimous for the good of the party and the organisation.' When a few speakers made it clear that a unanimous vote was out of the question, Haughey demanded an open roll-call vote. This was a flagrant violation of the party's own rules which stipulated that all votes should be secret, but nobody protested. Yet another roll-call vote was taken and the motion to expel O'Malley was passed by 73 votes to 9.

When the Limerick TD came out into the street and into the glare of the television lights, there were scenes which recalled the GUBU days of three years earlier. As O'Malley supporters, journalists and members of the party's national executive jostled around on the street, Haughey left the building to a few scattered boos and a solitary chant of *Sieg heil, sieg heil* from one protester. O'Malley himself was one of the calmest people present. He kissed his wife in front of the cameras remarking: 'I hope that is not conduct unbecoming.'[9] But the jocularity could not disguise the seriousness of the situation for him and it appeared to many that night that a brilliant political career had come to a premature end. At 46 years of age O'Malley had served as a cabinet minister or a front bench member for 14 years and had been tipped by many people, including Jack Lynch, as a future Taoiseach. Certainly, the omens were not good. Fianna Fáil ministers had resigned or been expelled before, only to vanish into the wilderness. A striking example was Neil Blaney, expelled in 1971 on exactly the same grounds as O'Malley. Like O'Malley, he had been in the top echelons of Fianna Fáil for a decade and a half but, once expelled, he never came back from the political fringes. There was some irony in the fact that the two men would now for a while sit together on the Independent benches in the Dáil – they represented the divergent strands of opinion that had dragged Fianna Fáil in opposite directions for 20 years.

O'Malley's expulsion marked the final step in Haughey's take-over of Fianna Fáil. With leading opponents dead, expelled or cowed, he had total control of the party he had taken over in December 1979. His supporters were delighted with the move and claimed that Fianna Fáil was now a unified and cohesive political party for the first time in just over five years. 'There is a unity of purpose now that hasn't been there since Charlie took over. We have a united party again,' said Albert Reynolds a few weeks later. The few remaining deputies with doubts about his leadership, like David Andrews, were simply too weary of the struggle to carry on. The outsiders of 1979 had now become the party establishment and they looked forward to government when the increasingly unpopular Fine Gael-Labour coalition had run its term. Doherty was now back in the party. MacSharry had won election to the European Parliament and was immediately installed as leader of the Fianna Fáil group in Strasbourg, though he still retained his seat in the Dáil. Albert Reynolds and Pádraig Flynn were leading members of the front bench. The plotters of 1979 were finally in command of Fianna Fáil, while O'Malley and all that he represented had been banished. It seemed only a matter of time before Fianna Fáil under Haughey would win a comfortable overall majority and take over the reins of power without any strings attached.

On the night Des O'Malley was thrown out of Fianna Fáil, a leading Fine Gael activist, Michael McDowell, was at home looking at television. Watching the events unfold on the news, McDowell commented to his wife that if the former minister started a new political party he was sure to get a fair degree of support because the time was right for it. McDowell's wife, Niamh, said to her husband that if he felt that way about it he should make his views known to O'Malley. So he sat down and wrote a letter encouraging O'Malley to form a new political party and offering whatever help he could give.

Michael McDowell was an up-and-coming young barrister who at this stage was growing increasingly disillusioned with Fine Gael's role in government. He had served three years as the chairman of the party's organisation in Garret FitzGerald's constituency of Dublin South-East and had made no secret of his view that the coalition with Labour was a disaster. A year before O'Malley's expulsion from Fianna Fáil, he had deeply irritated FitzGerald by using the occasion of his last speech as chairman at the constituency annual general meeting to make clear his view that the party was going nowhere and that he had decided never again to vote for Fine Gael if what it was offering to the electorate was a coalition with the Labour Party.

In the Law Library he regularly discussed politics with Michael O'Leary, who had performed the remarkable feat of getting elected as a Fine Gael TD only weeks after quitting as Labour leader because of a humiliating rejection of his policies at the party's annual conference. It did not take long, however, for disillusionment with his new party to set in and O'Leary was highly critical of the way the Fine Gael-Labour government operated. At a meeting in McDowell's house shortly before Christmas 1984, the two men drew up a list of the seats Fine Gael would lose at the next election. They arrived at the grand total of 21 – in the event, when the election came over two years later, the loss was 19 – and concluded that there was no way of stopping a Fianna Fáil landslide. It was not long after that – in February 1985 – that McDowell wrote to Des O'Malley. He got no immediate response but after Easter he was contacted by a Fianna Fáil TD, Mary Harney, who had been a close ally of O'Malley and who also knew McDowell through student debates a decade earlier. She asked him if he was serious about joining a new party and he said he was. Subsequently, McDowell invited O'Malley around to his house for dinner and the two men met for the first time.

In the meantime, Fianna Fáil friends of O'Malley were also considering the option of a new political party. Seamus Brennan, the former Fianna Fáil general secretary who had been an anti-Haughey TD since 1981, Mary Harney and David Andrews were chief among them. An opinion poll was organised by Brennan and financed by Barra Ó Tuama, the Cork hotel owner and concert promoter. The result, published on 18 April, showed that 39 per cent of people asked were in favour of a new political party headed by O'Malley while 35 per cent were against it. An interesting feature of the poll, carried out by Irish Marketing Surveys, was that the most positive reaction to a party led by O'Malley came from the AB social category and the large farmers. The strongest support was located in Munster, not surprisingly in view of O'Malley's home base and the continuing sympathy for Jack Lynch. At the time, there were mixed views on the significance of the poll. Haughey dismissed it as irrelevant. But for those planning a new party it appeared hopeful, particularly as it was published only a few days after another poll which showed a big drop in Fianna Fáil support because of O'Malley's expulsion.

In the following months, however, the steam seemed to go out of the plan to establish a new party. At the beginning of summer Seamus Brennan began to feel lukewarm about the project and eventually dropped out, apparently more interested in pursuing his political career within Fianna Fáil. O'Malley's supporters in Limerick were also reluctant to get involved in a new party, most of them preferring him to stay on as a sort of Independent Fianna Fáil deputy who might one day be reconciled with the party. Mary Harney remained a strong advocate of a new party. She was supported by an other Fianna Fáil TD, Charlie McCreevy, who had been a Haughey supporter in 1979 but had quickly become a die-hard opponent of the leader, and Paul MacKay who had been treasurer of the Fianna Fáil organisation in Haughey's constituency but had resigned in protest at the way the accounts were kept. O'Malley himself, however, still remained very reluctant to commit himself to the move.

A crucial meeting of the conspirators took place in Michael O'Leary's house in Wellington Road, Dublin, in September. At the meeting besides O'Leary were O'Malley, Harney, McDowell, MacKay and McCreevy. O'Malley advised doing nothing about the project, at least for the moment. Showing his impatience at the delay and indecision, McCreevy told the others that if the new party did not go ahead that night he would have nothing more to do with it. O'Malley was very wary of McCreevy, regarding him as a bit reckless because of the way he had put down the motion of no confidence in Haughey in October 1982 without consulting anybody, and he was unwilling to respond to such an ultimatum. A crucial factor in the indecision was the way in which the three attempts to remove Haughey had been botched. 'I think there was a lack of trust among some of us about the reliability of the others because of the way the heaves against Haughey had gone. At this stage each regarded the other as wimps because of what had happened before,' said one of the plotters later.

Some strongly anti-Haughey TDs in Fianna Fáil, like Bobby Molloy and Pearse Wyse, had had their fill of conspiracies and were not involved in any way at this stage. A serious car crash in November gave O'Malley a severe shock and that put back discussion yet again. While they waited to see if a new party would get off the ground, McDowell and O'Leary drafted a Divorce Bill, which O'Leary introduced in the Dáil. Only five TDs supported it but the move added to the pressure on the Fine Gael-Labour coalition which was theoretically committed to holding a referendum on divorce. Shortly afterwards, the Anglo-Irish Agreement, signed by Garret FitzGerald and Margaret Thatcher on 15 November 1985, was denounced in the strongest terms by Haughey. The Fianna Fáil leader had earlier dispatched Brian Lenihan to the US to lobby leading politicians against the planned Agreement. This attempt to sabotage an Anglo-Irish accord infuriated Irish American politicians, particularly the Speaker of the House of Representatives, Tip O'Neill, and did nothing to enhance Haughey's reputation.[10]

When the Agreement was announced the old divisions in Fianna Fáil were exposed once again. It was welcomed by O'Malley and by the former Taoiseach, Jack Lynch, and on 20 November Mary Harney issued a statement in favour of the Agreement, saying she would vote for it. She followed this up by going through the government lobby along with O'Malley. Expelled from the party a week later, she now joined O'Malley as an Independent and continued to encourage him to form a new party. Harney's strong advocacy of the move, coupled with Fianna Fáil's utterly negative attitude towards the Anglo-Irish Agreement, rekindled O'Malley's enthusiasm and he now committed himself fully to the project. At a meeting in Paul MacKay's house in late November the decision was finally taken to launch the party. MacKay and McDowell leased premises at South Frederick Street. A discussion paper was also prepared on the aims of the new party, to be called the Progressive Democrats. Soon, rumours began to circulate in political circles that something was up.

The Progressive Democrats party was publicly launched on 21 December. At this stage it had only two TDs, O'Malley and Harney. In acknowledgement of his work in establishing the party, McDowell was appointed chairman, the move serving to emphasise that the PDs were not simply a Fianna Fáil dissident rump. Michael O'Leary had been willing to join, but O'Malley thought this might give the impression that the PDs were simply a refuge for people who couldn't find a home elsewhere. Despite the fact that he had been in on the planning of the new party, there was no room for him in it. It was a decision that the founders of the PDs were later to regret, not just on a personal level but because O'Leary, whatever his political inconsistencies, was an effective vote-getter and a potential seat was thrown away.

Gemma Hussey records in her cabinet diaries how the involvement of McDowell came as a blow to Fine Gael. 'Dessie O'Malley's new party, the Progressive Democrats, was announced today. Michael McDowell is the chairman. Will it hurt Fianna Fáil more than us? It is depressing that Michael did this; it must be hurtful to Garret'.[11] Four days before Christmas seemed an odd time to launch a political party but the timing actually worked to great advantage. The PDs dominated the headlines and the news bulletins and O'Malley sounded very confident as he went on radio asking for donations of £150,000 a year to make the PDs a viable prospect. In the early days of the new year the party took off. Advertisements were placed in the papers on 2 January seeking money and supporters, and the party headquarters was inundated with people wanting to get involved. By 6 January over 4,000 people had enrolled as members and £25,000 was contributed by public subscription. Over 1,000 people attended the first party constituency meeting in the Marine Hotel in Sutton and the major parties began to sit up and take notice. Haughey went on radio a few days later and expressed the view that the PDs were not acting in the national interest. But the crowds continued to flock to their public meetings. At these early meetings O'Malley hammered home the core message of the party that the state was strangling the economy through an involvement only matched by the Communist countries of Eastern Europe. He committed the PDs to cutting taxes as the essential first step in putting the economy right. To an electorate crippled with personal taxation, disillusioned with a stagnant economy and rising unemployment, the new party's message sounded attractive. O'Malley's imposing presence and Mary Harney's abilities as a speaker contributed to the air of excitement generated at those meetings.

It was a very unsettling time for Fianna Fáil. A significant number of activists in constituencies like Dún Laoghaire, Dublin South and Cork city began to desert to the PDs. The question was whether the deputies for those areas, some of whom had been close to O'Malley, would follow suit. There was a wide expectation, both in Fianna Fáil and the PDs, that Dún Laoghaire TD David Andrews would switch parties and there were rumours about Seamus Brennan from the neighbouring constituency. Brennan, however, set his face completely against joining and spent a lot of time trying to persuade wavering Fianna Fáil deputies to stay in the party. In the middle of January, when rumours developed that Cork TD Pearse Wyse was on the verge of leaving to join the PDs, Brennan and Bobby Molloy were dispatched by Haughey to get him to stay on. Despite their efforts, Wyse turned up to the first major PD rally in Cork on 20 January and announced he was joining.

The Cork meeting, which overflowed the Metropole Hotel into the street outside, confirmed the revivalist air which now attended PD rallies. Three days later, a rally in the Leisureland complex in Salthill, near Galway, was even more sensational. At this rally, Bobby Molloy, who just a week earlier had joined Seamus Brennan in trying to persuade Pearse Wyse not to leave Fianna Fáil, jumped ship himself. The move stunned Fianna Fáil. Molloy had given no inkling of his plans to anybody in the party leadership. On the day of the PD rally, he left Dublin in the early afternoon and rang his secretary from a phone booth along the road. He told her to open his filing cabinet, take a letter he had left there and bring it to Haughey. The letter contained his resignation from the party he had served as a TD for 20 years. The Dáil was sitting that day and the shock among Fianna Fáil TDs was palpable. Labour TD Frank McLoughlin remarked that the party front bench looked like 'a crowd of cut calves' and it was hardly much of an exaggeration. Over the following days, Fianna Fáil TDs wondered who would be the next to go. David Andrews and Joe Walsh seemed the most likely as they were friends of O'Malley. Others like Noel Davern from Tipperary, Charlie McCreevy and many others were mentioned as possible defectors but when, after another few weeks of uncertainty, none of them had left, the mood in Fianna Fáil settled down and confidence gradually flowed back. The trauma of Molloy's defection actually marked the end rather than the beginning of the drift from Fianna Fáil to the PDs. Over the next few months the opinion polls confirmed the impact of the PDs on the public imagination. The first major poll published in the *Irish Times* gave the new party 25 per cent of popular support, putting them ahead of Fine Gael on 23 per cent while Fianna Fáil had come down to 42 per cent and Labour was just 4 per cent.

The PDs appointed two well-known journalists to run the party organisation. Pat Cox, a reporter with the prestigious RTÉ current affairs programme *Today Tonight,* was appointed general secretary with responsibility for developing the organisation. Cox, a former member of young Fianna Fáil, had in fact been in on the founding of the party and was one of O'Malley's closest confidants. The other journalist appointed to the party backroom staff was Stephen O'Byrnes. He was news analysis editor with the *Irish Independent*, having worked previously on the political staff of the *Irish Press*. Ironically he had just completed a book, not yet published at that stage, on the development of Fine Gael under Garret FitzGerald. Unlike Cox, O'Byrnes had no involvement in the founding of the party and did not know Des O'Malley particularly well at that stage. Both Cox and O'Byrnes were from Limerick, giving rise to comments about a Limerick Mafia running the new party.

Michael Keating was the only Fine Gael TD to join and he had an uneasy relationship with his PD colleagues from the start. The party did attract a number of people from well-known Fianna Fáil families. Anne Colley, daughter of George, joined in Dublin South and was quickly selected as a prospective candidate. Members of the Gibbons clan from Kilkenny also joined, with Martin, a son of Jim, emerging as the likely Dáil contender. The prominent names in the PDs – O'Malley, Molloy, Colley, Gibbons and Wyse – now read like a litany of the defeated faction in Fianna Fáil. Deep antipathy to Haughey was a strong motivating force among this group and the feeling was reciprocated by Haughey and his cronies and by most people in Fianna Fáil. Even though they would be in a coalition government with Haughey in the future, the antipathy between the two parties never really went away.

15. THE U-TURN

BY THE BEGINNING OF 1987 as the country moved towards a general election, Haughey was convinced that his hour was finally at hand. Fianna Fáil attacked every aspect of the coalition's record, particularly the harsh economic policies aimed at controlling the national debt. For months before the election campaign even began, placards with the message 'Health cuts hurt the old, the poor and the handicapped' were plastered up on billboards all over the country. While the party did accept the basic arithmetic of the outgoing Government's Budget, the populist nature of the slogan indicated that Haughey had no intention of addressing the issue in a serious fashion. His record over the previous four years of fighting the Government tooth and nail on every single public spending cut suggested that he would adopt a much more relaxed attitude towards public spending. He had maintained again and again that spending cuts were unnecessary and, as almost all professional economists were also preaching the need for control of public spending, Haughey attacked them as well. He had spelled out his opinion of them in June 1984: 'The failure of this government has been significantly contributed to by the invasion of the corridors of government by a coterie of professional economists, preaching defeatist, monetarist doctrines and peddling unrealistic and unacceptable policies,' he declared. 'No previous Government has given so much patronage and influence to a whole troupe of economists who seem determined to re-establish economics as a dismal science.'

His continuous and sustained criticism of the coalition's policies was not merely misplaced; it was based on a wilful misreading of the economic situation. The FitzGerald government's failure lay not in its desire to cut public spending but in the fact that it was not cutting that spending by nearly enough. It was not just through Dáil speeches that Haughey, during his period as Opposition leader, hampered the government's ability to convince the electorate of the need for cutbacks. He also offered open support to any and every interest group which engaged in confrontation with the government. Fianna Fáil supported pay demands by the country's teachers and encouraged the teaching unions to take industrial action in pursuit of those demands. It supported the Irish Shipping workers' protest against the closure of the state company because of a disastrous financial performance. It backed the farmers in their battle to avoid paying a land tax. Every instance of public dissatisfaction was used as a stick to beat the government.

Towards the end of its term of office, the FitzGerald coalition came up with two dramatic revenue-raising schemes which, if they had been introduced earlier in the government's life, would have made its job a whole lot easier. One was the National Lottery which brought in extra funds for social developments of many kinds and reduced demands on the national exchequer. The other was the Deposit Interest Retention Tax, quickly labelled DIRT, which was levied directly on the interest accrued by depositors in banks and building societies. Fianna Fáil attacked DIRT on its introduction and Haughey pledged to abolish it when he returned to office. Of course he did nothing of the kind because DIRT was a massive income earner for the exchequer and enabled him to cut borrowing quite dramatically. The Lottery money was also to play a big part in helping Fianna Fáil cope with the national finances.

In June 1986, in line with his policy of opposing the government on every possible issue, Haughey took delight in helping to torpedo the coalition's efforts to introduce divorce. In theory, Fianna Fáil was neutral on the issue but the party organisation was the mainstay of the anti-divorce campaign in many parts of the country. Haughey claimed not to be taking sides but he made his position clear enough. 'For my own part,' he declared, 'I approach this issue from the point of view of the family. I have an unshakeable belief in the importance of having the family as the basic unit of our society. My experience of life tells me that this is the best way in which to organise a society ... I want to make the valid point that there is a price to be paid for the introduction of divorce and that people must decide on whether they wish to pay that price. It is not reasonable to suggest that there is some form of divorce that could be introduced which would not have many definite consequences for society, for the stability of the family and for the rights of existing family members.'[1] The proposal to introduce divorce was defeated decisively in a referendum, with 63 per cent voting against it.

The setback further demoralised the Fine Gael-Labour coalition and, in the autumn of 1986, Labour's resistance to further spending cuts began to pull it apart. By Christmas of that year it was becoming obvious that the government parties would not be able to agree on a Budget. The inevitable break came on 20 January when the four Labour ministers left the government because they could not agree to the Fine Gael Budget proposals. Some Fine Gael deputies favoured unilaterally introducing the party's proposals as they stood and, in hindsight, such a strategy might have exposed Fianna Fáil's lack of policy. Instead FitzGerald asked President Hillery to dissolve the Dáil and an election was set for 17 February. Fine Gael published its Budget proposals and FitzGerald decided on an unusually long four-week campaign in the hope that it would give him time to bring the electorate around to approving them.

The Fianna Fáil strategy involved an outright refusal to make any commitments while at the same time trying to convince each segment of the electorate that things would be better under a Fianna Fáil government. When Fine Gael and the PDs announced they were in favour of selling off shares in semi-state companies, Haughey immediately sent a letter of reassurance to the Irish Congress of Trade Unions, pledging that a Fianna Fáil government would never countenance the privatisation of state enterprises.

Fine Gael concentrated heavily on Haughey's record on the North, particularly his attitude to the Anglo-Irish Agreement. Haughey had denounced it a number of times since it was signed in November 1985 and had pledged to renegotiate it if elected. At the start of the campaign he changed tack and pledged to continue working the Agreement though he maintained he still could not accept the constitutional implications of recognising partition.

The first opinion poll of the campaign confirmed the widespread belief that Fianna Fáil was on course for a resounding victory. The MRBI poll in the *Irish Times* gave the party 52 per cent with Fine Gael away back on 23 per cent, Labour on just 5 per cent and the PDs with a very impressive 15 per cent. As the long campaign wore on, however, Fianna Fáil's commanding lead in the opinion polls began to slip just as FitzGerald had hoped. But the benefits did not go to Fine Gael. As the campaign developed, it became clear that it was no longer a straightforward contest between Fianna Fáil on the one side and a Fine Gael-Labour combination on the other. For a start, Labour had decided not to go into another coalition. More importantly, there was a new party on the scene and it was difficult to anticipate how it would affect the situation. Despite the fact that support in the polls for the Progressive Democrats was still showing up at between 12 per cent and 15 per cent, few people, even in their own ranks, expected the party to get more than ten seats. During the campaign they managed to attract a lot of attention. A surprise candidate, Geraldine Kennedy, political correspondent of the *Sunday Press*, joined well-known names like Michael McDowell, Anne Colley, Martin Gibbons and Pat O'Malley on the PD ticket as first-time candidates. Both Fianna Fáil and Fine Gael initially attacked the PDs but as the campaign wore on it became clear that the new party was going to make a significant impact.

The strength of the PD campaign continued to disconcert Fine Gael.

The new party was staffed mainly by former Fianna Fáil activists who were bitterly anti-Haughey, but it was poaching votes not from their old party but from Fine Gael. On the other hand, FitzGerald's party recognised that the PDs represented the only chance of stopping Fianna Fáil from getting an overall majority. In the event the PDs mopped up Fine Gael seats, astonishing themselves as much as everyone else with their performance. Leading figures in the party were later to bemoan the fact that had they realised they were doing so well they could with a little extra effort have gained another three or four additional seats.

When the votes were counted on 18 February the result was a bitter disappointment for Fianna Fáil. Haughey's party had won 81 seats, three short of an overall majority. Fine Gael won 51 seats, the PDs 14, Labour 12, the Workers' Party 4 and Others 4. Fianna Fáil had confidently expected to sweep into power with an overall majority and from the grassroots membership up they were shattered at their failure to achieve that objective. It was the fourth time in a row that Haughey had failed to deliver an overall majority and some senior figures now began to despair of his ever being able to do so. The big winners were Haughey's old enemies in the PDs. Their 14-seat total exceeded their most optimistic expectations and enabled them to achieve one of their major objectives – depriving Charles Haughey of an overall majority. But the PDs failed in their second strategic objective. Many in the party had harboured the ambition of holding the balance of power so that they could force Fianna Fáil to ditch Haughey as the price of their support. They narrowly failed and though Haughey was deeply disappointed he did not show it. Instead he acted as if he had won an overall majority and as if there was no question but that he would succeed FitzGerald as Taoiseach.

He took the initiative and correctly read the mood of the electorate by announcing that he was not going to do deals with anyone. This gave him some room for manoeuvre. For a start, Fianna Fáil could hold on to its full voting block of 81 TDs as the Ceann Comhairle would not have to come from the party's ranks. Former Labour TD Seán Treacy, who had been Ceann Comhairle for the 1973-77 period, let it be known that he was available for the post. But as the Dáil was due to meet, Haughey's chances of becoming Taoiseach grew more uncertain. Fine Gael, the PDs, Labour, the Workers' Party and Jim Kemmy were all committed to voting against him. That meant there were 82 certain votes against Haughey as opposed to 81 Fianna Fáil votes. Haughey's fate, therefore, was in the hands of two Independents, Neil Blaney and Tony Gregory. As Haughey was sticking by his pledge not to do any deals and was known to have turned down Blaney's demands to end the Anglo-Irish Agreement and scrap extradition, the situation was very volatile.

In this uncertain atmosphere there were some murmurings about Haughey's position as Fianna Fáil leader. It was clear that any other Fianna Fáil nominee but Haughey for the Taoiseach's post would easily be elected with support from the PDs. Seeing the possibility of a challenge from within his own ranks, Haughey moved to quash any such move before it got off the ground. Just two days before the Dáil was scheduled to vote in a new Taoiseach, Ray Burke went on radio to warn off possible challengers. 'Let nobody outside Fianna Fáil have any feelings that since they've left the party they can influence our leadership,' he declared. 'They tried that when they were on the inside and they're not going to do it from the outside. He will remain leader, and let there be no misunderstanding for any member of the Dáil – the only alternative to Mr Haughey being leader and being Taoiseach is a general election.'

On the day of the Dáil vote, Haughey repeated the warning. To ensure that there would be no attempt to put forward another Fianna Fáil nominee for Taoiseach, he called his front bench together and told them to prepare for an immediate election. In fact, in the event of no nominee for the position of Taoiseach winning an overall Dáil majority, Haughey was in no position to call an election. That was the prerogative of FitzGerald, who would have continued as acting Taoiseach and certainly had no intention of asking the President for an immediate dissolution. In the circumstances, the President also had the right to refuse a dissolution to FitzGerald because he no longer commanded a majority in the House. As the country lurched towards a constitutional crisis, Haughey was determined, whatever the outcome, not to relinquish his leadership of Fianna Fáil and the chance of being Taoiseach again.

In the event, when the critical moment came, Seán Treacy was elected Ceann Comhairle unopposed. Treacy then presided over the election of Taoiseach and surprisingly, given that Garret FitzGerald was the outgoing holder of the office, he allowed a vote on Haughey's nomination to take place first. Blaney voted for Haughey while Tony Gregory abstained, leaving the vote tied 82-82. Treacy then gave his casting vote in favour of the Fianna Fáil leader, on the basis that he was the only contender with a chance of winning, and Haughey was Taoiseach again. Twice before he had demonstrated a total inability to run the national finances: could Haughey possibly do it third time around? The opportunity he needed had been created by his long-term political adversary, Garret FitzGerald. Near the end of the election campaign, FitzGerald came up with the interesting idea of creating an all-party Economic Forum, along the lines of the New Ireland Forum. Its objective would be to devise an economic strategy outside party politics which could get the country out of the economic mess. At that late stage in the campaign, when Haughey still believed that outright victory was within his grasp, he brusquely dismissed the idea on the grounds that it was the government's job to govern and make economic decisions. On the night of the election count, when the indecisive nature of the result began to emerge, FitzGerald, adopting a patriotic position totally alien to Haughey, said on television that Fine Gael would support a Fianna Fáil government if it adopted the correct approach to the economy.

One of the few people who read the political situation correctly was former Labour leader, Frank Cluskey. Joining a group of journalists and politicians of all parties in the Dáil bar on the day after the election result had been declared, Cluskey listened to the speculation that a new minority Haughey Government would collapse in a matter of months. 'Lads, you have got it all wrong,' he declared. 'All Charlie has to do is to be twice as tough as Fine Gael and the PDs and they won't be able to touch him. If he keeps his nerve he can govern as long as he likes.'[2] The logic of the Cluskey argument was impressive but his listeners were sceptical. In the realm of practical politics it was nearly impossible to believe that Haughey, having denounced spending cuts for the previous four years, could turn around and adopt more stringent financial policies than Fine Gael. Yet that is precisely what he did. Once it became the safest way of retaining power, the great survivor showed no qualms about adopting Fine Gael policies. The Minister for Finance, Ray MacSharry, not only swallowed the Fine Gael Budget whole; he actually made it harsher and aimed at more ambitious spending cuts than the outgoing government had dared to suggest. The new Fine Gael spokesman on Finance, Michael Noonan, did not mince his words about Fianna Fáil's latter-day conversion to fiscal rectitude: 'I have great pleasure today in welcoming Fianna Fáil's acceptance of the Fine Gael analysis of the problem and of the targets which we have set down. This is a grand larceny of our policy as put before the electorate.' The Fianna Fáil change of heart was politics at its most cynical but it set in train a real turn-around in the Irish economy and provided the basis of the Celtic Tiger of the 1990s.

Garret FitzGerald did not stay as Opposition leader to see the implementation of his policies by Haughey. On 11 March 1987, the day after he was replaced as Taoiseach, he took nearly everybody by surprise by announcing his decision to step down as Fine Gael leader. The decision came as such a shock because he had stoutly maintained in the immediate aftermath of the election that he had no intention of resigning. One person who didn't appear to be surprised by the move was Alan Dukes. Within an hour of the resignation announcement he was canvassing support from Fine Gael TDs and senators in Leinster House. Ivan Yates, the young Wexford deputy, immediately took over as Dukes's campaign manager, going to the political correspondents' room in Leinster House that same day to tell them his man had it in the bag.

The other candidates for the leadership were Peter Barry, the deputy leader of the party who received the support of most of the former cabinet ministers, and the two-time Finance Minister, John Bruton, who was the last to declare. The main support for Dukes came from the class of 1981 who had entered the Dáil with him after Garret FitzGerald's first campaign. Significantly, though, he had virtually no support among his former cabinet colleagues. Nevertheless, he emerged as the winner after less than six years in the Dáil. Over time it became clear that he got the leadership too early in his political career and he was not able to cope with all its demands.

As Dukes tried to get to grips with the role of party leader, Haughey was revelling in his third term as Taoiseach. Having begun by cutting public spending, he was determined to continue the process. On 17 May he circulated a letter to all government departments spelling out in clear language the kind of cut-backs he wanted for 1988. The letter was aimed not just at the ministers, who already knew what he wanted, but at the senior civil servants in each department who traditionally sought to squeeze extra money out of the exchequer each year regardless of the overall financial position of the state. Setting down the philosophy to underpin his administration until 1989, he stated: 'We must begin to identify the specific programmes and expenditures for further cuts now if we want to get results for the remainder of 1987 and 1988. I am anxious to get this process underway as soon as possible. I therefore ask you to submit to me, and to the Minister for Finance, a paper by Friday 22 May at the latest, identifying the proposed reductions to expenditure. The proposals must have the effect of achieving a significant reduction on your Department's present level of spending ... In arriving at your proposals all options should be considered, including the elimination or reduction of particular schemes and programmes, rooting out overlaps and duplications between organisations, the merger of organisations, the closure of institutions which may have outlived their usefulness, the scaling down of the operations of organisations and institutions and the disposal of physical assets which are no longer productively used. A radical approach should be adopted and no expenditure should be regarded as sacrosanct and immune to elimination or reduction. We do not want a series of justifications of the *status quo* or special pleadings.'[3]

The Haughey letter was leaked to the media by the Workers' Party and published in the national newspapers on the day when ministers were due to deliver their proposals for cuts to the Taoiseach. The Workers' Party was rumoured to have some senior civil servants in its ranks in the secret Ned Stapleton branch of the party, which catered for high-flying media people and public servants who did not want to be publicly identified. If they wished to thwart further cuts, the plan backfired because Haughey now felt himself publicly committed to the policy outlined in the letter and he was determined to live up to it. Another pivotal development in getting economic strategy right was the establishment of the Expenditure Review Committee, which became known as An Bord Snip. On the committee were the Secretary of the Department of Finance, Seán Cromien, an assistant secretary of the department, Bob Curran, and an independent economist, Colm McCarthy. Among civil servants the committee was likened to a Star Chamber because each department in turn was called in to justify every item of expenditure proposed for the following year. This committee put strong pressure on departmental officials to come up with ideas for spending cuts and it also made its own suggestions, drafting a number of memoranda which were presented to the cabinet in the name of the Minister for Finance. What gave the committee such influence was not that the range of cuts it suggested was particularly clever or original, but that the political will was now there to implement its proposals. 'The vital thing was that MacSharry was prepared to back the committee to the hilt and insist that his cabinet colleagues bit the bullet in relation to the suggested cuts,' said one senior official who observed the process. In fact, many of the suggestions for spending cuts had been circulating in the Department of Finance for a number of years and had been presented as options year after year only to be turned down by the cabinet. This menu of cuts had become known among coalition ministers as 'the Asgard List' because the scrapping of the sail-training vessel *Asgard* was a recurring item on it. Now, however, former Fine Gael and Labour ministers were astonished to see cuts they had rejected as being politically impossible to implement being recycled by Haughey's government and being accepted with the minimum of political flak.

A few months after the MacSharry Budget, Dukes announced his adherence to FitzGerald's policy of offering support to the government when it adopted Fine Gael policies. It quickly became clear that Fine Gael were prepared to support the government in a much more positive way than the PDs were. A variety of measures including the Health estimates for the year was passed through the Dáil by huge majorities. Most of the disgruntlement at the cuts came from the Fianna Fáil backbenchers whose TDs had not been prepared in advance for the scale of the U-turn. Despite the grumbling, the government kept its TDs in line, though it backed down on issues such as the immediate abolition of housing grants where it looked that they might run into real political difficulty. The Fine Gael position was eventually formalised in the 'Tallaght Strategy', so called because it was announced by Dukes at a speech in Tallaght, Co. Dublin, pledging support for the government as long as it stayed on the economic straight and narrow. It was a brave initiative in the national interest which changed the traditional adversarial nature of politics between the two big parties. The strategy worked for the country but it did not do a lot for Fine Gael, and it ultimately cost Dukes his job.

Everybody found something strange in the fact that a minority government was regularly able to command majorities of more than 100 in Dáil divisions. TDs on all sides of the House were puzzled by what was going on. Fianna Fáil backbenchers had not expected to be implementing public spending cuts even more severe than those of the Fine Gael-Labour coalition and the last thing Fine Gael TDs ever expected was to end up supporting a government led by Charles Haughey. Garret FitzGerald, now a backbencher, summed it up well. 'There seemed to be two Fianna Fáil parties, Fianna Fáil in opposition and Fianna Fáil in government, and any resemblance between them has become totally coincidental; in fact not only coincidental but almost unfindable at this stage.'

Having set the mechanisms in place for coming up with ideas for significant public spending cuts, Haughey then opened talks with the Irish Congress of Trade Unions, the employers and the farmers' bodies on a new national agreement to cover the following three years. The trade unions were the key to the deal as control of public service pay was a vital requirement for the government if it wished to keep inflation down and begin to get borrowing under control. Any other government would have found it difficult, if not impossible, to proceed with two apparently contradictory policies at the same time – one that involved huge cuts in public spending and the other which involved doing a deal with the trade unions designed to effectively tie them into the process of government.

Haughey managed to follow both these roads simultaneously. His overriding concern in the talks with the unions was to get a national pay deal. He started off with the great advantage that the trade union leaders liked him. They had fought bitterly with the Fine Gael-Labour government because they expected the Labour party to be an arm of the union movement rather than of government and could never establish a proper working relationship with the coalition. Haughey, on the other hand, in his first term of office, had been generous, far too generous for the national good, but generous nonetheless in his dealings with the unions.

'Haughey just mesmerises them,' said a Labour politician, appalled at the way the unions responded to the Taoiseach. 'When we were in office they wouldn't forgive us for not delivering everything they wanted and they just didn't take us seriously. They seem to regard Fianna Fáil as the real party of government and are prepared to deal with them in a way they would never deal with us,' he added disconsolately. While Ray MacSharry and Albert Reynolds were also involved in the talks, the minister who, apart from the Taoiseach, did most to bring the process to a successful conclusion was Bertie Ahern, the Minister for Labour. Having served Haughey well as chief whip during the three leadership heaves, Ahern had been newly promoted to the cabinet and his low-key conciliatory approach was suited to the delicate task. Another close confidant of Haughey, Pádraig Ó hUiginn, the secretary of the department, also came into his own in the negotiations. During the coalition's term of office, he had persuaded the social partners to agree to the National Economic and Social Council report on the future of the economy. Now he used his skills to keep talks going between the social partners on a national programme, despite all the publicity about the government's programme of public spending cuts.

The deal agreed between the social partners become known as the Programme for National Recovery and was the first of a series which guaranteed industrial peace for more than a decade. The nub of the Programme was an agreement with the unions on a public service pay deal which pinned back wage increases to just 2.5 per cent a year for three years and deferred a range of special pay awards. Taken in tandem with the public spending cuts it was just the medicine the economy needed.

16. HAUGHEY IN POWER

IN OFFICE BETWEEN 1987 AND 1989, Haughey repeatedly showed what he was capable of. His tragedy is that other aspects of his career will always overshadow his achievements in this period. One initiative taken by him at this time was to have enormously beneficial effects on the economy in the years ahead. This was the decision to establish the International Financial Services Centre in Dublin's dockland. The proposal was the brainchild of financier Dermot Desmond, the founder of NCB Stockbrokers, who had first put it forward at a dinner in the Shelbourne Hotel hosted by Ruairí Quinn, a Labour minister in the coalition government of 1985. Desmond told Quinn about the trend towards the globalisation of finance on the back of modern telecommunications and argued that it offered a great opportunity for Ireland. Dublin could undercut London on cost and, with a plentiful supply of well-educated young Irish people coming on the jobs market every year, a tailor-made workforce was available.

Quinn sanctioned a full-scale analysis of the plan costing £150,000, with half the cost to be paid by the state and the other half by NCB. Price Waterhouse completed the feasibility study in 1986 but Quinn, though very enthusiastic about the plan, was not able to sell it to his cabinet colleagues who put it on the long finger. However, Haughey heard about it and was immediately sold on it and ordered it to be included in the Fianna Fáil manifesto for the 1987 election. Desmond and his NCB colleague, Michael Buckley, a former top civil servant, duly wrote it up. When Haughey took power he pushed the idea through a reluctant bureaucracy. The highly ambitious plan aimed at creating 7,500 full-time jobs over five years and it was not envisaged that it would bring in any revenue to the exchequer. In fact, so successful did the Financial Services Centre become that by 1999 the 11,000 people employed there contributed £1 billion in taxation to the exchequer. By any standards the IFSC was a triumph of forward planning and Haughey deserves huge credit for making it happen. Without his single-minded drive it would never have got off the ground.[1]

Between 1987 and 1989, the Tallaght Strategy marked a fundamental change in Irish political life that enabled Haughey to govern comfortably without an overall majority. As time went on it became apparent that the strategy was mainly 'give' on Fine Gael's part and mostly 'take' on Fianna Fáil's, but Haughey banked on the fact that Alan Dukes did not have the nerve to bring the government down and cause an early general election.

The business of the Dáil is arranged by the government of the day through its chief whip who consults with the whips of the other parties about the scheduling of legislation and the timing and duration of debates. As a result of the Tallaght Strategy, the Fianna Fáil whip Vincent Brady and his Fine Gael counterpart Fergus O'Brien met a few times a week to arrange Dáil business and then presented a united front to the other whips at the official meetings. If Fine Gael had problems with legislation, O'Brien arranged for the party spokesman to have a meeting with the relevant minister and amendments to various Bills were agreed in this way. Finance Minister Ray MacSharry held many such meetings with his Fine Gael counterpart, Michael Noonan, to head off potential trouble. The Dáil now became a very different institution to the kind of one it had been before or since. The PDs and Labour became increasingly angry at what they regarded as collusion between the two big parties to arrange business behind their backs, but there was nothing they could do except kick up a rumpus in the Dáil.

Meanwhile, Haughey had reversed engines not only on economic policy but on the North as well. Despite his hostility to the Anglo-Irish Agreement, whose terms he had excoriated in 1985, once in office he proceeded to use it for all it was worth. He even managed to establish a reasonable working relationship with the Department of Foreign Affairs whose personnel he had long despised. He once referred to Ireland's diplomats as 'dog-handlers' and never concealed his dislike of them. One example of his attitude was expressed in the Dáil in March 1984. 'Can we now hope that all the sophistry, ambivalence and self-deception that has oozed out of Iveagh House for some time now will cease and that the cold harsh reality will be accepted that Ireland's interests are best defended by Irish men and women and that all the appeasement, the platitudes and the honeyed words mean nothing when the chips are down?' he said in a debate about the outcome of an EU summit. For good measure, he added that the summit had exposed 'the current favour-currying type of Iveagh House diplomacy for what it is.'[2]

Haughey's attitude in Opposition had been coloured by his hostile relationship with the department's chief, Seán Donlon, who had wisely moved into the private sector before the change of government. After an initial attempt to control the department's press relations through P.J. Mara failed, Haughey settled down to a working relationship with

Iveagh House. The amiable style of the Minister for Foreign Affairs, Brian Lenihan, helped to smooth things over, but so did Haughey's *volte face* on almost every aspect of foreign policy. He did move in on the department's power base by taking more control of Northern and European policy in his own department, but there was no significant change of policy in either area.

The management of the government's minority position in the Dáil did, however, pose problems for Haughey. During the weekly debates in private members' business, Labour and the PDs regularly tried to outmanoeuvre Fine Gael by attempting to force the party into voting against the government. In contrast, Fine Gael attempted to frame motions which would either be acceptable to the government or unacceptable to Labour. Fine Gael was embarrassed every now and again into voting with the other Opposition parties and the government suffered a series of defeats in private members' time. However, these did not carry any weight and the government was never threatened on an issue of substance.

A more threatening development was that Fianna Fáil backbenchers began to cause trouble on the issue of extradition. As on so many other issues, Haughey had to confront a problem of his own making because his attitude to extradition in Opposition was the direct opposite of what he was required to do in government. At the end of 1986 Haughey and Fianna Fáil had been instrumental in preventing the Fine Gael-Labour coalition sorting out the extradition issue once and for all.

While the Supreme Court had already extradited a number of people by disallowing the political defence in certain terrorist cases, FitzGerald had agreed in the negotiations on the Anglo-Irish Agreement to put the system on a legislative basis by incorporating into Irish Law the European Convention on the Suppression of Terrorism. The sustained Fianna Fáil objections prompted left-wing Labour TDs like Michael D. Higgins to threaten a revolt on the issue, so as a compromise the Extradition Bill was passed into law in December 1986 with a stay of execution for one year.

This left Haughey in the unenviable position as a Fianna Fáil Taoiseach of having to preside over the introduction of the legislation. A carefully orchestrated campaign developed in the months before the deadline in December 1987 and a number of Fianna Fáil backbenchers came under severe pressure on the issue. It became a much more contentious issue with Fianna Fáil TDs than any of the public spending cutbacks, the exact opposite of the public's priorities. With the pressure mounting on his TDs, it appeared that Haughey would not be able to stand over the introduction of extradition. P.J. Mara, on Haughey's behalf, accused the British ambassador, Nicholas Fenn, of over-zealous interference in local politics because of a briefing he gave to Peter Barry and Des O'Malley about the British position on extradition. It appeared as if Haughey was preparing the ground to postpone ratification of the Extradition Bill.

The whole situation was changed utterly in early November. In the early days of that month two of the most horrific terrorist outrages in the whole litany of violence since the Troubles began shocked the nation. Dublin dentist John O'Grady, who had been kidnapped in October, was finally rescued by Gardaí on 5 November and it emerged that two of his fingers had been hacked off by his kidnappers in an effort to force his father-in-law, Austin Darragh, to pay a £1.5 million ransom. The kidnappers had threatened to cut up Dr O'Grady piece by piece until a ransom was paid, and under this pressure Haughey agreed to let Darragh organise the payment of the ransom. Luckily the Gardaí captured the gang shortly before the transfer was to take place, but the brutality of the episode horrified the country.

Another horror followed three days later with the IRA bombing of the Remembrance Day ceremony in Enniskillen, which left 11 people dead. The moving account of the explosion by Gordon Wilson, whose daughter Marie died in the blast, made a profound impact on the whole country. As these two events came only days after an IRA arms shipment from Libya was captured on board the *Eksund* off the coast of France, and it became known that over £20 million worth of bombs and guns had got through in earlier consignments, the public attitude towards terrorism hardened considerably. In Fianna Fáil, however, the mood was still strongly against extradition in any circumstances.

At a meeting of the parliamentary party on 18 November, no fewer than 57 deputies and senators spoke out against extradition. Some were against it in any circumstances: most argued that it should not be introduced unless it was accompanied by very tough safeguards such as an insistence on *prima facie* evidence being provided to Irish courts in all cases. Even seven junior ministers joined the chorus of protest, with one of them, Denis Gallagher, telling the meeting he had been warned by his local organisation not to come back to Mayo if he agreed to the measure. One of the TDs most strongly opposed to the introduction was Noel Dempsey of Meath, who had just been elected as a TD in 1987. He articulated the views of a number of younger TDs who were unhappy at the way Haughey was reversing virtually every policy he had stood for in Opposition.

In the face of the internal opposition Haughey came up with a formula that allowed extradition to come into operation, alongside certain safeguards that involved the Irish Attorney General vetting all extradition applications. It was much less than most of the Fianna Fáil TDs had demanded but it was accepted with hardly a whimper.[3]

This process would be repeated again and again in the following few years. Fianna Fáil TDs would express outrage, Haughey would express concern at their predicament, follow that by doing precisely the opposite of what they wanted and the process would be completed by his back-benchers mutely accepting that which they had so strenuously objected to in the first place.

At the end of 1988 Haughey's right-hand man in the cabinet, Ray MacSharry, sought and obtained from the Taoiseach the nomination as Ireland's European Union Commissioner. Haughey did not want him to go but MacSharry was adamant. He was replaced as Minister for Finance by Albert Reynolds who, although he had always been loyal, had a more distant relationship with his party leader and was not blind to his faults. This change of personnel was to have profound consequences over time.

By early 1989, as a result of tough economic policies, the Tallaght Strategy and that most valuable of all commodities, luck, Haughey had never been in a stronger position. The PDs were in decline, Fine Gael was making little headway and neither was the left. Opinion poll ratings of 50 per cent and more painted a rosy picture for Fianna Fáil and indicated that the electorate was happy with Haughey's minority government. Yet it was during this period that the first public hints emerged that Haughey might be using his position to help himself to some extra wealth. The visit of a Saudi prince, a member of that country's royal family, caused a politi-cal storm when it emerged that Haughey had been presented with a jewel-encrusted dagger and that Mrs. Haughey had received a valuable necklace. This was not only unethical but also in flagrant contravention of the Government Procedure Instructions, which were binding on every member of the government. The instructions stated that while there were no formal guidelines on the subject of gifts, 'the practice has been for Min-isters and Ministers of State to accept relatively inexpensive gifts to mark occasions such as official openings etc and not to accept expensive gifts or when presented return them. Any gift of national significance would be regarded as the property of the state and dealt with accordingly.' Ironi-cally the instructions added that in any case of doubt the Taoiseach should be consulted. Haughey, however, consistently refused to give any explana-tion to the Dáil about the gifts.[4]

Another development that drew the fire of the Opposition was the decision by the Minister for Energy and Communications, Ray Burke, to establish the Independent Radio and Television Commission (IRTC) to oversee the establishment of commercial radio and television. A strange feature of politics during this period was that Burke took the Communica-tions portfolio with him through three departments – from Energy to

Industry and Commerce and then on to Justice. Some of the Opposition concern related simply to left-wing opposition to ending the state monopoly on broadcasting, but there were other, deeper worries about the way the licences were dealt with. When the IRTC was set up in 1988 the government appointed as chairman a retired Supreme Court judge, Seamus Henchy. In 1988, the IRTC under Henchy's direction handed out a number of radio licences, mainly for new local stations. Its most controversial decision was the allocation of the national commercial radio licence to the Century consortium, headed by a well-known Fianna Fáil supporter and concert promoter, Oliver Barry. It emerged over a decade later that Barry paid a donation of £35,000 to Ray Burke during the 1989 election campaign, which followed shortly after Century went on air. Rumours about that donation circulated for years, before being confirmed by the Flood Tribunal in January 2000. The tribunal also confirmed that Haughey's son-in-law, John Mulhern, was a major shareholder in Century. Ironically the granting of the licence to Century resulted in a financial disaster for Barry and his partners, who lost a lot of money on the ill-fated national station before it eventually closed down. On the positive side, many of the local stations quickly established themselves over the next few years as an integral part of Irish broadcasting.

Another friend of Haughey's who enmeshed the government in controversy was the beef baron, Larry Goodman, whose rags-to-riches story was as remarkable as Haughey's rise to the top in Fianna Fáil. On 18 June 1987, within months of achieving power, Haughey gave a major press conference to promote a massive development of the beef industry, involving the biggest investment programme ever devised for the food industry. The programme was to consist of £60 million in assistance from the Industrial Development Authority and the European Community to Goodman companies, a £30 million investment by Goodman himself and a £170 million package of loans under Section 84 of the Finance Act.[5] Despite continuous prodding of Goodman by the state agencies involved, the ambitious plan never got off the ground. No government agency made any direct investment in the abortive plan but the Goodman companies did draw down a considerable portion of the Section 84 loan finance.

One result of the massive publicity surrounding the project was to link Haughey and Goodman inextricably in the public mind. This association became a political issue in the early months of 1989. Firstly the Oireachtas Committee on State-sponsored Bodies became embroiled in controversy when it emerged that Goodman was interested in buying the state-owned Sugar Company through one of his own companies, called Food Industries. The chairman of the Oireachtas committee, Liam Lawlor, was also a director of Food Industries, and the PD committee member Pat O'Malley raised the issue of a potential conflict of interests. Lawlor was forced to resign. Agriculture Minister Michael O'Kennedy also came under attack in the Dáil and faced a series of questions on the issue.

At this stage, the media were pursuing various stories about the Goodman operation but because of the fear of libel a number of them were suppressed. RTÉ was forced to issue a cringing apology for an item carried on its 'Farm News' programme, containing allegations made against Goodman in New Zealand. The *Sunday Press* did carry a report about a raid by Department of Agriculture officials on a Goodman plant in Dublin's North Wall.[6] Then Labour TD Barry Desmond took the bull by the horns and made a series of damning allegations in the Dáil about the way the Goodman companies were operating. He spoke about a Garda fraud squad investigation and claimed that £20 million in export refunds had been withheld from the company because of its fraudulent practices. Desmond added that the newspapers had not reported these matters because 'writs were flying around all over the place.'[7]

Haughey immediately sprang to Goodman's defence, deploring the attacks and saying they could damage employment and growth. A national controversy quickly developed and Goodman challenged Desmond and Workers' Party TD Tomás Mac Giolla to repeat their allegations outside the legal privilege of the Dáil. 'We'll leave no stone unturned. It was an abuse of Dáil privilege and we're not going to stand for it,' said Goodman.[8] RTÉ broadcaster Gay Byrne leapt to Goodman's defence and accused Desmond of indulging in malicious publicity-seeking. Desmond was not deterred. The following week he told the Dáil that the Department of Agriculture had imposed a fine of over £1 million on one Goodman company arising from a number of offences, including over-statement of weights, incorrect declarations in relation to the export refund scheme and the aids to the private storage scheme, both of which were funded by the EC.

Desmond again raised the issue in the Dáil on 15 March and challenged Haughey or O'Kennedy to deny his allegations. Haughey reacted angrily. 'I, in turn, accuse Deputy Desmond, with a full sense of responsibility, of trying to sabotage the entire beef industry in this country,' he declared. O'Kennedy issued a statement denying that his department had initiated any court proceedings against Goodman companies but within a week he was forced to admit that irregularities amounting to £7.5 million in the beef industry had been notified to his department over the previous three years. In the midst of all these allegations Bobby Molloy of the PDs established the embarrassing fact that Goodman's private jet was being parked at Casement Military aerodrome at Baldonnel. This military facility was not open to private individuals and questions arose about why Goodman was being given the facility and what he was paying the state for the privilege.

It was not long before another controversy arose concerning Goodman. This time it involved the operation of the state export credit insurance scheme and the way in which Goodman's meat exports to Iraq were being underwritten. In 1986, the Fine Gael Minister for Industry and Commerce, Michael Noonan, had withdrawn cover for all exports to Iraq because of the risks of trading with that country. A series of Dáil questions from PD deputy Pat O'Malley (cousin of Des) in April 1989 established that on Fianna Fáil's accession to office in 1987 the cover had been restored. The vast bulk of that cover went to Goodman companies. In 1987 export credit for beef exports to Iraq was £41.2 million and in 1988 it had risen to £78.5 million. In fact, Goodman's trade with Iraq absorbed almost one third of all the available export credit insurance for all Irish exports. The figures also showed that the export credit insurance cover provided for the trade with Iraq in 1987 and 1988 actually exceeded the total value of beef exports to that country by £57 million.

The Opposition demanded to know why the Fianna Fáil government had provided such cover for Goodman. 'Members of this present Government, from the Taoiseach down, are extremely close personally to the leading figure in the group concerned,' Des O'Malley told the Dáil. The Minister for Industry and Commerce, Ray Burke, who had cancelled the export credit insurance for Iraq on taking over the department from Albert Reynolds in January 1989, responded by attacking O'Malley and accusing him of being out to get the Goodman group. 'Throughout it has been my impression – and it has been confirmed tonight – that many of the questions raised on this matter have been characterised by insinuation, innuendo and hints of abuse regarding the operation of the scheme.'[9]

The rows over the Saudi jewels and the allocation of the radio licence took some of the gloss off Haughey but it was the Goodman controversy that caused genuine public disquiet. Labour and the PDs latched on to the issue and pursued Haughey relentlessly over it. He fought back with equal vehemence and the political atmosphere heightened during the spring of 1989.

17. CORE VALUES ABANDONED

BY MAY OF 1989 the Fianna Fáil minority government had been in power for over two years and, despite the growing smell of corruption, Haughey seemed to never have had it so good. Amazingly, he threw it all away in a fit of pique, demonstrating once again that, far from being the political wizard of legend, his political judgement was often appalling. A master of tactics when it came to getting himself out of a crisis, he proved himself a poor strategist, plunging himself into one unnecessary crisis after another.

In the early summer, Haughey seemed secure in office for the rest of his term by virtue of the Tallaght Strategy. His government's genuinely remarkable performance on the economy had impressed the public, despite the various cutbacks that achievement entailed. Government borrowing, much of it carried out by Haughey himself in his first spell as Taoiseach, had finally been brought under control. Under the FitzGerald coalition borrowing had stabilised at around £2.5 billion a year or just under 13 per cent of GNP. In 1987 Fianna Fáil yanked the figure down to 9.9 per cent of GNP and in 1988 broke the back of the problem by bringing it down to a remarkable 3.3 per cent of GNP, the lowest for more than 20 years. The windfall of the tax amnesty helped this achievement but the key to the solution was the political will to cut public spending. The dismal scientists, as Haughey used to call economists, were universal in their praise. Apart from occasional private members' time defeats in the Dáil, which did not count as confidence issues, it appeared as if there was not a dark cloud on the horizon. Then out of the blue Haughey chose to make one of the biggest blunders of his political career. He returned from a successful visit to Japan on 27 April to discover that his government was about to lose a Dáil vote on a private member's motion calling for an allocation of just £400,000 to help haemophiliacs who had been infected with AIDS through contaminated blood. Though he had instructed Health Minister Rory O'Hanlon, before he went to Japan, to deal with the issue he can hardly have been too surprised, in view of the tight situation in the Dáil, that a trap had been set for him.

On his return, RTÉ reporter Charlie Bird met the Taoiseach at the airport. Instead of beginning the interview with the expected questions about the Japanese trip, the reporter asked Haughey for his response to an impending Dáil defeat. After the interview, the Taoiseach appeared overcome by rage. He made a quick visit to his Kinsealy home near the airport, where he consulted a few friends, and then insisted on going into Leinster House. He had just completed an arduous 16-hour journey from the other side of the earth and there was no need for him to be in the Dáil, as he was paired with Fine Gael leader Alan Dukes. On his arrival in Government Buildings the Taoiseach summoned the available ministers and subjected them to a tongue-lashing for allowing the situation in the Dáil to develop as it did. At the informal cabinet meeting which ensued, Haughey strongly expressed the view that he would not tolerate a defeat and would call a general election if the government was beaten. Most of his ministers were shocked. They saw no need for such an extreme response to what was only a political embarrassment and not a political crisis.

As news of the threatened election spread to TDs gathered in the Dáil chamber, journalists flocked to the press gallery. The public gallery also filled up with party activists, including P.J. Mara, Frank Wall, the party's general secretary, and Seán Sherwin, the party organiser, as well as officials of the other Dáil parties. The stage looked set for a drama but nobody was sure what would happen. After the critical vote was called Haughey's humour appeared to have improved considerably as he bowed Japanese-style to some colleagues and chaffed the Opposition. When the votes were counted, however, the government had lost by 72 to 69. Brady told Brendan Howlin at this stage that the game was up and the Dáil would be dissolved. However, as the TDs waited for the second vote, on the Opposition motion, Albert Reynolds sat down beside Haughey and spoke earnestly to him for ten minutes, urging him strongly not to make a hasty decision to call an election but to sleep on the matter.

Most of the cabinet was against an election and that view was put most strongly by Reynolds. Haughey's refusal to take that advice opened a breach which was to get wider over the following years. Two ministers, Pádraig Flynn and Ray Burke, were strongly for going to the country on the basis of opinion polls which showed Fianna Fáil getting an overall majority. In any case, the European elections were scheduled for 15 June and they argued that it would be the ideal opportunity to free Fianna Fáil of its dependence on Fine Gael's Tallaght Strategy. Both men were close to Haughey. As we now know, they also shared Haughey's ability to raise large sums of money and election time was the ideal opportunity for fund-raising. Flynn was particularly close to Haughey. He often wandered into the Taoiseach's office for a chat and had an unusually casual and frank relationship with him. Burke had not been an uncritical loyalist like

Flynn and had voted against Haughey during the latest heave in 1983. Nonetheless, he made it back into Haughey's good books and re-established himself with the Taoiseach, whose Kinsealy home was in his constituency of Dublin North.

Urging Haughey to go for an election, both men pointed to Fianna Fáil's privately commissioned opinion polls which gave the party 51 per cent. They also pointed to the low standing of the PDs and expressed the view that the time was ripe to wipe out O'Malley's party. Even though Haughey had calmed down in the days after the Dáil defeat, he couldn't resist the temptation to go for the overall majority that had eluded him on four previous occasions.

Though he waited for weeks, Haughey moved inevitably towards that decision and he dissolved the Dáil at 7 p.m. on 25 May, setting the election for 15 June, the same day as the European contest. The weeks of speculation in the lead-up to the calling of the election had given the Opposition plenty of time to prepare. Drafts of party policies, advertising strategy and the preparation of election literature and posters had all been completed by the Opposition parties before Haughey dissolved the Dáil and printing houses all over the country were on standby, geared up and ready to go on 25 May. In fact, the Opposition parties seemed far better prepared than Fianna Fáil. It was not just a matter of nuts and bolts; the Opposition had a strategy while the government appeared confused and was content to rely on its record.

During the campaign vague rumours circulated in the rarefied atmosphere of Leinster House suggesting that Haughey had gone to the country simply as an excuse to raise money for himself under the guise of electioneering. This appeared too fantastic even for Haughey and the rumours were dismissed out of hand. Almost a decade later, the information obtained by the tribunals about the money-raising activities of Haughey and some of his chief lieutenants put those rumours in a new light. Two days before the election of 15 June, Haughey drew down a £150,000 contribution from Ben Dunne, part of the £1.3 million he was given by the supermarket tycoon between 1987 and 1992. Also in early June, the Minister for Justice and Communications, Ray Burke, received £30,000 in cash from James Gogarty at his home. During the course of the campaign the minister also received another £30,000 from a company called Rennicks, a subsidiary of the Fitzwilton group and Century Radio boss, Oliver Barry, gave him £35,000.

Meanwhile the Minister for the Environment, Pádraig Flynn, was also busy. During the campaign he met the property developer Tom Gilmartin, who gave him a cheque for £50,000 and left it up to the minister to fill out the name of the payee. Gilmartin says the donation was meant for

Fianna Fáil but the party never got it.

A flavour of what was going on at the time was given to the Dáil in 1998 by Laois TD Seán Fleming, who was then a party official involved in fund-raising operations. 'On 8 June 1989 Fianna Fáil had a fund-raising luncheon in the Westbury Hotel,' Fleming told the Dáil. 'Mr Paul Kavanagh, chief fund-raiser for Fianna Fáil at that time, and I were in the entrance foyer of the hotel to meet the various people attending the luncheon. I was aware since the previous evening that Fitzwilton was to make a large contribution to the Fianna Fáil party through Mr Ray Burke. When he arrived we asked him for the cheque and he gave the envelope to Paul Kavanagh or myself. On opening it we saw it contained a bank draft for £10,000 and a photocopy of a Rennicks compliment slip. I was not satisfied that £10,000 was the full amount of the contribution. Both of us asked Mr Ray Burke where was the balance. He told us that £10,000 was the amount that was being given to party headquarters and the rest would be used for his constituency purposes.

'Immediately after that Mr. Paul Kavanagh and I spoke to the then party leader, Mr. Charles Haughey, who was at the luncheon. We pointed out to him that we believed the party's national fund-raising committee had been left short in respect of this donation. Mr Charles Haughey indicated that we should leave the matter with him. I took the contribution back to head office on 8 June 1989. It was receipted to Rennicks on 9 June 1989, lodged to our bank after the weekend and presented for payment to the Ulster Bank through the banking system in the normal manner. I hope that explains the sequence of events in relation to the receiving, receipting and lodgement of the bank draft.'[1]

This fascinating insight reveals that the official Fianna Fáil fund-raisers, desperate for funds in an increasingly difficult campaign, had to go chasing ministers who they had heard on the grapevine were collecting money. It is clear that there was a free-for-all pursuit of cash by some senior Fianna Fáil people in the course of that campaign. At the time the public and the media were completely in the dark about what was going on.

Within the past year it has emerged that Charles Haughey received £100,000 at his Kinsealy home from property developer, Mark Kavanagh, on the day of the election. Kavanagh's company had won a lucrative contract to develop the financial services centre. Haughey also received £50,000 from Michael Smurfit at this time with the money being channelled to his Ansbacher account, while beef baron Larry Goodman gave £50,000. All these people say they believed the money was going to Fianna Fáil, and some of it did end up in the party's accounts, but some ended up in Haughey's personal accounts.

On the day of the election count a cheque for £25,000 made out to cash and drawn on the Fianna Fáil leader's account was issued. The cheque, which also ended up in Haughey's personal account, was signed by Haughey and Bertie Ahern. Ahern told the Moriarty tribunal in 1999 that this cheque must have been one of the many he presigned and left to be filled up by Haughey. The Fianna Fáil fund-raising effort, headed by Paul Kavanagh, was based in P.V. Doyle's Westbury Hotel for the entire campaign and there was a steady stream of business people in and out every day to contribute money to the campaign. On the day of the count Haughey hosted a lunch in the Westbury for some of his key political associates and campaign staff.

In the campaign itself, the Opposition parties, particularly Labour and the Workers' Party, hounded Fianna Fáil on the health cuts which quickly became the dominant issue of the campaign while the economic achievements of the previous two and a quarter years were pushed into the background. The delay in calling the election also gave Fine Gael and the Progressive Democrats an opportunity to negotiate a pact to put an alternative government before the people. The deal was announced two days after the election was called but as things turned out it failed to capture the public imagination. It did, however, unsettle Fianna Fáil and prevented the two Opposition parties attacking each other during the campaign. Instead they joined in a systematic assault on the government along with the left-wing parties. This assault from all sides began to eat into the government's lead in the opinion polls. As had happened in almost every election since polling began in 1977, Fianna Fáil lost support as the campaign progressed.

The turn-out on 15 June was one of the lowest turn-outs of any recent general election, with just 68.5 per cent of voters going to the polls. When they came in the following day, the results proved a bitter blow for Fianna Fáil. The party ended up with just 44 per cent of the vote and dropped four seats in the process, from 81 to 77. There was a feeling of devastation in the party, not just because of the losses but because an election was so unnecessary. 'Of all the mistakes Haughey has made this has to be the biggest,' said one minister privately on the night of the count. Fine Gael improved only marginally, from 27 per cent to 29 per cent, gaining four seats. The PDs suffered badly, dropping from 14 seats to 6, losing some of its brightest stars, including McDowell, Geraldine Kennedy, Anne Colley, Pat O'Malley and Martin Cullen and the party seemed headed for oblivion. Ray Burke, smarting from his own party's failure to win a majority, said bitterly: 'It couldn't happen to a nicer bunch of people.'[2] Both Labour and the Workers' Party gained votes and seats by eating into working-class Fianna Fáil support, but it was hardly the big breakthrough for the left that had been predicted.

The most immediate issue when the result became clear was how a government could be put together. Fianna Fáil had 77 seats, Fine Gael 55, Labour 16, the Workers' Party 7, the PDs 6, the Greens 1 and Others 4. In a radio interview as the results came in, Labour's Barry Desmond maintained that there was no problem. Fianna Fáil and the PDs had the numbers between them so Des O'Malley should go back to Fianna Fáil from whence he had come and they could form a government. At the time that appeared far too simplistic an analysis.

After the final result became clear, Haughey stated his willingness to form a government and said he was prepared to consult with the other political parties before the Dáil resumed on 29 June. He gave the clear impression that he felt he could form another minority administration and that Fianna Fáil could simply take up where it had left off under the Tallaght Strategy. Next day, the prospects for that looked good when one of the surviving PDs, Mary Harney, said publicly her party would support Haughey if that was necessary to provide the country with a government. The fact that the six surviving PDs were all ex-members of Fianna Fáil added to the belief that they might step into Fine Gael shoes and support a Haughey minority government.

Haughey quickly began a series of meetings with the other party leaders. He met O'Malley to ask for support for a Fianna Fáil minority government and promised a very generous arrangement. Harney's intervention had provoked a very hostile reaction among PD supporters and at least three of the party's six deputies were adamantly against voting for Haughey as Taoiseach. A meeting between the Taoiseach and Alan Dukes the following day, 21 June, brought home to many in Fianna Fáil for the first time that things had changed fundamentally and that the party would have to pay a stiff price for its decision to call an election. Dukes said he was prepared to help Haughey form a government but only if Fine Gael got 7 of the 15 cabinet posts and the office of Taoiseach was revolved between them during the lifetime of the government. Dukes's tough line showed just how difficult forming a new administration was going to be. That brought the PDs into the picture as the only realistic option for a deal. With just six deputies, the PDs did not appear to be in a position to make the same kind of demands as Fine Gael, but there was intense opposition within the party to voting for Haughey in any circumstances. Their six deputies may all have been ex-Fianna Fáil but they had left the party precisely because they could not accept Haughey's leadership.

There was still no conclusion to the negotiations when the twenty-sixth Dáil met on 29 June. Haughey was beaten in the vote for Taoiseach although nobody else had the votes either. For the first time in the history of the state, the Dáil failed to come up with a majority for the election of a Taoiseach. As if that wasn't sensation enough, Haughey added to the drama of the day by initially refusing to tender his resignation to the President as the Constitution implied he should. The issue was raised by Dick Spring who challenged Haughey as to why he was not proposing to go to Áras an Uachtaráin to tender his resignation. Dukes had earlier been advised by his former leader Garret FitzGerald to raise that precise point with Haughey but had declined to do so on the basis that he had his own legal advice which suggested Haughey need not resign immediately. Establishing a pattern that was to be repeated again and again in the twenty-sixth Dáil, Spring seized the initiative from Dukes and the Fine Gael leader was then obliged to follow.

The Dáil was adjourned for two hours while Haughey met his cabinet and considered the position. His Attorney General, John Murray, was adamant that Haughey need not resign but should retain the office of Taoiseach until he was replaced. It was a stormy cabinet meeting as Haughey insisted that he would not resign. For the first time some of his ministers were prepared to challenge The Boss. Albert Reynolds lost patience with Haughey and demanded that whatever the legal niceties of the situation he should formally resign. They were extremely worried that an apparent attempt to flout the Constitution would only make it more difficult than it already was to form a minority government.

After a great deal of argument and persuasion at cabinet, Haughey finally agreed to resign. He went back into the Dáil to announce his decision and then drove to Áras an Uachtaráin where he handed a written note of resignation to President Hillery. As the Constitution states that an outgoing Taoiseach should remain in place until a successor has been appointed by the Dáil, Haughey and his ministers remained in office. However, there was considerable debate about the powers of an 'acting Taoiseach' and whether he had the authority to get a dissolution of the Dáil to hold another election. The Constitution does not appear to make adequate provision for the situation that arose after 29 June and there is considerable ambiguity about the role of the 'acting Government'. One way or another Haughey was still in power, but it had been brought home to him and his party that they would remain in that position only if they really got down to business and made some real compromises with the other parties. The one unmentionable compromise, then and later, was the possibility of Haughey stepping down as leader of Fianna Fáil to let somebody else take over and try to put a government together. Members of the cabinet and most Fianna Fáil TDs knew that with almost any other leader besides Haughey, they would have been able to retain office as a minority government. But the memory of the bitterness and divisiveness caused by the heaves of the early 1980s meant that nobody in the party dared to broach the subject.

The first real break in the logjam developed the day after the first meeting of the twnty-sixth Dáil. The PDs, who had voted for Alan Dukes as Taoiseach in fulfilment of their pre-election pledge, now offered to open talks with Fianna Fáil on a nine-point framework for dialogue which had as its core the principle that everything was up for discussion. The key point was number seven – 'that prior to any negotiations taking place, all discussion on all matters be open and that nothing be ruled in or ruled out in advance.' Haughey agreed and the two negotiating teams met on the evening of 30 June. The PD negotiators were former Fianna Fáil minister Bobby Molloy and newly elected MEP Pat Cox. The government team was Minister for Finance Albert Reynolds and Labour minister Bertie Ahern. Any issues that could not be resolved between the negotiators were to be referred to the party leaders. A number of TDs, particularly Joe Walsh and Charlie McCreevy of Fianna Fáil, and Mary Harney of the PDs, also kept up contacts during the negotiations and helped to facilitate dialogue when the process ran into trouble.

Entering negotiations, the central tactic of the PDs was not to agree a policy programme until Fianna Fáil had first accepted the central issue of coalition. 'Our main fear was that Fianna Fáil would agree to every policy proposal we put forward but in the last analysis refuse to give us cabinet posts,' said Stephen O'Byrnes of the PDs. 'They could then have broken off the talks, pointed to the agreed programme and put us in the dock as the party which had wrecked the prospect of stable Government out of a naked desire for Mercs and perks.' This determination to ensure that the coalition issue was tackled head-on torpedoed the first session of talks. The two negotiation teams met in Dublin's Mansion House. Pat Cox put the PD side. Then Bertie Ahern put the Fianna Fáil view, including the bottom line that they had no mandate to agree to participation in government with the PDs. Molloy, sticking rigidly to the tactic of getting agreement on coalition before discussing anything else, immediately intervened to say coalition had to be part of any deal. This effectively scuppered the talks but the negotiators agreed to meet formally the following morning so that the talks and their breakdown could be publicly announced.

Haughey and O'Malley met later in the day at the Mansion House to see if there was any possibility of a breakthrough, but had no success. Both men spoke to the media and their comments indicated that agreement would be extremely difficult. 'Coalition is completely ruled out,' Haughey told journalists as he left the Mansion House meeting. He added: 'We went before the electorate on the basis that we wouldn't form a coalition.

A majority of the people voted for Fianna Fáil Government and our position was always that if we hadn't an overall majority we would form a minority Government.' Developments over the next week or so showed that he didn't mean what he said at all, but his TDs were as gullible as ever and for a time they believed another general election was inevitable.

When the Dáil sat on Monday, 3 July there was still no change in the situation. The Fianna Fáil parliamentary party met that morning but there was no indication of any way out, and the report was that it could only endorse the efforts being made by the Taoiseach to form a government. The Dáil adjourned again for three days but speculation was rife about another election.

It dawned on some people that Fianna Fáil's only option might be to put forward somebody other than Charles Haughey as the party nominee for Taoiseach. Haughey could see that scenario more clearly than anybody else and on Tuesday, 4 July, he made the decisive move. That morning Haughey contacted O'Malley to arrange a meeting with the PD leader in the Berkeley Court Hotel for 5 p.m. and then called a cabinet meeting at which, for the first time, he broached the subject of coalition with his ministers. When they realised that it was coalition with the PDs which was under consideration, most of them were stunned. A clear majority of the cabinet, led by Reynolds, was strongly opposed to a coalition arrangement of any kind. Pádraig Flynn, Michael O'Kennedy, Rory O'Hanlon, John Wilson, Michael Noonan and Brendan Daly all spoke against a deal. Flynn was the most vehement and shocked everybody by accusing Haughey of opting for coalition out of a personal pursuit of power. Two key ministers, Gerry Collins and Ray Burke, took the opposite view and in coded language spoke in favour of a deal with O'Malley, even if the price was coalition. As ever, Brian Lenihan supported Haughey and said they would be able to sell coalition to the organisation, if that was the ultimate decision. The cabinet took no formal decision on a change of policy and Flynn went on radio that evening to say that refusal to enter coalition was a core value for Fianna Fáil.

At about the same time as the interview was broadcast, Haughey was meeting O'Malley in the Berkeley Court and making it clear to the PD leader that he was prepared to concede on coalition. Another meeting was arranged for the following day to formalise the decision. Pat Cox and Bobby Molloy accompanied their leader to this meeting but Haughey didn't bother to invite either of his two negotiators along. At the meeting, Molloy challenged Haughey about Flynn's widely-publicised remarks of the evening before that coalition wasn't on and also about anti-coalition views expressed by Reynolds that morning. 'It's all right. I just haven't told them yet,' was Haughey's cryptic response. The audacity of the

Taoiseach's reply didn't surprise the PD team who knew his form only too well and, if anything, they were impressed by the utter confidence and self-belief with which he conducted himself.

Having agreed to coalition in principle, Haughey then went back to put his cabinet in the know. But still he did not give them the full picture. He hinted that a coalition deal might be on but he didn't spell out the concession he had made to the PDs. Some of his ministers were appalled at the news and Reynolds in particular was deeply indignant at the effrontery of Haughey in making the fundamental concession without letting his negotiators know. Salt was rubbed into the wound when Reynolds and Ahern subsequently learned that the two PD negotiators had met Haughey along with their leader while they were not even aware that a meeting was taking place. Despite the misgivings of some ministers there was no clear objection to an announcement that evening that the negotiations with the PDs would resume. Haughey told his two negotiators to go back to the discussions about policy but the actual make-up of the government, and hence the question of coalition, would be left to the Taoiseach himself. There was little doubt in anybody's mind what that meant in practice, but some ministers tried to avoid facing up to the reality.

When the public announcement of the talks was made around 5 p.m. the media had no doubt about what had happened and that a Fianna Fáil-PD coalition was now on. Some ministers still clung to the belief that any deal would have to come back to the cabinet for final approval and they comforted themselves that they would have the last word. Of course, this never happened, Haughey correctly assuming that while they might huff and puff behind his back none of them would do anything about it. His attitude to his ministerial colleagues was summed up in an encounter with one backbench TD who asked him if his cabinet would agree to coalition. 'They are only a crowd of gobshites,' Haughey responded.

The announcement on the evening of 5 July that the principle of coalition had been conceded came as a severe shock to many in Fianna Fáil, particularly ordinary party members. Many TDs had already come to terms with the reality that if they didn't form a coalition another election was the only alternative and such an election would probably reduce the party's strength even further.

When the Dáil met the following day, 6 July, another adjournment was agreed to allow Fianna Fáil and the PDs to negotiate their programme for government. Haughey who a few days earlier had ruled out coalition in any circumstances told the Dáil that the 'higher national interest' required an arrangement to put a government in place. With the Dáil adjourned for six days to allow the two parties to conclude an agreement, there was intense pressure on both sides. Fianna Fáil tried to limit the PD representation at the cabinet table to just one minister, but again the PDs, and particularly Bobby Molloy, adopted a very tough negotiating stance, demanding that Haughey concede two cabinet posts. The Fianna Fáil parliamentary party met twice to debate the issues involved, but on both occasions gave Haughey a free hand without being told how many cabinet places the PDs were getting. Some deputies were still opposed to coalition at any price, among them Junior minister Máire Geoghegan-Quinn, Dick Roche of Wicklow and newly elected Meath TD Noel Dempsey. While the majority didn't like it they were anxious to avoid another election at all costs and were prepared to let Haughey make whatever decisions he thought necessary to avoid one. In the Fianna Fáil organisation as a whole, the mood was very different and there was total and utter astonishment that Haughey had given way to O'Malley of all people.

Fianna Fáil morale suffered a blow when the news about coalition was announced. Haughey continued to manoeuvre to avoid giving two ministerial posts to his junior coalition partner, but the PDs, at the insistence of Molloy, held out to the end and got what they wanted. Meanwhile the talks between the two negotiating teams resumed but they were relegated to the status of a side-show. The PDs produced their own policies while Fianna Fáil relied on briefing documents from the Department of Finance. A number of expert advisers was brought in by the PDs, including former Fianna Fáil minister Martin O'Donoghue. As these negotiations continued, Haughey met O'Malley regularly to iron out difficulties. The PD negotiating team were kept abreast of what went on at these leaders' meetings but Haughey didn't even tell his negotiators that they were taking place, never mind informing them fully of what transpired.

Meanwhile, Haughey set up a meeting with individual ministers and TDs to sound them out about how they felt. This threw the ranks of the anti-coalitionists into confusion because no one was sure what the other was saying directly to the Taoiseach. Junior minister Geoghegan-Quinn was so adamantly opposed to the prospect of her constituency colleague Bobby Molloy getting a cabinet post that there were rumours she would resign in protest. There were also dark hints that Flynn might resign from the cabinet and he certainly had a stormy face-to-face session with Haughey during which he repeated his suggestion that the Taoiseach should step down as Fianna Fáil leader and let somebody else try to form a government, rather than share power with the PDs. The Fianna Fáil parliamentary party met the day before the Dáil's crucial session on 12 July. Haughey told the deputies and senators that the negotiations with the PDs had not concluded and he did not deal with the issue of how many posts they were to get at cabinet. The anti-coalitionists, Noel Dempsey, Geoghegan-Quinn and Noel Treacy from Galway East, spoke against any deal. Geoghegan-Quinn said that she had sold a number of U-turns to the organisation on extradition, the Anglo-Irish Agreement, the Single European Act and spending cutbacks, but she drew the line at selling this one. She refused to accept that what the Taoiseach was doing was in the national interest.

In the final hours before the Dáil met, Haughey demonstrated all the old political skills which had helped him through earlier crises. He first met O'Malley at around 10 a.m. that day and half an hour later went into a cabinet meeting to tell his ministerial colleagues there were still some problems to be cleared up before the coalition arrangement could be finalised. No one challenged Haughey about the precise nature of the deal and there was no discussion on the number of PD cabinet seats. Radio interviews with Reynolds and Ahern had been broadcast that morning, the two ministers saying the PDs should get only one cabinet seat.

From the cabinet meeting Haughey went straight to the final meeting of the parliamentary party. He also told his backbenchers there was no final agreement but he did circulate a document, 'Fianna Fáil-Progressive Democrats Programme for Government 1989-1993'. The TDs didn't have time to digest the details and anyway the crucial question of cabinet representation was not mentioned in it. There were no objections and Haughey left the meeting before lunchtime. He was now completely in the clear: the cabinet, the parliamentary party and the national executive had not given him a precise instruction that he was not to concede two cabinet posts to the PDs. His deftness in avoiding an open confrontation meant that he had a free hand to act as he saw fit, even though he knew the deep-seated hostility in the party to what he was planning. At 1 p.m. he met O'Malley and the PD negotiating team of Molloy and Cox. As before, the Fianna Fáil negotiating team was not even informed of this meeting. Haughey formally agreed to two PD cabinet positions and to one junior ministry for the party. The four men then shook hands on the deal. 'Nobody but myself could have done it,' remarked the Taoiseach good-humouredly to the PDs, and they could only agree with that pronouncement.

When the Dáil met that afternoon Haughey was duly elected Taoiseach with the support of the PDs. In the short debate, O'Malley and Haughey publicly buried the animosity which had divided them for so long as they paid fulsome tribute to each other. 'I want to acknowledge the courage and skill exhibited, particularly by Deputy Haughey, in recent weeks, courage and skill which I know he possesses in abundance and which has been utilised in the national interest during this time,' the PD leader told the Dáil. After his election Haughey responded: 'I want to say about them all, particularly Deputy O'Malley, that I was able to conduct my conversations with them in a way that was always not just courteous but constructive, and I shall always remember that as one of the most important developments in this new Dáil as it went about its arduous and complicated business.'[3] After a visit to President Hillery, Haughey returned to announce his cabinet to the Dáil. It had taken a full 27 days since the election to put a government together, but in the end the logic of political arithmetic proved irresistible.

There were enormous stresses and strains in Fianna Fáil as the party sought to come to terms with the notion of coalition. Things eventually settled down, but one result was a decisive shift in the balance of power within Haughey's cabinet. ministers like Reynolds and Flynn, long-time Haughey supporters, who made up the old inner circle of the cabinet, were excluded from favour because of their opposition to coalition. Ahern remained as close to Haughey as ever by playing his usual ambiguous role of appearing to side with both camps.

Reynolds was deeply disillusioned and very angry over the whole process. He felt that Haughey had treated him with contempt by carrying out all the important negotiations himself without revealing anything of importance that was going on. The experience of being treated in this fashion did not come as a total surprise. While he backed Haughey in three early leadership heaves a coolness had developed between the two men since 1987, particularly as Reynolds began to emerge as a strong runner in the succession stakes. With his prominent supporters feeling aggrieved, Haughey had to rely for a while on Ahern and two of the most experienced ministers in the cabinet, Gerry Collins and Ray Burke. They occupied a position of trust they had not experienced since Haughey became leader of Fianna Fáil in December 1979. It was ironic that Haughey was now closest to the two Fianna Fáil members of his cabinet who voted against him the last time there was a leadership contest, while he brought into the government, out of necessity, two others who had left the party because of his leadership.

As Minister for Industry and Commerce, O'Malley now had responsibility for the operation of the export credit insurance scheme. He immediately set up a departmental inquiry into the discrepancies revealed by PD parliamentary questions back in April, which showed that the insurance cover given to Goodman companies for beef exports to Iraq was for a value greater than the total exports in 1987-88. Having got the results and discovering that 38 per cent of the 'Irish' beef covered by export credit insurance had been sourced in Britain and Northern Ireland, he cancelled policies worth nearly £40 million. Goodman responded by beginning a legal action against the state for £50 million.

O'Malley's action was taken after consultation with Haughey, and the Taoiseach made no objection. Neither were obstacles put in his way when O'Malley's inspectors concluded that Goodman was the beneficial owner of Classic Meats and the meat baron was ordered to dispose of it. O'Malley's ability to take independent action surprised many people but it appeared the parties in government could learn to live together in harmony. This impression was confirmed by the appointment to the Seanad of three PD senators. Again there were murmurings in Fianna Fáil, but they amounted to nothing. The PDs, on the other hand, showed their mettle by refusing to vote for the Fianna Fáil nominee for Cathaoirleach of the Seanad, Seán Doherty, because of his role in the GUBU controversies of 1982.

By the end of 1989 Haughey was back in the driving seat despite his disastrous decision to call a general election in June. However, his hold on power now depended on Des O'Malley and the PDs. That was something which rankled with Fianna Fáil members up and down the country, but all they could do was swallow their pride and accept the situation. Fianna Fáil TDs were relieved when 1989 drew to a close because they never wanted to see another traumatic year like it again. It was just as well they did not have the benefit of being able to see into the future because 1990 held even worse in store.

18. A HEAD ON A PLATE

HAUGHEY WAS BACK ON TOP OF THE WORLD in the first half of 1990. Ireland held the presidency of the European Community and he relished the opportunity of playing a part on the international stage at a time of historic change in Europe. He won the gratitude of Chancellor Helmut Kohl, which was to benefit Ireland in the long term, by doing everything possible to facilitate German unity. All in all, Haughey's handling of the EU presidency was a considerable success but another presidency, the Irish one, brought him tumbling down to earth. The presidential election campaign of 1990 turned into one of the most sensational in the history of the state, and it plunged Fianna Fáil into another crisis.

Yet again, Haughey managed to survive what can only be described as a calamity for his party. In January, the leader of the Labour Party, Dick Spring, announced his determination that there would be a presidential contest, even if he had to stand for president himself to ensure it. The post had not been contested since 1973, being filled on three occasions by agreement among the Dáil parties. Spring did not have to act on his threat because he was able to persuade a former Labour senator, Mary Robinson, to accept the party's nomination. Getting the party to agree was more difficult since there had been an earlier move to run Noel Browne. Left-wing TDs like Emmet Stagg and Michael D. Higgins still wanted Browne, but Spring got his way when the parliamentary party selected Robinson in early April. She spent the spring and summer slogging her way around the country building support, while the major parties waited complacently until autumn to select their candidates. One evening in July, Labour strategist Fergus Finlay was in the Dáil bar when he heard a rumour that Austin Currie was being mooted as the Fine Gael candidate. Convinced that Robinson could beat Currie and probably win on his transfers, Finlay contacted a bookmaker next morning about the betting. Quoted odds of ten to one on Mary Robinson, he was the first to put a bet of £100 on her.

Over the summer, the Robinson campaign soon began to capture the public imagination and the strong response of women had become the central feature. Before the major parties got around to nominating their candidates, another sensation emerged in the shape of the threatened collapse of the Goodman group. The Dáil was hurriedly recalled on 28 August to pass special legislation so that the company would not collapse immediately with devastating knock-on effects for farmers. O'Malley told the Dáil the stark facts. Goodman International owed a consortium of international banks an incredible £460 million and, in turn, was owed £180 million from meat exports to Iraq, which had just invaded Kuwait and was unlikely to be in a position to pay. Massive losses of £200 million had also been run up by Goodman in an ill-fated foray into the British stock market to buy sugar shares. Goodman tried to put pressure on the government to come up with a rescue package for his operation. He helicoptered into Kinsealy ten days before the special Dáil sitting to try to persuade Haughey to bale him out, but the scale of the losses was so great that the Taoiseach was in no position to attempt a rescue. All the government could do was pass the legislation to put an examiner into the company so that the debts to the banks could be rescheduled. In view of his close association with Goodman in the past, the whole affair was an embarrassment to Haughey. However, the decisive handling of the issue by O'Malley helped to calm public disquiet. It was an instance of where the participation of the PDs in coalition worked to the advantage of both parties in the government.

It was not until September that Fianna Fáil got around to nominating the Tánaiste, Brian Lenihan, for the presidential contest, and Fine Gael selected Austin Currie. Lenihan had been talked about as the likely Fianna Fáil runner for nearly a year. However, there were worries that a man who had had a liver transplant might not stand up to a gruelling campaign or survive for seven years in the Áras. There was also concern at the prospect of Fianna Fáil losing the seat in the Dublin West by-election that would be necessitated by his election. Less than a week before the party was due to confirm its candidate, the Marine Minister, John Wilson, mounted a late challenge to Lenihan. He got support from some Ministers of State like Máire Geoghegan-Quinn and Pat 'The Cope' Gallagher but the only cabinet colleague to back him publicly was constituency colleague Rory O'Hanlon. Wilson also attracted support from party TDs most hostile to the PDs. The Finance Minister, Albert Reynolds, who had bitterly opposed coalition, caused some worry in the Lenihan camp when it became known that he was considering coming out in open support of Wilson, but cabinet colleagues Bertie Ahern and Pádraig Flynn persuaded him to stay neutral. Wilson was ultimately defeated by 51 votes to 19.

Fine Gael had nominated the former SDLP politician Austin Currie, but only after the nomination had been turned down by several people in the party, including Currie himself at an earlier stage. Although poll research showed Currie didn't have a chance, his candidature enabled Dukes to head off his internal opponents; in the event, this was to prove only a stay of execution. Meanwhile, Robinson was barnstorming her way up and down the country. It was already a two-horse race between her and Lenihan, and there was nothing Currie could do about it.

Before polling day the country was rocked by a controversy which sent Lenihan's campaign into a tailspin. The problem arose on the 'Questions and Answers' television programme when a Fine Gael activist asked about the discretionary powers of the President to refuse dissolution of the Dáil to a Taoiseach who had lost his majority. Lenihan, who was one of the panellists, concluded his answer by saying an Irish President had never exercised this option. Garret FitzGerald, who was also on the panel, intervened to ask: 'Why were there phone calls to try to force him to exercise it?'

'That is a fiction of Garret's,' said Lenihan.

'It is not a fiction, excuse me,' FitzGerald replied. 'I was in Áras an Uachtaráin when these phone calls came through and I know how many there were.'

From there the controversy took flight. Later in the discussion, the Fine Gael activist Brian Murphy intervened to ask Lenihan directly if he had made a phone call to Áras an Uachtaráin when Garret FitzGerald was seeking a dissolution of the Dáil. 'No, I didn't at all. Nothing like that ever happened. I want to assure you that it never happened,' replied Lenihan. With his answer, a time bomb began ticking under his campaign and his political career. Brian Murphy, the Fine Gael questioner in the audience, knew something that neither Garret FitzGerald nor any of the other Fine Gael activists present knew at this stage. This was the existence of tape on which Lenihan had spoken freely of how he had phoned Áras an Uachtaráin on the night in question and detailed a conversation he said he had with the President. The person who had made that tape was a postgraduate politics student at UCD, Jim Duffy. He was watching 'Questions and Answers' that night and looked on in growing disbelief as Lenihan flatly contradicted his own colourful account a few months earlier about a conversation he had with President Hillery that night.

To compound the issue, Duffy had written a series of articles for the *Irish Times* a month earlier about the presidency and, on the basis of the taped information, had referred to phone calls by Lenihan, Haughey and Sylvester Barrett. Following Lenihan's denial on television, Duffy contacted the *Irish Times* and events began to take an inevitable course. In the meantime, Lenihan went on television again on Tuesday night to say that he had no hand, act or part in phoning Áras an Uachtaráin on the night in question. By Wednesday morning, in advance of the Dáil's resumption after the long summer break, rumours about the taped interview were circulating freely in Leinster House. The *Irish Times* carried a lead story saying they had independent evidence that Lenihan had phoned the President. For his part, Lenihan assured his director of elections, Bertie Ahern, and other ministers that there was nothing in the taped conversation that could cause embarrassment. The action then moved to the Dáil where Dukes made a comprehensive speech on the role of the presidency in which he outlined the various documentary references to the phone calls made in 1982. Next day, replying to Dukes's allegations, an angry Haughey told him 'to look behind at Deputy Garret FitzGerald who has been completely exposed as telling lies'. Only hours later the bombshell finally exploded when the *Irish Times* released the text of a portion of the taped interview.

On the tape, Lenihan was quite specific about what he had done on the night of 27 January 1982. He referred to a conversation he had with President Hillery and said that Haughey and Sylvester Barrett, as well as Lenihan himself, had rung the Áras. Asked if he had got through to the President, Lenihan replied: 'Oh yeah, I mean I got through to him. I remember talking to him and he wanted us to lay off. There was no doubt about it in his mind. In fact, looking back on it, it was a mistake on our part because Paddy Hillery would be very ... what's the word? ... strict or conventional in that way, you know. He wouldn't want to start breaking new ground. He's not that sort of man. He's a very cautious man, the sort of fellow that wouldn't. It didn't break new ground. But, of course, Charlie was gung ho.'[1]

In his book *For the Record*, published a few months after the election, Lenihan explained that when he gave the interview to Duffy on 17 May he was on heavy medication to counteract a complicated medical condition arising from his liver transplant. He cited medical evidence to show that he was in a confused state at the time and had no recollection of ever giving the interview. Lenihan had not given this explanation when the Dáil was discussing the matter. Fianna Fáil TDs were visibly reeling when they read the transcript of the tape and most of them quickly headed for their constituencies in a deep state of shock.

Lenihan himself returned from the campaign trail for a discussion with Haughey. He also consulted P.J. Mara and decided to go on television and radio immediately to rebut the clear evidence of the tape. Interviewed on the RTÉ 6 p.m. news by Seán Duignan, he tried to convince the bemused electorate that what he had said on tape to Duffy was not true and he stuck by his original story that he had never phoned the President. Looking directly into camera, he declared: 'My mature recollection at this stage is that I did not ring President Hillery. I want to put my reputation on the line in that respect. I have sought a meeting with President Hillery tomorrow and I intend to confirm that with him. That is the situation.'

When Duignan put it to him that either he had not told the truth to the nation or he had not told the truth to Jim Duffy, the Tánaiste responded: 'I must have been mistaken in what I said to Duffy on that occasion. It was a casual discussion with a research student and I was obviously mistaken in what I said.'

The performance knocked the wind right out of Lenihan's campaign. The combination of what he said and how he said it destroyed his credibility. The general reaction was well put by former rugby international Tony Ward, who was a member of Fianna Fáil. 'The whole thing made me cringe. It was pathetic to see someone continuing with a lie when the truth was there for everyone to hear. I just wanted to say "Stop, Stop. Get off the television screen".'[2] A subsequent radio interview with Seán O'Rourke only compounded the damage and another television appearance later that night added to Lenihan's woe. By the end of the evening, the Lenihan campaign was in tatters.

Dukes then raised the stakes. In an attempt to exploit the clear disarray in Fianna Fáil and, in to process, to shore up his own leadership, he put down a motion of no confidence in the government. 'I have put down a motion of no confidence in the Government because it is now clear and beyond any doubt that lies have been told this week by the Tánaiste, Mr Lenihan, and that those lies have been supported by the Taoiseach and three other ministers,' he said. The motion was designed to test the unity of the coalition and it succeeded in putting immediate pressure on the PDs. O'Malley rang Haughey to express concern at the development and asked the Taoiseach not to say anything which would commit the government as a whole in relation to the pending motion of confidence. O'Malley also told O'Byrnes to issue a statement on his behalf saying he found the situation 'very disturbing'. The PD leader then left for Luxembourg before the 6 o'clock news and Lenihan's 'mature recollection' interview.

The following morning, Fianna Fáil got itself into another mess in relation to Lenihan's proposed request to meet the President to discuss what had happened in 1982. President Hillery would almost certainly have refused to meet him in any event, but the request of itself put unacceptable political pressure on the President. The confusion originated in a statement from Lenihan's director of elections, Bertie Ahern, at Dublin airport where he had arrived ahead of the candidate for a flight to Cork for a day's campaigning. Ahern told journalists that the whole notion of seeking a meeting with the President had been dropped. When Lenihan arrived and was asked for his comment, he said the plan still stood. Told of what Ahern had said, he went off to consult with his director of elections, returning a short time later to ask RTÉ reporter Charlie Bird to play him the tape of his interview with Ahern. Having listened to it, Lenihan then confirmed that he had dropped the request for a meeting with the President.

From then on the focus was on how the coalition would cope with the confidence motion. O'Malley met Haughey at Kinsealy before the Taoiseach flew off to Rome for an EU summit meeting. He again emphasised the seriousness of the situation for the PDs, adding that it was not a problem of their making but one for Fianna Fáil. He did not say that Lenihan would have to go, but the clear implication of his remarks was that the PDs could support the government only if he left the cabinet.

Haughey returned from Rome to find things going from bad to worse. The following day at noon, O'Malley travelled out to Kinsealy for another meeting with Haughey. The Taoiseach was now keenly aware of the full scale of the crisis that threatened to bring down his government. He called a special meeting of the Fianna Fáil members of the cabinet that afternoon. Neither Lenihan nor his sister, the Minister for Education, Mary O'Rourke, was informed of the meeting. The ministers who did attend discussed the options facing them and there was broad agreement that Lenihan's resignation was the only course of action that would save the government. Haughey decided that he would have to meet his Tánaiste to sort out the situation and late that evening newsdesks at RTÉ and the national newspapers were informed anonymously that Lenihan had been summoned for a meeting at Kinsealy. P.J. Mara and Bertie Ahern spent much of the day at the Taoiseach's house planning the next move.

When Lenihan arrived by helicopter at Kinsealy the following morning, Haughey told him that O'Malley and the PDs wanted his resignation and he bluntly told his Tánaiste that he should resign from the government. In his book *For the Record*, Lenihan recounts how he resisted this pressure and countered by offering to resign if he lost the election. Haughey asked Lenihan to meet his ministerial colleagues, as he himself had to leave Kinsealy for Dublin airport to greet Queen Beatrix of the Netherlands who was beginning a state visit to Ireland. After the Taoiseach left, Lenihan was driven to Leinster House where he was confronted by a group of senior Fianna Fáil ministers. In the room were Bertie Ahern, Pádraig Flynn, Ray Burke, Albert Reynolds and the party chief whip, Vincent Brady. The issue of resignation was raised and strong pressure was applied to Lenihan. Vincent Brady in particular was insistent that the Tánaiste would have to resign from the cabinet by 5 p.m. that afternoon, and he demanded that the rest of the day's electioneering in Longford and Westmeath should be cancelled. Haughey, meanwhile, was being interviewed by reporters at the airport and he rejected suggestions that he would fire his Tánaiste. He said that Lenihan had not offered his resignation nor had it been sought. 'I want to make it clear that anything of that nature is entirely a matter for my old friend, Brian Lenihan, himself. I would not exert any pressure of any kind on any of my colleagues,' the Taoiseach told the journalists and his comments were carried on the lunchtime news bulletins.

Back at Leinster House, Lenihan again met Haughey who had returned from his lunch with Queen Beatrix. The Taoiseach repeated his request to Lenihan to resign and handed his Tánaiste a three-page resignation statement, which had been prepared by one of Haughey's staff. It expressed regret for the embarrassment caused to the government. 'Accordingly, I have today tendered my resignation as Tánaiste and Minister for Defence in order to enable the Government to continue with its successful programme.' To add insult to injury, the statement went on: 'This decision is mine and mine alone. I have not been subject to pressure from any quarter.' Lenihan refused to sign on the spot and asked for time to consider his position.

He insisted on going ahead with the day's campaigning and shortly after 2 p.m. he left by helicopter for Granard in Co. Longford with Albert Reynolds. At Granard, Lenihan's wife and family and his sister, Mary O'Rourke, were waiting to set out on the campaign trail for the day. They immediately took Lenihan into what amounted to protective custody and told him not to be pressurised into doing anything he didn't want to do. Reynolds gave him similar advice as the bus headed across Longford. At every stop along the way there were phone messages from the Taoiseach's office but the cordon of protection around him kept the callers at bay. The crowds were getting bigger at each town and by the evening people were shouting 'Don't resign' when he alighted from the campaign bus at each stop.

As darkness fell and the entourage drew near Athlone to bigger and bigger crowds, Lenihan made up his mind firmly that, come what may, he would not resign and said so in a television interview.

In Moate, two cabinet ministers, Pádraig Flynn and Bertie Ahern, were spotted in the crowd. 'Am I welcome to Westmeath?' called out Flynn above the hubbub. 'No, you are not,' shouted Mary O'Rourke, who told him to clear off back across the Shannon.[3]

The Lenihan family were deeply indignant at the pressure. Reynolds was the only senior Fianna Fáil figure who stood by them and continued to insist that the Tánaiste should be allowed to make his own decision in his own time. Ann Lenihan stuck to her husband's side and refused to allow him to be put under any pressure by Mr Haughey's messengers. Meanwhile, Haughey and O'Malley met again that evening at a state banquet in

Dublin Castle for the Dutch queen and both of them became resigned to the fact that Lenihan was not going to go. With the Dáil motion due for discussion the following day it looked as if the coalition was doomed.

Yet, at 7.30 a.m. the next morning Mary Harney was woken by a phone call from Charlie McCreevy who urged her not to take any action until after a meeting of the Fianna Fáil parliamentary party which, he hinted, could change the picture. The no confidence debate was due to begin in the Dáil at 10.30 a.m. Shortly after first light, a helicopter, piloted by the Taoiseach's son Ciaran Haughey, came into view over Athlone and circled ominously above the Lenihan house where the Tánaiste had spent the night. Inside the house, members of the Lenihan family received a stream of phone calls appealing to the Tánaiste to consent to board the aircraft for a journey to Kinsealy to meet the Taoiseach. Fianna Fáil deputy general secretary, Michael Dawson, and press officer Niamh O'Connor called at the door of the house. As angry exchanges raged along the telephone line the helicopter clattered around in circles overhead, young Haughey waiting to see if Lenihan would consent to make the journey to Dublin for a final showdown with his father. Lenihan's family, particularly his wife Ann, angrily rejected the appeal for a meeting at Kinsealy and eventually the helicopter turned and flew off back to Dublin, leaving the family to consider their position. The telephone calls continued, however, but Mrs Lenihan refused to let anyone from the Taoiseach's office speak to her husband and he remained incommunicado in Athlone all morning.

Back in Dublin, Haughey was in consultation with P.J. Mara and McCreevy and they urged him to do the unthinkable – to sack Lenihan. Haughey was still agonising when the Fianna Fáil parliamentary party met at 11.30 a.m. to consider the position. Gloomy deputies and senators heard the Taoiseach begin the meeting by saying: 'As of now there will be a general election.' He went on to state just how serious the position facing them was since it appeared there was no way they could win a vote on the motion of no confidence. Bertie Ahern induced even more gloom when he outlined the prospects facing the party in both the presidential election and in a possible general election. He told the TDs that the party's private polls put Mary Robinson at 45 per cent of the vote with Brian Lenihan trailing behind on about 39 per cent. The IMS poll published that morning in the *Irish Independent* painted an even gloomier picture, putting Robinson a massive 21 per cent ahead, at 52 per cent to 31 per cent. While Ahern said that the poll predictions looked a lot better for a general election, he predicted that an election caused in by the current circumstances would see a big slump in party support and another hung Dáil where nobody would be able to put a government together. Senator Eddie

Bohan, a friend of Lenihan's, stood up to say that he had a message from the Tánaiste to the effect that he would not be turning up to Leinster House until 7 p.m. that night when it was time for the vote of confidence.

The Fianna Fáil meeting adjourned and resumed in the late afternoon without contact having been established between the Taoiseach and his Tánaiste. After a lot of agonised discussion, the general tenor of which was against forcing Lenihan to resign, Haughey intervened to ask if he had the approval of the meeting to take the necessary steps to ensure an election was avoided. Kildare TD Seán Power responded by saying that they were discussing sacrificing Brian Lenihan's head and he demanded to know if the Taoiseach would give the same advice in six months if his head was the only thing that would save the government. M.J. Nolan, Noel Dempsey and Ned O'Keeffe also argued strongly against forcing Lenihan's resignation.

'Lest there be any doubt about what is at stake here, I cannot contact my Tánaiste; he won't talk to me,' Haughey told his colleagues, adding that a cold decision had to be made. Backing Haughey as usual, the chairman, Jim Tunney, summed up by saying that it was the feeling of the meeting that it should be left to the Taoiseach to do his best to avoid an election and with that he ended the meeting without a vote. Immediately afterwards, at around 5 p.m., the Taoiseach rang O'Malley and asked him to come to his office. There he solemnly told the PD leader that he had decided to terminate Lenihan's membership of the government. The meeting between Haughey and O'Malley, like all their meetings since the crisis started, was correct and formal with no hint of the emotions that were seething under the surface.

Just after 5.45 p.m., Lenihan eventually picked up the phone and rang the Taoiseach. Haughey formally asked his Tánaiste to resign and Lenihan refused. Haughey then said it was with great regret that he was terminating Lenihan's membership of the government. Brian Spain, the minister's Private Secretary at the Department of Defence, was dispatched to Leinster House with a letter signed by President Hillery removing Lenihan from office. There were emotional scenes in the chamber two hours later when Lenihan made his way there to listen to Haughey read out his formal dismissal.

Labour leader Dick Spring used the debate to launch a scathing attack on Haughey and everything he stood for. 'This debate is not about Brian Lenihan, when it is all boiled down. This debate, essentially, is about the evil spirit that controls one political party in this Republic and it is about the way in which that spirit has begun to corrupt the entire political system in our country. This is a debate about greed for office, about disregard for truth and about contempt for political standards. It is a debate about the way in which a once great party has been brought to its knees by the grasping acquisitiveness of its leader. It is ultimately a debate about the cancer that is eating away at our body politic – and the virus which has caused that cancer, An Taoiseach, Charles J. Haughey.' He then went on to compare Haughey's Fianna Fáil to that of his predecessors. 'This last week would not have happened in the days of Seán Lemass or Jack Lynch. It would not have happened if there had been a George Colley or any person of stature and honour left on the Fianna Fáil benches. How can anyone conceive of all this happening in the days of the founder of Fianna Fáil and the author of our Constitution, Eamon de Valera? But they have all gone and the party is now dedicated to the greed and unprincipled behaviour of its present leader, who is bent on creating a party entirely in his own image. When the world watched Ceaucescu and Honecker fall, we knew it was because people could no longer tolerate tyranny, but how much longer will the members of Fianna Fáil tolerate the internal tyranny that rules their party with an iron hand and that has brought it to a point where it is an object of shame and revulsion for so many?'[4]

While there were tears in the eyes of many Fianna Fáil deputies as they marched through the lobbies, they did not hesitate to vote confidence in Haughey's government. After the vote, Haughey, his face like a mask, sat stonily on his seat, many of his colleagues avoiding contact with him. Afterwards he asked Lenihan to meet him and the two old friends had an emotional get-together for a few minutes.

After the sacking there was a wave of public sympathy for Lenihan and in the final days of the campaign there was a dramatic swing in his favour. However, it was just too late and Flynn, true to form, put a huge spanner in the works shortly before polling day. On RTÉ's 'Saturday View' programme with PD chairman Michael McDowell and Brendan Howlin of Labour, he raised, with some justice, the subject of how Robinson had remodelled her image for the election campaign. But he went on to say that for electioneering purposes she had discovered a new interest in the family whereas those who knew her for years couldn't remember her talking about the family before. His ill-judged comments might not have attracted too much attention in the middle of a radio discussion programme were it not for the fact that McDowell exploded on air. The PD chairman pounced on Flynn, calling his attack on Robinson disgusting and demanding its withdrawal. Within hours, the Robinson camp focused in on the issue, with the candidate herself demanding a withdrawal. Eventually that night Flynn did apologise, but only after the Taoiseach had intervened to put pressure on him to do so. In the meantime, he had handed a hostage to fortune which Robinson played for all it was worth. As she had already planned to conclude her campaign with an appeal to

Fianna Fáil women voters, the issue was a godsend. Robinson kept it going for the remainder of the campaign, with RTÉ highlighting it on the news bulletins for the last three days of the electioneering.

Fianna Fáil tried a last major effort to grab the headlines with a campaign rally in the National Stadium on the last Sunday before polling. There was visible hostility between the Lenihan family and the Taoiseach in the hospitality room before the speeches began and Haughey was booed by some sections of the audience when he appeared on the platform. He kept his cool nonetheless and launched into a strong criticism of Robinson, saying that she could not escape from her backers, Labour and the Workers' Party. He told the audience that the Marxist Workers' Party would have an influence in the Áras if she was elected and he also cited her *Hot Press* interview where she had threatened a confrontational presidency.

When the election took place on 7 November, Lenihan got just over 44 per cent of the vote on the first count with Robinson following with just under 39 per cent and Currie trailing on 17 per cent. The strength of the Currie transfers gave Robinson victory in the end. It was the first time in the history of the presidency that a candidate not backed by Fianna Fáil had become President.

Ironically, there was a political upheaval in Fine Gael rather than Fianna Fáil as a result of the Robinson victory. Alan Dukes was blamed by many in the party for its ignominious showing and Dublin TD Fergus O'Brien immediately tabled a motion of no confidence in him. Dukes was intellectually brilliant but remote, and had alienated a majority of his parliamentary party after less than four years as party leader. After a traumatic few days he was persuaded to resign without a contest and was replaced by his deputy leader, John Bruton, who was widely regarded as a representative of the more traditional wing of Fine Gael.

19. Death of a Thousand Cuts

THE SACKING OF LENIHAN marked the beginning of the end for Haughey. Reynolds and Flynn had been alienated from 'The Boss' since the coalition with the PDs but the removal of Lenihan was the last straw. On the day of the presidential election count, Reynolds put Haughey's future on to the political agenda in an oblique fashion. Speaking to party supporters in Cork, he said that he would be a contender for the leadership of the party when a vacancy arose. While there was no direct challenge to Haughey, the message was clear – Reynolds was preparing to push his leader if he did not go within a reasonable time frame. What followed over the next 12 months was reminiscent of Haughey's campaign to destabilise Jack Lynch just over a decade earlier.

Haughey knew there was a threat and prepared himself carefully for an inquest into the presidential election at a parliamentary party meeting on 28 November. It turned out to be a damp squib, although it had been hyped in advance by the media and this lulled Haughey into a false sense of security. At the meeting 35 TDs and senators spoke, but only Liam Lawlor told Haughey it was time to go. Many others made coded speeches that Haughey, the master of codes, curiously failed to read properly or chose not to read. He defused the fears of his deputies by telling them he was setting up a special commission to examine the party's operations and he assured them that not only would his government last but that Fianna Fáil would be in power for the next ten years.

After the meeting Haughey went into the Dáil chamber where he skipped down the steps, paused for a moment, clasped his hands together and held them aloft like a winning prizefighter. Fine Gael's Ivan Yates, who was speaking at the time, stopped in surprise. 'I see you have survived yet again, Taoiseach,' he remarked. Haughey smiled broadly in return.[1]

The obvious sense of relief showed how worried Haughey had been. He regarded Reynolds's expression of interest in the leadership as a quickening of the campaign to oust him that Reynolds had been building up gradually. Back in February 1990, Reynolds, at a Fianna Fáil meeting in Kanturk, Co. Cork, had referred to the coalition with the PDs as 'a temporary little arrangement'. The remark, which was picked up by the media, went down well with the party organisation. Later, Reynolds had toyed with the idea of supporting Wilson against Lenihan for the presidential nomination.

Haughey never believed that Reynolds would become a real threat but he began to treat his Finance Minister with great caution. P.J. Mara was openly dismissive of the Longford man, saying that because of Haughey's patronage Reynolds had already risen to a position well beyond his capabilities and wasn't remotely qualified to be Taoiseach.

Reynolds was the opposite of Haughey in virtually every respect. A self-made millionaire, he earned his own money. In the 1950s, he gave up his safe job as a CIÉ clerk in Co. Leitrim to move into the showband scene. Later he sold his interests in dancehalls and started a pet food business in Longford. He also involved himself in a number of other business ventures, including a bacon factory in Dublin, an unsuccessful fish exporting operation and a hire purchase company in Longford. He liked life as a risk-taker and treated politics in the same way as business. He was 45 years old when he entered the Dáil, a late start to national politics by modern standards, but he didn't waste much time catching up with his peers, spending only two years as a backbencher. His involvement with the Haughey campaign in 1979 was a typical Reynolds 'all or nothing' ploy. If his man lost, then Reynolds would have no political future; if Haughey won, Albert was on the inside track to the top. The gamble paid off and Reynolds was Minister for Posts and Telegraphs after a little over two years in the Dáil.

Where Haughey was remote and imperious, Reynolds was the soul of affability, although this disguised the steely quality that had brought him far in business. As a minister, he was available at all times to backbenchers, ready to listen to their concerns and give them the information about constituency developments that could be of help to them. He was so accessible to Fianna Fáil backbenchers that many of them referred to him as 'Uncle Albert'. A traditional family man, he had a happy home life with his wife Kathleen and his seven children. Reynolds was a tee-totaller, although, as a hangover from his dance-hall days, he liked to stay up very late chatting half the night over cups of tea. He also frequented the Dáil canteen and bar and talked to everyone. He got on well with journalists as a group and was always available for a quote, a briefing or a simple chat. Haughey despised most journalists, although he did have a small coterie of influential media admirers with whom he indulged in scabrous gossip and plotting.

The battle lines for Haughey's last-ditch stand as party leader were drawn at the end of 1990. The so-called 'Country and Western' ministers like Flynn, Geoghegan-Quinn, Michael Smith and Noel Treacy gravitated towards Reynolds as the heir apparent. Other senior party figures like Ray Burke, Bertie Ahern, Gerry Collins and Mary O'Rourke were firmly in the Haughey camp. So too, surprisingly, was Brian Lenihan. After the indignity of his sacking by Haughey in the presidential election campaign there was speculation that he might challenge Haughey for the party presidency at the Fianna Fáil Árd Fheis in March 1991. P.J. Mara reacted by threatening publicly that any challenge to Haughey would trigger a general election. Privately he moved to patch things up with Lenihan.

Haughey felt confident enough about his position to indulge in a public sideswipe at Reynolds at a press conference after the December 1990 EU summit in Rome. 'We all know that Chancellors of the Exchequer and Ministers for Finance are neurotic and exotic creatures whose political judgement is not always the best,' he said as Reynolds sat stony-faced beside him.[2]

Haughey now re-established control over Fianna Fáil, and the coalition deal with the PDs continued, despite occasional tension between the partners. Reynolds continued with popular tax-cutting measures in the Budget while Bertie Ahern presided over the successful negotiations for a new national agreement between the social partners. The deal, called the *Programme for Economic and Social Progress (PESP)*, provided generous pay increases to public servants and was launched with an elaborate fanfare. Haughey also began to adapt his social policies to changing mores and instructed Burke to prepare a White Paper on marital breakdown and to decriminalise homosexuality. He withstood a minor storm in the parliamentary party about changes in the contraception legislation to allow 16-year-olds to buy condoms. Bertie Ahern, intervening as Haughey's fixer, averted a potential revolt by getting agreement on a compromise age limit of 17. Haughey also faced a revolt from the PDs over allegations about practices operating in the Goodman meat plants. After days of controversy and uproar in the Dáil, the government agreed to the establishment of a judicial tribunal at the behest of the PDs. Haughey gave way on condition that the tribunal should be into the beef industry as a whole and not just into the Goodman plants. That decision was to have its own unforeseen consequences down the line, but it bought Haughey some time.

By the summer of 1991, Reynolds and his supporters were getting impatient. Flynn toured the country talking to Fianna Fáil TDs in an attempt to establish how many of them wanted Haughey to go. He tried to drum up support for Reynolds who was now something of a hero in the Fianna Fáil organisation because of his opposition to the PDs. One key figure who appeared to straddle the Haughey and Reynolds camps was Bertie Ahern. Although he was barely 40, Ahern regularly headed opinion polls as the most favoured choice of the public to be Haughey's successor. Reynolds wanted Ahern on his side and proposed a deal whereby Ahern would back Reynolds for the leadership and, in turn, the Longford man would back Ahern to succeed him when he retired five or six years later. However, Ahern never left the Haughey camp and remained his most trusted lieutenant.

The end of the Haughey era really began on 1 September 1991, when the *Sunday Independent* published a story by Sam Smyth which broke the news of a row between key executives of Greencore, the recently privatised Irish Sugar Company, over the ownership of a Jersey-based company. The upshot of the story was that the managing director of Greencore, Chris Comerford, and the company secretary, Michael Tully, were forced to resign. The age of the business scandals had begun and the effect on Haughey was to prove disastrous. Ironically, he had no real connection with Greencore, but the controversy opened the door on a range of other business scandals which did have some connection with him. The veil had been lifted, if only ever so slightly, on the world of the golden circles and Haughey was the spider at the centre of that web.

Hot on the heels of the Greencore resignations came the Telecom affair. The issue here was the purchase by Telecom of the old Johnston, Mooney and O'Brien bakery site at Ballsbridge for £9.4 million. The role of financier Dermot Desmond, who had been a close associate of Haughey since 1986 and the inspiration behind the financial services centre, became a source of public controversy. A property company established by Desmond, called UPH, had initially bought the site but had sold it on to another developer who in turn sold it to Telecom. When it emerged that the Telecom chairman, Michael Smurfit, one of Ireland's most respected business figures, had an interest in the property company, the political storm gathered force.

As pressure grew on Smurfit, on Desmond and on the government, Haughey summoned his closest associates to a council of war at his Kinsealy home on 21 September. At the meeting were Bertie Ahern, P.J. Mara, Pádraig Ó hUiginn and Seamus Brennan. Haughey sought their advice on how to handle a major radio interview scheduled for the next day at which he intended to put an end the controversy. They decided that the best way out for Haughey and the government was to force Smurfit out as chairman of Telecom. It was also suggested that Haughey should ask the former chairman of the Revenue Commissioners, Séamus Paircéir, who had an involvement with UPH, to step aside from his position as chairman of the Custom House Docks Development Board.[3]

In his RTÉ radio interview with Seán O'Rourke the next day, Haughey called on the two men to step aside in view of the controversy. Neither had been consulted and both were extremely angry. Paircéir responded immediately by announcing his resignation while Smurfit sought a meeting with Haughey to tell him that, in view of the fact that he had been asked publicly to step aside without prior consultation, he had decided to resign from Telecom. Haughey had hoped to dampen down the controversy by sacrificing the two men, but in the course of his interview he stoked up further trouble for himself within Fianna Fáil by repeating his intention to lead the party into the next election. 'Some of these Chinese leaders go on till they are eighty or ninety – but I think that is a bit long,' he said jocosely. The remark was not treated as a joke by some of his TDs and it only added to the problems created by his interview.

With rumours now circulating about plots being hatched by the Reynolds faction, other ministers reaffirmed their support for Haughey. In an attempt to scare Reynolds off, Mary O'Rourke, John Wilson and Michael O'Kennedy joined Collins and Burke in publicly backing Haughey. It was all too much for four Fianna Fáil backbench TDs who took the bull by the horns and issued a statement expressing their unhappiness with Haughey's leadership. The four brave men were Noel Dempsey, Liam Fitzgerald, M.J. Nolan and Seán Power. 'We have watched with growing disquiet the events of the past three weeks in the semi-state sector ... We are particularly concerned at the manner in which these matters were dealt with by An Taoiseach in his radio interview last week.' Haughey moved to quash the dissent as quickly as possible, summoning a meeting of the parliamentary party for 2 October, even though the Dáil recess still had some time to run. Of the 101 TDs and senators at the meeting, 42 spoke, but only Power and Dempsey had the courage to challenge Haughey head on. 'The people of Ireland are disgusted with the scandals and the relationship you, Taoiseach, have with some of the people at the centre of those scandals,' said Power. Many of his colleagues were astounded at his outspokenness and, although they didn't back him, it was clear that Haughey's authority was slipping.[4]

More scandals, which appear quite minor in the light of what we now know about Haughey, although they didn't seem so minor at the time, emerged in the following weeks. Fine Gael leader, John Bruton, disclosed that a confidential report carried out by Dermot Desmond's NCB stock brokers for an Aer Lingus subsidiary called Irish Helicopters had, mysteriously, found its way into the hands of Ciaran Haughey's rival Celtic Helicopters. There was also controversy over the installation by the ESB of a wind generator on Haughey's island home of Innishvickillane.

Anticipating a concerted Opposition attack when the Dáil resumed, Haughey moved quickly to protect his position. He put pressure on his key ministers in charge of renegotiating the programme for government with the PDs to wrap things up as quickly as possible. The talks between the two parties were fraught with difficulties. Some of the PDs, like Michael McDowell, took the view that they should get out of government before they were dragged down by the controversies besetting Haughey while Reynolds on the Fianna Fáil side refused, as Finance Minister, to accept a deal which didn't protect the exchequer. Reynolds had considerable backing in Fianna Fáil for his determination to stand up to the PDs but Haughey believed his minister was simply trying to further his own leadership ambitions by collapsing the government. In the face of a real threat to his position, Haughey called on Bertie Ahern to solve the difficulties. In the course of a long night of negotiations, Ahern managed to persuade Reynolds, O'Malley and Bobby Molloy to put aside their various reservations and do a deal on a renewed programme for government. Haughey was safe and he knew who had delivered for him. The next day P.J. Mara arranged a briefing in the Taoiseach's Department for Sunday newspaper journalists, Gerald Barry, Sam Smyth and myself about how the deal was done. In the middle of the briefing, Haughey put his head around the door. Grinning, he pointed at Ahern, 'He's the man. He's the best, the most skilful, the most devious and the most cunning of them all.' When Haughey withdrew, Ahern remarked, 'God, that's all I need.' But there was no disguising the important role he had played in saving Haughey's skin.[5]

The deal itself was a victory for the PDs. Tax cuts were recognised as the political priority rather than social spending as favoured by Fianna Fáil. A commitment was made to reduce the basic rate of tax from 33 per cent to 25 per cent by 1993. Although the deal was not what Fianna Fáil wanted, the party's TDs backed it without a murmur. Haughey had crossed a major hurdle in his battle to hold on to power.

However, the Country and Western group had not given up. Reynolds himself was reluctant to be drawn into a confrontation, particularly as Ahern appeared to be firmly in the Haughey camp, but Flynn and Geoghegan-Quinn pushed him towards a showdown. The enthusiasm of his allies and the increasingly dismissive attitude of the Haughey camp towards him left Reynolds with little option. One associate of Haughey, overly influenced by American terms of abuse, went over the top and dismissed Reynolds as 'trailer park trash'.

In November 1991, the sleaze factor continued to dog Haughey. The beef tribunal opened in Dublin Castle and heard a steady stream of evidence about irregularities in the meat-processing industry that made a mockery of Haughey's statements in the Dáil on the issue in 1989. Questions were also raised in the Dáil about the allocation of exchequer funds to University College Dublin to purchase Carysfort College at the end of 1990. A central ingredient in the controversy was the surprising fact that

'Pino' Harris, a businessman close to Haughey, had made a profit of almost £1.5 million on the land in just six months. On top of this, the relationship between Haughey and the chairman of Greencore, Bernie Cahill, caused uproar in the Dáil. At the end of 1991 John Bruton and Dick Spring renewed their attacks on Haughey over the golden circle allegations.

Against this background the Fianna Fáil parliamentary party met for its regular weekly meeting on 6 November. The meeting is usually routine but on this occasion there were heated exchanges between Charlie McCreevy and Brian Lenihan, who was standing in as acting chairman. McCreevy told the meeting that all the uncertainty arising from the scandals would have to be cleared up and he had suggested publicly that Haughey should seek a vote of confidence from his TDs. He tried to raise this issue at the meeting but Lenihan, who had reverted to his old role as Haughey's staunch defender, peremptorily ruled him out of order. Lenihan told the meeting that if TDs wanted to discuss the leadership somebody should put the matter on the agenda. Some of the younger TDs were angered by Lenihan's conduct of the meeting and one of them, Seán Power, there and then put down a motion of no confidence in the leader. He handed in his motion to the whip's office that afternoon and Haughey faced the fourth challenge to his leadership.

The situation now was that some of Haughey's old friends, who had stood by him during the heaves of 1982-83, were looking for his head while his old enemies, like O'Malley and Molloy, were propping up the government. Lenihan, who had been dismissed by Haughey only a year earlier, was firmly in his leader's camp on this occasion as were senior ministers like Collins and Burke. Reynolds was taken a bit by surprise by the way the challenge to Haughey had come about, but he had no choice but to fight at a special meeting of the parliamentary party called for the following Saturday. He issued a statement in which he declared: 'For some time now there has been considerable political instability which has led to an erosion of confidence in our democratic institutions. This uncertainty must not be allowed to continue. The well-being of our country requires strong and decisive leadership of government and of the Fianna Fáil party. I am not satisfied that such leadership now exists. In the circumstances, I will be supporting the motion tabled for the party meeting on Saturday next.'[6]

Reynolds did not resign from the cabinet as O'Malley and O'Donoghue had done in 1982. Instead he followed the Lenihan precedent and waited for Haughey to fire him. He didn't have long to wait. Within an hour the Taoiseach requested President Robinson to terminate the appointment of the Finance Minister and the battle for the leadership was on in earnest. The following day the process was repeated when Flynn came out in favour of Reynolds and was fired. The same happened to junior ministers Geoghegan-Quinn, Michael Smith and Noel Treacy, although the process took longer for technical reasons.

Those in the Reynolds camp were not sure they would win but they were confident that at least 30 of the 77 TDs would vote against Haughey. It was significant, though, that the rest of the cabinet held firm behind Haughey. Ahern told Reynolds that he would not support him, as he didn't have the numbers. Other ministers like O'Rourke, Collins and Burke publicly backed Haughey. Collins gave a bizarre television interview in which he tearfully appealed to Reynolds not to 'burst the party'. By the morning of the meeting the Reynolds camp knew that the game was up. A number of TDs on whose support they were relying, including some who had encouraged Reynolds to make a challenge two weeks earlier, now made it clear they were not going to vote against Haughey. In typical fashion Haughey called TDs to his office and left many of them believing they were in line for promotion to the cabinet or to one of the vacant junior ministries.

The meeting began at 11.30 a.m. on 9 November and continued until after 2 a.m. the following morning. The worst fears of the Reynolds camp were realised when Haughey, by 44 votes to 33, forced through a motion that the decision be taken by an open roll-call vote, rather than a secret ballot. In the late afternoon Reynolds made a speech in which he said P.J. Mara had orchestrated a campaign of disinformation against him. He also claimed that a prominent business associate of Haughey's had tried to dig up dirt on his business affairs in the midlands, that people in a white Hiace van had conducted surveillance of his house in Longford and that a man acting suspiciously had been seen near his Dublin apartment. Parliamentary party chairman Jim Tunney intervened to suggest that a special commission be set up to examine the Reynolds allegations as well as those of two backbenchers, Noel Dempsey and John Ellis, that their phones were being tapped.

The claims made by Reynolds provoked a mixed reaction from the meeting. His own supporters regarded them as evidence of a conspiracy to discredit him, but the Haughey camp poured scorn on the claims. Outside his own immediate circle, few took the Reynolds claims seriously and a majority swallowed the Haughey line. Debate became unreal as the knowledge that Haughey was going to win the vote regardless of what was said began to permeate the meeting. A number of TDs who had been complaining bitterly about Haughey behind his back to colleagues and journalists vied with each other to praise the leader.

'How can you speak like that when you can't say a good word about him in the Dáil bar?' piped up a voice as one TD expressed his impassioned support for Haughey.

As the meeting moved towards its inevitable conclusion, the principal Reynolds supporters insisted on stating their case for the record. Geoghegan-Quinn made one of the longest speeches but the most riveting of the day came from Flynn who, in characteristic style, referred to himself throughout in the third person as 'P. Flynn'. He spoke of the mounting problems facing the Fianna Fáil party, including the prospect of bankruptcy with debts running at £2.3 million, the poor performance in the general election, the presidential contest and the local elections. He said the Taoiseach must take responsibility for all those problems and for breaking the sacred principle of not entering coalition. 'Pee Flynn would be doing himself a disservice if he did not support the motion to discontinue the leadership forthwith of Charles J. Haughey,' he announced.

It was nearly 2 a.m. on Sunday morning before Haughey stood up to reply to the debate. He had spent nearly 14 hours in the Fianna Fáil party room with just one break for tea and sandwiches. His stamina had impressed everybody but his speech was quite subdued. He told his TDs that he would not be around forever, but there was important business on European union coming up and he wanted to be around to deal with it. When he sat down to general applause all that remained for the weary deputies to do was participate in a roll-call vote.

The first name called in alphabetical order was that of Bertie Ahern. It was no surprise that he voted for Haughey. The only real surprise was that a number of those who had been expected to vote for Reynolds chickened out at the last moment. Haughey won the vote of confidence by 55 votes to 22. There was something symbolic in the fact that Haughey was opposed by precisely the same number of TDs who had voted against him nine years earlier, but only three of the new 'Gang of 22', McCreevy, David Andrews and Willie O'Dea, were survivors of the old gang. Most of the others who were still in the Dáil backed Haughey while most of the new 'Gang of 22' had been Haughey supporters back in 1982.

After his victory, Haughey gave a press briefing for political correspondents in the Taoiseach's office at 2.30 a.m. that Sunday morning. He shook hands with each of the journalists present and a glass of champagne was pressed into the hands of everyone in the room to celebrate his victory. It was a rare display of magnanimity towards journalists he regarded as his enemies. 'Well, you got it wrong now, admit it. Didn't you?' he remarked good-humouredly. In fact, given his ability to survive in the past, nobody had dared to write him off, although a number of journalists, including this one, made the mistake of over-estimating the likely level of support for Reynolds.

It seemed that despite his age, his health, the welter of business scandals and the privately expressed desire of many of his closest colleagues that he shouldn't lead them into the next election, there was nothing they could do to stop Haughey doing precisely that. He was still 'The Boss' and most of his ministers and a majority of his TDs were perfectly happy with that.

20. THE FINAL DAYS

THE ROUT OF HIS INTERNAL OPPONENTS IN NOVEMBER 1991 restored Haughey's belief in his own invincibility. This was to prove fatal because it prompted him into a series of unforced political errors and, more importantly, it lulled him into underestimating his enemies. The first big mistake, which took a lot of gloss off his victory, was the cabinet reshuffle caused by the departure of Reynolds and Flynn. Instead of doing the obvious and cautious thing, as he normally did in these situations, and promoting junior ministers like Vincent Brady and Joe Walsh who had proved loyal, Haughey catapulted two backbenchers into the cabinet. They were Noel Davern from Tipperary and Dr James McDaid from Donegal. Though they were two of the most popular members of the parliamentary party, their promotion seemed unfair to many of the junior ministers who had carried the burden of defending unpopular government policies and who had all been given strong hints by Haughey that they would be promoted. The appointment of Dermot Ahern and John O'Donoghue to fill the two vacant junior ministerial posts did not cause as much surprise, as both were widely regarded as young men of ability who had also proved their loyalty to Haughey by backing him against Reynolds. As usual, though, the jobs had been promised to a whole range of other backbenchers and some of the more gullible were naturally aggrieved.

Resentment at the promotions was quickly overtaken by a mini political crisis. McDaid had been given Defence, but Fine Gael and the Workers' Party quickly raised his involvement in an extradition case a year earlier concerning a leading member of the IRA, James Pius Clarke, who was wanted in Northern Ireland. McDaid had been one of a number of people on whom Clarke relied for an alibi and, after the hearing in the Supreme Court which refused the extradition request, he was photographed with Clarke and anti-extradition campaigners on the steps of the court. The issue quickly became a hot potato and when PD leader Des O'Malley sought a meeting with Haughey to explain his concern, it became a crisis. The nomination was postponed for a day as the coalition partners squared up to each other again. However, the crisis was quickly defused by McDaid himself who withdrew his name from consideration for the cabinet vacancy. There was renewed uproar in Fianna Fáil, this time at the fact that the PDs had effectively scuppered Haughey's nomination for the cabinet. The outcome was that Haughey, having outfoxed his internal enemies only days earlier, had created a fresh crisis and reopened all the questions about his allegedly failing judgement. A number of TDs who had voted for Haughey but had not been rewarded by office went back to Reynolds to say they wanted a change of leadership after all. It was the signal for the 'Country and Western gang' to regroup and prepare to strike again.

This time they found a weapon with the capacity to pierce Haughey's defences. Seán Doherty, the ill-fated Minister for Justice who had taken the rap for the phone-tapping episode in Haughey's GUBU phase, had never recovered from the experience. After the controversy became public, he had resigned from the front bench. Haughey had promised him reinstatement when the fuss died down but the call to rejoin the front bench never came. Doherty was deeply wounded by his continuing isolation, particularly since Ray MacSharry, who had also resigned in 1983, was elected to the European Parliament in 1985, took over as leader of the Fianna Fáil group and re-established himself in the highest councils of the party. When Fianna Fáil returned to power in 1987, Doherty did not get even a junior ministry. He felt he had become the sin-eater of the party who bore the guilt for what happened in 1982 while his colleagues went on to new respectability. In 1989 he had tried to follow the MacSharry route to rehabilitation by standing for the European Parliament but the strategy came horribly unstuck when he not only failed to get elected but also lost his Dáil seat in the simultaneous elections. It was some consolation when he made it to the Seanad and managed to get the backing of his Fianna Fáil colleagues for the position of Cathaoirleach, with some limited assistance from Haughey.

Though he was an intelligent man with a roguish wit and, better than most, understood the devious nature of Fianna Fáil politics in the Haughey era, he continued to blame Haughey for his misfortunes. For years he had given dark hints to colleagues in the party that he might some day spill the beans about what really happened in 1982. His pent-up resentment found a focus at the end of 1991 when the Minister for Justice, Ray Burke, published the Phone Tapping Bill.

The commitment to the Bill had been contained in the Programme for Government with the PDs, but when Burke produced the legislation Doherty regarded it as a personal affront. He asked Burke to withdraw the Bill or at least stall its passage so that he would not face the embarrassment of having to deal with it in the Seanad. Burke refused and also rejected a request from Doherty to be allowed to look at the files in the

Department of Justice relating to the controversial incidents of 1982. This was the last straw. Doherty was seething with anger when he met P.J. Mara in the bar of Jury's Hotel just before Christmas 1991. Late into the night, the two men had a bitter stand-up row in full view of a group of Fianna Fáil colleagues.

Reynolds and Flynn continued to plot against Haughey and were keenly aware that Doherty was now a loose cannon with the capacity to bring The Boss down once and for all. Events unfolded in a strange way during January 1992. 'Nighthawks', an innovative and trendy television programme on RTÉ's Network 2, decided to do a special edition on Doherty. The programme format involved the presenter, Shay Healy, talking to guests in a relaxed pub-like atmosphere in a makeshift bar in RTÉ. For the Doherty programme, the production team travelled to Roscommon and Doherty was interviewed among a group of friends and supporters in a local pub. For a while, it was an easy-going discursive interview, but in the middle of it Healy asked Doherty about his involvement in the phone-tapping scandal of 1982.

'There was a decision taken in cabinet that the leaking of matters from cabinet must be stopped,' Doherty replied. 'I, as Minister for Justice, had a direct responsibility for doing that – I did that. I do feel that I was let down by the fact that people knew what I was doing.'

Doherty's statement initially threw more heat than light on the situation. It had been known since 1983 that the cabinet of which he was a member had discussed leaks. But his comment that people knew what he was doing opened up the possibility that somebody else was aware that he had authorised the tapping of journalists' telephones. Details of the 'Nighthawks' interview had been leaked to the *Irish Press* beforehand so that by the time the programme was transmitted on 15 January it received a lot of attention. A number of the ministers who had served during 1982, including Des O'Malley, reacted by saying that the phone-tapping issue had never been discussed at cabinet so who else, apart from Doherty, was in on the act?

Some of Doherty's Fianna Fáil colleagues in the Seanad issued a public rebuke and indicated that they might not back him if the Opposition put down a motion of no confidence in the Cathaoirleach. Doherty kept his own counsel for six days as various members of Fianna Fáil taunted him to put up or shut up. Then on 21 January the time bomb that had been ticking for nine years exploded. Journalists were summoned to a hastily arranged press conference in the Montrose Hotel near RTÉ. Doherty arrived at the hotel with his wife Maura, walked rapidly to the small conference room, sat down and began to speak before conversation among the assembled journalists had died down. The talking stopped instantly after the first few devastating words.

'I am confirming tonight,' he began, 'that the Taoiseach, Mr Haughey, was fully aware in 1982 that two journalists' phones were being tapped and that he at no stage expressed a reservation about this action. Here are the details.' Speaking rapidly, Doherty outlined the circumstances in which he authorised the Deputy Garda Commissioner, Joe Ainsworth, to tap the phones of Geraldine Kennedy and Bruce Arnold. He said that he had done so against the background of continued leaks from the cabinet.

'I did not seek nor did I get any instruction from any member of the cabinet in this regard, nor did I tell the cabinet that this action had been taken. Telephone tapping was never discussed in the cabinet. However, as soon as transcripts from the tapes became available I took them personally to Mr Haughey and left them in his possession. I understand that the Taoiseach has already denied that this happened but I wish to reiterate it in specific terms. Mr Ainsworth forwarded to me the transcripts relevant to the cabinet leaks problem, numbering some four or five out of the roughly twelve or thirteen total. Each and every one of those relevant transcripts was transported by me to Mr Haughey's office and handed to him directly. He retained all but one of them, making no comment on their content. At no stage did he indicate disapproval of the action which had been taken.'

Doherty went on for about ten minutes. He referred to Haughey's statement, made when the phone tapping was revealed in January 1983, that he 'would not have countenanced any such action' and that it was 'an abuse of power'. Doherty said he felt pressurised at that time by Haughey's response to back his leader's public position. 'Not only did I take the blame but when Mr Haughey claimed not to have been aware of the tapping while it was in progress I did not correct this claim, and indeed supported it. However, the truth is that the Taoiseach, as I have already stated, had known and had not expressed any reservations during the several months in which he received from my hands copies of the transcripts of the taped telephone conversations.' Doherty then announced that he would resign as Cathaoirleach of the Seanad. He left the room without answering any questions.[1]

The effect of the Doherty statement was electrifying. A substantial chunk of the press conference was transmitted on the RTÉ television news less than an hour later. The fact that a journalists' strike at the station prevented the statement from being edited and packaged increased rather than detracted from its impact on an unsuspecting public. Immediately after the press conference, the senior RTÉ journalist Shane Kenny, one of the skeleton staff keeping the news bulletins on air, phoned Des

O'Malley and played the tape of the Doherty press conference down the line to him. The PD leader expressed his shock and consternation to Kenny and then summoned an emergency meeting of his closest advisers and parliamentary colleagues. As they watched the 9 o'clock news they knew that there was no way the PDs could continue to serve in government with Haughey.

Next day, the PD ministers refused to attend a cabinet meeting on budgetary issues and the writing was clearly on the wall. Haughey gave a press conference and delivered another of his bravura performances. He rejected Doherty's claims as absolutely false and pointed to the fact that Doherty was now saying the exact opposite of what he said in 1983. 'Are the Irish people more entitled to believe me, who has been consistent in everything I have said about this affair from the beginning, or someone who has been inconsistent and by his own words untruthful on countless occasions with regard to it?' he asked. Unfortunately for Haughey the answer to that question was that the PDs, at least, believed Doherty and a majority of the Irish people probably did as well. This was long before judicial tribunals exposed the fact that Haughey frequently lied.

Answering questions from the journalists, Haughey made it clear that he regarded Doherty's intervention as part of a plot by disaffected elements of Fianna Fáil. He singled out Pádraig Flynn for mention and drew attention to a *Sunday Tribune* interview given by the former minister which indicated that he was aware of what Doherty was going to say. Haughey referred derisively to the plotters as 'The Country and Western alliance' but made an error of judgement by insisting that he did not have any time frame in mind for stepping down as leader. Some of his TDs were not too happy to hear that he had no plans to resign but most were desperate to find a reason to justify their support for Haughey just two months earlier. Michael Noonan of Fine Gael accurately summed up the situation after Haughey's press conference by remarking: 'Charlie did enough to reassure his own crowd but not enough to win over the PDs.'

The PDs held another meeting after the Haughey press conference and issued a statement saying: 'It is not for the Progressive Democrats to decide as between the conflicting accounts given by both the Taoiseach and Senator Doherty in relation to the telephone tapping affair. The plain fact is that this is but the latest – and almost certainly the most serious – in a long list of unhappy and politically unacceptable controversies which undermined the capacity of the Government to work effectively ... While the Progressive Democrats will not interfere in the internal affairs of another party we are anxious to see that the acute dilemma facing the Government is speedily resolved.'[2]

The statement did not spell it out, but it was clear that the price of continued PD participation in government was that Haughey should step down as Taoiseach. The parallels with the departure of Brian Lenihan a little over a year earlier were uncanny and the wording of the PD statement bore a striking resemblance to the phraseology used on the earlier occasion. To make sure there was no ambiguity about the issue, Harney and Molloy met Bertie Ahern to spell out what lay between the lines. Ahern then passed the message on to Haughey, who might well have recalled a remark made by Kildare TD Seán Power during the Lenihan crisis when he asked if Haughey would sacrifice his own head for the good of the party if that was required. That night, 22 January 1992, Haughey made up his mind that he would step down rather than dissolve the Dáil and call another election which was the only alternative course open to him. Over breakfast with his family in Kinsealy the following morning, he told them of his decision and they fully approved.

Haughey then went into the Taoiseach's office where he met Ahern and the Tánaiste, John Wilson, to discuss the situation. They looked at all the options facing them and the prospect of a general election if the PD demand was not complied with. As the two Fianna Fáil ministers stood up to leave, O'Malley and Molloy came into the office to outline their position. They told Haughey they would have to withdraw from government unless he resolved the situation. The Taoiseach in turn told them he would not be the cause of a general election, signalling clearly that he intended to go. All he asked for was that the PDs should give him a short breathing space so that he could depart with dignity. The meeting in the Taoiseach's office broke up and the ministers present then adjourned to the cabinet room for a routine government meeting on the Budget. Haughey presided as if nothing had happened and the loose ends of the Budget, due to be delivered by Ahern the following week, were wrapped up. If Haughey felt bitter towards the PDs he didn't show it; his real animus at this stage was reserved for the people within Fianna Fáil who had finally taken him out. Speaking at an emotional meeting of the party national executive that evening where a lot of hostility had been expressed towards the PDs, Haughey focused on a different target. 'We have nothing to fear from our enemies without. It is the enemies within we must fear,' he said at the close of the meeting.

The details of the plot which finally unseated Haughey have never emerged although rumour abounded about its genesis. Ahern shared Haughey's view that Doherty did not act in isolation. 'I don't know who set it up but Albert, Flynn and the boys obviously knew about it, because Flynn had gone on the radio the previous Sunday about the same thing,' Ahern said a few years later. Ahern had tried to keep on good terms with Reynolds up to November 1991, but when the Longford man made his challenge Bertie was forced to show his colours and he was unequivocally in the Haughey camp. 'The first time Albert, Flynn and the boys had a go in November I led the campaign openly to keep Haughey in power and we succeeded. The second time they came after him with the Doherty interview about the telephone buggings Haughey was gone.'[3]

For the next week Haughey entered a twilight zone. News of his impending departure quickly filtered through to the media but the absence of full RTÉ radio and television coverage, due to the continuing journalists' strike, allowed things to proceed at a sedate pace reminiscent of an earlier generation. It was not until a week later on 30 January that Haughey rose to his feet at a meeting of the Fianna Fáil parliamentary party to announce his resignation. While none of the deputies and senators present was surprised at the announcement they still found it difficult to absorb. After all the drama, the controversies, the splits, the sackings and the sheer excitement of his 13-year reign, it was hard to believe that it was all over. (Those present would really have been stunned if they knew that Haughey would come back to haunt Fianna Fáil before the decade was out.) Haughey made a short speech in which he called on the party to select a new leader in an orderly and dignified manner and he said he would not take sides in the leadership contest. After that came an outpouring of tributes to the departing leader. A total of 84 TDs and senators got to their feet to eulogise his leadership, demonstrating that there was still enormous affection for Charlie within the parliamentary party.

When it came to his last day in the Dáil as Taoiseach on 11 February 1992, Haughey was at his charming best, even if his words ring a little hollow now. 'The work of Government and of the Dáil must always be directed to the progress of the nation, and I hope I have been able to provide some leadership to that end in my time. I have always sought to act solely and exclusively in the best interests of the Irish people. Let me quote Othello: "I have done the state some service; They know't. No more of that".'

The other party leaders paid Haughey the traditional courtesy of wishing him well. John Bruton was brief and avoided hypocrisy; Dick Spring reflected on Haughey's 13-year reign and then looked to the future. 'I have to say that if the next 13 years enable politics to be restored to a more honourable and consistent ground, our country will be the richer. If we can bring an end to the style and substance of politics that enables a few to benefit at the expense of the many we will be better off.'[4]

When it came to the succession, Haughey informed his TDs that he would not take sides in the leadership contest but his intense antipathy to Reynolds was obvious. Ray Burke, Gerry Collins and all the others who had stood by Haughey through thick and thin also wanted to block

Reynolds at any cost and they egged on Bertie Ahern go for the job. Haughey, too, wanted Ahern to take over from him but now he would no longer be around to instil that mixture of awe and fear that made the parliamentary party bend to his will in every crisis. Haughey did provide covert support for his protégé but essentially it was up to Ahern himself to win the big prize. Opinion polls had consistently shown him to be considerably more popular than Reynolds, but would Fianna Fáil TDs take the same view? Which of the two would the majority prefer to run the party, Haughey's old gang or Reynolds's 'Country and Western brigade'?

IV

THE REYNOLDS YEARS

21. THE 'LONGFORD SLASHER'

REYNOLDS AND AHERN BEHAVED COMPLETELY IN CHARACTER in the race to succeed Haughey. Reynolds ran an open, up-beat campaign, confidently asserting from the beginning that he had it in the bag. Ahern moved cautiously, weighing up his level of support and his options, never showing his hand and not even declaring that he was seeking the leadership. Reynolds was 59 years old at this stage, almost 20 years older than Ahern, and he knew that this was the only chance he was going to get to win the big prize. He also knew that Haughey had wanted to hang on until he could be sure of passing the succession on to Ahern. He had always been a risk-taker and a dealer, so with the biggest deal of his life on the table he went for it bald-headed. Seán Duignan, the RTÉ broadcaster who became his government press secretary, had his first lengthy conversation with Reynolds around this time. He could not help being attracted by the direct, uncomplicated style of the Longford man: 'I found his breezy blend of small town mateyness and "up she flew" optimism appealing. Here was one of my own Western breed who made no apologies for his background or the kind of grafting he had to do to climb to the top. "Keep 'er going, Patsy, and fuck the begrudgers".'[1]

Reynolds was on good terms with many journalists who generally liked him because he was prepared to discuss political issues frankly without pushing an obvious party line. Duignan was surprised to find that Reynolds knew far more journalists on a one-to-one basis than he did himself. However, some elements of the media treated him with the same snobbish disdain as that displayed by Haughey and his Dublin northside mafia. *Irish Times* columnist Fintan O'Toole reflected this negative approach: 'When Mary Robinson said, "Come dance with me in Ireland", and the people accepted the invitation, knowing what would fill a ballroom on a wet Tuesday night in Rooskey was not part of the equation.'[2] It was ironic that the urban liberals and the Haughey toughs found common cause in sneering at Reynolds as an 'unlettered culchie' from Longford. Reynolds was more wounded than he ever cared to admit by the sneers but he pressed on regardless, confident that the majority of Fianna Fáil TDs would back him. However, the sneering did colour his generally benign attitude towards the media and he issued writs against the *Irish Times* on a number of occasions.

Ahern was a different kettle of fish in every respect. If Reynolds was an open book, Ahern was a paradox. He was a politician who craved public approval and got it; opinion polls consistently showed him more popular with the public than Reynolds. He was elected a TD at the age of 25, having worked in the accounts department of the Mater Hospital since his Leaving Cert, and he built up a strong political base in Dublin Central. He was a Haughey man from the beginning and helped The Boss by undermining the electoral base of his constituency colleague, George Colley. Independent socialist TD Tony Gregory remembers campaigning in the early 1980s and being rudely introduced to the bitterness of internal Fianna Fáil politics. Gregory canvassed a row of houses not long after Ahern had done so. At one door an elderly woman, clearly a Fianna Fáil voter, gave him a better than expected reception. 'Mr Ahern said we were to vote for him number one and Tom Leonard number two, but he told us to give you the number three, ahead of George Colley,' the voter told an astonished Gregory.

Ahern's loyalty to Haughey throughout the leadership heaves was rewarded by his appointment as chief whip. He made a good public impression by remaining calm and courteous even in the most difficult of circumstances throughout those trying times. He became one of Haughey's inner circle, so much so that in 1982 he was made a co-signatory on the controversial party leader's bank account, which was to become the subject of investigations by the Moriarty tribunal. Ahern was initially a signatory because of his position of chief whip but his name remained on it for five years after he left that post in 1987 until Haughey finally departed the leadership. Cheques from that account signed by Ahern ended up in Haughey's personal accounts while others went to buy Charvet shirts and pay for meals at Le Coq Hardi. Questioned by the Moriarty tribunal in 1999 about how his name came to be on cheques used for such unorthodox purposes, Ahern said it was the practice to sign blank cheques which were completed by the party leader.

As Minister for Labour in the late 1980s, Ahern became a popular figure with the general public and was a huge vote-getter in his constituency. Yet, despite his popularity, both parliamentary colleagues and journalists knew far less about him than about his rival. Unlike Reynolds he did not mingle much in the Dáil, preferring the company of his friends in Drumcondra who formed a formidable political organisation dedicated to his interests. People found it difficult to get behind the mask, but in the constituency his political opponents both inside and outside Fianna Fáil found him to be a ruthless operator. He built up a powerful and exceptionally well-funded organisation in Dublin and even acquired a permanent headquarters in Drumcondra. Located in a large red brick house called St Luke's, Ahern lived there for considerable periods follow-ing the break-up of his marriage in the late 1980s. He became involved in a relationship with a Fianna Fáil activist, Celia Larkin, who went to work for him as his constituency secretary in the Department of Labour. The run-ning costs of the St Luke's operation are partially funded by an annual dinner in the Royal Hospital Kilmainham run by the O'Donovan Rossa cumann of Fianna Fáil of which Ahern is a member. Since the late 1980s the prominent businesses in Dublin Central and beyond have been invited to buy tickets for the dinner. This enabled Ahern to run the full-time con-stituency office and to spend considerable amounts of money at election time. He estimated his expenditure on the 1989 election as around £20,000 and the 1992 election at around £30,000.[3]

Ahern always seemed to get an easier ride from the media than any of his colleagues. Maybe it was the slightly hurt, even bemused way he reacted whenever he suffered criticism that disarmed journalists and political opponents alike. Strangely enough, he had no real friends in the parliamentary party apart from Haughey and a handful of the old Haughey loyalists.

In the undeclared leadership battle with Reynolds, Ahern moved with extreme caution. He later claimed his reticence was due to the fact that he had a Budget to prepare but this had actually been delivered to the Dáil by the time the race formally began. The real reason for his caution was political calculation. He wanted to go for the top prize, but he was keenly aware of the perils of a bitter contest. If he fought a hard fight and lost, he was likely to earn the enmity of Reynolds, who gave every indica-tion of being vindictive in victory. On the other hand, there was a strong temptation to do a deal with Reynolds that would make him the number two and the clear heir apparent.

There was intense pressure on Ahern, not least from Kinsealy itself, to throw down the gauntlet to Reynolds.'The boys were saying you've got to go, you've got to go. All the senior guys – Lenihan, Ray Burke, Rory O'Hanlon, Gerry Collins – I had them all with the exception of John Wilson. I had good rural support down the western seaboard. I had all the senior people outside the parliamentary party as well,' said Ahern later.[4] What deterred him, he added, was that a number of Dublin TDs like David Andrews, Seamus Brennan, Ben Briscoe and Tom Kitt were in the Reynolds camp.

Reynolds, by contrast, threw his hat into the ring immediately Haughey announced his resignation. He already had a lot of preparatory work done before the formal race even started. Real canvassing for him had been going on since the summer of 1991. Backbench TDs like Charlie McCreevy and Brian Cowen were firmly in his camp and worked on their colleagues to come over to his side. Not surprisingly, perhaps, the model for the Reynolds campaign strategy was Haughey's own campaign for the Fianna Fáil leadership between 1977 and 1979. Reynolds and Flynn were key figures in the 1979 campaign and they well remembered the lessons learned at that time. Along with Michael Smith, Geoghegan-Quinn and Noel Treacy, they formed the inner caucus of the Reynolds team. The Ahern camp, which had remained loyal to Haughey, forgot the lessons of the earlier campaigns and was taken unawares by the strength of Reynolds's tactics. Reynolds made himself available to tour the constituencies and, like Haughey before him, didn't spare himself the chicken-dinner circuit where he met and impressed ordinary party supporters. 'The leadership race didn't begin when Haughey announced his resignation to the parliamentary party. It was all over by then because Reynolds had enough pledges in the bag at that stage,' said one member of his campaign team.[5]

The result of the challenge the previous November had given a misleading impression of Reynolds's level of support because a number of his supporters switched sides when they saw he could not win while others were just not prepared to change the leadership in that way. When Haughey resigned, those supporters flocked back to the Reynolds camp and from the beginning of the succession race proper he had a clear majority in the parliamentary party. Smith, McCreevy and Cowen did most of the campaigning; Flynn took a back seat because of his own perception that he would rub some people up the wrong way.[6]

Much of the impetus for the Reynolds campaign came from a feeling of frustration among younger TDs at the lack of opportunity under Haughey. The prospect of sweeping changes at the top and the opening up of career opportunities was a decisive factor in the mood for change. By contrast, the endorsement of Ahern by the Haughey loyalists in the party hierarchy indicated that there would be minimal changes at the top if Bertie took over as leader. Those Haughey loyalists became frantic as Ahern continued to dither about entering the contest. According to Ahern's biographers they all but squatted in his constituency headquarters in Drumcondra, imploring him to run.

Ahern's personal life became an issue for a time. Michael Smith, then Minister for the Environment, was quoted in his local newspaper, the *Tipperary Star,* as saying that there were question marks over Ahern's suitability for the Taoiseach's office because of his unclear marriage situation. Reynolds himself was quoted as saying, 'People do like to know where the Taoiseach of the day is living.'[7] Both men later claimed they were misquoted but the barbs stung Ahern. 'Michael Smith came out and gave an interview to the *Tipperary Star,* and Albert Reynolds apparently said, "We should like to know where the Taoiseach lives",' Ahern said later, paraphrasing Reynolds.[8]

The fact that the breakdown of his marriage became a public issue was not altogether the fault of his opponents. Ahern himself had given very contradictory accounts of his personal life to the media over the previous few months. In a number of interviews he referred to the fact that he was separated from his wife and claimed he had no stable second relationship even though his relationship with Celia Larkin was common knowledge. In a *Sunday Press* interview with Brenda Power, he was not only evasive about whom he was living with, he also refused to be pinned down about where he was living, saying that he spent the night at different places. One way or another there is no doubt that Ahern's personal life and the use likely to be made of it by his enemies was a factor at this stage in his calculations about whether to go for the leadership. His supporters were desperate for him to announce his candidacy and Lenihan even told the radio station 98 FM that he was in the race. Ahern, though, continued to keep his options open.

On the Saturday morning before the parliamentary party vote for the leadership, Reynolds and Ahern met in the Berkeley Court Hotel, where Reynolds had the use of a suite. 'You know I'll win it,' Reynolds told his younger colleague immediately. He went on to tell Ahern that he would not remain in the leadership indefinitely and wouldn't try to do a Haughey on it and hang on. The message to Ahern was clear. If he dropped his challenge he would become the number two and the anointed successor. If he insisted on a fight and lost he would have to suffer the consequences. Ahern went for the safe option and agreed to withdraw from the race, which he had never even formally entered in any case. When the news broke, the Haughey camp was furious. Ahern's supporters were even more annoyed when the newspapers reported that during their meeting the two men had compared lists of supporters and discovered that a good number of TDs had promised their votes to them both. Some of them felt their chances of promotion under Reynolds had been ruined as a result.[9] Two other candidates, Mary O'Rourke and Michael Woods, had already declared their interest, but neither could muster any significant support. With Ahern out of the running, the race was all over.

When the Fianna Fáil parliamentary party met on Thursday, 6 February, Reynolds's margin of victory was even greater than people had envisaged. He got 61 votes as against 10 for Michael Woods and six for Mary O'Rourke. The margin was remarkable considering that just two months earlier he had been able to mobilise only 22 supporters to take on Haughey. The pitiful performance of Woods and O'Rourke was also surprising in the light of the earlier result. In the scramble to get into Reynolds's good books, the Haughey camp had obviously deserted the battlefield. After his victory Reynolds gave a confident press conference at which he surprised most people by saying that peace in the North was his top priority. He had hardly ever made a reference to the North during his political career, which had been dominated by economic concerns. The sceptics would find out before too long just how serious he was.

Reynolds was now Fianna Fáil leader, but he did not become Taoiseach until 11 February when Haughey formally resigned. Reynolds was then elected Taoiseach with the support of the PDs, and the Dáil adjourned while he went to Áras an Uachtaráin to get his seal of office and appoint his ministers. The new cabinet created a sensation. Reynolds fired eight of Haughey's ministers, including such household names as Ray Burke, Mary O'Rourke and Gerry Collins. It was a savage purge that stunned the political world. Back to office came Flynn, Geoghegan-Quinn and Smith. Long-serving backbenchers David Andrews and Charlie McCreevy were promoted to the cabinet for the first time as were young TDs Brian Cowen and Noel Dempsey. Probably the biggest surprise of all was the appointment as Minister of Health of Dr John O'Connell, a former Labour TD and friend of Haughey's who joined Fianna Fáil after years as an Independent. It was the scale of the purge that took the breath away, particularly as Reynolds followed it up by sacking nine out of the 12 junior ministers, including young Haughey loyalists like Dermot Ahern and John O'Donoghue.

Seán Duignan recalled how he listened with fascination to members of the Taoiseach's staff as they recounted the details of 'the great chainsaw massacre' in the days after the event. 'I was fascinated by how he went about it. Before leaving for Áras an Uachtaráin to receive his seal of office he informed staff he wanted to see most of the above upon his return. He was reminded that by then he would have not much more than half an hour to spare before leading his new ministerial team into the Dáil. That, he assured everybody, would give him plenty of time. Private secretary Donagh Morgan, conscious of the time element, reasoned that, whatever their fate, the ministers would have to be dealt with *en bloc,* but some sixth sense told him to double-check, so he went back into the Taoiseach's office. 'You'll see the Ministers all together then, Taoiseach?' he asked. 'Oh no, one at a time, please.' It was all over in less than a quarter of an hour. Almost all of them took it on the chin without a murmur. Only Mary O'Rourke and chief whip Dermot Ahern demanded an explanation, but they were given short shrift.[10] O'Rourke angrily declined to become a junior minister with responsibility for Women's Affairs, but did accept a junior post at Enterprise and Employment. The manner in which Reynolds dispatched the majority of the old cabinet earned him the nickname 'The Longford Slasher', after the local GAA team in his home town. His purge created ample room to reward his own supporters and bring on talent in the party, but it also earned him the undying enmity of those he had fired. 'I remember thinking at the time that those who live by the sword are liable to die by the sword. Now, having lived through the Reynolds era, I am convinced that he himself fully appreciated that, and even included it in his calculations,' wrote Duignan.

Duignan added that Reynolds once talked briefly to him about that day and gave a hint of his thinking by referring to the problems Haughey had faced when he appointed his archrival, George Colley, to the cabinet. 'The main thing to remember about being in this job is that you're here to make decisions and that involves taking risks,' Reynolds told his press secretary. 'You cannot get all the decisions right but you'll have no hope at all if you try to play it safe and duck taking them. You've got to be prepared to take the responsibility and also, if you get it wrong, to take the consequences.' That philosophy did not make for an easy life but it made for exciting politics. Everybody in the political world quickly discovered that the departure of Haughey did nothing to lower the temperature of Irish politics. If anything, things became even more stimulating.

22. BREAK-UP OF A COALITION

FROM THE BEGINNING Albert Reynolds had a fundamental problem. He had become leader of Fianna Fáil by capitalising on the widespread discontent in the organisation at the coalition with the PDs. Yet it was by courtesy of the PDs that he was Taoiseach. The 'temporary little arrangement', as he had insultingly described the coalition with them, had put him into the highest office in the land. If Fianna Fáil had been in government on its own when Seán Doherty made his allegations, the party's TDs would certainly not have pressurised Haughey to go. It was the PDs who put the gun to Haughey's head so it was ultimately thanks to Des O'Malley that Reynolds landed the big prize. Reynolds ignored that fundamental fact and it ultimately cost him and his party dearly.

A more immediate problem for Reynolds on his first day in office was the 'X' case. On the very day that he took over, news first broke of the move by Attorney General Harry Whelehan to prevent a 14-year-old rape victim from travelling to Britain for an abortion. Whelehan, in his role as the guardian of the Constitution, took the case to the High Court and got a decision upholding his right to do so. The country was convulsed by the case, less than a decade after the bitterly divisive referendum which resulted in the insertion of an anti-abortion clause in the Constitution. It was the last thing the new Taoiseach needed, but Whelehan was single-minded in his determination to do his duty as he saw it and appeared blithely unconcerned about the political consequences.

'Nobody is wild about Harry around here,' Seán Duignan confided to his diary. 'Practically every member of Dáil Éireann is castigating him for not having turned a blind eye. They won't admit it publicly but that's what they mutter in corners. That is how they want the chief law officer of the state to operate, but not one of them will openly admit it.'[1] Ultimately the Supreme Court decided that the girl was entitled to travel to Britain for an abortion, on the basis that as she had threatened to commit suicide there was a threat to her life. In the event, the girl did travel but suffered a miscarriage before any abortion was performed.

The abortion issue immediately strained relations between the two parties in government as they tried to come to grips with the implications of the X case and it was to bedevil their relationship as long as the coalition lasted. The pressure from the Fianna Fáil grassroots was for a new referendum to copper-fasten the pro-life provision in the Constitution while the PDs emphasised the right of a woman to receive information about abortion and to travel freely outside the jurisdiction. Pressure groups sought to make abortion an issue in the June referendum to endorse the Maastricht Treaty. After an early scare, Reynolds, with the support of the main Opposition parties, carried the referendum by getting EU agreement to add a protocol recognising Ireland's pro-life constitutional provision. The issue did not go away, however, and after a great deal of agonising the government decided to hold another referendum on the complicated issues involved. The people were asked to vote on three separate issues – the right to travel, the right to information about abortion, and a proposal to make abortion illegal except where the life of the mother was in danger. The first two propositions were not that contentious and were passed comfortably, but a proposal to deal with the so-called 'substantive issue' whipped up a major controversy and the government suffered an embarrassing defeat.

Reynolds's good relations with journalists ensured that he readily agreed to give a weekly on-the-record briefing to political journalists when it was suggested to him by his media adviser, Tom Savage. It was a decision he lived to regret. No Taoiseach, before or since, provided such access to the media and, given the Reynolds experience, it is not difficult to see why. The journalists harried him week in, week out on the abortion issue. It was a subject about which he was clearly uncomfortable as he tried to find a path through the legal and political morass that would not conflict with his own traditional Catholic views and those of his supporters. Committed to giving the briefings, he found himself making unwanted headlines again and again just as the story began to die down. He also discovered that the free-and-easy relationship he had enjoyed with journalists no longer translated into the same level of positive media coverage. As Taoiseach he was regarded as fair game and he had some difficulty in coming to terms with the fact.

He also adopted a strategy of taking legal action against newspapers he believed had libelled him and this soured his relations with a number of media people. Even before he took over the Taoiseach's office he was involved in a legal action against the *Irish Times* over an article by anti-EU campaigner Raymond Crotty who had accused him of attempting to use his position as a minister to secure European funding for his family pet-food firm. 'I am not going to take that kind of thing lying down,' he declared. 'Charlie felt there was nothing he could do about it but if they tell lies about me I will sue them and to hell with the consequences.'[2] This attitude was inexplicable to journalists who had been used to Haughey's policy of never suing. It also appeared to fly in the face of Reynolds's attitude towards journalists and his ability to roll with the punches without complaint most of the time.

The touchy and litigious Taoiseach seemed to be a different person to sunny Uncle Albert who was hail-fellow-well-met around Leinster House and in his constituency. But there was something many journalists, used to writing about politics as a blood sport, did not understand about Reynolds. While he was as good a political schemer as anybody in Leinster House, he did not usually indulge in personal abuse of opponents inside or outside the Dáil. Neither did he engage in the even more insidious black art of undermining his opponents through rumour and character assassination which was second nature to some of the more cunning political operators. Behind his affable mask Reynolds was extremely touchy and often insisted on regarding political abuse as attacks on his personal honour. He knew that as Taoiseach he was bound to come in for far more abuse than he had ever received as a minister, but he could not accept that the best policy was to grin and bear it. As a result, his relations with sections of the media deteriorated rapidly. 'I can live with them questioning my competence. I will not abide an attack from whatever quarter on my personal integrity. I will fight that to the bitter end, even if its costs me my job,' he told Duignan.[3] This attitude turned some influential people in the media against him but he was impervious to advice on the subject from his own advisers.

On abortion, Reynolds found it increasingly difficult to deal with the PDs. The wording of the constitutional amendments on travel and information was no problem but the third leg of the referendum, which proposed to make abortion illegal unless it was necessary to save the life of the mother, brought the extremists of the liberal and conservative fringes together. Liberals saw the amendment as a rowing back from the Supreme Court decision, which allowed the threat of suicide as sufficient reason for abortion. They argued that a threat to the health, rather than the life, of the mother should also be grounds for abortion. The conservatives claimed the amendment would allow abortion in limited circumstances for the first time. Reynolds had got the private approval of most senior Catholic church figures for his wording, but the zealots would have none of it and an unholy alliance of pro-life and pro-choice campaigners gleefully joined forces against the amendment. The PDs put their oar in, siding with the liberals and claiming the amendment was dangerous for women. For a time the issue threatened the stability of the government, but ultimately O'Malley backed away from confrontation and argued that to plunge the country into an election on the abortion issue would be unforgivable.

Despite these tribulations the news was not all bad for Reynolds. One thing he did manage was to establish a very close relationship with the new British Prime Minister, John Major. Historically this would far outweigh any of the debacles of Reynolds's first year but at the time it passed relatively unnoticed. The two men had met while they were finance ministers and had established an immediate rapport and even then had discussed Northern Ireland. Major records that when Reynolds became Taoiseach in February 1992, relations between the Taoiseach's office and Downing Street really improved. 'He was easy to get on with, naturally cheery and loquacious and as keen as I was to see real progress in Northern Ireland,' wrote Major later. 'I liked Albert a lot and I thought we could move things forward together. I invited him over for supper a fortnight after his election as Taoiseach.'[4]

One thing that caused Major some unease was Reynolds's liking for giving media interviews at every opportunity. 'Albert never walked past an open microphone in his life,' one of the Taoiseach's aides told the Prime Minister at an early stage. Major himself added: 'There was never any malice in this. Albert pitched his line so as to ensure a good reception from his nationalist audience, but unfortunately this invariably had the reverse effect on Unionists. This nearly derailed the process on one or two occasions but it was a price we were willing to pay for Albert's readiness to strike deals,' said Major.[5]

For much of 1992 the Irish public also warmed to Reynolds. Opinion polls revealed a high degree of public satisfaction with the government, with Fianna Fáil being supported by 50 per cent of the electorate that summer while the PDs registered only 4 per cent. These figures lulled Reynolds and other senior Fianna Fáil people into the false belief that the PDs would have to avoid an election at any cost, no matter what the provocation from Fianna Fáil. That provocation had started almost as soon as Reynolds had taken over. At the Fianna Fáil Árd Fheis in March, he had an unambiguous message for his coalition partners. 'Fianna Fáil does not need another party to keep it on the right track or act as its conscience,' he declared. This was a reference to the PD pressure that had led to the sacking of Lenihan and McDaid. What Reynolds seemed to forget was that the PD pressure had also resulted in the departure of Haughey and his own elevation. His young cabinet favourite, Brian Cowen, was even more blunt in his warm-up to the leader's address. 'What about the PDs?' he asked rhetorically, before providing an answer the delegates loved. 'When in doubt leave out,' he declared to great applause. It was good crowd-pleasing stuff but it was bad politics. It helped to lock Reynolds and O'Malley on a collision course that was in the long-term interest of neither.

   The tribunal of inquiry into the beef industry provided a pretext for both parties to stretch the coalition to breaking point. The original motivation for the establishment of the tribunal came from the suspicion among the Opposition leaders and the PDs that Haughey and Larry Goodman had an unhealthy special relationship. By the middle of 1992, however, it was clear that the tribunal might undermine Reynolds instead. The Taoiseach believed that the PDs were out to get him through the tribunal. 'The PDs set up the tribunal to get Charlie. He went down before it really got underway. So, now, they've decided that I'm the next best thing,' Reynolds told an associate.[6] The PDs for their part sensed the deep hostility of Reynolds and they believed that a number of issues were being manipulated by Fianna Fáil in order to embarrass them and that O'Malley was being kept in the dark by his cabinet colleagues on important matters.

   In June O'Malley gave his evidence to the beef tribunal. The critical issue for the stability of the government was how he would back up his claim, made while he was in Opposition and later in his written submission to the tribunal, that Reynolds had shown favouritism to Goodman in the way he operated the export credit insurance scheme as Minister for Industry and Commerce in 1987 and 1988. In the early days of his oral evidence O'Malley did not mention Reynolds by name but he stood over his view that the export credit scheme was abused to benefit Goodman International and Hibernia Meats. On his fifth day in the witness box he made a more direct attack on the Taoiseach, describing decisions taken by Reynolds on export credit as 'wrong ... grossly unwise, reckless and foolish'. Reynolds was livid. Although he did not let that show in public, those around him had a sense of foreboding as he spoke of a day of reckoning when he would set the record straight.

   Reynolds was not due to be called until after the summer and the tension mounted as the day approached. Duignan accompanied Tom Savage to a briefing with the lawyer Gerry Danaher, a colourful barrister and passionate Fianna Fáil supporter, who was an adviser to Reynolds at the tribunal. Danaher tried to give the two media men an inkling of the complex legal issues involved but Duignan was left scratching his head in confusion. After the meeting he remarked to Savage that it was a hundred times more complicated than abortion. 'I don't know about that but it's certainly a hundred times more dangerous for Albert,' replied Savage presciently.[7] His senior civil servants and political advisers urged caution on Reynolds before his tribunal appearance, but he was having none of it. An array of senior Fianna Fáil people, Haughey, MacSharry, Ray Burke, Seamus Brennan and Michael O'Kennedy, had given evidence to the tribunal and come away unscathed. Reynolds was anxious to express his views and stand up to O'Malley and some of the Fianna

Fáil witnesses who had been notably unhelpful to him.

Early at the tribunal, Reynolds gave a hostage to fortune when he described his *modus operandi* as a minister. 'I operate a Department on the basis of no long files, no long reports; put it on a single sheet and, if I need more information, I know where to get it ... the one sheet approach has got me through life very successfully in business and politics,' he told the tribunal. It was a reasonable statement but his enemies in the media distorted the sentiment and labelled Albert as 'the one page man'. It was a tag that stuck and it did nothing to improve his image.

On the central issue of how he operated the export credit insurance scheme Reynolds blustered and stonewalled when asked questions by hostile lawyers, particularly O'Malley's counsel, Adrian Hardiman. He might have survived that but he could not resist having a direct go at O'Malley, describing his evidence as 'reckless, irresponsible and dishonest'. There were many senior Fianna Fáil people who believed that O'Malley would put up with this abuse. But shrewder observers who knew O'Malley's true character realised that he was on his way out of government, whatever the consequences, the moment Reynolds described him as dishonest. He did give Reynolds a chance to retract. On a number of occasions during the cross-examination Hardiman offered the Taoiseach the option of modifying his description of O'Malley's evidence from 'dishonest' to 'incorrect'. On one occasion Reynolds appeared to waver. Duignan recorded the event in his diary: 'I kept willing him to say yes, to get back to defending his own decisions, to leave O'Malley out of the damn thing, get the show back on the road. Albert paused for what seemed ages (we all held our breath) and then he said that one word ... "dishonest". I think we're bollixed.'

That about summed it up. After a couple of days of shadow-boxing, the PDs announced that they would vote in favour of a motion of no confidence in the government of which they were a part. There was no way to avoid an election on the worst possible issue for Fianna Fáil and for Reynolds himself. He had ignored the advice of any of his paid political advisers, senior civil servants and cabinet ministers about the decision. Instead, the Taoiseach worked out his tribunal strategy with an advisor who suggested that it was legally permissible to call O'Malley dishonest and that the PD leader would have no choice but to grin and bear it. Later, with the benefit of hindsight, Reynolds regretted the move. 'Looking back on it from a political point of view, and I stress the word political, I was badly advised,' he said.[8]

The Dáil was dissolved on 5 November and Reynolds lashed into the PDs in his final speech of the twenty-sixth Dáil. He did manage to do one thing right in that speech. He carefully avoided having a go at the Labour

Party. It didn't get much notice at the time but Reynolds, having pulled the plug on his government, showed some foresight in throwing out a lifeline in the midst of the storm.

The softly, softly approach to Labour was generally ignored because Dick Spring didn't respond in kind. Instead he attacked Fianna Fáil in no uncertain terms. 'We will not get involved in any Government that is willing to bring politics into disrepute as this Government has done ... I believe one party in this House has gone so far down the road of blindness to standards and blindness to the people they are supposed to represent that it is impossible to see how anyone could support them in the future without seeing them first undergo the most radical transformation. We will not support any Government with the track record of this one.'[9] On the face of it Reynolds could expect no deal of any kind with Labour after the election but he had a gut instinct that something might be possible if the worst came to the worst.

There was consternation in Fianna Fáil that the strategy of confronting the PDs had precipitated an election. The first opinion poll of the campaign in the *Irish Independent* confirmed their worst fears as it showed a massive drop of 20 per cent in the Taoiseach's satisfaction rating. The voters clearly blamed Reynolds rather than O'Malley for the break-up of the government. Some of the old Haughey gang could not disguise their glee at the fact that Reynolds's strategy had come so spectacularly unstuck, but they did not have much time to enjoy his discomfiture. It was every man for himself in the battle to hold on to Dáil seats as the tide moved strongly against Fianna Fáil. As if things were not bad enough Reynolds dismissed the arguments of his opponents as 'crap' in the first weekend of the campaign. The resultant publicity was so bad that he had to apologise for his indelicate language.

The Fianna Fáil election manifesto itself was not at all bad but nobody was interested in the details. From the beginning, the campaign lacked the buzz that was so characteristic of Fianna Fáil's electioneering style. In Kerry the crowds melted away as Reynolds took his campaign to the south. ministers and TDs who saw the writing on the wall concentrated on their own constituencies and left the Taoiseach and his entourage to their own devices. Things were so bad that many leading Fianna Fáil figures, including some well-known Reynolds supporters, refused to go on television to defend the government. One of the exceptions was the Minister for Transport, Energy and Communications, Brian Cowen. The young, combative and capable Offaly man was stunned when the party press office told him that some of his colleagues were ducking out of interviews. He offered to go on television and radio anywhere, any time to defend his leader and try to put the party's election manifesto across.[10]

Seán Duignan summed up the mood. 'I could see, talking to FF Ministers, that they already regarded themselves as primarily conducting a damage limitation exercise. If, in addition, the Reynolds era was about to end, personal survival would take precedence over all else. The air was thick with fear, frustration and fault-finding ... I was struck by signs of indiscipline and even insubordination in the organisation at large. A steady stream of HQ instructions to FF notables recommending particular responses to opposition criticisms were being widely ignored. Certain Ministers and other personages who had been requested to represent Fianna Fáil on various TV and radio elections were begging off with all manner of specious excuses.'[11]

As the polls got progressively worse for Reynolds, senior party figures began to prepare themselves for the post-Reynolds era. It looked as if the Haughey gang would be back in town, less than a year after The Boss had been shafted. The Haugheyites could hardly contain their glee and middle-ground TDs scrambled to dissociate themselves from Reynolds. The pressure began to tell on the Taoiseach, particularly as the battering he was taking in the media traumatised his wife, Kathleen, who was recovering from breast cancer. 'None of this is worth what it's doing to Kathleen,' he remarked at one stage. Kathleen, in an interview with Anne Cadwallader of the *Irish Press,* poured out her anguish. 'I just can't take it. I can't believe what's happened over the past few days. I can't recognise the man I married in what's being said about him. In three weeks he's gone from being the best man around to someone none of us recognises.'[12]

During the campaign, the Fine Gael leader, John Bruton, suffered almost as much media hostility as Reynolds. After the heady days of the 1980s the party had simply become unfashionable and Bruton, the Meath farmer, represented the most unfashionable side of it. His campaign took a nose-dive after his proposal for a 'rainbow coalition' alternative, including Labour but excluding the Democratic Left, was given a cool response by Spring. He had foolishly made the proposal without any prior consultation with the Labour Party and as a result had aroused Spring's ire. The two men had had a strained relationship in government during the 1980s and Spring and his advisers believed Bruton was taking them for granted in his unilateral announcement of the rainbow proposal.

The star of the election campaign was Spring who had been so effective over the previous two years in taking on first Haughey and then Reynolds. He capitalised brilliantly on the anti-Fianna Fáil mood and the polls showed a big swing to Labour as the campaign progressed. Spring was not pressed by the media about what he would do after the election in terms of coalition, but his proposal that he would have to have a turn at Taoiseach grabbed the headlines. The polls showed that he would be a

more popular Taoiseach than Bruton and the notion of a rotating Taoiseach in the event of a rainbow coalition was seriously entertained in the
media.

Before the end of the campaign it was obvious that Fianna Fáil was
going to lose seats and that the big winners would be Labour. Even before
polling day Reynolds was thinking of a coalition deal with Labour
although all the media speculation at the time was on a rainbow coalition
as an alternative to Fianna Fáil. When it came, the result was terrible for
Fianna Fáil. The party dipped below 40 per cent of the vote for the first
time since 1927 and dropped ten seats into the bargain. Surprisingly, Fine
Gael also dropped 10 seats, the big winners being Dick Spring and Labour
which gained 17 seats to finish with a record 33. The PDs also did well,
defying the pundits and almost doubling their numbers to ten. Democratic Left had five and others six seats.

Initially, Reynolds took the result very badly. At home in Longford
for the count he retreated to his bedroom and literally 'took to the bed' for
a few hours. His election agent, Mickey Doherty, tried to explain his
absence from the count by saying the Taoiseach was engaged in urgent
consultations about the Irish pound which was then in the throes of a currency crisis. Journalists reported the comments on the wire services and
the pound dropped by a couple of pfennig against the German mark. Seán
Duignan has famously told the story as 'the day Mickey Doherty took a
pfennig off the pound'. Eventually his fellow constituency TD, Seán
Doherty, had to force his way into Reynolds's room and tell him to snap
out of it. Reynolds did pull himself together by clinging to the consolation
that nobody had a clear majority and that coalition with Labour might be
on. Many of the people close to him thought he was totally out of touch as
a number of party big guns like Flynn, MacSharry and Seamus Brennan
had come out publicly against coalition even before polling day. On the
night of the count they and many others argued that Fianna Fáil needed to
re-group in Opposition. Only Brian Lenihan, who had always favoured a
deal with Labour rather than the PDs, publicly advocated the Labour
option. It seemed like a long shot at the time but, as the Harold Wilson
maxim has it, a week is a long time in politics.

23. SPRING SAVES THE DAY

IN THE DAYS AFTER THE ELECTION, Albert Reynolds's grip on the leadership of his party appeared to be slipping from his grasp. With the majority of politicians and the media strongly of the view that a rainbow coalition was inevitable, questions began to be asked about the Fianna Fáil leadership. Most of the senior party figures were strongly opposed to any coalition deal to get back into government. Flynn, MacSharry and McCreevy publicly refused to even contemplate the idea. More ominously, a string of anti-Reynolds TDs, including Ray Burke, Gerry Collins, John O'Donoghue and Ned O'Keeffe, were also against a deal. The sub-text for this group was that they wanted a change of leader but only the former party whip, Vincent Brady, had the courage to preach mutiny openly. There was a move to float the name of David Andrews as a potential successor but he quickly quashed it by describing the idea as unprincipled and obscene. Everybody looked to Bertie Ahern but he remained enigmatic and declined to get involved.

As time passed, however, the rainbow simply refused to materialise, despite the favourable conditions. Fine Gael stuck to its policy of excluding Democratic Left while Labour placed a similar exclusion on the Progressive Democrats. The simple fact of the matter was that without the two smaller parties the numbers were not there for a government. Labour opened negotiations with DL in the hope of forming a left-wing alliance to pressurise John Bruton into a U-turn but the demand for a rotating Taoiseach was simply unacceptable to Fine Gael. The last straw for the potential rainbow was the eventual outcome of the seesaw recount in Dublin South-Central that elected Ben Briscoe of Fianna Fáil rather than Eric Byrne of DL after a week of confusion. The result meant that a three-party coalition of Fine Gael, Labour and Democratic Left would not have a majority. Meanwhile Labour treated the PDs with scorn and made it clear they would not deal with them in any circumstances.

The key to the failure to form the rainbow was Labour's attitude to Bruton, which was 'almost eerie in its intensity', as one observer recorded.[1] There was no disguising Spring's deep-rooted hostility to the Fine Gael leader because of repeated clashes during the FitzGerald coalition. When the two men met in the Shelbourne Hotel after the election, the Labour leader gave Bruton a dressing-down, accusing him of taking Labour for granted during the campaign. Spring was the one in pole position because of his brilliant election performance and Fine Gael was too demoralised to come up with a coherent strategy to get off the hook on which the outright rejection of DL had impaled the party.

Reynolds played it coolly and bided his time as first one and then another Opposition party scuppered the rainbow. He remained uncharacteristically reticent in public about his chances of holding on to government, but in private he maintained that he might just be able to do a deal with Labour. Questioned by reporters in the days after the election he was non-committal. 'We haven't had an approach from anybody. Labour are talking to the other parties. The sooner a Government is formed the better,' he responded. But, he was asked, what if Labour and the other parties could not agree? 'Well, I suppose when they've talked to the rest, if they don't agree, they'll come and talk to us then,' he said.[2]

As the rainbow began to fade slowly Reynolds was kept informed of what was going on. He was particularly fascinated by the scornful way Spring treated Bruton and knew by it that Labour was not going to do business with Fine Gael. In fact, back-door talks about a coalition between Fianna Fáil and Labour had already begun immediately after the election when Brian Lenihan met Ruairí Quinn. In his book *For the Record*, written after the presidential election, Lenihan had strongly advocated the move. 'There was a shared understanding between Labour and Fianna Fáil in the 1930s when de Valera was Taoiseach. That understanding must be recast for modern times to ensure future stability in the political system. It would be a stability based on the principled support of people sharing similar social and national values,' he wrote.[3] Another tentative exploration of the possibilities of a Fianna Fáil-Labour deal came when Bertie Ahern as Finance Minister briefed all the Opposition leaders on the country's financial situation. Ahern used his meeting with Spring and Quinn to establish just what Labour's bottom line was on a number of issues including privatisation.

Another minister who did not believe that the jig was up for Fianna Fáil after the election was Agriculture's Joe Walsh. He had been involved in the contacts that led to the formation of the previous Fianna Fáil coalition with the PDs and always believed there was a chance of a deal with Labour. At the first cabinet meeting after the election he proposed that they should prepare a policy document so that they would be ready for talks at any stage. He warned that one of the flaws in the approach to the PDs after the 1989 election was that Fianna Fáil had no policy document of its own, but had to rely completely on the civil service, while the PDs had a detailed shopping list of demands. Although a number of ministers, including Flynn, McCreevy, Brennan and Andrews, did not want any truck with Labour, Reynolds was delighted with the Walsh proposal and, even though most ministers thought it was an academic exercise, the cabinet approved the move. The task of preparing the approach was given to the Taoiseach's adviser, Martin Mansergh. He trawled through every policy statement produced by Labour for over a decade and put together proposals which he felt would be compatible with the positions adopted by both parties in the election campaign.[4]

Reynolds sat patiently on the document until Labour exhausted the rainbow option. Finally Spring made the move the Taoiseach had been waiting for and sent him a copy of the joint Labour/DL policy, and asked for a meeting. Reynolds was about to go to Edinburgh for one of the most crucial EU summits ever held, from Ireland's point of view. On the agenda was a huge expansion in the money available for structural funds. In the light of this, Labour did not expect a reply for a few days but they got it in less than an hour. The Mansergh 20-page document was dispatched to Labour and shortly afterwards Reynolds took off for Edinburgh feeling real hope for the first time since the middle of the election campaign. Spring and his colleagues were completely taken aback not just by the speed of the response but at the content of the document which went a very long way to meet their position on a whole range of issues. For instance, Fianna Fáil's plans to privatise the ACC, the ICC and the Trustee banks were dropped in favour of Labour's election idea for the creation of a third banking force by the state sector, and a whole range of infrastructural projects to create jobs was promised. 'We certainly never expected Fianna Fáil to come back with such a comprehensive policy document by that evening,' said Ruairí Quinn.[5]

The Edinburgh summit provided Reynolds with his trump card. He went to the summit committed to doubling Ireland's entitlement and securing an unprecedented £6 billion over a five-year period. Labour was, in Bertie Ahern's words, 'watching for a sign', so the negotiations became a matter of political life or death for Reynolds. The prevailing view was that the Taoiseach had gone over the top by publicly committing himself to getting £6 billion, but friends and enemies again underestimated his ability as a dealer. Even as Seán Duignan hosted a 'farewell dinner' for the press on the theme 'You won't have Diggy to kick around any more', the Taoiseach and his civil servants were pulling off an astonishing deal. They did not get £6 billion; they got a commitment for £8 billion in structural and cohesion funds. It was an astonishing achievement and while there were quibbles later about whether it was actually £6 billion over five years or £8 billion over seven there was no taking away from the impact. 'Eight billion, Diggy, eight billion. Tell that to the begrudgers. Now watch me put a Government together,' remarked an ebullient Reynolds to his press secretary immediately after the meeting.[6]

Spring had agreed to meet Reynolds on his return from the summit the following day. The two men met in a penthouse suite in the Berkeley Court Hotel on 13 December. Fergus Finlay, who accompanied Spring to the meeting, expected to meet a politician with a hunted and hangdog look. After all, Reynolds had been under intense pressure for months and the knives were out for him in the media and in his own party. If he did not do a deal with Spring he could kiss goodbye to the Fianna Fáil leadership. Finlay's initial surprise was to discover that far from being downbeat and defensive Reynolds was his usual bright and breezy self. He behaved like a man without a care in the world. Reynolds and Spring retired for a private chat, leaving Finlay and Duignan to shoot the breeze while keeping an eye through a glass partition on how things were going in the other room. The two politicians chatted for an hour with Reynolds doing most of the talking.[7]

After the meeting a chirpy Reynolds left the hotel while Spring retired to another suite where he was joined by his closest political allies and friends. He told them about his conversation with Reynolds and asked for their advice on what to do. Should the party make history and do a coalition deal with Fianna Fáil? Spring told them that Reynolds was anxious to do business but the question was, should Labour do business with him? Ruairí Quinn asked his leader whether there was anything in the beef tribunal which contained a time-bomb with the potential to destroy the government. Spring gave his view that at worst Reynolds would be found careless or incompetent but nothing more than that. Quinn also asked if they had talked about anything else. 'We talked about Northern Ireland,' Spring answered. 'I promised him I wouldn't elaborate but you can take it that there are real possibilities there. The other thing he told me was that I was getting a briefing that Des O'Malley never got.' His listeners were intrigued but they were more preoccupied with the practical issue. To deal or not to deal, that was the question. Quinn, who strongly favoured a coalition with Fianna Fáil, was happy at the account of the meeting.

Apart from Spring and Quinn, the other people present were Barry Desmond, Brendan Howlin, Fergus Finlay, Pat Magner, James Wrynne the party's financial secretary, and two economic advisers, Willie Scally and Greg Sparks. Spring's closest friend, John Rogers, and his brother Donal made up the group. Quinn and Howlin were the leading supporters of the Fianna Fáil option, while Desmond and Finlay still thought that on balance it was worth exploring the option of a four-party rainbow, including the PDs. After the pros and cons had been weighed up again and again, Spring asked the ten other people present to vote on which was the best option to pursue. Five people supported the Fianna Fáil option and five voted for a rainbow coalition as long as it involved the Democratic Left as well as the PDs. 'That's a great help,' remarked Spring wryly and the meeting broke up with the issue still in the hands of the party leader. However, there was little doubt what was going to happen.[8]

The Dáil met the following day to elect a Taoiseach. Reynolds, Bruton and Spring were all proposed and defeated for the post by increasingly bigger margins. The failure of the Dáil to elect a Taoiseach had happened for the first time after the 1989 election so it now caused little excitement. That night the Labour parliamentary party met to consider whether it should give Spring a mandate to open talks with Fianna Fáil. There was really no argument and formal negotiations between the two parties began on 16 December. The two party leaders did not get directly involved in the talks. Reynolds appointed Ahern, Dempsey and Cowen to do the deal for Fianna Fáil while the Labour team was made up of Quinn, Howlin and Mervyn Taylor. The key negotiators were Ahern and Quinn, who had both been Ministers for Labour. Despite facing each other across the floor of the Dáil as minister and Opposition spokesman they had developed a good relationship and trusted each other. Both were extremely anxious to do a deal. Howlin and Dempsey also knew each other quite well, being whips of their respective parties, and they had also established a level of mutual trust. The final members of each team, Mervyn Taylor and Brian Cowen, were not as comfortable as the others. While Taylor was reserved, Cowen emerged as the hard man of the talks. He played it tough right through, insisting on as much Fianna Fáil policy as possible going into the joint programme and refusing to budge on basic budgetary targets. Ahern played his customary conciliatory role, while Dempsey facilitated the talks by ensuring that the Labour team had access to any information they needed from the Department of Finance or other Departments. The talks never ran into serious problems and unlike the discussions between Fianna Fáil and the PDs in 1989 there was no great mutual suspicion between the teams or among members of the same team. One reason for this was that while Reynolds and Spring were waiting in the wings to deal with any problems that emerged, neither of them pulled the rug from under the feet of their negotiating teams to speed the process. One of the main problems for Fianna Fáil in 1989 was that Haughey negotiated directly with Des O'Malley without telling his own team what he was up to. This time around, there was unity on both sides and a healthy atmosphere around the table.

On the question of the spoils of office there was also an early understanding. Spring accepted that he would not get the Taoiseach's job on a rotating basis. It was a big climbdown from the demand he had made of Bruton, but given the respective Dáil strength of the parties he did not have much choice. He also backed down from the demand that the DL be included in any arrangement. In return, Reynolds agreed to formalise the new partnership through the establishment of a special office for the Tánaiste which would have its own staff and budget. There was agreement that Labour would get six of the 15 cabinet posts. Fianna Fáil fully expected Labour to demand Finance and would have conceded it, but the push never came. Surprisingly, Spring opted instead for Foreign Affairs.

Relations got off to such a good start that the Labour team and its advisers were issued with the special plastic security keys which enabled them to enter the Taoiseach's Department from Leinster House at will. Not only that, but Fergus Finlay was given the office inside the department which had been occupied by Stephen O'Byrnes of the PDs, who had been Assistant Government Press Secretary in the previous coalition. Although the talks were amicable, they were also lengthy and it took a full four weeks from the first Spring-Reynolds meeting to the final acceptance of the deal by the Labour Party at a conference in the National Concert Hall in Dublin. Meanwhile, the country was experiencing a currency crisis, with Irish interest rates rising higher and higher in the aftermath of Britain's withdrawal from the EMS the previous September. The absence of a permanent government at such a period provided grounds for criticising the lengthy talks.

Before the coalition had been agreed, the Dáil met again on 22 December without electing a Taoiseach and again on 5 January with the same result. On the second occasion, John Bruton hammered away at Spring for being ready to do a deal with Fianna Fáil. He cited the Labour leader's speech on the dissolution of the Dáil in November. 'Deputy Spring did receive a mandate; he received a mandate for change. Now he proposes to give us that change by putting back in office the same Taoiseach, the same ministers, the same political party against whom he spoke with such precious and high-flown rhetoric here in this house on 5 November last and for the previous five years,' said Bruton.

During the debate, Des O'Malley made obscure references to the Taoiseach's access to documents. It transpired later that O'Malley had gone to Spring's office that very morning with a curious tale. He referred back to an approach Spring had made to him the previous October in relation to a story going the rounds of the Bar library. This was to the effect that Gerry Danaher, the barrister who had represented Reynolds at the beef tribunal, had tried to intimidate O'Malley's counsel, Adrian Hardiman, before Hardiman's cross-examination of Charles Haughey and

Press conference to announce the first social partnership agreement, 1987, (from left): Ray Burke, Pádraig Ó hUiginn (looking away), Ray McSharry, Charles Haughey and Bertie Ahern

Press conference announcing the first Fianna Fáil-Progressive Democrats coalition, 1989, (from left): Bobby Molloy and Des O'Malley (PD), Charles Haughey and Albert Reynolds (Fianna Fáil)

Taoiseach Charles Haughey with British Prime Minister Margaret Thatcher
at the European Community summit in Dublin, 1990

On the presidential campaign 1990, Brian Lenihan (right) and his son, Conor (facing him)

Fianna Fáil Dáil members listen to their leader Charles Haughey
at the party Árd Fheis, 1991

Bertie Ahern, Charles Haughey and Pádraig Flynn on the local elections campaign, 1991

Former Taoiseach Charles Haughey and Minister for Finance
during the Fianna Fáil Presidential

Above: Charles Haughey, after his retirement,
sits beside Minister for Finance Bertie Ahern at
the Fianna Fáil Árd Fheis, 1993

Right: Former Taoiseach Charles Haughey and
Taoiseach Albert Reynolds at the Fianna Fáil Árd
Fheis, 1993

Below: Taoiseach Albert Reynolds with
President Mary Robinson

Taoiseach Albert Reynolds meets US President Bill Clinton at the White House, 1993

Progressive Democrat TDs Michael McDowell and Mary Harney (party leader)
reading the report of the Beef tribunal, 1994

Taoiseach Albert Reynolds with Labour leader Dick Spring in September 1994,
shortly before the break-up of the Fianna Fáil-Labour coalition

Celebratory handshake, shortly after the historic announcement of the IRA ceasefire in 1994,
(from left): Sinn Féin leader Gerry Adams, Taoiseach Albert Reynolds, SDLP leader John Hume

Right: A young Bertie Ahern as Lord Mayor of Dublin, 1986

Left: Taoiseach Bertie Ahern with British Prime Minister Tony Blair, 1998

Charles Haughey enjoying his expensive lifestyle – riding at his estate, at Dingle regatta

July 2000, Charles Haughey attends the Moriarty tribunal which exposed details of his financial affairs

Albert Reynolds. The PD leader said that he now had further serious information to impart about other incidents and he wanted the Labour leader to be aware of them. The central incident involved a claim that Fianna Fáil had access to privileged documents prepared by a member of O'Malley's legal team at the beef tribunal, Gerard Hogan. O'Malley said that these documents had been photocopied and delivered to Fianna Fáil headquarters and subsequently made available to Danaher.

He gave as the source of this information a Christmas Eve conversation in the bar of the Shelbourne Hotel between one of his barristers, Diarmaid McGuinness, and Danaher. McGuinness, apart from being O'Malley's barrister, was a member of the Labour Party and well known to Spring. O'Malley also mentioned a burglary at the Department of Industry and Commerce the previous November and the fact that notes about Hardiman's travelling arrangements to and from the beef tribunal were found by the Gardaí in the possession of a suspected subversive. The Labour leader was taken aback by these allegations and immediately consulted his friend and legal adviser John Rogers. Together with Rogers and Mervyn Taylor, another lawyer, he went to see Reynolds. The Taoiseach acted immediately by calling in the Attorney General, Harry Whelehan, and the Garda Commissioner and asked them to investigate the claims. Spring was reassured by the Taoiseach's quick response and some Labour people actually came to the conclusion that the timing of the revelations was a last-minute attempt by the PDs to scupper the formation of a Fianna Fáil-Labour government. While the controversy continued for some time and eventually resulted in a Bar Council investigation into the various allegations, it quickly fizzled out as a political issue, but it spurred the negotiators to move ahead as quickly as possible with the formation of a government.

The Fianna Fáil and Labour *Programme for a Partnership Government 1993-1997* was published two days later and immediately presented to two specially convened meetings of the respective parliamentary parties. The 58-page document was given to TDs of both parties only as they began their meetings, but there was a widespread welcome for it from both camps. Reynolds was happy to adopt the bulk of the Labour agenda on issues like ethics in government, Dáil reform, the introduction of divorce, the decriminalisation of homosexuality and extra health and social welfare spending. In return, he insisted that Labour accept the budgetary constraints necessitated by the Maastricht Treaty. This was a major modification of Labour's position in the election campaign but Labour bit the bullet of fiscal rectitude.

When the Dáil met on 12 January, Reynolds was elected Taoiseach with the biggest majority in the history of the state. It was an incredible turn-around for a man who had stared defeat in the face on the night of the election count. Instead he made room at the cabinet table for six Labour ministers. It was not all that difficult to do. The departure of the PDs created two vacancies, while Fianna Fail's John Wilson had retired; Flynn was dispatched to Brussels as EU Commissioner, much to Labour's relief, Seamus Brennan was demoted to the junior ranks and John O'Connell was dropped. There had been a lot of speculation that Reynolds was going to drop McCreevy, but the two men got on too well for that to happen, even if they disagreed about coalition. 'You couldn't bring yourself to drop me – the girls [the Reynolds's daughters] wouldn't let you,' joked McCreevy. 'At least I've got you out of Social Welfare,' responded Reynolds, referring to the wave of controversy McCreevy's attempts to reform the welfare system had caused. In Trade and Tourism he was in an area for which he had more empathy. Ahern stayed at Finance, Geoghegan-Quinn went to Justice, Cowen took over Transport, Energy and Communications, but Andrews had to move from Foreign Affairs to Defence to make way for Spring. Smith remained at Environment and Woods went back to Social Welfare.

Labour had six cabinet posts, headed by Spring in Foreign Affairs, as well as the Tánaiste's office in Government Buildings. One of the reasons for his choice of Foreign Affairs rather than Finance was because Reynolds had briefed him about important developments taking place on Northern Ireland and he wanted an input into the process. In any case, he was never very interested in economics. One of the shortcomings of Labour under Spring was that the party failed to develop new economic policies and remained stuck with the old Labour anti-enterprise culture. Quinn, who was interested in economic reform, got Enterprise and Employment, the most senior economic ministry ever held by a Labour politician since William Norton in 1953. Howlin, Taylor, Michael D. Higgins and Niamh Bhreathnach made up the rest of the team.

Now the pundits began to talk of Fianna Fáil and Labour governing together for the remainder of the century and into the new millennium. The Opposition was demoralised and divided and it seemed that all Reynolds had to do was to steer the ship straight ahead and nothing could go wrong. Unfortunately for Reynolds it was not that simple. While the Labour ministers settled down comfortably with their Fianna Fáil cabinet colleagues, the same was not true of the all-important government advisers. One of the key parts of the 'Programme for Government' was the institution of a new system whereby every minister had a programme manager whose job it was to ensure that the coalition deal was implemented. All six Labour ministers appointed political activists to this position and they also appointed additional special advisers. Fianna Fáil made the mistake of relying on civil servants as programme managers. The programme managers held a weekly meeting, generally the day before Tuesday's cabinet meeting. Over time it became clear that this Monday meeting was, if anything, more important than the cabinet meeting itself.

It did not take long for Fianna Fáil to resent this while Labour began to share the same feelings in time. Reynolds was especially angry at what he regarded as media leaks designed to further Labour's position on major issues of conflict between the two parties. In particular, he came to develop an obsession with Finlay whom he regarded as the orchestrator of negative publicity against him. Seán Duignan agreed with the assessment of his boss. 'Finlay was highly intelligent, astute and volatile. He had extraordinary influence over Spring; he decided quite early on in my view that the Reynolds-Spring union wasn't working, that Reynolds could not be let have his way to the extent that he desired and, if that were not achievable, Spring would have to be prepared to pull out of Government.'[9]

This is obviously a partisan view but it began to gain currency in Fianna Fáil. The myth developed that Finlay was a closet Fine Gaeler and would do anything to get out of the Fianna Fáil embrace. Nothing could have been further from the truth. If anything, Finlay had an even greater contempt for Fine Gael and particularly for John Bruton than he had for Fianna Fáil. On Northern Ireland he was always very much on the 'green' wing of the Labour Party and much closer to the Fianna Fáil position than he ever was to the Fine Gael one. It was no accident that he developed such a good working relationship with Martin Mansergh, who was Reynolds's closest adviser. This was based on a shared analysis of the Northern problem as well as on growing mutual respect.

It is certainly true that Spring and the people close to him were wary of Fianna Fáil from the beginning of the partnership. They were particularly aware that the beef tribunal was going to pose difficulties in time and they watched Reynolds like a hawk. The rest of the Labour Party, ministers and backbenchers who were not in the Spring loop, were much happier with the alliance and good personal relations quickly developed.

On the Fianna Fáil side, Reynolds and those around him were delighted to have made it back to government after such a disastrous election. However, a significant rump of the party remained out in the cold. Powerful and experienced figures like Ray Burke and Gerry Collins, as well as younger TDs like Dermot Ahern and John O'Donoghue, were left on the back benches to brood and plot. For them, Bertie Ahern was the Bonny Prince Charlie, the standard bearer of the old regime, on whose accession to the leadership they pinned their long-term hopes. In the early months of 1993, though, a change of leadership looked like something that would not happen for a considerable time. Nobody could have foreseen what would happen next.

24. THE PEACE PROCESS

ALBERT REYNOLDS WAS EXTREMELY LUCKY to get a second bite at government. It might have been expected that his brush with political disaster would have taught him caution, but caution was foreign to his nature. He proceeded to govern with the same devil-may-care attitude that had characterised his first year in office. The result of his audacious style of political leadership was the crowning achievement of the peace process, which nobody else but Reynolds would have had the courage to attempt. But that very same reckless quality would ultimately blow his second coalition apart.

When he first became Taoiseach in 1992, Reynolds had startled everybody by expressing a burning desire to do something about Northern Ireland. Behind the scenes, tentative moves had already begun, following a meeting in Dublin between Charles Haughey and the new British Prime Minister, John Major, in December 1991. Haughey had then proposed the notion of a Joint Declaration between the two governments, setting out the principles for an eventual settlement based on bringing republicans into the mainstream of politics on condition that violence should end for good. The initiative was made at the prompting of John Hume who had been engaged in talks with the Sinn Féin leader, Gerry Adams, over the previous two years. Major was non-committal but said he was prepared to look at the merits of any proposal. A month later, in January 1992, he got a text from Haughey. In February a different version, which appeared to have originated with Sinn Féin, came from John Hume. Major regarded both texts as being so utterly one-sided, and based on the presumption of a united Ireland, that they did not even have merit as a basis for negotiation. 'I was frankly surprised that John Hume and Charles Haughey, both very experienced politicians, should have lent themselves to such an unrealistic approach,' said Major.[1]

However unsatisfactory the moves had been, Reynolds grasped their importance and, immediately on taking office, he sought to build on them. In public, the focus was on the talks process with the parties in the North and the historic decision of the Ulster Unionists to come to Dublin for the first time to negotiate with the Irish Government. In private, Reynolds was far more engaged in efforts to get republicans involved on a realistic basis in the process of formulating a Joint Declaration. He kept the Prime Minister up to date on the progress of his tactics and built on his good relationship with Major. With so many other things on the political agenda, however, progress was slow.

Reynolds's efforts had the enthusiastic support of Dick Spring. One of the reasons the Labour leader was so interested in doing a deal with Fianna Fáil and in choosing Foreign Affairs rather than Finance was that Reynolds had confided in him since the start about the discussions, pledging him to complete secrecy.

In the early part of 1993 the peace process, as it became known, gathered momentum. Reynolds put a huge amount of effort into convincing republicans that democratic politics offered them a far better way of pursuing their political agenda than random terrorism. But he had to shift them from the belief that they could get the British to agree to a timetable for Irish unification. Instead, he let republicans know that they would get the broad support of democratic nationalist Ireland if they accepted the principle of consent, involving the agreement of all the people of Ireland to future political structures.

Effectively what Reynolds did was to synthesise all the various strands of nationalist policy that had developed since the outbreak of the Troubles. He accepted the crucial importance of the consent principle, something Haughey had always refused to do, but he did so in the context of a new expression of self-determination by all the people of Ireland, something that was crucial for republicans. The truly original core of the policy pursued by Reynolds was to argue that everybody else had put the cart before the horse in trying to get a political solution in order to bring about peace. He proposed instead to concentrate all efforts on bringing about peace first, in the belief that a political solution would inevitably flow from that. It was an idea whose time had come. Republicans were weary with a campaign of violence that had got them nowhere and the British were weary of a war they could not win.

With the new Irish Government in place, the Hume-Adams talks which had been meandering along since 1989 developed a fresh impetus and an agreed document was submitted to the Irish Government in the early summer of 1993. Reynolds and Spring believed it could provide the basis for a deal, but the British were adamant that it contained fundamental flaws, particularly because it required them to become persuaders for a united Ireland. The British regarded it as a variation on the old Haughey call on them to offer a timetable for withdrawal and it just was not acceptable.

Reynolds decided that, regardless of British reservations, he had to put the document to John Major to test his response. 'Whatever his inner misgivings, Albert presented it in effect on a take-it-or-leave-it basis – this was his habitual style of negotiation,' said Major.[2] Major also records that he had to deflect what he regarded as a bizarre suggestion from the Taoiseach that the two men should meet somewhere in the United Kingdom. Instead he sent the Cabinet Secretary, Robin Butler, to Dublin to receive the letter directly from the Taoiseach. Butler travelled to Reynolds's apartment in Ballsbridge to pick up the document and was told that it represented the basis for 'a lasting cessation of violence'. Republicans had accepted the consent principle and separate self-determination for the people of Northern Ireland.

Major was still sceptical and there were divisions on the Irish side between Reynolds and Hume. Nonetheless, despite a series of ups and downs, the initiative gradually built up momentum through the remainder of 1993. Reynolds and his officials gradually modified the original Hume-Adams document to make it an acceptable basis for negotiations with Major, and the Taoiseach kept prodding all the negotiators into further compromise. Then in November 1993, the IRA bombed a shop on the Protestant Shankill Road, killing ten people as well as the bomber. 'Feelings of horror, shame and revulsion are everywhere. But above all despair,' wrote Fergus Finlay. 'For many weeks now there has been a growing feeling that, perhaps, some sort of breakthrough is possible. Perhaps whatever is going on between John Hume and Gerry Adams has the seeds of peace in it. And now the IRA has sent what seems like a definitive answer.'[3] When Gerry Adams carried the coffin of the IRA bomber Thomas Begley, it appeared to confirm the notion that republicans had no interest in peace. Further violence then followed as Loyalist paramilitaries retaliated. The massacre of a group of people in a pub in Greysteel was the worst of these atrocities.

Yet John Major believed that in a paradoxical way the wave of violence helped the process in the long term. 'I think it would have broken down had not the Shankill and Greysteel tragedies intervened,' he wrote later. 'In the wave of revulsion that followed the Shankill bomb the Irish Government took a more critical attitude to the Hume-Adams process.'[4] Dick Spring gave expression to the feelings of the Irish electorate by setting out six principles on which any settlement would have to be based, including the principle of consent. Reynolds met Major on the margins of the EU summit in Brussels and agreed a toughly-worded communiqué which said that the two governments would take matters into their own hands. It also accepted that there could be no question of the two governments adopting the raw Hume-Adams proposals. It was a courageous move by Reynolds and showed that he was prepared to take on Adams and Hume if need be, regardless of the political consequences for himself. The dispossessed ex-ministers and their allies within Fianna Fáil who hated Reynolds with a vengeance prepared to savage the Taoiseach if his strategy failed.

But Reynolds kept his nerve. In the next round he went on the offensive and challenged Major at a special Anglo-Irish summit in Dublin Castle. A fierce row developed between the two men when the British proposed yet another new draft of the Declaration rather than the working text which had been painfully put together by officials from both sides. 'You are trying to make a fool out of me, John, and I won't have it. We'll not do business on the basis of this,' said Reynolds, throwing the British draft into the middle of the table during a meeting of the two leaders and their respective delegations. The language got so heated that Major, who was holding a pencil, snapped it in half. He then suggested a private meeting and the two men retired to an anteroom. When they emerged after half-an-hour they both looked pale.

'How did it go, Taoiseach?' asked Fergus Finlay.

'It wasn't too bad. He chewed the bollix off me but I took a few lumps out of him,' replied Reynolds.[5]

Just a little over a week later, on 15 December 1993, Reynolds and Major signed the Joint Declaration in the cabinet room at Downing Street. It was the same room in which Michael Collins and Arthur Griffith had signed the Anglo-Irish Treaty in 1922. It was a truly historic occasion that paved the way for the IRA ceasefire and the Good Friday Agreement. It would never have happened without the drive and bravado of Albert Reynolds and the patience and intelligence of John Major. 'The great point about my relationship with Albert Reynolds was that we liked one another and could have a row without giving up on each other. The air was clearer when we left the room,' recorded Major in his memoirs.[6]

Unfortunately for Reynolds, his relationship with Dick Spring was never remotely as good. The two men were like chalk and cheese and seemed always prepared to think the worst of each other. In contrast to Reynolds's bright and breezy style, Spring was thoughtful and reserved and quick to take offence. Throughout the 1980s he fought a long and courageous battle to get control of the Labour Party and, at times, had barely survived. By the end of 1992, although he was still only 42, he had been leader for ten years and was one of the most experienced politicians in the Dáil. Although he had the triumph of the election behind him, Spring knew that he was taking a big risk by going into coalition with Fianna Fáil. The opinion polls seemed to suggest that the public approved the deal, but many long-time Labour supporters were shocked, and the media, which had been uncharacteristically indulgent towards Spring for the previous two years, suddenly reversed its position and began attacking Labour on a number of fronts. The most spectacular anti-Labour coverage appeared in the *Sunday Independent* but, more ominously as far as the party leadership was concerned, the *Irish Times*, which had long been regarded as at least somewhat pro-Labour, began to turn against the party. Its new-found hostility really disconcerted Spring and his senior colleagues. 'Dick recognised the signs as I did. The media was doing it again,' wrote Finlay. 'Everything we did in opposition had been fully supported by the commentators and the experts. But Labour fighting for implementation of its policy, instead of recognising its natural place as a mudguard for some other, bigger party, simply wasn't acceptable.'[7]

In order to prove that the coalition could work as a partnership, Spring wanted more than the implementation of the agreed 'Programme for Government'. He required Reynolds to act with tact and to treat Labour publicly with respect. For his part, Reynolds quickly came to believe that Spring wanted to dominate the partnership, even though Labour had only half Fianna Fáil's number of seats. He saw Finlay's hand in a spate of newspaper stories suggesting that Labour ministers were really running the show in government and he came to resent it. 'Reynolds was manipulative and impatient of opposition to his wishes. Spring was moody and quick to take offence,' wrote Seán Duignan who famously recorded in his diary: 'I kind of like Spring but he's touchy and, when he's not being touchy, Fergus is touchy for him.'[8]

Finlay's views about Reynolds were not all that different. 'Albert Reynolds had the potential to be truly great. A lot of the criticism levelled against him was unfair – especially in relation to his style and use of language. And I was one of the people who levelled those criticisms. But other criticisms are valid – that he couldn't take no for an answer, that sometimes pride clouded his judgement ... His bottom line was respect and he felt he never got enough.'[9]

The niggling controversies had started right away, at the beginning of 1993. Spring insisted that plans to begin the privatisation of Telecom through a sale of 25 per cent of the company to Cable and Wireless be scrapped. He also demanded a commitment that no sale of state assets would take place during the lifetime of the government. Reynolds gave the commitment after a lot of Labour pressure and threats, but it rankled.

Strangely, Labour took a more low-key approach to what was a far bigger issue – a proposal for another tax amnesty. The previous such amnesty, only five years earlier, had brought in over £500 million to the exchequer. A second amnesty did not appear to make any sense and most Labour ministers were opposed to it, as were the Revenue Commissioners. Why, they asked, should large-scale tax evaders be given a second chance in a few years to have their liabilities written off, particularly as the Revenue were closing in on many of them? Reynolds talked about the extra revenue that would come into the exchequer as a result and offered the carrot of an extra £200 million from the amnesty to fund cherished Labour spending projects.

Spring was caught in a quandary. His economic adviser, Willie Scally, was strongly against the amnesty, but Spring was reluctant to confront Reynolds openly and took comfort from the fact that Bertie Ahern, who brought the formal proposal to cabinet, also opposed it privately on the advice of his officials in Finance. Spring believed a majority of the cabinet shared his view and that there was a good chance Reynolds would be talked out of it by his own people, particularly as the Attorney General, Harry Whelehan, also advised against.

On the day the cabinet was to make the decision Spring's programme manager, Greg Sparks, reported to a routine meeting of Labour ministers, held in advance of cabinet, that he had received a very unusual call at 1 a.m. that morning. The caller was Ahern. The Minister for Finance told Sparks he was still resolutely opposed to the amnesty and determined to ensure that it did not go through: could he be assured that the Labour ministers would back him? Sparks told him he could depend on Labour support.[10] After this briefing, the six Labour ministers trooped into the cabinet meeting. When the agenda item on the amnesty issue came up, the Labour ministers waited for Ahern to express his opposition. They were astounded when, instead of expressing his opposition to it, Ahern actually proposed the amnesty.[11] The Labour leadership was baffled and confused by Ahern's behaviour, but they continued to have good relations with him. Some of the Fianna Fáil ministers, who had longer experience of Ahern's style, were amused at the Labour confusion, but they kept their thoughts about the matter to themselves.

In publicity terms, the tax amnesty was a disaster for both government parties, but particularly for Labour. Even though Reynolds privately insisted that he had achieved a victory over the Department of Finance and not over Labour, the media and the public saw it in different terms. Spring was denounced for allowing the 'cheats' charter' to pass unchallenged. While he subsequently won concessions from Reynolds on other issues, like a reduction in the threshold for the now vanished Residential Property Tax, it did not help him to recover lost ground. The tax amnesty was also a political disaster for Reynolds. There was simply no justification for it so soon after the earlier one. Opponents claimed that the Government had promoted it to look after the interests of a handful of prominent business people who were Fianna Fáil supporters. There was certainly a great deal of public suspicion about the move and it undoubtedly damaged the credibility of the Taoiseach.

The following year another financial issue caused a bitter row between the two leaders. This time it was over proposals for incorporation in the Finance Bill of arrangements to ease the residency requirements for the Irish super-rich. When he was made aware of the proposals shortly before Easter 1994, Spring was infuriated. Reynolds went off for a family holiday in Cyprus, but Spring faxed him an angry warning that he would not stand for a legislative move which Labour interpreted as being designed to benefit people such as Tony O'Reilly, Michael Smurfit and Dermot Desmond. The fax concluded with the blunt threat that Labour would pull out of government if the measure went ahead.

The Taoiseach was furious at being 'dictated to', but he sent a seven-page, hand-written, conciliatory letter to Spring who was meeting in Tralee with his advisers. Out of the blue, Ahern also arrived in Tralee for talks with Spring and the two men spent an hour together in the Brandon Hotel. Ahern told Spring that he did not agree with the proposals either but said Reynolds was refusing to back down. Everybody apart from Spring returned to Dublin that night, and the crisis was defused when Ahern telephoned the Labour leader to say that an angry Reynolds had changed his mind.

Curiously, the proposals to ease the tax residency requirements were not dropped completely, as both Duignan and Finlay recorded in their memoirs. At the committee stage of the Finance Bill, Bertie Ahern introduced a complex amendment providing that tax exiles could spend half the year in Ireland while still retaining their non-resident status for tax purposes. The minister said this was simply bringing Irish practice into line with that in other western countries and the amendment went through with curiously little comment, considering the fuss that had been going on behind the scenes.

Fergus Finlay believes that the row between Reynolds and Spring on the issue marked the beginning of the end for the government. For weeks afterwards, relations between the Taoiseach and the Tánaiste were extremely tense, but no word of the row escaped into the public domain. Before he agreed to modify his original proposals, Reynolds had insisted that he would do so only on condition that there were no leaks. Any hint in the newspapers of a 'Reynolds backs down' story and the deal was off. It was the only time during the Fianna Fáil-Labour government that a serious row did not leak to the press. Behind the scenes, though, the stresses and strains were beginning to show after a little over a year in government.

The tax residency issue had barely died down when along came another damaging row, this time over the 'passports for sale scheme'. The media and the public had previously known little or nothing about this issue, but in June 1994 the news broke that under the scheme the Reynolds family pet food firm had benefited from a £1 million investment. The money had come from a Saudi family called Masri and in return they had been granted Irish citizenship. Reynolds could not see what the fuss was about, arguing that his family business was just as entitled to avail of the scheme as anybody else. The media fulminated about conflicts of interest, Labour agonised and then Spring announced that he had inspected the file on the matter in the Department of Justice. He pronounced that the deal had been conducted in an 'ethical, above board and arms length way'. Another avalanche of criticism poured down on Labour. Michael McDowell, then a PD deputy, told the Dáil that Spring was now 'morally brain dead'. In an attempt to deal with the criticism, the Labour leader announced that the scheme would henceforth be put on a statutory basis. However, when the Fine Gael leader, John Bruton, pressed Reynolds about the matter in the Dáil, the Taoiseach responded by saying that no legislation had been promised. It was a technical response designed to avoid answering Opposition questions, but it infuriated Spring. To those uninitiated in the complexities of parliamentary procedure it seemed that Reynolds was publicly vetoing Spring's announcement.

By this time the PDs also had problems. O'Malley stepped down as party leader in the autumn of 1993 to make way for a younger leader. Mary Harney won the leadership election, beating the MEP and TD Pat Cox. The contest caused considerable bitterness with Cox believing that O'Malley had given Harney an unfair advantage. Then in 1994, after the PDs had nominated O'Malley to run as a European election candidate for Munster, Cox decided that he wanted to run again, and he announced he would be contesting the campaign as an Independent.

Meanwhile the government parties continued to squabble in the run up to the European elections and the two by-elections which were scheduled for the same day in June 1994. All the media focus was on the European result which was bad for Labour. The party's vote was down considerably and Spring's candidate for Dublin, Orla Guerin, was beaten by her running mate, Bernie Malone. Fianna Fáil did well, winning eight seats out of 15, the first time the party had won a majority of Euro seats. On the same day, however, Fianna Fáil lost the two by-elections. Eric Byrne of Democratic Left recaptured his seat in Dublin South-Central following the resignation from the Dáil of John O'Connell, while in Mayo Fine Gael's Michael Ring sensationally beat Beverley Cooper-Flynn for the seat vacated by her father when he went to Brussels. The results meant that the numbers could now be assembled in the Dáil for the rainbow coalition if the need arose. Spring and his advisers immediately spotted the significance. For the first time he was able to toy with the idea that, if the worst came to the worst, an alternative coalition could be formed without the need for a general election. This political consideration was totally lost on Fianna Fáil. Instead, Reynolds and his colleagues interpreted the results as indicating that Labour could not afford a general election in any circumstances. This contradictory reading of the election results proved fatal for the coalition. Just as Spring spotted his escape hatch, Reynolds decided to take no more nonsense from Labour, believing that his junior partner in government had nowhere else to go.

25. COALITION ON THE ROCKS

FROM THE BEGINNING OF THE COALITION Reynolds and Spring were acutely aware that the beef tribunal was a time bomb which had the capacity to destroy the government. To limit the potential for damage, the Taoiseach and Tánaiste agreed at the outset that the recommendations, whatever they were, would be fully implemented. The tribunal had been forced on Fianna Fáil by Spring from the Opposition benches and by Des O'Malley from within the government in 1991. The original intention was for the tribunal to investigate the relationship between Larry Goodman's beef empire and the government, particularly Charles Haughey. However, its terms of reference were drafted so widely by the Department of Agriculture that it was obliged to investigate the whole beef industry. The result was that it trundled along for years, at enormous cost to the taxpayer. At last, by the summer of 1994, the tribunal judge, Mr Justice Liam Hamilton, was ready to report and the political temperature began to rise in anticipation.

Fine Gael's Jim Mitchell caused a sensation in the Dáil by calling attention to a potential conflict of interest involving Hamilton. He said that the public could be forgiven for thinking that judges dependent on the government for promotion might not be as independent as they should be in discharging their duties in relation to the behaviour and performance of serving ministers. 'The president of the High Court is an illustrious judge and is only second in rank to the Chief Justice. It would not be unnatural for him to expect promotion to a vacancy in that office. For such promotion he is depending on the nomination of the present ministers, some of whom have a vested interest in his findings as sole member of the tribunal of inquiry into the beef industry,' said Mitchell.[1] His remarks caused a furore and he was forced to make a personal statement the following day making it clear that he was not impugning the integrity of anyone on the bench. Nonetheless, the message was clear.

With publication of the tribunal's report imminent, media speculation increased and a story by Emily O'Reilly in the *Sunday Business Post* caused immense irritation to Reynolds. The headline ran: 'Spring Ready to Leave Coalition if Tribunal Report Censures Reynolds'. The

Taoiseach immediately detected the hand of an 'unidentified, bearded Labour source', in other words Fergus Finlay.[2] 'No Government can survive this kind of thing,' he remarked. He was particularly annoyed because it followed a serious row at cabinet between Brian Cowen and Ruairí Quinn over the future of Team Aer Lingus.

Finlay was indeed the source of the *Business Post* story. He said later he had no intention of winding up the pressure on Reynolds, that he believed he had only been stating the obvious in a casual conversation in the Dáil bar and that he had no inkling of how his remarks would be used. He offered to meet the Taoiseach to explain the background, but was not taken up on the offer. Weary after a long Dáil session, Finlay went off on holidays with his family to England in the middle of July.[3]

The tribunal report eventually landed on the Taoiseach's desk late in the evening on the last Friday in July, at the start of the bank holiday weekend. It had firstly been delivered to the Department of Agriculture but was quickly dispatched to the Taoiseach's office for assessment. Reynolds went into conclave with his legal team from the tribunal, Henry Hickey and Conor Maguire, who were summoned to the Taoiseach's office. Also there were the Secretary General of the Department, Paddy Teahon, and the cabinet secretary, Frank Murray. Political advisers Tom Savage, Donal Cronin and Seán Duignan joined the effort to make a quick assessment of the 900-page report, a task made hugely difficult because it did not have a conclusion, a set of recommendations or an index. Hickey, Maguire and Savage divided the report into a number of sections and dissected them quickly to try and establish the nature of the verdict. After half-an-hour or so a quick check around the table produced a consensus that the findings did not question Reynolds's motives or impugn his integrity, even though it did offer some criticism of his actions. 'You're in the clear,' remarked one of the advisers. 'Are you sure?' asked Reynolds. 'Yes,' came the reply. 'OK,' said the Taoiseach, 'I've taken this shit long enough. I'm not taking another minute of it. Tell the pol. corrs I'm vindicated, Diggy,' he said, turning to his press secretary.

Duignan hesitated. 'Taoiseach, Labour are going to go spare. They've warned me against this,' he remarked. Teahon supported Duignan: 'You don't need to do this, Taoiseach. You don't need to have a row with Labour. You've won.' Reynolds was not to be swayed. 'They told the dogs in the street they would bring me down on this if they didn't like the judgement. Now I've been cleared and I don't need their permission to tell it as it is.' When Duignan still made no move to go and brief the political correspondents, Reynolds became impatient. 'You're already losing the country editions of the papers, Diggy. Now, if you don't do it, I'll bloody well do it myself.' Duignan bowed to the pressure but insisted that he would have to inform his Labour counterpart, John Foley, what he was going to do. In a phone conversation Foley strongly advised against the move, saying a deal had been made at cabinet that that there would be no individual party reaction to the report. However, Duignan was under orders and proceeded to scribble down selected quotes from different parts of the report to feed to the media.[4]

On the Labour side, Spring decided to stay in Tralee when he heard the news that the report had been handed over to Agriculture, but Finlay flew home from holiday. Spring told him over the phone that an agreement had been reached at cabinet earlier in the week and that no comment would be made by the government until the report had been studied. Spring told Finlay to go to Government Buildings as soon as the report was available along with his private secretary, Niall Burgess. They were to collect Spring's copy and then summon Greg Sparks and Willie Scally to analyse it with them. They learned early in the evening that the report had been handed over by Agriculture to the Taoiseach's Department, but they were unable to obtain a copy in the department where Spring and his staff had an office. Spring was told of the situation and tried, without success, to contact Reynolds by phone.

There are widely differing accounts on either side about what happened next. Having entered Government Buildings, Finlay tried unsuccessfully to gain access to Reynolds's office. He maintains that a set of double doors on the corridor, which he had never noticed before, had been pulled over and locked. He knocked on the doors, to no avail. Fianna Fáil people present that evening are adamant that this never happened and that the doors were certainly not locked.

One way or another Finlay failed to make contact with Reynolds or any of his senior staff. He looked into Duignan's office but found it empty. The phone was ringing and Finlay decided to pick it up. On the line was RTÉ's political editor, Donal Kelly, who was very surprised to hear Finlay on the other end of the line.

'What are you doing there at this time of night?' asked Kelly.

'Why not?' was all Finlay could think of to say in response. 'I work here, after all,' he added.

'Well, can you tell me when we're going to get the statement that's been promised?' asked Kelly.

Before Finlay had time to answer, Duignan came striding into the room and was astonished to find the Labour adviser on the phone in his office. Duignan took the phone and told Kelly he would call him back. It was a tense moment for the two advisers who had had a good personal relationship. Finlay felt Duignan was deeply embarrassed and unhappy at the situation, while Duignan thought Finlay looked like an 'Old

Testament whirlwind of wrath, biblical beard quivering' and was about to flip. Both men have written since about that scene in the government press secretary's office and they disagree about whether Finlay actually flung the phones around the office in a rage or whether he merely tripped over the extension chord and dragged it to the floor. The one thing Duignan is certain about is hearing Finlay proclaim fiercely: 'This could mean the end of the Government – you have been warned.'⁵

The rest of the night was filled with fraught exchanges as the various participants responded to the events. 'That's it. Collective responsibility, my eye! How can I stay in a Government where I'm told that I cannot speak to my Taoiseach about an absolutely crucial matter like this?' remarked Spring to Finlay. The media too played a part in fuelling the animosity between the two sides. Duignan rang around the various newsrooms to give the Reynolds line, but he was challenged by Jackie Gallagher, then a financial journalist with the *Irish Times*. 'Gallagher insists that I'm purporting to speak on Spring's behalf as well as Albert's,' Duignan noted. 'He subsequently tells this to Labour which drives Dick around the twist. He [Spring] rings Frank Murray and warns of implications for the Government.'⁶

Eventually at around 1 a.m. Reynolds and Spring finally spoke on the phone. The Labour leader was furious and he accused the Taoiseach of indulging in improper behaviour. There were further angry exchanges before Reynolds asked: 'Would you deny me my hour in the sun?' Spring's reply was ominous. 'There may be no sun, Albert. This is bad.'

The following day Fine Gael leader John Bruton pointed out publicly that Spring could leave the government and form an alternative administration involving Fine Gael and Democratic Left. The suggestion was treated as absurd by the media and many in the Labour Party, but Spring had been thinking about it since the by-election results in June. It was not an option that he wanted to take but he was keenly aware that it was there if he needed it. It had never been done in the history of the state and would be very difficult to pull off, but the Labour leader drew some comfort from the fact that he had more options available to him than anybody in Fianna Fáil was prepared to recognise.

In the days following the publication of the report tempers cooled a bit and the Taoiseach and Tánaiste managed to patch things up. However, the incident stretched their relationship to breaking point and they never recovered from the stress. Reynolds was the one to suffer in the public eye because the media focused on the row over his 'I'm vindicated' leak rather than the actual content of the report itself. While the report was hardly a total vindication for him it was certainly not the damning indictment his political opponents and much of the media had expected. If he had not jumped the gun, Reynolds would have been on strong ground as there was nothing in the report that would have done him serious damage. His premature reaction gave the public the impression that he had something to hide and that proved very damaging.

Reynolds was under pressure on another front in the summer of 1994. The foot-dragging by the republican movement in response to the Joint Declaration had gone on for much longer than anyone had expected. Endless requests by Sinn Féin for clarification were punctuated by random acts of IRA violence. All eyes were on the Sinn Féin Árd Fheis in Letterkenny for a signal that an IRA ceasefire was on the way. Instead the tone was extremely negative and many people began to despair about the prospects of peace. Reynolds, though, maintained a buoyant optimism. He was in possession of information from senior republican sources which gave a very different perspective, and he got his officials to persuade the British to be restrained in their response. However, at a reception for political journalists at the beginning of July, the Taoiseach found it impossible to convince them that there was still a real chance of a ceasefire. 'Nobody believes me. Even Diggy won't believe me any more but I know there's still a chance,' he told his sceptical listeners.

A few weeks later the debate within the republican movement entered a critical phase. In late August a delegation of Irish-Americans who had huge influence with the republican leadership came to Ireland to establish what the IRA was going to do. The key figure in the delegation was businessman Bill Flynn, accompanied by journalist Neil O'Dowd and former Congressman Bruce Morrison. Before they went to Belfast to find out from Gerry Adams what had been decided, the delegation met Reynolds and Spring in Dublin. They raised the possibility of a temporary ceasefire, but were stunned by Reynolds's emphatic reaction.

'Permanent,' snapped the Taoiseach. 'No pussy-footing. I haven't devoted two years of my life to this in order to be insulted with a temporary ceasefire. And another thing: I want their announcement to be written in language that an 11-year-old can understand. No messing, there's to be no messing.'

Reynolds was also firm on another issue that later bedevilled the peace process for a considerable amount of time. He was asked about the issue of arms and the desire of the IRA to hold on to them, even if there was a ceasefire. 'What do they need weapons for?' he asked. He was told that they would argue that some were needed for defensive purposes. 'Look. They're either at war or they're in politics. If they're in politics they don't need guns. Full stop.'[7]

The Taoiseach's blunt message clarified things for the American delegation and for the republican movement. It was all or nothing as far as Reynolds was concerned. It was typical of his style not to tolerate half-measures but to go for broke at the decisive moment. This time, on the biggest issue of them all, his tactics worked. He had a few sticky moments, the biggest of them getting President Clinton to sanction a US visa for IRA veteran Joe Cahill to allow him to travel to New York to talk republicans there into agreeing to a ceasefire.

The long-awaited IRA announcement came on 31 August. 'A complete cessation of military operations' from midnight on that date was announced. 'We believe that an opportunity to secure a just and lasting settlement has been created,' declared the IRA who went on to demand inclusive negotiations on a political settlement. Almost immediately a debate began as to whether 'a complete cessation' amounted to a permanent ceasefire. However, there was no disguising the historic significance of the IRA announcement.

Clinton rang Reynolds to congratulate him. Then John Major rang. 'We did it together,' Reynolds told the Prime Minister. Major was cautious about counting his chickens at that stage but the Taoiseach was ebullient. Hindsight has proved Reynolds right. Whatever his other political triumphs and disasters, the Joint Declaration and the IRA ceasefire were monumental achievements. It was Charles Haughey who once remarked that nobody would go down in history for getting the economy right, but the individual who settled the Irish question would go into the history books. Many politicians, including Haughey himself, played a part in the evolving peace process in the 1990s but Reynolds deserves more credit than anyone else. Without his drive, his tunnel vision and, indeed, his recklessness, it would probably never have happened. The announcement of the IRA ceasefire was his finest hour but, for him, it was a heartbreakingly brief hour in the sun. The highest point in Albert's political career was followed by a sickeningly rapid descent into the political abyss.

On the day the ceasefire was announced the Dáil had been recalled to debate the beef tribunal report. In the light of the IRA announcement the debate was postponed for 24 hours and instead the Dáil debated the implications of the ceasefire. It was a day of glory for Reynolds as he received the congratulations of all sides. Bruton accepted the Taoiseach's contention that the ceasefire was permanent even if that precise word was not used in the IRA announcement.

'Every Irish person at home and abroad will welcome with relief and thanksgiving the decision announced today of an end to the 25-year-old IRA campaign,' said Reynolds. 'It is a day that many had begun to fear they might never see. We all hope that it will be swiftly followed by an end to paramilitary violence on all sides and consolidated by a gradual and general process of demilitarisation and that it will facilitate the achievement of a comprehensive negotiated political settlement. A long nightmare is coming to an end.'[8] Reynolds went out of his way to pay tribute to Spring for his contribution to the process and the Labour leader returned the compliment, congratulating the Taoiseach on what had been achieved.

The following day the honeyed words were set aside as the Dáil debated the beef tribunal report. Reynolds was adamant that the tribunal chairman, Mr Justice Liam Hamilton, had given the final word on the truth or otherwise of the allegations he was asked to investigate and that it was 'dishonourable and improper to seek to go behind his final report'. The Taoiseach again claimed vindication. 'First and last the tribunal was about integrity. The integrity of the Government and of the public administration formed the main focus of the tribunal's inquiries and its findings are clear. I have been fully and totally vindicated, both personally and as a Minister. My decisions at the time, the report confirms, were taken in the national interest.'[9]

Fine Gael leader John Bruton, in the course of a detailed critique of Reynolds's behaviour, also took Spring and his colleagues to task. 'I say to the Labour Party: If you believe in accountable Government you must be willing to call people to account. If Deputy Reynolds is demonstrated in this debate to have breached the trust given to him as a Minister then he should not continue as Taoiseach. Otherwise there will be no accountability. If you, the Labour Party, for the sake of political convenience, try to avoid that issue, you will be burying the concept of public accountability deeper than it has ever been buried in the history of this House. Ethics Bills are only window dressing if transgressors are not called to account at the highest level.'[10]

Spring was clearly uncomfortable at his position in the debate and he spoke publicly for the first time about Reynolds's handling of the report on the night of publication which, he said, failed to reflect the principle of trust on which the Government was founded. 'In that sense it was completely unacceptable to me. It was also counter-productive. The Taoiseach is aware of my strong feelings in the matter ... We have discussed the leaking of sections of the report candidly with each other. He knows that the action damaged trust. The Taoiseach knows that I am prepared to work to restore it and I believe he is too.' Spring then issued his final warning. 'The truth is that if both sides in this Government are willing to see it as a genuine partnership which puts the interests of the people first, this administration will succeed in its many tasks. If delicate and sensitive situations are to be played for party or personal advantage this Government will fail. I do not want that to happen – but it is not up to me alone. It will require a new commitment on all sides.'[11] Spring's public message to Reynolds was crystal clear but, for a variety of reasons, the Taoiseach failed to grasp it. He lived to rue the consequences.

26. ALBERT PULLS THE HOUSE DOWN

WITH THE BEEF TRIBUNAL DEBATE OUT OF THE WAY Reynolds again basked in the glow of his successful Anglo-Irish policy. Spring departed the country to brief a series of notables, including President Clinton and German Foreign Minister Klaus Kinkel, about the implications of the ceasefire. It was on the government jet on the way back from Berlin that the Labour leader was given the first intimations of a problem that led to the destruction of the coalition. His private secretary handed him the agenda for the following day's cabinet meeting. One of the items was the appointment of the new Chief Justice. Accompanying it was a memorandum from the Minister for Justice, Máire Geoghegan-Quinn, recommending the president of the High Court and author the beef tribunal report, Mr Justice Liam Hamilton, for the position. The agenda also referred to filling the subsequent vacancy as president of the High Court but no names were mentioned.[1]

Spring was surprised because he had discussed the issue with Reynolds some time before and the two men had disagreed. Reynolds had made it clear that he wanted Hamilton; Spring had made it equally clear that he wanted the eminent judge Donal Barrington, then serving in the European Court, to come home to fill the position. There was some irony in all of this because Hamilton, the Fianna Fáil nominee had, in his younger days, been a member of the Labour Party and contested the 1965 local elections as a party candidate. He was appointed to the bench at the instigation of Labour during the 1973-77 coalition. By contrast, Spring's nominee, Barrington, had Fianna Fáil links in his younger days and the party backed his promotion to the bench.

Spring's plan to promote Barrington's cause foundered because a legal technicality, subsequently repealed under pressure from Labour, prevented a judge moving directly from a European Court to the Irish Supreme Court.

The Attorney General, Harry Whelehan, then told Spring that he would be interested in filling the vacancy as president of the High Court if Hamilton were promoted. The convention is that a serving Attorney General has first option on senior judicial vacancies so Whelehan's ambition to take a High Court position was not all that surprising. However, his desire to become its president, the second most senior position after the Chief Justice, without first serving as an ordinary judge of the courts came as a big surprise to Spring. When he told Fergus Finlay about the approach and was asked in return whether he had given Whelehan any satisfaction, Spring replied, 'You must be joking.'[2]

The Labour leader's succinct and negative response was based on a number of grounds but the fundamental reason was that Spring wanted the job to go to someone with liberal, leftish credentials. The Labour side regarded Whelehan as a conservative Catholic who would bring that perspective to the bench.

As Attorney General, Harry Whelehan had been at the centre of controversy on a number of occasions, most notably because of his intervention in the X case. Some Fianna Fáil politicians felt that he should have followed the well-worn Irish tradition by turning a blind eye to the case. He himself saw it as his clear duty, as guardian of the Constitution, to act once the matter was brought to his attention. A polite and pleasant man, Whelehan did give the impression at times of being an innocent abroad in the cut-throat atmosphere of Leinster House. 'Harry doesn't have a political bone in his body,' was a refrain frequently heard from Fianna Fáil TDs. However, Labour and the PDs regarded him as very much a Fianna Fáil Attorney General.

This was the background to the item on the cabinet agenda of 7 September. Spring was taken aback by its appearance without prior notice, even though there had not been any agreement on the matter. He met Reynolds before the cabinet meeting and it was agreed to withdraw the item from that day's agenda. Over the following days, the two men discussed the issue again. Spring told Reynolds that Labour would accept the appointment of Whelehan to the High Court, but not as president. His choice for the presidency was Susan Denham, a 48-year-old High Court judge who had been appointed to the court by Haughey and who was widely regarded as a liberal. A week later, when Spring was in Japan and Reynolds about to go to Australia, the original proposal re-appeared on the cabinet agenda. Ruairí Quinn got through to Spring at a public coin box in Tokyo airport and it was agreed that Labour ministers would not accept the appointment.

The cabinet meeting was delayed for three hours while Quinn and Brendan Howlin negotiated with Reynolds. Seán Duignan, who joked at the time that, like Inspector Clouseau's boss, his right eyelid began to twitch every time he heard mention of Harry Whelehan's name, recalled the atmosphere in the Taoiseach's office that morning: 'Cabinet delayed for hours. Quinn comes back up looking like death. I do my Diggyshrugging bit as he passes out from the Taoiseach's office. He looks right through me.' Reynolds was adamant that the matter was rightfully on the cabinet agenda, as it had not been taken the previous week. 'I'm going down there and I'm going to appoint Liam Hamilton without conditions. They walk out, they walk out. They want to bring the thing down, so be it,' he told Duignan.[3]

This, of course, was Reynolds purposely missing the point. Labour's main objection was not to Hamilton's promotion but to the proposed Whelehan appointment. Eventually Quinn came back to Reynolds to say that Labour would agree to Hamilton's appointment without conditions but the filling of the subsequent vacancy should be deferred until the two leaders sorted matters out. Afterwards Finlay approached Duignan to emphasise that Spring would resign from the government if the appointment of Whelehan went ahead. 'I'm just telling you that if he tries to force Harry on us we will make the beef tribunal row look like a storm in a teacup.'

Reynolds then departed to Australia while Spring was still in the Far East. It did not take long for the row over the Whelehan appointment to leak out and it filled the newspapers the following Sunday. The story was that Labour had blocked Whelehan and wanted Susan Denham to fill the position. Most Fianna Fáil and Labour TDs regarded the controversy as a storm in a teacup. The late Pat Upton summed up the mood around Leinster House by facetiously wondering aloud whether the row would stir the public into 'Whelehanite and Denhamite' factions. The bemusement of TDs was shared by the general public, who could not figure out what the controversy was all about. What nobody appreciated was that as far as Reynolds and Spring were concerned the issue had become a point of honour on which they were prepared for a duel to the political death.

As media controversy and speculation developed into a frenzy at home, Reynolds made a triumphant tour of Australia and New Zealand on the strength of his achievement regarding the peace process. Spring, too, was travelling most of the time and the two men managed only one phone conversation in ten days. The call settled nothing. On a farcical note, Reynolds finally arrived home on 30 September by way of Shannon to keep an appointment with the Russian President, Boris Yeltsin, who was on his way back from the US. Yeltsin refused to disembark to meet the Taoiseach, the general assumption being that he was too drunk to come down the steps, and Reynolds had to wait around for hours as Yeltsin remained inside the plane. Eventually the deputy prime minister emerged to fill the gap and shake hands with Reynolds, who, tongue in cheek, offered to go aboard the plane to meet Yeltsin. This caused consternation in the Russian camp and was hastily refused. It was a moment of light relief in an increasingly gloomy political landscape.[4]

The general media mood now swung in favour of Reynolds. He basked in the unexpected glow of *Irish Times* approval as the newspaper chided Spring in an editorial for making such a fuss over a judicial appointment. But if Reynolds began to feel things were going his way, he was soon disillusioned. On his first weekend home, a headline in the *Sunday Press* read: 'Spring to Walk if Harry Gets Job.' The story cited Labour sources as saying that Spring would bring down the government rather than agree to Whelehan's appointment. It added that Labour now regarded Reynolds as a bully who would never learn how to behave.[5]

Two days later, Reynolds made a stern public riposte which worried some of his own leading ministers, like Charlie McCreevy and Máire Geoghegan-Quinn, who feared he was risking his position needlessly. Finally, the Taoiseach and Tánaiste met face-to-face to sort out the problem, falling back on the tried and trusted political method of kicking to touch – they established a sub-committee. Then, as the mood continued to swing against Labour, the party backbenchers panicked. A string of them queued up to go on radio saying it was time for Spring to back off. Their anxieties were heightened by an opinion poll that showed a serious slippage in Labour support. The ground appeared to have been cut from under Spring when he met Reynolds for a secret midnight summit at Baldonnel airport. 'God, Dick, we must be mad to be in this job when we have to meet like this in an airport at all hours of the night; it's no way to live,' Reynolds breezily remarked, arriving nearly two hours late.[6] The two men agreed not to allow the situation to spill over into a general election and made a deal to revamp the whole judicial appointments system. Spring accepted that when the details of the court reforms were worked out in a matter of weeks, the issue of judicial appointments could come back to the cabinet table. He did not specifically agree to the appointment of Whelehan, but even Labour sources conceded that it was implicit in the deal.[7] As far as Reynolds was concerned he had won, but he was prepared to give Spring time to eat humble pie. It was one of the biggest mistakes of his political career.

Within a week of the Baldonnel accord Reynolds was made aware that there had been some problem about the response of the Attorney General's office in Dublin to an extradition request from the RUC relating to a paedophile priest, Fr Brendan Smyth. At this stage, Smyth was in jail in Northern Ireland for his activities but a television programme about him heightened public awareness of the matter. Then the story broke in the Irish newspapers that an extradition warrant for Smyth had been with the Attorney General's office for seven months, without any action being taken. Spring suddenly had a weapon in his hands to renew his resistance to the appointment of Whelehan to the presidency of the High Court. 'The priest changes everything,' Labour's John Foley told Duignan. Reynolds could not see why and kept repeating, 'Dick and I have a deal.' Spring demanded a report on the delay from Whelehan and got one that he considered unsatisfactory.

Finally Reynolds lost patience and demanded that the issue be decided by cabinet. It was due for decision on 10 November but was put back for a day because of the murder by republicans of a post-office worker in Newry. Reynolds knew that Spring was still determined to resist the appointment of Whelehan. In fact, the Labour ministers agreed to attend the cabinet meeting only because Reynolds persuaded them that they should listen to the Attorney General's explanation for the extradition delay. The explanation did not mollify Spring, but Reynolds, manifesting the same risk-taking qualities that had proved so successful in the peace process, pressed ahead with the appointment regardless. This time, they proved his undoing.

Without demur the Fianna Fáil ministers present approved the appointment of Harry Whelehan as president of the High Court. Not one of them raised an objection, not even Geoghegan-Quinn who was privately seething at the decision. McCreevy, the most outspoken and independent-minded of the Fianna Fáil ministers, was out of the country at the time and the others felt they had no option but to go along with Reynolds and call the Labour bluff. The Labour ministers watched in silence as the Fianna Fáil majority approved the appointment. Believing that dramatic action would force Reynolds to reconsider, Spring took the unprecedented step of leading his ministers in a walkout from the cabinet room. 'Jesus Christ! Albert gambled and lost. We finally got caught,' was Duignan's reaction when Noel Dempsey told him of the development.[8] That afternoon the results of two Cork by-elections were announced. Fine Gael won one of the seats and Democratic Left the other. Fianna Fáil did badly but Labour was trounced in both constituencies and their setback encouraged Reynolds to go for broke. Some of his more short-sighted ministers and TDs believed that the bad result would deter Spring from pulling the plug. Other, more astute, players of the game like Duignan knew that the decision was disastrous.

Reynolds was calm now that the die had been cast. After a time he picked up the phone and rang Spring who was closeted in his Leinster House office with his ministerial colleagues and top advisers. 'What'll we tell the press? Is it over, or what?' asked Reynolds. Spring told him the situation was grave and that he would be consulting his parliamentary party. The Taoiseach, undeterred, headed for Áras an Uachtaráin with his new High Court president and the Minister for Justice,

Geoghegan-Quinn, for the official ceremony with President Mary Robinson at which Whelehan's appointment was formally made. The atmosphere in the Áras was cold and unreal with everybody, apart from a beaming Whelehan, conscious that they were in the middle of a major political crisis. The President was glacial and even the new Attorney General, Eoghan Fitzsimons, who was there to get his seal of office, looked grim. 'Extraordinary haste,' muttered the President's special advisor, Bride Rosney.

After the short ceremony Geoghegan-Quinn marched over to a still beaming Whelehan and hissed, 'When I'm out in the snow on the election trail in Galway and people on the doorsteps ask me "What about Harry Whelehan?" I'm going to reply, "Fuck Harry Whelehan".' It was a sentiment shared by some of the other Fianna Fáil ministers but none of them had spoken up an hour earlier to try to deter Reynolds from his folly.

Why did Reynolds do it? The appointment of Whelehan made no political sense and there was no internal political pressure on Reynolds to make it. The reason none of his ministers or advisers made a strong stand against it was that they could see Albert's determination to get his way, regardless of the consequences. The assessment from the Taoiseach's special adviser Martin Mansergh was simple: 'The Taoiseach was engaged in a power play that went hideously wrong – what he wanted, he had to have, and that was the end of the matter.'[9] The assessment from Spring's special adviser Fergus Finlay was not very different: 'Albert felt he had been bested in relation to residency tax changes, made beholden in relation to the Masri affair and abandoned in relation to the publication of the beef tribunal report. In my opinion he was wrong on all counts, but that didn't matter. He decided that the battle over Harry Whelehan was one he had to win.'

Whether Reynolds was right or wrong in his list of grievances against Labour is a matter for debate, but Finlay is basically right in his assessment of Reynolds's motivation. Of course the Fianna Fáil ministers felt that Spring was equally obdurate and pig-headed. They believed that in government they had given Labour more scope than the party had ever had in any previous coalition with Fine Gael and that Spring was prepared to throw it all away because of pride.

The appointment of Whelehan and the Labour walkout happened on a Friday evening. That weekend the media were full of hostile comment on Reynolds's behaviour. It was an eerie rerun of the breakdown with O'Malley two years earlier. Just as on that occasion, the media was reasonably neutral until the actual breakdown but then the scorn and derision was poured on Reynolds for forcing the breach. He decided over the weekend that his only chance of saving the government was to address the Dáil the following Tuesday to explain the position and hopefully to persuade Labour to come back on board.

The Labour backbenchers, who had been distinctly cool about Spring's strategy in risking so much over the appointment of a judge, rallied to the party flag. Spring called an emergency meeting of the parliamentary party for Jury's Hotel on Sunday, 13 November and made a powerful speech pointing out the achievements of the government, including the peace process, but, notwithstanding the successes he stated: 'Last Friday collective cabinet responsibility broke down. The ethos of partnership, which has informed the achievements of this Government, was abandoned.' That was the nub. Spring went on to tell his TDs that he would have to make the final decision on what to do but he proposed to attend the next scheduled cabinet meeting on Tuesday morning with his Labour colleagues. Spring then turned to the Fr Brendan Smyth affair.

'At the end of the day, when all other questions have been dealt with, one remains. We have allowed a child abuser to remain at large in our community, when we had it in our power to ensure that he was given up to justice. Is no one to explain why? Is no one to take responsibility? Is no one to account to the people of this country for so grievous a lapse?'[10] The speech was made in private but when garbled versions were published in the media Reynolds and Fianna Fáil interpreted it as an unfair charge that they were in some way prepared to cover up for a paedophile. Fergus Finlay said subsequently that this was an absurd reading of Spring's speech, which was essentially about accountability, but it was a reading that suggested itself to many of the Labour TDs present. In media interviews they laid heavy stress on the issue of child abuse and Fianna Fáil's perceived failure on that issue. Spring was backed to the hilt by his backbenchers who vied with each other to express their loyalty and support, just weeks after they had tried to out-do each other expressing the opposite view.

Many of the TDs believed that an election was the only possible outcome at this stage, but some people in the leadership had different views. In the corridors of Jury's Hotel an alternative option was being bruited about. If Fianna Fáil dumped Reynolds and installed Bertie Ahern in his place then Humpty Dumpty could be put together again.

27. ALBERT AT BAY

THE FINAL DAYS OF THE REYNOLDS GOVERNMENT were some of the most extraordinary in Irish politics. They were made more remarkable by the fact that most of the events unfolded out in the open for everybody to see. Over the course of three days of Dáil debate, broadcast live to the nation, Reynolds, like a fox with the pack in full cry behind him, dodged this way and that. Supposedly strong leads, which were invested with all sorts of importance at the time, proved ultimately to be false trails. Once, Reynolds even doubled back and came within a whisker of freedom but, just as he appeared to have reached safety, the cry went up and the motley pack was after him again. Eventually he was run to ground and his political life destroyed in full public view over the course of a working week. It was painful to watch and even some of the Labour top brass, who were the architects of his destruction, winced at the end. The only people whose joy was unconfined was the Haughey faction within Fianna Fáil.

The final act in the drama began on Monday, 14 November 1994 with an emergency meeting of Fianna Fáil ministers that morning. The mood had changed completely over the weekend and the imperative now was to find a way of patching up a deal with Labour. On the previous evening the Minister for Justice, Máire Geoghegan-Quinn, had asked the new Attorney General, Eoghan Fitzsimons, to go back over Harry Whelehan's handling of the Smyth case to see that everything that been done properly. When the cabinet met, Seamus Brennan informed Fianna Fáil colleagues about contacts with Labour's deputy leader, Ruairí Quinn, who had suggested a way out of the quandary for Reynolds. This involved the Taoiseach gorging himself on vast quantities of humble pie. He would have to come into the Dáil the following day and apologise to the Irish people for the handling of the Smyth case, promise a total reform of the Attorney General's office and under no circumstances defend the handling of the case by Whelehan. On top of that, he would have to pay tribute to the contribution of Dick Spring and Labour to the government and express regret to Spring at the way he had broken trust. It was a tall order and there was no guarantee that, even if the conditions were met, Labour would come back.[1]

Work was begun on the draft of a speech to mollify Labour but Reynolds and his ministers were also furiously searching for other avenues of retreat. Fitzsimons, the tall and aesthetic-looking new Attorney General, was a central figure in this search for an escape. He had no political experience worth speaking of but came to his new job with a reputation for being as straight as a die. Some of his more political colleagues in the Law Library even regarded him as too inflexible. On his first working day in the job, he was plunged into the middle of an extraordinary political crisis. He started work shortly after 8 a.m. and within a couple of hours of consultation with his legal staff had unearthed information which suggested that there was a possible flaw in his predecessor's handling of the Smyth case. Whelehan had stated in his report to the cabinet that the Smyth case was the first one in which a section of the Extradition Act relating to lapse of time had been considered in the handling of the case. Fitzsimons reported that the files showed there had been an earlier extradition request for a man called Duggan, in which the time factor had been considered. If Fitzsimons was right then Whelehan had been wrong to say that the Smyth case was the first. However, the senior legal officer in charge of the Attorney General's office, Matt Russell, strongly rejected the suggestion that the two cases were comparable. Whether or not the two cases were is a matter of legal opinion. In hindsight some lawyers agreed with Russell while others agreed with Fitzsimons. Whether the cases were comparable or not, within weeks nobody could remember clearly what the row was about but, in the frenzied atmosphere of those November days, the Smyth affair assumed a central importance.

Fitzsimons met Reynolds and the Fianna Fáil ministers and broke the news of the Duggan case to them that Monday morning. Whether the Taoiseach and his ministers understood the full legal and political implications became a matter of dispute later. What is not in dispute is that Fitzsimons was asked to approach Harry Whelehan to see if he would consent to postpone for a few days his swearing in as a judge, due to take place the following morning. The new Attorney General called out to see Whelehan at his home in Howth and told him about the discovery of the Duggan case and its possible implications. 'Mr Fitzsimons came to my home and conveyed to me the suggestion that I consider my position and/or postpone taking the oath of office,' recalled Whelehan, who was shocked at the suggestion. He said he considered it 'inappropriate and constitutionally incorrect and improper' that members of the government should bring pressure to bear on a judge to resign from office. Fitzsimons went back to Government Buildings and reported his conversation to the Fianna Fáil ministers.[2]

The Taoiseach and his ministers met late into the night. Reynolds balked at the suggestion from Labour intermediaries that he should apologise to Spring. However, even though he felt Labour was intent on a split, he wanted to go as far as he could to meet their demands. A number of ministers, including McCreevy and Cowen, along with the Taoiseach's adviser, Martin Mansergh, and his media guru, Tom Savage, worked on the draft of his speech until 5 a.m. on Tuesday morning. It was decided that Reynolds would use the word 'regret' rather than 'apologise' but the five points demanded by Labour intermediaries would be included.

When the normal working day began, Harry Whelehan was formally sworn in as president of the High Court. As the tired Fianna Fáil ministers drifted in to Government Buildings during the morning, the word was that four Labour ministers – Quinn, Brendan Howlin, Michael D. Higgins and Mervyn Taylor – were prepared to accept the proposed speech from Reynolds. Ominously though, Spring's feelings on the matter were unknown when the division bells began to ring to summon deputies to the Dáil chamber shortly before 2.30 p.m. Seán Duignan has a vivid recollection of the walk across the tunnel from Government Buildings to the Dáil chamber. 'Albert like a boxer flanked by handlers filing down the long corridor to the arena: words of encouragement, Noel Treacy at his shoulder, McCreevy whispering in his ear.'[3]

In the meantime Fitzsimons arrived at the Taoiseach's office, just after Reynolds had left, with a letter containing his definitive advice on the significance of the Duggan case and other documents, including a suggested answer to a possible Opposition question on the issue. Some ministers, including Geoghegan-Quinn, were still there and the Attorney General spoke to them. He understood from Geoghegan-Quinn that she was not willing to take the documents down to Reynolds, but she later claimed that he was wrong about this. Fitzsimons then gave the documents to the Taoiseach's private secretary, Declan Ingoldsby, who copied them and tried to get them to Reynolds. Ingoldsby handed copies to Paddy Teahon, the secretary of the department, who passed them on to cabinet secretary Frank Murray. He passed them to the chief whip, Dempsey, who in turn passed them to Bertie Ahern who was sitting beside Reynolds. Ahern never passed the documents on to Reynolds. Amazingly, a second copy of the possible reply to an Opposition question was also in Ahern's file, placed there by Geoghegan-Quinn, but neither copy was brought to the Taoiseach's attention.

In his speech to the Dáil, Reynolds tried to undo the damage of the previous Friday. He made no bones about the fact that the delay in exercising the extradition warrant in the Smyth case was inexcusable. 'There was an unacceptable delay in the handling of this case for which we all in Government must take responsibility. On my behalf, and on behalf of the

Government, I wish to express my deep regret to the Irish people for the delays that occurred. I give a solemn assurance in this House today that such a situation will never arise again on the part of an organ of state whose special duty it is to look after the rights of citizens. I want to take this opportunity of confirming categorically to the House that I have been assured by the then Attorney General that he did not know and was not made aware of the existence of a request for the extradition of Fr Brendan Smyth until recent weeks.'[4]

Reynolds then told the Dáil of his decision to institute an immediate review of the operations of the Attorney General's office to be completed within three weeks. Turning to the politics of the issue he defended his decision to appoint Whelehan, giving details of the deadlock between himself and Spring over the matter. 'It would be a great pity if a Government that is achieving rapid economic progress, that has achieved the biggest breakthrough in Northern Ireland in over 25 years and that has a fine legislative programme, should be placed in jeopardy over misunderstandings surrounding a single judicial appointment. In particular, it is my profound conviction that we have to give the fragile Northern peace process the best possible chance of permanent consolidation. I believe the national interest requires continuity at this time. We must all work to restore the spirit of partnership, which is the cornerstone of this successful Government. I solemnly commit myself as Taoiseach and leader of Fianna Fáil to restoring that spirit of partnership and trust.'[5]

Finally, in an attempt to persuade Spring to return, Reynolds referred to the Labour leader's indispensable contribution to the peace process. 'I want again to pay tribute in particular to the dedication and expertise which he brought to these delicate and protracted negotiations, the success of which will underwrite the future of this country. History will recall Deputy Spring's essential contribution to that success. We can go forward from here and build on that success. I know that Deputy Spring and the Labour Party are the right partners to achieve that goal.'[6]

Fianna Fáil ministers were confident that the speech would do the trick and they were shocked when word came back to the Taoiseach's office almost immediately that it would not do. Duignan met Spring's programme manager, Greg Sparks, in the corridor and was told it was not enough. In response Duignan muttered something about a general election and was surprised when Sparks paused and merely conceded that one would probably happen. 'Jesus. "Probably", my arse. Suddenly, it's clear, They're going to go for it. Gambling just like Albert. The trick is no election. Shaft Albert but stick with Fianna Fáil? Albert may have walked into a trap,' thought Duignan.[7]

That night the atmosphere became even more hysterical. The

Duggan case was back at the centre of the political agenda. Reynolds now said that its significance had not been made clear to him earlier in the day and he complained bitterly that the note from Fitzsimons on the issue had not been passed on to him. He did not read the documentation from Fitzsimons until 9 p.m. that evening. The Taoiseach stunned Duignan by saying he felt betrayed by Whelehan. 'Harry could become the first senior member of the judiciary in the history of the state to be impeached,' he added to an incredulous Duignan. That evening Fitzsimons was dispatched back out to Whelehan's house but was again rebuffed.

Back in Government Buildings, Duignan joined Cowen, McCreevy, Dempsey, Woods and Smith as they held a running council of war with Reynolds and reported back on their contacts with Labour. McCreevy had met the Labour senator Pat Magner, a key figure in the party, who had indicated that if Reynolds were prepared to say certain things the next day all might not be lost. Around 11 p.m. the phone went in the Taoiseach's office. It was Howlin ringing for McCreevy, but as he was in another room drafting the speech, Noel Dempsey took the call. The message was a hopeful one for Reynolds, as long as he was prepared to deliver a number of specified remarks to meet Labour concerns in his speech the following day. 'Howlin indicated to me that he and other people in the Labour Party were anxious that the government should continue ... He indicated a certain reluctance, as he said himself – maybe he put it a little bit stronger – to going into Government with Fine Gael.' The question was whether Howlin was speaking for the Labour Party. Dempsey rang him back at 1 a.m. to say there was no problem in principle with accepting the statements Howlin wanted included in the speech. Again the question was whether Howlin could deliver Spring. The Labour minister told Dempsey that his 'arse was out the window on this one' but he believed he could deliver.[8]

Reynolds and his ministers kicked the issue around. They now believed that all was not yet lost if the Taoiseach went into the Dáil the next day to say he would never have appointed Whelehan if he had only known then what he knew now about the Duggan case and that Spring was right all along.

Duignan was aghast at the strategy. 'Why go out this way? If we stick with Harry, you at least go out with your head high,' he told the Taoiseach. Reynolds's faced hardened. 'It has to be done,' he replied. Later in the conversation when the significance of the Duggan case was being discussed a thought struck Duignan and he intervened again. 'What about knowing it on Monday? What about Eoghan Fitzsimons telling you all about the Duggan case?' he asked Reynolds. 'We couldn't take it in then. Fitzsimons couldn't make up his mind about its actual significance and effect. I told him to go away and study it in detail, then give me a full written report,' replied the Taoiseach. The other ministers thought this was a distraction from the central issue of framing an acceptable statement. Only Cowen picked up on the possible pitfalls in the strategy. Back in his own office Duignan ruefully remarked to the head of the Taoiseach's Department, Paddy Teahon, 'Spring is on for the treble. He gets rid of Harry; he gets rid of Albert, and gets into bed with Bertie without any election.'[9]

Meanwhile Fitzsimons was woken at home at 1.30 a.m. on Wednesday morning by a phone call from Michael Woods who asked him to come into Government Buildings. Earlier in the evening Fitzsimons had again gone to see Whelehan at the instigation of Woods. He delivered a message suggesting there was good reason to believe that if the government fell the peace process could break down. Whelehan, who was also roused from his bed again, refused the 'invitation', as he delicately put it, to resign.[10] When Fitzsimons arrived in Government Buildings, Reynolds told him he was going to make full disclosure of the Duggan case to the Dáil. The Attorney General was asked to read a draft of the Taoiseach's speech and he made some minor changes. He left for home at 4.30 a.m.

At 8 a.m. the contacts between Dempsey and Howlin resumed. Labour ministers met an hour later and just before 10 a.m. McCreevy showed Howlin the draft speech containing a number of sentences drafted by Labour. The relevant sentences read: 'I now accept that the reservations voiced by the Tánaiste are well founded and I regret the appointment of the former Attorney General as president of the High Court. I also regret my decision to proceed with the appointment against the expressed wishes of the Labour Party.' There was also a sentence about trust. 'I guarantee that this breach of trust, a trust on which the partnership Government was founded, will not be repeated.' Howlin told McCreevy that the speech with those inclusions would be an acceptable basis to go back into government.

This was not good enough for the Fianna Fáil ministers who were gathering in the ante-room of the Taoiseach's office and they demanded a written agreement from Spring that, if the sentences were used, Labour would come back into government. 'Look, do you not trust me?' Howlin asked Dempsey. 'Yes, Brendan, I trust you, but some of my colleagues don't trust some of your colleagues, or some other people in the Labour Party,' came the reply. McCreevy and Dempsey then accompanied Howlin over to Mervyn Taylor's office and Spring was brought in. He read the draft speech and said: 'Yes, fine. What do you want me to sign?' Dempsey produced a short note which read: 'On the basis of the statement prepared by me being incorporated in the Taoiseach's speech, I will lead my

Ministerial colleagues back into Government to complete the Programme for Government.' The Labour leader took the note from Dempsey and signed it 'Dick Spring, 16 November, 10.22 am.'[11]

For a brief period it seemed as if Reynolds had pulled the iron out of the fire and saved the coalition and his job. The cost, though was extraordinarily high; not only was he pledged to undermine his own credibility but he was also committed to making an unprecedented attack on a senior member of the judiciary.

Fergus Finlay, who was told the terms of the deal by Spring just moments after it was signed, was dumbfounded. 'He can't do it. Albert can't say these things about the president of the High Court,' said Finlay. 'But he's going to,' Spring replied. 'He believed all Harry's reasons for the delay and now he feels let down.' Finlay tottered off out into the street in a state of shock at the notion that the offices of Taoiseach, the Attorney General and the President of the High Court were all to be dragged through the mud for political expediency. He went to St Stephen's Green, sat down on a park bench and wept.[12]

When the Dáil met at 10.30 a.m. the Taoiseach sought an adjournment so that arrangements for putting the pieces back together again could be worked out with Labour. The Opposition parties were outraged and Labour strangely silent. Suddenly the penny dropped with the Opposition – a deal was being cobbled together. There were hoots of derision as Spring agreed to the adjournment but just as everybody began to come to terms with the notion that the Fianna Fáil-Labour coalition might survive, after all, it received its deathblow.

The Labour version of events is that while he was still in the Dáil chamber Spring was approached by his colleague from Louth, Michael Bell, who slipped him a note containing a name and a phone number. 'I think you should ring this number. He knows something about the Brendan Smyth case.' After the adjournment Spring rang the person named on the note: Paul Murphy, editor of the *Drogheda Independent* and election agent for Bell. Murphy told Spring there was another case involving a monk. Spring knew that but asked Murphy how he knew. The reply was that the *Irish Independent* gossip columnist, Angela Phelan, who was friendly with the Reynolds family, had told him that she had been in Albert's house on Monday night. At that stage the Taoiseach had expressed annoyance with Whelehan because he had been told of a new case (Duggan) which changed the picture. The significant point for Spring was that the conversation had taken place on Monday evening, before Reynolds's Dáil statement defending Whelehan and making no reference to the Duggan case. There have been suggestions that Spring also received the information about Monday's events from another source that Wednesday morning, but that has never achieved more than the status of rumour.

In any event, Spring contacted the Taoiseach's office and asked for a meeting with Eoghan Fitzsimons. Reynolds asked his AG if he would be willing to discuss the Duggan case with the Tánaiste and he agreed. Fitzsimons went to Spring's office and sat down at a table with the Labour leader who took notes about the details of the Duggan case. Spring asked when the file had been found. 'I informed him that it was found on Monday,' said Fitzsimons in his evidence to the Dáil committee. 'He then asked me when the Taoiseach was told but also said that I need not tell him if I did not wish to do so. I informed him that he was the Tánaiste and that I would tell him. I then told him that the Taoiseach was informed of the Duggan case on Monday.' Fitzsimons expressly recalled Spring's response to this information: 'Oh Lord, Eoghan, we will both be back in the Law Library.'

Accompanied by Quinn and Howlin, Spring then went to see Reynolds who was in his office with McCreevy, Geoghegan-Quinn and Dempsey. Spring immediately asked Reynolds when he had been told about the Duggan case. The Taoiseach said it had been mentioned on Monday and went on to explain the circumstances surrounding the disclosure and the confusion it caused. He also told Spring about the letter from the Attorney General and tried to get him to read it but Spring was not interested. Quinn suggested that Whelehan should resign as President of the High Court, but Reynolds pointed out that efforts had been made to bring this about on Monday and Tuesday night, but to no avail. Quinn then suggested that the government should call for his resignation in the Dáil or seek to have him impeached, but Reynolds said that he could not do either. The Labour ministers got up to leave and Quinn then uttered a phrase that passed into political folklore. 'We have come for a head, Harry's or yours [Reynolds's]. It doesn't look like we are getting Harry's.' Howlin supported Quinn but Geoghegan-Quinn looked at Spring. 'What are you looking for, Dick?' she asked. Spring threw his hands up and said, 'I think it's all over.' It certainly was all over as far as Reynolds was concerned, but Spring and Labour had further options.[13]

Duignan, who slept late that morning after so many exhausting late nights, arrived in Government Buildings just moments after the deal had unravelled. 'I meet Dempsey who is almost speechless, suddenly aged for such a young guy, and he tells me what happened. It's just unbelievable. Máire Geoghegan-Quinn like I've never seen her before, utterly shattered. Smith as if he has been hit between the eyes with a hammer. All standing around Albert, beating their breasts saying: "We let you down." Albert occasionally taking out the sheet of paper (the note signed by

Spring) and looking at it bemusedly. A dud cheque …'[14]

As the drama was being played out behind closed doors Leinster House was gripped by wild rumours. Cardinal Daly was falsely accused of having had some involvement in the Smyth case and felt it necessary to issue a formal denial. The government stoked the speculation by adjourning the Dáil three times during the day in the forlorn hope that some way could be found to bring Spring back on board. This time around, though, Labour refused to bite. Spring was furious with himself for having signed the 10.22 a.m. note and ordered an end to all contacts. As far as he was concerned there was now no going back with Reynolds, but he waited for the Dáil to resume before putting that on the record.

Reynolds spent the day agonising over what had gone wrong. Who had leaked the information about the link between Brendan Smyth and the Attorney General's office to scupper the Baldonnel deal? Why had he not been given the Fitzsimons letter in the Dáil by Bertie Ahern? Who had phoned Dick Spring after the 10.22 a.m. deal? All the agonising led nowhere and eventually Reynolds conceded that the Dáil business would have to begin. In an unedifying end to a grim day he marched into the chamber and delivered the speech as agreed with Labour, including the unprecedented attack on the president of the High Court he had insisted on appointing the previous Friday. Saying that he would have expected the Attorney General to inform the government of the significance of the Duggan case, Reynolds said: 'This information was not made known to me and the Government by the former Attorney General. Had my colleagues and I been aware of these facts last week we would not have proposed or supported the nomination of Mr Harry Whelehan as President of the High Court.' He then referred to the actions of the Labour Party. 'I now accept that the reservations voiced by the Tánaiste are well founded and I regret the appointment of the former Attorney General as President of the High Court. I also regret my decision to proceed with the appointment against the expressed opposition of the Labour Party. I guarantee that this breach of trust, a trust on which the partnership Government was founded, will not be repeated. I hoped that these assurances would form the basis of an agreement and I still hope it will.'[15]

Reynolds was clutching at straws in the hope that Labour would relent, but the situation had gone far beyond that point. In response, Spring delivered a carefully crafted speech that heightened the sense of drama because he did not reveal his hand until the last possible moment. The Dáil, and the nation watching on television and listening on the radio, hung on every word, not knowing what he was going to do. He went over all the twists and turns of Whelehan's appointment, the discovery of the Duggan case and the events of the previous 24 hours. Eventually he delivered the *coup de grace*. 'For the reasons I have outlined it will be obvious to the House that neither I nor any of my colleagues can vote confidence in the Government at the conclusion of this debate.'[16] It was all over for Reynolds. Across the tunnel in Government Buildings, the wake began and it went on all night as the bottles came out in Duignan's office. Brian Cowen cried, Charlie McCreevy kept repeating, 'Albert is being hung for the wrong crime,' and Seán Doherty told jokes in between bouts of recrimination.

Events then happened with extraordinary speed as Reynolds, having lived on adrenaline for nearly a week, threw in the towel. He came into the Dáil the following morning and announced his resignation as Taoiseach. He delivered a short speech, totally lacking in self-pity. 'When I became leader of Fianna Fáil and Taoiseach I set myself two political objectives – to achieve peace in Northern Ireland and on the whole island and to turn the economy around. I was fortunate in such a short space of time to achieve those two political objectives.' The other party leaders then paid tributes, normally reserved for the dead, to the man they had just forced out of office. Reynolds wound up the short debate by reflecting on his own political style. 'I am what I am. I do not pretend to be something that I am not. We all have human feelings but we have a good sense of values as well ... I was straight up; I have never hidden anything. Give it as it was; tell it as it is, that is me. That is what I have been and that is what I always will be ... In life, in business and politics you cannot win them all. You win some, you lose some, but throughout my life in politics I have been delighted to be a risk-taker. If you are not a risk-taker you will not achieve anything.'[17]

Speeches over, the Ceann Cómhairle adjourned the Dáil but Reynolds was reluctant to leave the chamber. He waited as a long line of TDs from all parties walked over to shake his hand, some of his friends almost in tears. In Duignan's phrase, he acted as chief mourner as well as the deceased. Reynolds lingered until the chamber was finally emptied of every TD and then he looked around him from the Taoiseach's bench for the last time before heading for the exit. As he left he looked up at the still-crowded press gallery, shook his head sadly and remarked:'It's amazing. You cross the big hurdles and when you get to the small ones you get tripped.'[18]

V

THE AHERN YEARS

28. THE BOYS ARE BACK IN TOWN

ALBERT REYNOLDS SLEEPWALKED from his position as Fianna Fáil leader and was replaced almost before he realised it. After the calamity of the Labour Party's withdrawal from government on the evening of 16 November, Reynolds resigned as Taoiseach within 12 hours and set the wheels in motion for the appointment of his successor two days later. With hindsight, he could have moved more slowly, buying time to assess the lie of the political land. He could have tried for a dissolution of the Dáil and taken his chances in a general election. He could have hung on for a period to see what the other parties in the Dáil came up with as an alternative or to give his favoured successor, Máire Geoghegan-Quinn, time to build a support base. Instead, he took the honourable course and got off the pitch as quickly as possible, handing the Fianna Fáil leadership on a plate to Bertie Ahern.

Almost immediately afterwards he had reason to regret his decision to step down as leader of Fianna Fáil as well. When he came back from Áras an Uachtaráin after handing in his seal of office to President Robinson, he went to a meeting of his parliamentary party in Leinster House. He read out a letter from British Prime Minister John Major, paying generous tribute to him for the work done in the peace process. The party discussed meeting again two days later to choose a new leader. Later that day there was another bombshell with the resignation of Harry Whelehan as president of the High Court; if he had done this 24 hours earlier, Reynolds might have been saved. Even so, Reynolds's supporters in the parliamentary party tried to have his decision to step down as leader reversed. Reynolds toyed with the idea, even though he had said he would resign 'at the wishes of the party'. In the event, any thoughts he had about changing his mind soon disappeared. The Haughey faction had foreseen the possibility. As soon as Spring announced he was pulling the plug, Ray Burke, Dermot Ahern, P.J. Mara and other representatives of the *ancien régime* whipped up anxiety in the parliamentary party and contacted their friends in the media to ensure that the pressure on Reynolds to go was maintained. Reynolds himself was not in the least bit surprised. He fully expected the many people he had sacked on taking over in 1992 to come looking for his head at the first opportunity.

His own supporters were reeling from the tension of the traumatic events of the week and exhausted from lack of sleep. They were totally unprepared to do battle for control of the party and the Haughey faction had no difficulty in getting support for Bertie Ahern from the middle-ground TDs. Geoghegan-Quinn, who had resigned from the cabinet in the midst of the November crisis in an effort to save Reynolds, tried to make a fight of it but she was hopelessly outnumbered. Just before the vote was due to take place on the morning of 19 November, she withdrew from the race. Ahern ran a systematic campaign from his constituency office, and St Luke's in Drumcondra became well known as an important address to the Fianna Fáil backbenchers. Brian Lenihan, one of Ahern's strongest backers in the parliamentary party, was in the Mater hospital at the time and issued a statement from his bed urging his colleagues to select Ahern as the new leader. 'He has the right balance of ability, age and experience. Electorally he is ideally located to strengthen party support and personally he has the negotiating and consensual skills that are so required for national leadership in the modern age,' he declared.[1] Lenihan's statement summed up the attitude to Ahern within the party and he was chosen unanimously as the successor to Reynolds. At 43 he was the youngest leader in the history of Fianna Fáil. It was taken for granted that he would do a deal with Spring and take over the Taoiseach's office. After his election, at a meeting in the Burlington Hotel, he spoke of the need for party unity and for an end to the factionalism which had split Fianna Fáil into warring camps for more than two decades. He also dealt openly with questions about his private life, the break-up of his marriage and his partnership with Celia Larkin. It seemed that everything was rosy in the political garden and that nothing could go wrong.

Although he was elected unanimously, few of his colleagues knew Ahern at all well. In many ways he was the most enigmatic leader ever chosen by Fianna Fáil, a paradox on every level. A hugely popular politician loved by the public, he is also a ruthless behind-the-scenes operator. Often a hesitant and ungrammatical public speaker, he has an acute political brain. On a personal level he is also full of contradictions. He is the first Irish political leader since the foundation of the state who is separated from his wife and openly living with another woman. Yet in other ways he behaves like a traditional Catholic. In an age when the Church is in retreat and is certainly not fashionable, Ahern behaves in public like very few politicians of his generation. He blesses himself after the daily prayer in the Dáil before the order of business and on Ash Wednesday he displays the penitent's ash on his forehead. He is also very young, as political leaders go. This is often overlooked because he has been in national politics for nearly 25 years and has been in the front rank of political life since 1982.

Ahern's father was a native of Co. Cork but he himself was born in Dublin in September 1951. The family was involved in the War of Independence and supported Fianna Fáil since the foundation of the party in 1926. Ahern left school after the Leaving Certificate and worked in the accounts department of the Mater Hospital where he was an active member of the Workers Union of Ireland. He was still only 25 when he was first elected to the Dáil for the Dublin Finglas constituency in the Fianna Fáil landslide which followed the Cosgrave coalition. In 1979, he backed Haughey for the leadership and in 1981 he ran in the Dublin Central constituency, where his running mate was George Colley, who was Tánaiste and deputy leader of Fianna Fáil at the time. There was a bitter struggle between the two since Ahern was firmly associated with the Haughey camp and on election day the rival supporters clashed outside polling stations. Ahern won more votes than Colley, even though both were elected. This was the first indication of Ahern's aggressive electioneering style. His big vote also demonstrated his ability to cultivate the voters. His huge appetite for constituency work and his ability to organise a constituency machine completely loyal to him had become a feature of politics in Dublin Central. In the 1980s, Ahern set up his own annual fundraising dinner in the Royal Hospital at which most city-centre business houses were represented. With this political machine and the fundraising operation behind him, Ahern became one of the top vote-getters in the country. It has also enabled him to staff and run his own full-time constituency office.

After the 1981 election Ahern's star began to rise in the Fianna Fáil party. Haughey made him government chief whip after the election of February 1982 which brought Fianna Fáil back to power. It was a time of unparalleled turbulence within the Fianna Fáil party as Haughey had to fight three heaves against his leadership. In the midst of the passionate struggles which frequently brought frayed nerves to breaking point, Ahern remained dignified and calm while never wavering in his support for Haughey. The Boss developed a strong bond with his young chief whip and marked him down as a man for the future. Ahern raised his political profile by becoming Lord Mayor of Dublin in 1986 and was an automatic selection as a cabinet minister when Fianna Fáil returned to power in 1987. As Minister for Labour, Bertie's skills as a Mr Fix-it came into play. During his period in Opposition, when he was spokesman for Labour, he had established very good relations with the trade union leaders and he developed these contacts in office. His style was uniquely personal.

During one ESB dispute, one of the political correspondents asked government press secretary P.J. Mara if the minister was going to intervene. 'Well, Bertie will go out and have a few pints with the lads tonight and see what can be done,' replied P.J. Ahern's skills as a negotiator and the personal style were vital to the negotiation of the three national agreements with the social partners which delivered industrial peace for almost a decade.

Ahern again showed his political skills and his loyalty to Haughey in the negotiations with the Progressive Democrats after the 1989 election and in the re-negotiation of that deal in 1991 which saved his boss's bacon. This prompted Haughey's famous remark about his protégé being the most devious and the most cunning of them all.

Ahern became Minister for Finance when Reynolds was fired after his abortive *coup*. At this stage he was clearly Haughey's favoured son to succeed to the leadership, but he backed out of the challenge to Reynolds when Haughey lost power in February 1992. His dithering annoyed many of the TDs who had pledged their support to him while his opponents in the Reynolds camp dubbed him 'the rat in the anorak'. Nonetheless, Reynolds appointed him to Finance in his two governments and while they were not personally close they worked comfortably well together without any hints of tension or rivalry.

When Ahern was elected leader on 19 November 1994 there was general euphoria in Fianna Fáil that a young leader who appeared to represent a complete break with the past had been chosen. His popularity both inside and outside the party is undeniable. He has a compulsion to shake hands and treat every day as if it was the middle of an election campaign, but he wears a mask that has proved impenetrable to most of his colleagues in the Dáil. None of his colleagues is really sure whether he is possessed of all the deviousness and cunning attributed to him by Haughey or whether he simply suffers from chronic indecision disguised as political shrewdness.

It is precisely this 'Teflon' quality which was so appealing to Fianna Fáil supporters. After years of attack, crisis and division under controversial leaders, Ahern was seen as the man to bring the party into calming waters. 'I have no big houses or mansions or yachts or studs. All I've got is a mortgage. The only thing they have on me is the fact that my marriage has broken down and I'm with Celia,' he told the authors of a book about him in 1998. In an interview for that book he also dealt with rumours about his private life suggesting tensions between himself and Celia Larkin and allegations that his ex-wife, Miriam, had secured a barring order against him. 'I know all the rumours and so do Celia and Miriam. I can do sweet nothing about these things. You can sound me out till the cows come home: you'll find no Garda reports, no barring orders, nothing. I'll tell you, there's not a whole many things in my life that I can 110 per cent swear on, because I'm no more an angel than anyone else in this life, but of the barring orders there is zilch.'[2]

The rumours had no effect on Ahern's popularity before or since he became leader of Fianna Fáil. On his election as leader it appeared there were no obstacles to his becoming Taoiseach and a deal with Labour was regarded as a formality. Negotiations got underway and a deal was virtually signed, sealed and delivered when the wheels came off the wagon in the early hours of 6 December. Less than 24 hours before the government was to take office, Dick Spring dramatically called off the talks. By that stage Ahern had even picked his own cabinet and was photographed going into Government Buildings with a folder on the seat of his car with the clearly legible message on the cover 'Members of the Government'.

There had even been some background discussion between Fianna Fáil and Labour figures about whether Ray Burke should be in the cabinet. Geoghegan-Quinn and Michael Smith told Pat Magner and Brendan Howlin of Labour that Burke would be excluded if Spring objected to him. Burke, who had been cast into the wilderness by Reynolds, had backed Ahern to the hilt in the leadership contest and it was widely assumed that Ahern would reward his loyalty by bringing him back to the cabinet. Spring was puzzled as to why senior Fianna Fáil figures appeared to be giving him a veto on Burke. 'We knew that Ray Burke wouldn't have been popular – in fact he was hated – by many of the Fianna Fáil people who had been in the ascendancy under Albert Reynolds. But was there more to it than that? Burke had always been surrounded by rumours but there weren't any more going around at the time than usual,' was Fergus Finlay's reaction.[3] Spring took the view that it was not his business to tell Bertie Ahern who should be on the Fianna Fáil team and he made no effort to intervene.

At the very last minute Spring simply got cold feet about another deal with Fianna Fáil. A number of things happened to rattle him in the final stages of the negotiations. On radio, John Bruton accused him of being prepared to go back into coalition with Fianna Fáil under the leadership of one of those responsible for the collapse of the Reynolds Government. The *Irish Times* attacked Spring in an editorial and the Labour leadership decided that the negative attitude from the newspaper would continue as long as Labour was in government with Fianna Fáil. The real nail in the coffin, though, was a story by Geraldine Kennedy in the *Irish Times* the previous day confirming that 'the Fianna Fáil members of the Government [including Ahern] had full knowledge of the significance of the Duggan case on 14 November.' Even though many in the political world knew this was the case, and Geoghegan-Quinn as good as told the Dáil about it, the story prompted a rethink by Labour. Spring had to deal with the fact that if he was not prepared to stay in government with Reynolds, because of the alleged failure to disclose what he knew to the Dáil about the Duggan case, then the same standard would have to apply to Ahern.

On 5 December, when the story broke and Labour nervousness became clear, Ahern asked Eoghan Fitzsimons to draft a report on the events leading to the collapse of the Reynolds Government. Ahern himself was in Brussels and Reynolds was in Budapest for a meeting of the Organisation for Security and Co-operation in Europe. Through a day of utter confusion and on into the morning of 6 December, Fitzsimons prepared a report on the events of 14/15 November and faxed them to the Taoiseach in Budapest. Reynolds insisted that the report should not be passed on to Spring until he had a chance to go through it line by line. Back in Dublin, Labour advisers were screaming for the report and Ahern wanted desperately to give it to them to save his prospects. Eventually, in the early hours of the morning while Reynolds was still on the way back from Budapest, Ahern handed the report to Spring. According to the gossip, a furious Reynolds tried to fire Ahern as Tánaiste when he got back to Dublin in the early hours, but was dissuaded by Brian Cowen. It did not matter anyway because Spring felt he had no option but to pull out of the deal. With a little over 24 hours to go before becoming Taoiseach, Ahern had the rug pulled from under his feet. It took him a long time to come to terms with what had happened. Becoming leader of the Opposition rather than Taoiseach was not something he had planned for and it was a while before he found his feet. 'When Dick Spring called at 2 a.m. on Tuesday, 6 December to break it off, I was left shaken,' he said later. 'For about four minutes I dropped myself back down on the pillow and said "Hell". Within about five minutes I was down in my office and back on the phone ringing around the ministers.'[4]

It also took Reynolds time to come to grips with what had happened. He had given up the leadership of Fianna Fáil on the basis that that was necessary for the party to remain in power. Now they were out of power anyway, and instead of being leader of the Opposition he was a mere backbencher. He seemed to see plots and conspiracies everywhere. Ahern and Reynolds eyed each other suspiciously because of the series of amazing events that had deprived both of them of the Taoiseach's office. Ahern's failure to pass the note from Fitzsimons on to Reynolds during the critical Dáil debate of 15 November was analysed again and again. 'It's the one question I am always asked. In terms of me holding back anything, I didn't,' said Ahern later. 'In terms of us not copping the importance of the letter, I have to say I've read that letter many times since and if I read it today I still wouldn't cop the importance of it.'[5]

Meanwhile John Bruton was elected Taoiseach. The man everybody had written off and who was widely regarded by the media as having blown his chances in the irascible radio interview calling on Labour to stay away from another deal with Fianna Fáil had power dropped into his lap. It was the first time in the history of the state that government changed hands without a general election. Spring remained as Tánaiste and Minister for Foreign Affairs, badly bruised by the whole experience but still in office. As Duignan had forecast, he had pulled off the biggest gamble of them all.

When Ahern had got over his disappointment he knuckled down to his job as leader of the Opposition and did what he is best at; he took to the road and campaigned the length and breadth of the country, never forgetting his own constituency of Dublin Central. His front-bench appointments were designed to heal the rifts in the party. On the day of his election as leader he promised there would no longer be factions in the party and he did his best to fulfil that pledge. He brought his ally Ray Burke back from the cold to the senior position of Foreign Affairs spokesman and he also appointed other Haughey loyalists like Dermot Ahern and John O'Donoghue to the senior positions of Social Welfare and Justice respectively. However, he also gave senior appointments to leading members of the Reynolds camp. McCreevy got the key job of Finance spokesman while Noel Dempsey, Brian Cowen and Michael Smith were all rewarded with front-bench posts. A newcomer to the front rank was the bright Cork TD, Micheál Martin, who was made Education spokesman while Síle de Valera was given her first front-bench role, having first been elected to the Dáil in 1977. Her appointment was widely regarded as a shrewd one, providing a link between her grandfather who founded Fianna Fáil in 1926 and the party Ahern was now leading and which was gearing itself for a return to government.

29. BERTIE WINS POWER

AHERN TOOK SOME TIME to adapt to the role of Opposition leader and was often outshone in the Dáil by the PD leader, Mary Harney. A fluent speaker, Harney had performed brilliantly during the crisis which brought down the Reynolds Government and was full of confidence in the future. Fianna Fáil was also surprised at how comfortably the rainbow coalition, led by Bruton, settled down in office. Fireworks between Bruton and Spring, who had not got on together during the FitzGerald coalition, had been widely expected but the two men quickly achieved a good working relationship. Proinsías De Rossa and his Democratic Left party, the third component of the coalition, took to office like ducks to water and it soon became apparent that the rainbow would be around for a while. That brought home a sense of realism to Fianna Fáil and the party began a period of rebuilding. A large backroom staff was appointed and everybody prepared for a long slog. Ahern concentrated on touring the country and covered an amazing number of miles per year.

A rapport quickly developed between Ahern and Harney. The two realised that they would have to co-operate if they were to get into government. The PDs were bitterly angry with Labour for excluding them from the rainbow coalition and resented the fact that Fine Gael had so easily bowed to Labour pressure. That left Harney and her colleagues no option but an alliance with Fianna Fáil if they wanted to get into government. Over time Ahern showed more political skill than Harney in the way he cultivated the PDs and gradually ensnared them so firmly that the smaller party's options were effectively closed down by the time the election came around.

In his own first big test of leadership, though, on the government's Abortion Information Bill, Ahern did not do so well. Whether through indecision or cunning, he effectively refused to take a position on the Bill and abdicated to his parliamentary party on the issue. Despite the fact that his aides claimed he favoured the Bill, which provided for abortion information as required by the referendum decision of 1992, he allowed his backbenchers to determine party opposition to it. The government passed the Bill and Fianna Fáil unity on the issue was maintained, but the event demonstrated that Ahern was not prepared to lead from the front. It was a pattern he was to repeat on other major issues and in terms of *realpolitik* it proved a successful formula. Nobody was ever sure where precisely he stood on a controversial issue but he maintained a united party. The public had no complaints either and Ahern's popularity continued to rise, even though the rainbow government was widely credited with doing a good job.

As Ahern prepared for his first general election, he suffered the loss of a leading party stalwart when Máire Geoghegan-Quinn announced she was quitting Dáil politics. Her decision was prompted by media intrusion into her family life relating to problems one of her sons was having at school. However, the underlying basis of her resolve went deeper. She always had ambitions to be the first woman to lead Fianna Fáil and the first woman Taoiseach. When Ahern, who was slightly younger than her, took over the leadership she came to the conclusion that her chance of making it to the very top had passed. Her decision not to contest the next election was a blow for Ahern as it put paid to the chance of winning an extra seat in Galway West and he knew that every last seat was going to count.

Ahern had better luck with Albert Reynolds who was debating whether or not to stay on for another Dáil term. Ahern badly wanted him to run to give the party a chance of winning three out of four seats in Longford-Roscommon. The two men met for a tête-à-tête in the Berkeley Court Hotel and, over lunch, Ahern told Reynolds he would back him for the presidential election nomination if he would run for a Dáil seat in Longford. Mary Robinson had announced she would not be seeking a second term and speculation was mounting about who would be in the race to succeed her. Reynolds was clearly interested and had no problem agreeing to run again in Longford on the basis of Ahern's assurances.

By the end of his first two years in the leadership, Ahern had put himself in a strong position to contest the general election which was expected some time in 1997. But at the end of 1996 a scandal broke that initially threatened Bruton but ultimately posed even bigger problems for Ahern. Leaked extracts from court documents showed that Fine Gael minister Michael Lowry had had extensive renovations to his house in Tipperary paid for by supermarket tycoon Ben Dunne.[1] Lowry owned a refrigeration company that worked for Dunne but the publicity surrounding the payments for his house, which were routed in a complex way, fatally undermined his position and he quickly resigned from the cabinet. There was initial euphoria in Fianna Fáil at having inflicted what was undoubtedly a serious blow on Fine Gael, but the fickle finger of fate quickly pointed in another direction. Rumours began to fly that Dunne had also paid over large sums of money to Charles Haughey. The same court documents that did for Lowry also provided the first clues about a scandal that would truly stun the nation and bring Haughey's shadow back to haunt his favoured successor.

Throughout his political career there had been rumours about the source of Haughey's wealth. It was obvious to everybody that his Dáil salary came nowhere near funding his lavish lifestyle but he refused point blank to answer questions from journalists about it and it never became a real political issue. In general, people seemed happy enough to ignore troubling questions and instead there was widespread admiration of Haughey for having done so well. 'If Charlie did it for himself, he will do the same for the country,' was a common refrain, particularly in Dublin. Those who raised questions about his wealth were regarded as churlish and envious. After he had retired as Taoiseach it seemed that nobody would bother asking any more questions of the Lord of Kinsealy.

Then, in a classic example of the chaos theory which holds that the beating of a butterfly's wings in one part of the globe can cause a hurricane in another, Haughey was suddenly engulfed in a controversy not of his own making which was to destroy his political and personal reputation. The financial arrangements which had underpinned his lifestyle and which had been carefully concealed from the public and the tax authorities for decades were exposed to public view. The effect on Haughey was shattering and over time it also became clear that a whole swathe of the business community was implicated in massive tax fraud.

The incident which triggered Haughey's downfall happened in far-off Miami in 1992 when Ben Dunne had a brainstorm. In the company of a prostitute and under the influence of cocaine, he threatened to jump down from the twelfth floor into the hotel lobby. Better counsels prevailed and Dunne was talked down to safety but the resultant publicity caused a massive row among the members of the family who owned Dunnes Stores. Ben was removed from the board and in subsequent litigation payments to Haughey and Lowry were mentioned in affidavits. In a further twist to the story, it appears that the initial leak of the privileged information in relation to Lowry was organised by senior Fianna Fáil figures. They did not anticipate that the rocket designed to destroy the Fine Gael minister had the capacity to take out the much bigger target of Haughey as well.

Sunday Tribune editor Matt Cooper was the first to break the story about the references to Haughey in the court documentation.[2] That set the wheels in motion for the establishment by the rainbow coalition of the McCracken tribunal to investigate the payments by Dunne to Haughey and Lowry. When the formal hearings began in April 1997, the opening evidence of Ben Dunne to the tribunal was sensational. He revealed that in late 1987 Haughey's financial adviser Des Traynor approached Dunnes's accountant, Noel Fox, seeking a financial contribution to get Haughey out of financial problems. Traynor's story was that he was seeking to put together half a dozen people to contribute £150,000 each towards dealing with the difficulty. When Ben Dunne was told of this he remarked: 'I think Haughey is making a huge mistake trying to get six or seven people together ... Christ picked twelve apostles and one of them crucified him.' Instead Dunne offered to pay the entire amount of £700,000. Between 1987 and 1991 Dunne paid Haughey more than £1 million, most of it being routed through an associate of Traynor's, the Cayman Islands banker John Furze. Dunne's evidence revealed for the first time the existence of the Ansbacher accounts and things were never to be the same again in politics or business. One of the more colourful anecdotes told to the tribunal by Dunne was of a visit to Kinsealy in November 1991 as he was on his way home from a golf game at Baltray. Sensing that Haughey was a bit depressed, Dunne took three bank drafts totalling £210,000 out of his pocket and handed them to the then Taoiseach saying: 'Look, that is something for yourself.' Haughey took the money and replied, 'Thank you, big fellow.'[3]

The disclosure of this information in April 1997 in the run-up to the general election had the capacity to do serious damage to Ahern and Fianna Fáil. However, through very delicate political footwork and the failure of his political opponents to press home the point, Ahern managed to keep his long relationship with Haughey at the margins of political debate. Just before the opening of the tribunal he made a speech at the Fianna Fáil Árd Fheis putting as much distance between himself and his former mentor as possible and focusing on the future of Fianna Fáil, not the past. He made a commitment, which he repeated again and again during 1997, that he would not stand over wrongdoing no matter who suffered as a result. 'Certainly there would be no place in our party today for that kind of behaviour, no matter how eminent the person involved or the extent of their prior services to the country,' he declared. Ahern added that even if no favours had been sought or given, 'we could not condone the practice of senior politicians seeking or receiving from a single donor large sums of money or services in kind.'[4] The speech worked because it was welcomed by the media as a clear indication of a breach with the past. Yet Ahern made no attempt to disguise the fact that the past and present were inextricably linked. As he prepared for the general election, he appointed P.J. Mara as his director of elections. Mara was Haughey's former press secretary, who had gone on to success as a lobbyist and trouble-shooter for business clients after the departure of his boss and was a key member of Ahern's kitchen cabinet.

Fianna Fáil was put on an election footing from the spring of 1997. The rainbow parties played right into Ahern's hands by calling the election for June, just as the McCracken tribunal was getting into full flight. Bruton had wanted to wait but Labour insisted on a June election, mainly because their TDs were getting restive amidst all the election speculation. This suited Ahern on a number of levels. It allowed him full opportunity to do what he does best – to meet the people. In a campaign carefully plotted for him by Fianna Fáil general secretary Pat Farrell and director of elections P.J. Mara, he criss-crossed the country shaking hands with a sizeable proportion of the electorate. The television cameras following his every move and the nightly television news bulletin carried pictures of him meeting the people. In a campaign which had no real issues, as the Government and Fianna Fáil were agreed on the main issues of the economy and the North, PR was everything, and on that score Ahern walked away with it. By contrast, the rainbow leaders seemed to be in hiding for much of the time and their campaign lacked any buzz, even though they were generally considered by the electorate to have done a good job. The only real debate between Ahern and Bruton took place in the dying days of the campaign. The Fine Gael leader won the debate hands down but it came too late to reinvigorate the coalition campaign.

Right through the campaign the opinion polls favoured Fianna Fáil. This helped the feel-good aspect of the party's campaign but it would become apparent later that they seriously overestimated the level of popular support. The last poll of the campaign which, in a break with precedent, appeared in the *Irish Independent* only 24 hours before voting, gave Fianna Fáil 44 per cent of the vote and was widely taken as indicating that the contest was over. In another break with precedent, the *Independent* carried a front-page editorial on the same day strongly backing a Fianna Fáil-Progressive Democrat government on the basis that the two parties were promising big cuts in the tax rates. The editorial, headlined 'Payback time', was felt by Fine Gael in particular to be a serious blow, although it probably made little difference to the outcome.[5] The final ingredient that went Ahern's way was that a deal with the PDs on the formation of government had been announced early in the campaign. The PDs themselves went on to have a disastrous campaign but the pact helped to portray Ahern as a winner because he was assured of the support of the smaller party in the new Dáil. The collapse of the PD vote also helped Fianna Fáil to pick up substantial transfers from eliminated PD candidates all over the country.

Many people in Fianna Fáil believed that the campaign was the best that the party had run since 1977 but in the event the result was, like the Battle of Waterloo, a damn close-run thing. Despite all the plaudits,

Ahern and Fianna Fáil managed to win only 39 per cent of the vote, the same percentage won by Reynolds in the teeth of a howling gale of negative publicity in 1992. The big difference this time was that transfers from the PDs and Independents, plus a bit of luck, helped Fianna Fáil to victory in a number of crucial seats. The party wound up with 77 Dáil seats, an increase of nine on the previous election, although it had won only the same share of the first preference vote. The PDs had the opposite experience, winning almost the same percentage of votes as in 1992 but dropping from ten seats to just four. Between them, however, the two parties managed to win 81 seats, close enough to the magic figure of 83 to enable them to form a government. Seeing the way the wind was blowing, three Independents threw their support behind Ahern in the vote for Taoiseach and he was home and dry.

His next task was to form a government and there was speculation in the media as to whether he would stick with the front bench he had in Opposition or reward some younger TDs like Brian Lenihan (son of Brian Lenihan, now deceased) who had been given a high profile by the party during the campaign. There was also considerable debate as to whether front-bench spokesmen like John O'Donoghue and Micheál Martin, who had given numerous hostages to fortune in Opposition, might be better off getting cabinet posts unrelated to their previous jobs.

In private, Ahern had more difficult things to consider. The main one was what to do about his Foreign Affairs spokesman, Ray Burke. For the previous 18 months numerous stories had appeared in the media, mainly in the *Sunday Business Post*, concerning allegations of planning corruption being made by an elderly man called James Gogarty. Gogarty had come forward when a £10,000 reward was offered by Dublin environmentalists through a firm of Newry solicitors, Donnelly, Neary and Donnelly, for information about such corruption in the Republic. Gogarty made a statement to the solicitors saying that he had given a prominent politician a large sum of money for planning favours on behalf of a company called JMSE for which he had worked. He named Burke in his statement and stories subsequently appeared in the newspapers about the matter, though Burke was not named for fear of libel.

At a press conference in the middle of the election campaign, Ahern had been asked about the Burke allegations by Geraldine Kennedy of the *Irish Times*. Without naming Burke, Ahern replied: 'I have gone to that member and gone through it in detail on four separate occasions as the allegations continued to come up in one newspaper over a period of 17 months. Insofar as I possibly can be, I am satisfied.' He went on: 'We all know who we are talking about.'[6] The Fianna Fáil leader's apparent denial of the allegation against Burke defused the issue. It merited only a brief mention on page eight of the following day's *Irish Times* and was not referred to by the media for the rest of the election campaign.

After the election was over but before the Dáil met, Ahern asked his chief whip, Dermot Ahern, to travel to London to meet the chief executive of JMSE, Joseph Murphy junior, to ask whether there was any truth in the rumours about Burke. On 24 June, two days before the government was formed, Dermot Ahern met Murphy junior who told him that no money had been paid to Burke in return for political or planning favours. The relieved chief whip told Murphy that his party leader had been questioned about rumours and had responded by stating he had spoken to Burke on a number of occasions and that Burke had categorically denied there was any truth in them. It subsequently emerged that Bertie Ahern had done more than speak to Burke and send his chief whip to London. He had actually conducted his own inquiry by speaking to builder Michael Bailey, one of the key figures in the saga. Gogarty had named Bailey as being present when money was handed over to Burke. However, Ahern had told his chief whip nothing of his contacts with Bailey before asking him to travel to London to investigate the matter.

After getting the report from his chief whip and taking the precaution of clearing the move in advance with the PD leader Mary Harney, Ahern went ahead and selected Ray Burke as his Minister for Foreign Affairs. It was a decision which was to rebound on him later. Harney was the only PD in the cabinet, as Minister for Enterprise and Employment, while the rest of the team of ministers virtually picked itself. Ahern displayed enormous caution in his selection, nominating almost all the leading members of his front bench to the cabinet posts they had shadowed while in Opposition. McCreevy was given Finance, Andrews Defence, O'Rourke Public Enterprise, O'Donoghue Justice, Martin Education and Dermot Ahern Social Welfare. Former Reynolds loyalists Cowen and Dempsey got Health and Environment respectively. Michael Smith was the only front-bench member left out to make room for Harney, while Séamus Brennan was appointed chief whip.

Bertie Ahern made an initial blunder when he appointed David Andrews not only as Minister for Defence but also as a junior minister in Foreign Affairs. John Bruton, now back as Opposition leader, immediately denounced this as unconstitutional, on the basis that one cabinet minister cannot be subordinate to another. Ahern was forced into a rapid retreat and he dropped the notion. It was only a minor blemish on an otherwise joyous occasion. At the age of 46, Ahern had achieved his ambition of becoming Taoiseach. The bitter disappointment of 1994 had been well and truly buried.

In his first summer as Taoiseach Ahern experienced the highs and lows of political life. The high point was the renewal of the IRA ceasefire which had broken down in February 1996 when Canary Wharf in London was bombed, killing two people and injuring more than 100. The IRA shifted the blame for its murderous action to the British Government, which it held responsible for the failure of all-party talks to get underway. They had also attributed some of the blame to the then Taoiseach, John Bruton, for the failure of talks to begin, even though the Irish Government had worked tirelessly to get them going. A few months after the bombing the two governments had agreed a framework for talks, but it was contingent on another ceasefire. The election of Tony Blair and Labour in Britain in May 1997 raised new hopes, but nothing happened until after Fianna Fáil came to power in the Republic a little over a month later.

At the time, and since, suggestions have been made of shadowy contacts between Fianna Fáil and Northern republicans over the timing of a new ceasefire. The author has learned that key members of the Bruton government were informed, by an impeccable source, about a number of conversations between a high-level member of the Fianna Fáil front bench and a leading republican in the first half of 1997. In one of those conversations the Fianna Fáil politician was reported as stressing that the IRA should not call a ceasefire before the election in the Republic, as this might boost Bruton's chances and hinder Fianna Fáil's prospects of winning power.

In his recent book about the peace process, *The Far Side of Revenge*, Deaglán de Bréadún quotes republican sources in Belfast as saying that there were two occasions after the Canary Wharf bomb, during the lifetime of the Bruton government, when the ceasefire could have been renewed but the opportunity was lost: 'There was said to be a cynical element in Fianna Fáil which wanted the IRA to hold back the ceasefire until after the general election in the republic but, until they became disillusioned with Bruton and Major, this was not the attitude of republicans, who wanted to get into the talks as quickly as possible.'

The full story of what happened at this time will probably take years to emerge but there is conclusive proof, from a number of different sources, that a great deal of contact between Fianna Fáil and republicans took place in the 12 months before the election. It was no coincidence that just weeks after Ahern took office, the IRA declared its long-awaited second ceasefire. That initiative presented the new Taoiseach with a great opportunity to renew the work of building a solution to the Northern problem.

The downside for Ahern that summer was that the allegations about Ray Burke became much more persistent once he was installed in Iveagh

House. Within weeks of the government's formation, the story of Dermot Ahern's trip to London emerged and after the *Sunday Tribune* named Burke publicly for the first time it was also confirmed publicly that a political donation of £30,000 had in fact been paid to him in 1989, although government sources denied strenuously that any impropriety had been involved. In an interview with Gerald Barry on RTÉ's 'This Week' programme, the Taoiseach said that he had gone 'to extraordinary lengths' and had been 'up every tree in North Dublin' in his inquiries to find out about the payment before appointing Burke to the cabinet. 'I know the circumstances about it and I am quite satisfied with the matter,' he added.[7] Despite the fact that Mary Harney then rowed into the debate and publicly defended Burke, the pressure from the Opposition and the media mounted throughout the summer of 1997.

Burke was finally forced to issue a public statement on 7 August. He told how he had been visited at his home by Michael Bailey and Gogarty during the general election campaign of 1989. 'Gogarty told me JMSE wished to make a political contribution to me and I received from him in good faith a sum of £30,000 as a totally unsolicited political contribution,' he stated. 'At no time during our meeting were any favours sought or given. I did not do any favours for or make any representations to anyone on behalf of JMSE.' Claiming that he was the victim of a vicious campaign of rumour and innuendo, Burke added, 'I have done nothing illegal, unethical or improper. I find myself the victim of a campaign of calumny and abuse.'[8]

Far from ending the controversy as the government hoped, Burke's statement simply fuelled demands for a full explanation because it raised as many questions as it answered. Now that Burke himself had confirmed he had received £30,000 from JMSE, why had Ahern maintained all along that there was no truth in the allegation? The Opposition scented blood and began to bay all the louder for a fuller explanation. The Opposition was also galvanised by sensational developments in the final phase of the McCracken tribunal. Charles Haughey was called to give evidence in July. Even before he took the witness stand he was caught telling barefaced lies in his affidavits to the tribunal. When he appeared in person on 9 July he cut a sorry figure as he was forced to apologise not only to the tribunal but also to his own legal team for misleading them. It was widely believed that his lawyers had threatened to walk out on him if he did not make it clear to the tribunal that he had been misleading them as well. 'I now accept that I received the £1.3 million from Mr Ben Dunne and that I became aware that he was the donor to the late Mr Traynor in 1993 and furthermore I now accept Mr Dunne's evidence that he handed me £210,000 in Abbeville in November 1991,' said Haughey in the course of a short statement.[9]

When he reappeared on 15 July to give fuller testimony, Haughey was even more contrite. 'I accept that I have not co-operated with this tribunal in a manner which would have been expected of me. I deeply regret that I have allowed this situation to arise.' Haughey was blunt about the reason for his failure to co-operate. 'I was concerned as to the effect that the publication of these payments would have for me in the public mind and in hindsight I accept that a lot of the problems and embarrassment that I have caused would have been avoided if I had been more forthcoming at each and every relevant period.' He said that throughout his public life Des Traynor had been his trusted friend and financial adviser. 'I never had to concern myself about my personal finances. He took control of my financial affairs from about 1960 onwards. He saw it as his personal responsibility to ensure that I would be free to devote my time and ability to public life and that I would not be distracted from my political work by financial concerns. The late Mr Des Traynor had complete discretion to act on my behalf without reference back to me. In hindsight it is clear that I should have involved myself to a greater degree in this regard.'[10]

As Haughey was humiliated and forced to concede in public to the tribunal that he had told lies in the course of the inquiry, leading Fine Gael and Labour politicians ground their teeth in frustration at having called the election before Haughey gave his evidence. When the tribunal report was published at the end of August they were even angrier. Mr Justice McCracken was scathing in his criticism of Haughey and said bluntly that key portions of his evidence were 'quite unbelievable'. The report charted the manner in which money had been channelled to Haughey from Ben Dunne through the Ansbacher accounts in the Cayman islands. While it found no evidence of any favours that might have been done in return for the payments to Haughey, the judge was unequivocal in his assessment that such payments were very wrong. 'The tribunal considers it quite unacceptable that Mr Charles Haughey, or indeed any member of the Oireachtas, should receive personal gifts of this nature, particularly from prominent businessmen within the state. It is even more unacceptable that Mr Charles Haughey's whole lifestyle should be dependent upon such gifts, as would appear to be the case. If such gifts were to be permissible, the potential for bribery and corruption would be enormous.'[11] Finally the tribunal listed the series of lies it had been told by Haughey and referred the papers to the Director of Public Prosecutions to see if a prosecution should be brought.

The report was a devastating blow to Haughey's reputation and it prompted an immediate call by the Opposition parties for a recall of the Dáil to discuss the implications. Taken in tandem with the mounting pressure on Ahern over the Ray Burke appointment, the government faced an enormous test of its cohesion after a little more than two months in office.

As if that was not enough, Ahern had another problem to sort out at this time. Fianna Fáil had to decide whom it was going to nominate to contest the presidential election scheduled for early November. This time Ahern was determined to recover the office for Fianna Fáil.

30. THE SHAFTING OF ALBERT

WHEN IT CAME TO SELECTING THE FIANNA FÁIL PRESIDENTIAL CANDI-
DATE, Ahern conducted himself with the precision and ruthlessness of a
true follower of Machiavelli. The two leading hopefuls, Albert Reynolds
and Michael O'Kennedy, were taken out in one fell swoop. Reynolds was
his predecessor as a Fianna Fáil Taoiseach; O'Kennedy was a former
European Commissioner and an ally. Ahern dispatched them mercilessly
in the search for the perfect presidential candidate, without leaving as
much as his fingerprints on the stiletto. But neither of the discarded hopefuls was in any doubt about who ordered his political assassination.

For Reynolds the saga began back in January of 1997 when the
former Taoiseach was thinking of stepping down at the forthcoming
general election because he saw no future as a backbencher. But over
lunch in the Berkeley Court Hotel, Ahern urged him to fight the election
in the belief that only with him on the ticket could Fianna Fáil gain an
extra seat in the Longford-Roscommon constituency. He offered Reynolds two inducements – he would be named as a special 'peace envoy'
for the North if Fianna Fáil won the election and would be in a better
position to fight the presidential election if he held on to his Dáil seat. At
a second meeting in McGrattan's Restaurant, near Government Buildings, Ahern repeated his pledge of support for Reynolds's presidential
ambitions on condition that he ran for the Dáil again. On that basis Reynolds agreed.[1]

Even though there had been some coolness between the two men
since the departure of Haughey, Reynolds had no reason to believe he
was being led up the garden path. At the launch of the Fianna Fáil election campaign in May, Ahern surprised the media and many of his party
colleagues by referring publicly to the 'peace envoy' role for Reynolds if
Fianna Fáil won the election. Taking this as a clear signal that the deal
between himself and Ahern would be honoured, Reynolds ran for the
Dáil and retained his seat in Longford-Roscommon, but Fianna Fáil
failed to win the magic three out of four in the constituency. When
Ahern formed his government in June he had a change of heart. The
Minister for Foreign Affairs, Ray Burke, made it clear he would not

stand for a 'peace envoy'. In any case, the role had become redundant as a result of the new IRA ceasefire.

When Reynolds and Ahern next met, the Taoiseach again suggested the presidency and Reynolds jumped at it. As well as giving him private encouragement, Ahern went public to say he believed the former Taoiseach would be a very good president. Reynolds then began to organise for the race and hired Peter Finnegan, a PR consultant and former member of the Fianna Fáil national executive, to run his campaign. However, another candidate had entered the lists without anybody in political circles in Dublin taking much notice. Prof. Mary McAleese, a law lecturer at Queen's University, Belfast, announced in early July that she was seeking the Fianna Fáil nomination. In fact, she had been making behind-the-scenes moves ever since March when Mary Robinson announced that she would not be seeking another term. McAleese, an intelligent Belfast woman with a strong sense of self-belief, was no stranger to Fianna Fáil politics. After an unhappy stint as an RTÉ reporter in the early 1980s, when she felt pilloried inside the national broadcasting station for her Catholic views, she turned to law lecturing at Trinity College, Dublin. She advised the Catholic bishops during their appearance at the New Ireland Forum in Dublin in 1984. Three years later she ran as a Fianna Fáil Dáil candidate in Dublin South-East, having been imposed on the constituency by party headquarters with the endorsement of Charles Haughey. She did not get elected and returned to Belfast where she quickly moved up the ladder in the Law Department at Queen's.

McAleese was prodded into running by a friend from Meath, Harry Casey, a teacher at St Patrick's Academy in Navan and ironically a native of Co. Longford. She consulted a few friends about the idea and in April Fr Alex Reid, the Redemptorist priest who had acted as a contact between the IRA and Albert Reynolds during the peace process, mentioned McAleese to Ahern's special adviser, Martin Mansergh. Though her name began to circulate in the background, McAleese waited until after the general election in June before making her move. Casey contacted the newly-elected Fianna Fáil TD Mary Hanafin about how to approach the party and was given a run-down about the power structure in Fianna Fáil. McAleese then composed a letter to Bertie Ahern outlining her credentials for the presidency. Casey delivered it to the Taoiseach's constituency office in Drumcondra.

McAleese then began a round of senior Fianna Fáil figures. She met the chairman of the parliamentary party, Rory O'Hanlon, and also went to the Minister for Social Welfare, Dermot Ahern, following up an approach she had made to him while he was chief whip. McAleese and her husband, Martin, called to the Athlone home of the party deputy leader,

Mary O'Rourke, and spent a couple of hours discussing the presidency. 'I pledged my troth that night,' O'Rourke said later. 'I asked her whom she knew in the party and she mentioned Dermot Ahern and Rory O'Hanlon. I told her she would want to move quickly because others were moving as well. I advised her to get her name into the public domain.' O'Rourke followed up the meeting by lobbying Ahern on her behalf.[2]

Most of the senior figures McAleese met in the first stage of the campaign had a grudge against Reynolds as he had sacked them from ministerial office in 1992. The next stage in the campaign was to write a letter to Fianna Fáil TDs all over the country. These were followed up by letters from McAleese supporters suggesting her as somebody who would make a good president. Most TDs did not pay a lot of attention to these circular letters even when the Queen's University academic went public and declared she was interested in the office. This was the situation in mid-July when John Hume's name was suddenly floated as a possible agreed candidate. Reynolds insisted that he would not stand aside for the SDLP leader but McAleese announced that she would stand down if Hume decided to put his name forward. As Hume delayed giving a yes or no to the idea, stories began to appear in the newspapers suggesting that Ahern wanted him to go forward, but the Taoiseach refused to be drawn. He did, however, refuse to let David Andrews run because Fianna Fáil could not risk a by-election in Dún Laoghaire. Instead, Andrews went public saying he would back John Hume.

Then, in August, former EU commissioner Michael O'Kennedy, who was a little disappointed at being left out of the cabinet, went to see Ahern and expressed an interest in running for the Áras. He was encouraged to put his name forward and led to believe that he had the goodwill of the party leadership for his bid. About the same time, stories were appearing in the press suggesting that Ahern did not want Reynolds as a candidate. This caused some puzzlement in the Reynolds camp and Peter Finnegan wrote to the Taoiseach asking if there was a problem. Ahern rang Finnegan to reassure him that he was not part of any hostile campaign against Reynolds. The Reynolds camp was reassured, believing that P.J. Mara, Haughey's former press secretary who had been the party director of elections in June, was behind the negative newspaper stories. It was a fatal mistake because Mara was voicing what the Fianna Fáil leadership really believed. 'Anybody but Albert' was the general feeling and everybody but Albert seemed to be in on the secret in the last few weeks before the parliamentary party met to decide on the candidate.

The anti-Albert strategy took a knock when Hume finally announced that he was not a candidate. By that stage the race for the Fianna Fáil nomination had already hotted up, with Reynolds and

O'Kennedy canvassing hard among their parliamentary colleagues. On 28 August the Reynolds team delivered a letter from Albert to every member of the parliamentary party containing the findings of a privately commissioned opinion poll. 'As we all know, polls are more indicative than definitive in what they tell us,' wrote Reynolds, who included the figures and analysis. The result showed Reynolds on 45 per cent, Fine Gael's Mary Banotti on 20 per cent, Michael D. Higgins of Labour on 17 per cent with 18 per cent undecided. By this time Fine Gael had selected Banotti, but Labour had still to make up its mind.

McAleese, too, was back in the race with a vengeance. On 9 September, with just eight days to go before the vote, she met Bertie Ahern in the Taoiseach's office. Government chief whip Seamus Brennan and Martin Mansergh were in the room with the Taoiseach to listen as she made her pitch for the nomination. Hardly pausing to take breath, she delivered a 15-minute monologue on her vision of the presidency. It was a typically confident performance, but Ahern was his usual cagey self and gave her no firm commitment when she finished. 'Good luck' was all he said, but his adviser Martin Mansergh was a little more forthright. 'You went in a no-hoper and you have come out with some hope,' he said. Significantly, after the meeting Brennan handed her a list of Fianna Fáil ministers, deputies, senators and MEPs along with their private phone numbers. 'Get a team together to canvass the parliamentary party. You must talk to all of them. Starting from now you have one week to do it,' Brennan told her.[3]

When the Dáil met the following day McAleese came into Leinster House first thing in the morning with Mary Hanafin. She circulated around the restaurant and called at the offices of Fianna Fáil TDs and senators to canvass as many of them as she could. By now, she was beginning to look like the favoured candidate of the Taoiseach and the ministers close to him, but they tried to keep all options open in their 'Anybody but Albert' strategy. They still regarded McAleese as unlikely to beat Reynolds; she was the fall-back candidate rather than the first choice. A lot of pressure was put on Ray MacSharry to come into the frame and Jim McDaid, Mary O'Rourke and Dermot Ahern were deputed to issue public statements calling on the former EU Commissioner to enter the field. McDaid did go public but shortly afterwards a journalist contacted MacSharry to ask him about political contributions he might have received over the years. That was enough to make MacSharry decide that he wanted nothing more to do with public life and he rang the Taoiseach to say he would not be a candidate in any circumstances. The planned statements from O'Rourke and Ahern were then aborted and a new strategy emerged from the Taoiseach's office – a last-minute attempt to draft David Andrews.

Andrews, who was in Calcutta for Mother Teresa's funeral, was contacted and told that the earlier injunction not to stand had now been cancelled and he was free to enter the race. The Minister for Defence was furious that it had been left so late, particularly as the message to him coincided with the leaking of the news that Labour was going to nominate the environmental campaigner Adi Roche. Andrews rang the Taoiseach from London on his way back from Calcutta early on Monday morning to say he had not been given time to canvass or prepare for the parliamentary party meeting. 'You are probably right,' Ahern told him. In fact, by this stage the leadership had fixed on McAleese as the best candidate. Wicklow TD Dick Roche was drumming up support for her and ministers like Dermot Ahern, Mary O'Rourke and John O'Donoghue began to use their influence in her favour.[4]

Even with just 24 hours to go to the vote, Reynolds and his supporters were blissfully unaware of what was going on and were confident he had 70 votes out of 114 in the bag. There was something ominous, though, that out of the 15 members of the cabinet only Charlie McCreevy, Brian Cowen and David Andrews said they would support him. O'Kennedy, too, felt there might be something up so he rang both the Taoiseach and Dermot Ahern to check the position. He was looking for a signal of any kind that they did not want him to stand but he finished both phone calls under the clear impression that he had the goodwill of the leader for his nomination bid. However, when he read a story in the *Evening Herald* which quoted leadership sources as suggesting that McAleese was putting in a strong bid for the nomination he began to get suspicious. These suspicions were fuelled when he went to the Dáil restaurant for his lunch and found that Dermot Ahern, who was at an adjacent table, did not greet him as he normally would. After lunch, O'Kennedy followed Ahern into the corridor. 'I told you I need to know if I have support. Are you going to propose Mary McAleese?' asked O'Kennedy. When he did not get a satisfactory reply he became incensed. 'I will not be treated this way by you. I was entitled to be made aware what was going on but I have been treated with contempt.' The minister responded with equal anger. 'Nobody ever told you to stand,' he snapped and the two men parted. A furious O'Kennedy went back into the restaurant and told Séamus Brennan that he could not be part of a charade any more and he was going to withdraw. However, a statement he had drafted earlier was issued saying he was making a last vigorous attempt to win votes. That night O'Kennedy talked the matter over with his family and with Brian Lenihan, one of his strong supporters, and decided to let his name go forward after all though he was determined not to canvass. He rang his proposer, Brian Lenihan, and said: 'If you so much as canvass one vote for me tomorrow morning I will personally disown you.'

On Tuesday night the Taoiseach addressed a meeting of his ministers. In a typically ambiguous speech he said the time had come to face up to electoral realities. In an ideal world, it would be nice to have one of their own contesting the election but this was not an ideal world. The subtext was clear – he wanted them to go for McAleese. After the meeting the ministers backing McAleese and some party backroom figures carried out a last-minute canvass for her. It was cleverly conducted because the 40 or so certain Reynolds supporters were not contacted at all. On the eve of the nomination meeting most of them were unaware that their man was doomed. O'Kennedy was in a marginally better position because he at least knew his goose was cooked.

On the day of the vote Reynolds was still full of confidence, believing he had the pledges of a majority in the bag. Shortly after 10 a.m. he received a phone call to his Ailesbury Road home in Dublin. The caller was the Taoiseach. Reynolds asked Ahern if he would be required to make a speech and was told he would not; only the proposers and seconders would be asked to speak. 'Bertie rang me about 10.15 on the morning of the meeting to ask who I would like as my director of elections,' Reynolds said later. 'He suggested Martin Mackin [soon afterwards to be appointed party general secretary] and I agreed. He asked me if I was happy that I had the numbers to get me through and I said yeah.'[5] When he walked into the meeting half an hour later Reynolds was still blithely oblivious of his impending fate and he chatted amiably to Ahern before the meeting started.

There had been a last-minute change of plan, however, because the format did not suit McAleese. She had thought of having Mary O'Rourke as a proposer but dropped the idea, feeling that TDs might regard O'Rourke's involvement as simply part of a grudge against Reynolds. McAleese had then forgotten all about arranging for a proposer, concentrating instead on preparing a speech to the meeting, even though the ostensible format did not provide for speeches. In a panic just before the meeting started, Martin McAleese asked Dick Roche if he was proposing Mary but Roche said he thought O'Rourke was doing the job.

The next thing Roche remembers was being approached by the Taoiseach and the party chairman, Rory O'Hanlon. 'Are you proposing Mary?' they asked him and he replied that he was not. 'Well, that panicked me,' said Roche later. 'Then Rory said, "We won't have any proposers or seconders." That's literally what happened. It was confusion. It was cobbled together at the last minute.'

Reynolds was told about the new arrangements at the door of the

party room on his way in. Neither he nor O'Kennedy had anything prepared, believing speeches would not be required. When O'Hanlon
opened the meeting he outlined the new arrangements and said that each
candidate would speak for three minutes. The candidates were called in
alphabetical order and McAleese spoke first. She had spent hours the previous night preparing for this moment and delivered a typically fluent and
confident speech about her vision of the presidency. There was warm and
sustained applause when she sat down. O'Kennedy then made a curious
speech. He quoted the constitutional pledge of the president to serve the
Irish people and he hearkened back to the standards of honesty and integrity which pertained when he joined Fianna Fáil in the mid-1960s. Those
present did not know what O'Kennedy was on about until much later in
the day when the pieces of the jigsaw fell into place. When Reynolds's turn
came he was nervous. He had never been an inspirational speaker; he was
a doer rather than a talker. On his feet, without advance preparation, he
delivered what even his supporters agreed was a poor speech. He went on
for too long and he raised eyebrows by saying he would use the presidency
to be an ambassador for Irish business.

Even after the speeches Reynolds had no idea what was to come and
he told Senator Eddie Bohan, who was sitting beside him, that he
expected to get around 70 votes. There were some straws in the wind even
before voting started. Ray Burke, who was out of the country, not surprisingly left his anti-Reynolds vote behind him. MEP Mark Killilea faxed his
vote for Reynolds from Brussels, but, curiously, Environment Minister
Noel Dempsey, who had been given his first big political break by Albert
and was also abroad, chose not to vote at all. His action was in sharp contrast to the other protégé of Reynolds, Brian Cowen, the Minister for
Health. Cowen remained loyal to the last and rebuffed the blandishments
of cabinet colleagues suggesting that he should ingratiate himself with the
leadership by voting for McAleese. Cowen, McCreevy and David
Andrews were the only members of the cabinet to back Reynolds.

Then, in a final humiliation, Ahern twisted the knife in the wound
before dispatching the former Taoiseach. After the ballot papers were
handed out he came over to Reynolds and showed him his vote. He had
voted for the Longford man, but Reynolds suddenly felt a chill run down
his spine. The MEP Brian Crowley, sitting on the edge of the front row to
accommodate his wheelchair, saw Ahern's action and his heart sank. He
suspected that Ahern was so confident of a McAleese victory he could
afford to squander his own vote. 'You're finished now,' Crowley
remarked to Reynolds.[6]

When O'Hanlon announced the first-count result there was no outright winner but the outcome was clear. Reynolds was ahead with 49 votes

but McAleese was not far behind with 42 and O'Kennedy had 21. 'We knew then Albert was scuppered,' remarked Dermot Ahern.[7] O'Kennedy was eliminated and a second ballot ensued. At this stage Reynolds told Ahern he would not accept the nomination even if he won on the second ballot, but in the event McAleese was comfortably ahead, winning by 62 votes to 48. There was euphoria in the McAleese camp as she swept out of Leinster House amidst a crowd of supporters and across the road to Buswell's Hotel where the winner's press conference was scheduled. A shattered Reynolds followed in a daze, a dead man walking. All his previous setbacks in politics, even his loss of the Taoiseach's office, were nothing to the humiliation visited upon him that day.

Even though he got what he wanted, the result was also a defining moment for Ahern who had displayed a ruthlessness that etched itself into the political folk memory.

31. Burke Bites the Dust

AS THE CAMPAIGNING FOR THE PRESIDENTIAL ELECTION got under way, the Dáil was recalled on 10 September 1997 to debate the report of the McCracken tribunal which had brought Haughey into public disgrace over the Dunne payments. The report came at a bad time for Ahern as it coincided with mounting Opposition demands for another tribunal to examine the whole Ansbacher accounts scandal. Fine Gael leader John Bruton believed that a concerted push by the Opposition could topple the government before it had time to find its feet but others on the Opposition benches lacked the stomach for an all-out assault on the coalition so soon after the election.

Before the Dáil debate began, another scandal which was to do further damage to Fianna Fáil mesmerised deputies. The Ceann Comhairle gave precedence to a personal statement from Ray Burke about the circumstances in which he accepted a payment of £30,000 in 1989. 'I have come here today to defend my personal integrity, the integrity of my party, of this Government and the honour of this House. I have also come here to reassure the public and in particular my constituents that I have done nothing wrong,' said Burke. He then read into the Dáil record the public statement he had made a month earlier confirming that he had received a payment of £30,000 from James Gogarty on behalf of JMSE in June of 1989. He added that he had contributed £10,000 to Fianna Fáil headquarters during the 1989 election campaign and had handed over approximately £7,000 to his local party organisation. 'The remainder of the political contributions received by me, including the contribution Mr Gogarty gave me during our meeting in my home, were used to cover my personal election expenses. I did not and do not have separate accounts as regards either the election campaign in question or my subsequent political expenditure.' In a question and answer session with Opposition TDs little further information was elicited and the general media consensus on the day was that the Opposition had not laid a glove on Burke.[1]

Later that evening Ahern promised to establish another tribunal on foot of the McCracken findings which were limited by the terms of reference solely to payments to Haughey from Ben Dunne. Despite the indictment of Haughey in the McCracken report Ahern was reluctant to condemn his old boss. 'In many important areas valuable service by some-one of immense ability will be recalled. For the positive things he did he will always be held in high regard by many people,' said Ahern. He added that it was unfortunately inevitable that Haughey's achievements would be set off against the findings of the tribunal. 'I find that very sad for an individual that many of us know well and have honoured and admired ... It is sad for our democracy and our nation that a leader who, after Lemass, put more of his stamp on the Ireland of the second half of the twentieth century than possibly anyone else, should have demeaned himself and political life by accepting such huge sums of money for his personal bene-fit from Ben Dunne.'

Later in his contribution Ahern gave a hostage to fortune when he referred to the issue of the party leader's allowance. Throughout the 1980s there were strong rumours in political circles that Charles Haughey was pocketing the state grant made to political leaders to run their parties. During his period as leader well over £1 million had been paid over to Haughey. The Labour leader, Dick Spring, had raised this issue in a letter to Ahern following the publication of the McCracken report. In his Dáil contribution Ahern referred to Spring's query. 'Insofar as I could, with little available records, I am satisfied, having spoken to the person who administered the account, that it was used for *bona fide* party purposes, that the cheques were prepared by that person and countersigned by another senior party member.'[2] What Ahern did not tell the Dáil was that the other 'senior party member' who normally countersigned the cheques was no other than himself. When it later emerged that a significant sum of money from the account had ended up in Haughey's personal account or had gone to fund his expensive shirt-buying and wining-and-dining habits, Ahern claimed to have signed hundreds of blank cheques on the leader's account.

Under pressure from the Opposition and from the Progressive Democrats within the coalition, the government agreed to establish a new tribunal to look into other possible sources of Haughey's money, apart from Ben Dunne. The tribunal was headed by Mr Justice Michael Mori-arty. Attempts to open up all the Ansbacher account holders to scrutiny were resisted by the coalition and eventually voted down. Later, however, Mary Harney, as Minister for Enterprise and Employment, began inquir-ies of her own under the terms of the Companies Act and the findings eventually led to a full-scale inquiry into all the Ansbacher accounts.

The setting up of the new Moriarty tribunal did not buy much time for the beleaguered government because the Opposition and the media moved the focus back on to Burke and the payment he had admitted receiving from James Gogarty. The *Irish Times* published a story on the manner in which Burke, as Minister for Justice, had issued some of the 'passports for sale' and further stories suggested that Ahern had conducted his own investigation into this aspect of Burke's past.[3] The pressure on Burke was becoming intolerable and on 7 October, on the day of his brother's funeral, Burke resigned, not just from the cabinet but also from the Dáil. The decision to resign his Dáil seat initially left Fianna Fáil reeling but the government recovered its composure and agreed to Opposition demands to establish yet another judicial tribunal, this time into the Burke payment. The terms of reference it drafted were very wide, taking in the whole issue of planning in north County Dublin and not just the payment to Burke. The responsibility for chairing this tribunal was given to Mr Justice Fergus Flood.

As these political dramas were being played out in the Dáil the presidential election got into full swing. Despite the unpromising background, the campaign served to unify Fianna Fáil and stabilise the government. Ironically, Department of Foreign Affairs documents leaked by an anonymous source and purporting to show that the Fianna Fáil presidential candidate, Mary McAleese, had a cosy relationship with Sinn Féin, actually served to get the party behind her. The leak changed the focus of political debate away from internal problems in Fianna Fáil onto the national issue. The resulting political storm allowed Fianna Fáil to do what it is best at – to wave the green flag and to berate everybody else, particularly John Bruton, for being 'unsound' on the national issue. Bruton was even falsely accused of being behind the leaks. The scandals and tribunals were forgotten for a few weeks as the party rallied to McAleese who was a powerful campaigner in her own right. The election was held on 30 October and McAleese won comfortably, beating Mary Banotti of Fine Gael on the final count while Labour's Adi Roche trailed back in fourth place behind Dana Rosemary Scallon, while Derek Nally came fifth.

The outcome changed the political atmosphere quite dramatically. At the beginning of the campaign the coalition government was on the ropes but at the end it was the Opposition parties who were in disarray. Fine Gael was left bruised by the row that followed the leaked documents while Labour was in a bad way after a second thumping defeat in the space of a few months. Dick Spring decided it was time to call it a day and he announced his resignation as party leader. As his successor, Labour selected Ruairí Quinn ahead of Brendan Howlin. Quinn turned the focus away from trying to destabilise the government. His priority was to rebuild the Labour Party and begin the moves towards a merger with Democratic Left. Bertie Ahern and Mary Harney were given the breathing space they needed to stabilise the coalition relationship.

The lull gave Ahern the interlude he needed to concentrate on dealing with the increasing tempo of events in the North. At this stage, following the renewed IRA ceasefire, Sinn Féin had been admitted to talks involving all the other Northern parties and chaired by former US senator George Mitchell. It was a complicated and difficult process which at times came close to collapse, but it ended triumphantly on Good Friday 1998 with the so-called Good Friday Agreement, based on the principles of the Downing Street Declaration of 1993. Under its terms, an executive involving Sinn Féin was to be established in the North, decommissioning of paramilitary weapons was to conclude by 22 May 2000, terrorist prisoners were to be released and a referendum held on both sides of the border to ratify the Agreement. Part of the deal was that the territorial claim to the North in Articles 2 and 3 of the Irish Constitution would be abolished and replaced with provisions expressing an aspiration to unity.

The Agreement was a triumph of diplomacy and while it was by no means plain sailing afterwards, it gave Ahern a standing that he had not had before. The amendment of Articles 2 and 3 of de Valera's Constitution was a potential minefield for Ahern but he skilfully steered the changes through his parliamentary party and got the endorsement of the Fianna Fáil national executive. When the referendum in the Republic was carried with a 'Yes' vote of over 90 per cent, an opinion poll gave Ahern the highest satisfaction rating ever achieved by a party leader since polling began. After less than a year in office it seemed that he had established himself in the eyes of the voters as a statesman of some quality to augment his image as a glad-handing politician.

However, the referendum was barely out of the way when Fianna Fáil's past returned once more to haunt Ahern. Vincent Browne reported in *Magill* magazine that Fitzwilton plc had paid £30,000 in cash to Ray Burke in June of 1989, within a few days of the £30,000 payment by James Gogarty. The Flood Tribunal was investigating the payment, made through a subsidiary called Rennicks, and Fianna Fáil had made statements to the Tribunal and handed in documents relating to the payment.[4] A political row immediately erupted about the disclosure of this payment, not least because it emerged that Ahern had not kept his Tánaiste, Mary Harney, informed about the development when it first came to his attention. Seán Fleming, the Fianna Fáil TD for Laois-Offaly, who was an accountant with Fianna Fáil in 1989, gave an interesting account of the circumstances surrounding the 1989 payment to the Dáil and also outlined his involvement the previous year in helping the party investigate the circumstances of the Gogarty payment. 'In July or August 1997 the party general secretary, Mr Pat Farrell, contacted me and asked me whether Mr Ray Burke had given £10,000 to Fianna Fáil head office in June 1989. I visited party headquarters and checked the cash receipts book and was satisfied we had received £10,000 through Mr Ray Burke during the June 1989 election campaign and that this contribution had been from Rennicks. I informed the general secretary verbally of this matter and he was then able to confirm receipt of the £10,000. Mr. Des Richardson, the party's fundraiser, was in the room during some of this meeting.'[5]

Fleming's statement made no attempt to disguise the fact that both he and Pat Farrell were aware at the time of Burke's statement to the Dáil that the £10,000 he had handed over to the party did not come from Gogarty's contribution, as was strongly implied, but actually came from Fitzwilton. Opposition deputies also noted Fleming's reference to Des Richardson because Richardson was not only Fianna Fáil's fundraiser in 1997 but also a close associate of Bertie Ahern and his main political fundraiser for a considerable time. Amid the political uproar the government agreed to widen the terms of reference of the Flood tribunal to allow it to investigate other payments made to Ray Burke or any other politician. The amended terms of reference, published on 15 July 1998, considerably added to the task facing Mr Justice Flood and his legal team, but the move calmed the political storm.

The same pattern was repeated a number of times over the next two years. The coalition government achieved high popularity ratings as the economic boom went from strength to strength but every so often another ghost from the past would suddenly emerge to haunt Ahern and give the coalition a dose of the jitters. Later in 1998 it was the issue of Haughey's tax liability for the Dunne payments. Haughey was served with a tax assessment of £2 million by the Revenue Commissioners but on appeal to the Tax Appeals Commissioners the bill was reduced to zero. There was uproar in the Dáil when it emerged that the Appeals Commissioner who had made the decision was Ahern's brother-in-law, Ronan Kelly. Not only that but Kelly had been appointed to the position by Ahern in 1994. Pat Rabbitte sprang the information on the Dáil and there was bedlam as Ahern was caught on the hop, even though the decision had nothing to do with him.[6]

In January 1999 another voice from the past spoke up. Intermittent stories had appeared in the media in the autumn of 1998 about property developer Tom Gilmartin, a Sligo man living in Luton. The reports suggested that he had given information to the Flood tribunal about a payment of £50,000 he had made to Pádraig Flynn in the month of June 1989. However, it seemed that Gilmartin was unwilling to give evidence at the tribunal, until he was provoked into it by Flynn himself. In a startling performance on the 'Late Late Show' in January, Flynn dismissed Gilmartin's allegations and said that the developer was not well. That prompted an immediate reaction by Gilmartin who said he was now willing to give evidence at the tribunal. He also claimed to have told Ahern about the £50,000 payment to Flynn during one of a number of meetings.[7] In response Ahern said he had met Gilmartin only once but, as political pressure mounted, he revised his statement and conceded that he had met him on a few occasions. Ahern was then forced to submit himself to a long question and answer session in the Dáil about the matter and while he came through without suffering any serious embarrassment it put him back on the defensive for a time.[8]

Harney managed to live with Ahern's loss of memory in relation to the meetings with Gilmartin but she was presented with a more difficult problem a couple of months later during the so-called Sheedy affair. This was a complicated sequence of events which led to the unprecedented resignations of a Supreme Court judge, a High Court judge and a senior judicial officer. It began with the release from jail of a young architect called Philip Sheedy who had been sentenced to four years for dangerous driving causing death. However, Sheedy was released nearly three years early by Judge Cyril Kelly, who had not been the original sentencing judge. It then emerged that Supreme Court judge Hugh O'Flaherty had asked the county registrar to put the case back onto the list for hearing. In the resulting furore O'Flaherty and Kelly were effectively forced into resignation by the government. In the dramatic 24 hours before O'Flaherty resigned, Celia Larkin visited him at his Ballsbridge home along with a number of other well-wishers. Then the *Sunday Tribune* security correspondent, Catherine Cleary, uncovered the fact that none other than Bertie Ahern had made representations on Sheedy's behalf asking that he be released early.[9]

Luckily for Ahern he had informed Harney about the matter a few days before the news broke, but a row developed between Taoiseach and Tánaiste when Ahern publicly dismissed her concerns and denied that she had asked him to make a statement to the Dáil on the issue. Harney refused to attend a cabinet meeting and for 24 hours it seemed that the coalition might come apart, but Ahern publicly backed down and the cracks were papered over. He then answered questions in the Dáil about the affair and maintained that he had merely made representations on behalf of Sheedy as he would for anybody else who asked him. There the matter rested.

The Gilmartin story rumbled on and it put paid to any chance Flynn might have had of remaining on as a European Commissioner. It also put his daughter, Beverley, into an embarrassing position in the Dáil. She was already under something of a cloud because of her own role as a financial adviser with National Irish Bank before she entered politics. The bank was accused of facilitating a tax-evasion scheme based in the Isle of Man and this was the subject of a Department of Enterprise and Employment investigation and a number of court cases. When Fianna Fáil accepted an Opposition motion censuring Pádraig Flynn for refusing to give any explanation for the Gilmartin donation, Beverley refused to vote for the motion and lost the whip for a period as a result. In a debate on 10 February, Des O'Malley took the opportunity to make a few reflections on standards in political life. He referred back to the climate under Haughey and pointed out that many people had left Fianna Fáil because of it. 'However, there were many who did not leave, many who felt totally comfortable in the kind of party which Charles Haughey had created. Among them was Mr Pádraig Flynn.' He also made a reference to the Taoiseach as being another who had been comfortable in the house that Charlie built. O'Malley went on to recall that when he had been drummed out of Fianna Fáil in 1985, Flynn had 'addressed the nation through an RTÉ camera and pronounced that my conduct was "unbecoming a member of Fianna Fáil." Now it is Mr Flynn's turn to be dumped upon.'[10]

Meanwhile the Moriarty and Flood tribunals held intermittent public hearings throughout 1999 and the public finally began to hear chapter and verse about the scale of corruption that had flourished during the Haughey era. For a start the Moriarty tribunal learned how he had run up an overdraft of over £1 million with AIB during the 1970s; that amounts to over £5 million in today's values. When Haughey became Taoiseach, the bank wrote off nearly £400,000 of the debt. The complex web of bank accounts which sustained Haughey's lifestyle at this period and which allowed him to take over the leadership of Fianna Fáil was exposed for all to see.[11]

Later the tribunal heard how a list of prominent business people had invested in Celtic Helicopters, the firm owned by Haughey's son Ciarán. Some of the money ended up in the Ansbacher accounts managed by Des Traynor which funded Haughey's lifestyle. Among the investors was John Byrne, the property developer who had been linked with Haughey for decades. Another prominent figure mentioned at the tribunal was former chairman of Aer Lingus and CRH, Michael Dargan. It was revealed that £10,000 from him had provided start-up capital for the helicopter company, although he said he had no idea how his money had got there. Others who invested in Celtic Helicopters were former Bord Fáilte boss Joe Malone, the hotelier P.V. Doyle, the beef exporter Seamus Purcell and the politician and businessman Dr John O'Connell.[12] It also emerged that beef baron Larry Goodman had paid £25,000 to Haughey.

The tribunal uncovered the names of more and more of the people who had financed Haughey's lifestyle during the 1980s, including Patrick

Gallagher, the property developer jailed for fraud. When it seemed things could not get any worse the gossip columnist Terry Keane went public for the first time about her 27-year relationship with Haughey. Keane wrote in lurid detail about the champagne lifestyle which she enjoyed with him and chronicled the affair in a series of articles in the *Sunday Times* which were accompanied by intimate personal photographs.[13]

The Moriarty tribunal came up with further evidence of this lifestyle. The public was enthralled to hear that in 1991 alone Haughey spent over £15,000 from his exchequer allowance on dining out and buying shirts. Eileen Foy, Haughey's personal secretary for his entire period in office and the administrator of the leader's allowance account, told the tribunal that the second signatory on most of the cheques was Bertie Ahern. Asked by tribunal lawyer John Coughlan whether Ahern or Ray MacSharry, the other co-signatory on the account, would have considered this expenditure normal if it had been brought to their attention, Foy replied: 'I think so.'[14]

Called before the Moriarty tribunal himself during the summer, Ahern gave evidence about the operation of the party leader's allowance during the Haughey era and he confirmed that his name was on most of the cheques as a co-signatory with Haughey. Asked to account for his signature on a cheque for £25,000 signed in the month of June 1989 which ended up in Haughey's personal account, Ahern said that it was his practice to pre-sign most of the cheques.

And yet all the revelations about the sleaze of the Haughey era did not appear to do too much damage to Ahern. Fianna Fáil did reasonably well in the local and European elections which were held in June 1999. The party's share of the vote held up and it regained control of a number of county councils. However, by-elections continued to go against the party and in Dublin South-Central in October Labour's Mary Upton comfortably retained the seat held by her late brother, Pat, who had died suddenly earlier in the year. Opinion polls also showed the beginnings of a drift in Fianna Fáil support from the extraordinary ratings which followed the Good Friday Agreement. Nonetheless, Ahern remained comfortably ahead of Opposition leaders John Bruton and Ruairí Quinn.

At the turn of the millennium embarrassing revelations at the Moriarty tribunal involving two more Fianna Fáil TDs had no perceptible effect on the government's standing even though Ahern again displayed unaccountable tolerance for their behaviour. The first controversy related to Leitrim TD John Ellis when it was revealed at the tribunal in late 1999 that he had received £26,000 from Haughey ten years earlier to get him out of serious debt problems relating to his cattle-exporting business. The revelation provoked farmers in the west of Ireland who had lost money in the business collapse to renew their campaign for compensation. What added fuel to the fire was that Ellis had been appointed chairman of the Oireachtas Agriculture Committee following the 1997 election. There were calls on him to resign, but Ahern refused to put pressure on the TD and in fact ticked off the Minister for Tourism and Sport, Dr Jim McDaid, for publicly seeking his resignation. Eventually, pressure from the Opposition, the media and some of his colleagues forced Ellis to step down.

The Taoiseach adopted a similar non-committal role when the Moriarty tribunal disclosed at the end of January 2000 that Kerry Fianna Fáil TD Denis Foley had two Ansbacher accounts worth over £130,000. Not only that, but Foley, the vice-chairman of the Public Accounts Committee, had participated in the inquiry into the DIRT tax scandal in the autumn of 1999 without revealing to the committee's lawyers that he had a major conflict of interest. When the matter became public it emerged that Mary Harney had told Ahern about Foley's Ansbacher accounts before Christmas. There was a media hullabaloo but, as in earlier controversies, Ahern declined to take an attitude of any kind, at least in public. Instead he allowed pressure from all sides to build up on Foley. The Kerry TD eventually resigned the Fianna Fáil whip but only after a deal had been struck that he would continue to support the party in the Dáil.

On the political front, the government gained from a tax-cutting budget, despite a lot of controversy over the tilting of the benefits in favour of the better off. On the North, political progress followed a pattern of two steps forward, followed by one and a half steps back, as the parties inched towards a settlement. A power-sharing executive including Sinn Féin was finally established at the end of 1999 only to be suspended in February 2000 because of the failure of the IRA to begin decommissioning. Then in May the IRA finally stated that it would make a move on the issue and the political process resumed its slow progress. The Northern issue had little impact on political events in the Republic because of the all-party consensus on the issue, though the elections of summer 1999 indicated that Sinn Féin had begun to pick up support south of the border.

32. Serving Their Time

BY THE TIME THE DÁIL ADJOURNED for the Easter recess in the first year of the new millennium it appeared that the worst was over for Bertie Ahern and his government. The public seemed impervious to the drip-feed of revelations from the tribunals while the Opposition parties had failed to capitalise on the coalition's problems. There was even speculation that Ahern might try to wrong-foot the Opposition by calling a general election in the early summer of 2000, so that he would be safely ensconced for a second term in office before the tribunals got around to seriously embarrassing revelations.

The respite for the government was short-lived, however. A series of controversies, cock-ups and revelations rocked the coalition to its foundations during the next Dáil session and it survived by a thread. Far from thinking about a snap election in June on the third anniversary of coming to office, Ahern and his cabinet colleagues were grateful to limp into the summer recess without having to face a wrathful electorate.

The slide began on Easter Sunday when the *Sunday Business Post* claimed that in 1989 a member of Haughey's government had received £50,000 in a car park in the Burlington Hotel in Dublin, on the night of the All-Ireland football final, from an individual who was acting on behalf of a leading property developer. The following day, at the annual Fianna Fáil 1916 commemoration, Bertie Ahern said he believed that the allegation related to him, but he vehemently denied that it had happened. 'I am a straight, honest person. I got no money. I was in no car park. I wasn't in the Burlington Hotel that night. Owen O'Callaghan has given me nothing.'[1]

The Cork property developer, Owen O'Callaghan, who has been a major contributor to Fianna Fáil, issued a statement saying he was the individual alleged to have been behind the payment, but he was as vehement as Ahern in denying the allegation. It soon emerged that the person making the claims, Cork-based Denis (Starry) O'Brien, had been called a forger and a perjurer by a judge during a civil action a decade earlier. Opposition politicians were sceptical about the whole story; and ultimately (July 2001) Ahern won the case and was awarded £30,000 in damages against O'Brien.

This was quickly followed by series of revelations from the tribunals, some of which again featured Owen O'Callaghan. At the Flood tribunal the political lobbyist and former Fianna Fáil government press secretary, Frank Dunlop, was forced into admissions that he had spend hundreds of thousands of pounds in a campaign to get planning permission for O'Callaghan at the Quarryvale site on the west side of Dublin for a huge shopping complex. Dunlop listed more than 20 county councillors, some of them TDs and senators, to whom he said he had paid money to get them to vote for the project. By far the biggest amount of money was paid by Dunlop to Fianna Fáil TD Liam Lawlor.[2] Even though Fine Gael and Labour as well as Fianna Fáil Oireachtas members, were included on Dunlop's list, the revelations destabilised the coalition again.

Fine Gael conducted its own inquiry and found that while a number of its councillors had received £500 or £1,000 from Dunlop as campaign contributions in 1991 and 1992 they were not believed to have compromised themselves. The party found that three of its representatives could not provide adequate explanations for the contributions, and party leader John Bruton said none of them would be allowed to run as a party candidate again. Labour TD Pat Rabbitte also suffered embarrassment from the disclosure that he had received a contribution of £2,000 from Dunlop in 1992, even though he had sent it back after consultations with his party.

Nonetheless, the spotlight remained on Fianna Fáil for a number of reasons. The really big payments from Dunlop went to Fianna Fáil politicians, and O'Callaghan was a well-known party supporter who publicly stated that he had contributed over £100,000 in formal donations to Fianna Fáil on top of payments to individual politicians.[3] The involvement of O'Callaghan also reopened an earlier controversy about why Bertie Ahern, on his last day in office as Minister for Finance in 1994, had signed an order giving special tax designation for a site at Golden Island near Athlone in which O'Callaghan was also involved.

The controversy about the Dunlop payments caused further anxiety in the Progressive Democrats who announced that they would not continue in a government if it depended for its survival on the support of corrupt TDs. Fianna Fáil conducted its own inquiry, which took some time to report, but which eventually concluded that Liam Lawlor had questions to answer. Lawlor eventually resigned the Fianna Fáil whip and the party rallied around other TDs like G.V. Wright and Batt O'Keeffe, who had received substantial contributions from O'Callaghan. There was also some embarrassment for Minister for Health Micheál Martin, widely regarded as a future party leader, when it emerged that he had received £6,500 in political donations from O'Callaghan. However, as the money was donated over four election campaigns, the Martin amount was quite small in the scale of things.

Then at the end of May the Moriarty tribunal disclosed that according to its calculations Charles Haughey had received contributions amounting to £8.5 million from leading businessmen over the years. Tribunal barrister Jerry Healy SC said the funds in question did not include money from the party leader's allowance fund or the money paid to Celtic Helicopters. Included in the calculations were the £750,000 used to pay off Haughey's massive AIB overdraft in 1980 and payments from leading Irish businessmen, including supermarket supremo Ben Dunne, the hotelier P.V, Doyle, the stockbroker Dermot Desmond. The tribunal was unable to trace the ultimate source of a considerable portion of the funds which had been channelled through Des Traynor , but was able to identify some sources: 'The Tribunal has, however, heard evidence from which it would appear that the ultimate source of some of these funds can be identified as in the case of payments through Mr. Bernard Dunne, Mr. Dermot Desmond, Mr. Fustok, Mr. PV Doyle, Mr. Patrick Gallagher, Dr. John O'Connell; but the Tribunal believes that Mr. Charles Haughey may ultimately be able to be of assistance in either identifying or providing evidence which may assist in identifying the sources of some of the other payments, the ultimate sources of which have not yet been identified.'[4]

It was against this background of continuing revelations about sleaze that the government made the decision to appoint the former Supreme Court judge, Hugh O'Flaherty, as Ireland's vice president of the European Investment Bank, a post with a salary of £170,000 a year. The decision caused a level of public outrage that took the government and the Opposition parties completely by surprise. There were widespread demands to know why a person the government regarded as unfit to remain on the Supreme Court because of his involvement in the Philip Sheedy case a year earlier was now considered suitable for a lucrative EU position.

The O'Flaherty appointment, following so quickly on the heels of the Dunlop revelations, seemed to act as a lightning conductor for public disgust at the mountain of sleaze which had been uncovered by the tribunals. Two opinion polls showed that 70 per cent of voters were opposed to the government decision and the polls for the first time began to indicate a serious slippage in support for the government.

The appointment also caused a crisis in the PDs. Mary Harney was consulted in advance about the appointment by Minister for Finance Charlie McCreevy, and expressed no objections. Des O'Malley and Bobby Molloy, who had made no objection when they were consulted by Harney before the announcement, quickly came to regret the decision and expressed the view that the appointment was wrong. Junior minister Liz O'Donnell, who was not consulted at all, was furious, while Senator

Helen Keogh left the party and joined Fine Gael in protest. 'I have grown increasingly uneasy in recent times at the way in which the Progressive Democrats are melting back into Fianna Fáil,' she said. 'The party now lacks the hunger and the energy to fight for its relevance in this very unbalanced Government, where the domineering Fianna Fáil party has killed off any chance that the Progressive Democrats had to make an impact.'[5]

Serious tensions then developed between the two parties in government when Ahern said he agreed with the views of the majority of people in opinion polls who opposed the O'Flaherty appointment. He added that the government would nonetheless proceed with the appointment. The PDs regarded this as an attempt by Ahern to distance himself from the appointment and he made matters worse a few days later by saying in a radio interview with Eamon Dunphy on Today FM that O'Flaherty should at some time explain his role in the Sheedy affair. Harney saw red and phoned Ahern, demanding that he stop trying to have it both ways and either stick with the appointment as decided by the Government or make a decision to drop O'Flaherty. The Taoiseach went into the Dáil the next morning and met Harney's conditions by responding to a demand from Labour's Brendan Howlin that he clarify his position on the appointment. 'The Government is collectively responsible for the nomination of Mr. Hugh O'Flaherty to the European Investment Bank. As leader of the Government I fully stand over that decision. With all my colleagues we made the decision. The Government had no reason to believe anything untoward needed to be added by way of explanation with regard to the controversy surrounding the Sheedy affair. So that there will be no doubt about the subject of Deputy Howlin's question, I wish Mr. O'Flaherty well. I have no doubt he will do an excellent job in the bank and I hope he serves a long and full period.'[6]

Harney was placated, but the net effect of Ahern's intervention was that the controversy was still in full swing when the people of South Tipperary went to the polls on 22 June to fill the vacancy caused by the death of Labour TD Michael Ferris. In the run-up to the by-election, Fine Gael leader John Bruton was the politician under pressure because some of his TDs were looking for a scapegoat for the party's failure to attract more support, given the problems of the coalition. There was a lot of speculation in the media that Bruton would face a challenge if the Fine Gael candidate did not perform well in Tipperary.

In the event, it was Fianna Fáil that received a real pasting in Tipperary. The party's vote slumped by 15 per cent to just 22 per cent of the vote and, even more important psychologically, the Fianna Fáil candidate was eliminated before the final count. Independent socialist candidate Seamus Healy eventually edged out Senator Tom Hayes of Fine Gael for the seat, but this was enough to take the heat off Bruton. The result sent shock waves through Fianna Fáil because it was the first time in the history of the party since 1926 that a Fianna Fáil candidate had been eliminated in a by-election before the final count.

The election result should not have come as a complete surprise to the party faithful because the party's performance in by-elections during the lifetime of the twenty-eighth Dáil had been dismal. It was the fifth by-election loss in a row. Also, in the Limerick East by-election of 1998, the Fianna Fáil candidate had come third on the first count and barely avoided elimination. One of the reasons the result was such a shock was that national opinion polls had lulled Fianna Fáil into a false sense of security, continuing to give the party between 45 per cent and 50 per cent of the vote. While most people involved in politics had long since discounted the headline poll figure for Fianna Fáil, a collapse to 22 per cent was something for which nobody was prepared.

There was even more political instability in the wake of the by-election and, in the last week of the Dáil session before the summer recess, the coalition came close to collapse. The government was fortunate that there were only four sitting days left in the session because it would have had difficulty surviving for much longer if the pressure was maintained. Matters began to spin out of control with the decision of Judge Kevin Haugh in the Dublin Circuit Court to order the indefinite postponement of Charles Haughey's trial on charges of obstructing the McCracken tribunal. The judge made his decision on the basis that remarks made by Mary Harney in a newspaper interview had made a fair trial impossible. In the interview published in the *Irish Independent* in late May, Harney said Haughey should go to jail.[7] Haughey's legal team used the comment, made in response to a reporter's question, as the basis for arguing that a fair trial for the ex-Taoiseach had become impossible.

Judge Haugh announced his decision on 26 June. 'I believe that the views and assertions of the Tánaiste, as expressed by her in the course of the said interview, constitute an attack on the accused's character of a sort which I must assume would not be permissible to be made by the prosecution in the course of a trial. At their lowest, in my opinion, the statement made and the views expressed constitute attacks whose prejudicial value wholly outweigh any possible prohibitive value and are therefore inadmissible.'[8] The judge's decision astonished the country and was devastating for the PD leader. It was supremely ironic that Harney, of all people, should be responsible for allowing Haughey to escape indefinitely from the clutches of the law.

Harney was in Warsaw on an official visit to Poland when the news broke. She was stunned by the judgement and began to entertain serious doubts about whether she could continue as PD leader and Tánaiste. She found it really distressing that having spent so much of her political life opposing Haughey she should end up being the one to get him off the hook with respect to criminal prosecution. When Harney arrived back in Dublin on 27 June she immediately went to Government Buildings and offered her resignation to the Taoiseach in advance of that day's cabinet meeting. Unsurprisingly, he declined to accept it as it would mean the collapse of the government, but she was still not sure about continuing on and later in the day discussed her position with the first leader of the PDs, Des O'Malley, and her ministerial colleague, Liz O'Donnell. They both advised her strongly to forget about resignation as the judge's decision would face a legal challenge in any case. Having agonised over her position, Harney decided to remain in office.[9]

On the same day, Ahern and Fianna Fáil were rocked by developments at the Moriarty tribunal. The previous week, property developer Mark Kavanagh had given evidence in private to the tribunal that he had given £100,000 to Charles Haughey at Kinsealy on the day of the 1989 election. Kavanagh maintained that £75,000 of the money was intended for Fianna Fáil and £25,000 for the Brian Lenihan liver transplant fund. Curiously, though, he gave four bank drafts for £25,000 each to Haughey. One was made out to Fianna Fáil and the other three to cash. A few days after giving his evidence in private, Ursula Halligan, the political correspondent of TV3, revealed that in 1996 Bertie Ahern had carried out an internal investigation in Fianna Fáil following complaints from Kavanagh that his contribution had not been acknowledged.

The Moriarty tribunal only discovered this from the TV3 story and tribunal lawyers were furious on a number of counts. Firstly they were annoyed to find that while Fianna Fáil had given them access to its cash receipts book, another document, variously described as a list or an extract from the cash receipts book, had not been disclosed. This document was, in effect, a key to a relatively small number of donations which were handled personally by Charles Haughey in 1989 but which were listed as 'anonymous' in the main cash book. What annoyed the tribunal lawyers was that this list, which had not been provided to the tribunal, contained precisely the information they were mandated to investigate.

Secondly, they were angry at the Taoiseach for failing to disclose that he had made his own inquiries into the Kavanagh payment in 1996 when this was also a matter of direct relevance to their inquiries. Bertie Ahern was summoned to give evidence to the tribunal about these issues. With Ahern and Harney now both in hot water politically, the political temperature began to rise alarmingly. If the Opposition parties had known that Harney was on the brink of resignation their excitement would have been even greater. A meeting of the Joint Committee on Justice, Equality and Women's Rights then added another vital ingredient into the heady mix. The Labour Party had tabled a motion for debate by the committee, calling on Hugh O'Flaherty to come before it to explain his role in the Sheedy affair. Some Fianna Fáil TDs, including three committee members, publicly expressed similar views. There was outrage in the Fianna Fáil leadership and the dissenting TDs were called in and giving a severe dressing down in the chief whip's office. The Fianna Fáil members of the committee were ordered to toe the line or face dire consequences. It was both a shocking and eye-opening experience for the newer TDs involved and they were intimidated into voting down the motion. Labour deputy leader Brendan Howlin, also a member of the committee, was so incensed by what he saw happening that he urged his party leader, Ruairí Quinn, to table a motion of no confidence in the government. Quinn added to the air of tension by doing this the following day and the motion was scheduled for debate on the last day of the Dáil session.

The final days before the Dáil recess saw a return to the atmosphere of fear and loathing which characterised Haughey's GUBU government of 1982. Having intimidated their own backbenchers into toeing the line, Fianna Fáil ministers went on the warpath against enemies, real and imagined. The media suddenly became a target for abuse with a succession of ministers, including senior figures like Brian Cowen, denouncing RTE for allegedly failing to give an accurate report of proceedings at the Moriarty tribunal. The charge was ludicrous. The RTE news team, led by television reporter Annette O'Donnell, had provided superb and remarkably fair reports of the complicated tribunal proceedings for the previous 18 months. The Fianna Fáil assault indicated a government on the verge of a nervous breakdown. 'The party stepped back, took a hard look into its own heart and, after mature reflection, faced up to the awkward truth: it was all the media's fault. Over the next few days the public was presented with a Government so lacking in self-awareness that it thinks denial is a river in Egypt,' wrote Fintan O'Toole in the *Irish Times*.[10]

On the day the Taoiseach gave his evidence to the tribunal, the tribunal lawyer John Coughlan SC, responded to the Fianna Fáil hysteria by calmly outlining the basis for the tribunal's actions in calling the party to book. He took the unusual step of reading the correspondence between Fianna Fáil and the tribunal into the record. Then, addressing the tribunal chairman, Coughlan added pointedly. 'I am not concluding that there was any deliberate withholding of information from the tribunal but the facts need to be established in the public domain and it would be for you, Sir, as the tribunal, at the end of the day, to make any findings of fact or to arrive at any conclusions which you consider appropriate in accordance with the

Terms of Reference which you have been given for the purpose of this inquiry.'[11]

When the Taoiseach took the stand he was cross-examined in a much less deferential fashion than on his first appearance almost a year earlier. Coughlan quizzed him on two main issues. Firstly, he was pressed about why he had not informed the tribunal about the inquiry he had instigated into the Mark Kavanagh payment in 1996. Secondly, he was asked to account for the fact that as recently as ten days earlier he had not communicated to the tribunal information at his disposal about those events. Ahern did not have any really satisfactory answers to the questions, maintaining that despite a discussion he held with Kavanagh about the events in question he was never told that £100,000 was involved or that the money had been handed directly to Haughey in Kinsealy. However, he avoided getting himself into further trouble by saying anything that might frighten the PDs into bolting.

When it came to the motion of confidence the next day, Ahern was on safer ground in the more familiar surroundings of the Dáil. He defended his government's record, saying he had been faced with the responsibility of cleaning up a legacy from the past of unacceptable practices. John Bruton, in one of his best speeches for some time, remarked that while Ahern's speech had been very precise about what other politicians had done at various times 'that was in contrast with the very poor memory he seems to have of events affecting himself in 1996.'[12]

When the vote was called the government survived comfortably by 84 votes to 80. There was great relief among TDs of all parties that a summer election was not going to be sprung on them. Although they escaped an election, Fianna Fáil TDs had to endure a hot political summer as the O'Flaherty saga dominated the headlines day in, day out. At the end of August, when it became clear that the board of the European Investment Bank would not ratify his nomination, O'Flaherty withdrew his name from consideration. The whole affair did enormous damage to the credibility of both Government parties.

Yet when the Dáil resumed in October, after the summer recess, it was as if the whole O'Flaherty affair was just a bad dream. The Government settled back into the routine of preparing the budget while the Opposition flailed about helplessly, trying, but failing, to find another issue with the potency of O'Flaherty. The extraordinary resilience of Fianna Fáil, and the willingness of so many of its supporters to back the party through thick and thin, seemed to make it impervious to the normal rules of politics.

In December, McCreevy introduced another give-away budget. Tax rates were reduced again and bands widened, despite warning from the

EU against pumping too much money into the economy. It was another bonanza for voters and McCreevy gaily defended it against all criticism, suggesting that his critics were nothing better than killjoys. The voters agreed, with opinion polls showing they wholeheartedly endorsed the measures. It appeared that the extra pounds in the punters' pockets had far more potency than all the political scandals affecting Fianna Fáil put together.

As the year 2000 turned into 2001 the politician at the centre of tribunal investigations was Dublin TD, Liam Lawlor. He had resigned from Fianna Fáil some months earlier because of his starring role in the Flood tribunal investigation into planning in Dublin, although he vehemently denied any wrongdoing. Throughout the autumn of 2000 he had been playing ducks and drakes with the tribunal lawyers, challenging their authority and failing to provide the detailed documentation they were seeking. He was hauled into court on a number of occasions in an effort to make him comply with the tribunal's orders, but he pushed his luck too far. In the middle of January 2001 High Court judge Tom Smyth called a halt to the TD's gallop and sentenced him to jail for contempt.

In a withering judgement Mr Justice Smyth accused the TD of blatantly defying the tribunal. 'That he did so as a citizen is a disgrace; that he did so as a public representative is a scandal,' he said. 'No one is above the law ... there are no untouchables,' he added. Lawlor was taken to Mountjoy to serve the first week of a three-month sentence, but the remainder of the jail term was suspended on condition that he begin to cooperate fully with the tribunal.[13] Nonetheless, the fact of a TD going to jail sent shock waves through the political system.

There were amazing scenes outside Mountjoy as Lawlor began his sentence. But the media circus outside the gates was denied the sight of the TD being brought into the prison. He was driven in lying in the back of a landscape gardener's van to avoid being photographed, and he came out in similarly mysterious circumstances. Even though Lawlor was jailed for contempt rather than for any irregularities discovered by the tribunal, the episode focused the minds of many tribunal witnesses who had been dragging their heels. Fianna Fáil was fortunate that Lawlor had been pushed overboard from the parliamentary party some months previously and the party leadership was able to dissociate itself from him, despite his long years of service as a Fianna Fáil politician.

In fact it was Fine Gael, and not Fianna Fáil, which went through an upheaval at the beginning of 2001. A couple of months earlier maverick Waterford TD Austin Deasy had put down a motion of no confidence in party leader John Bruton and while the leader survived, thanks to some clever footwork by party chairman Phil Hogan, who arranged an immediate vote, before his enemies had time to go away. When an opinion poll in the wake of Lawlor's jailing showed a slump in the Fine Gael rather than the Fianna Fáil vote, the main Opposition party reacted in desperation. Michael Noonan and Jim Mitchell launched an all-out attack on Bruton's leadership and after a long and bitter debate the party leader was removed by 39 votes to 36. In a clear case of history repeating itself, what should have been a disaster for Fianna Fáil instead cost the sitting Fine Gael leader his position. Bruton was blamed by his own TDs for not capitalising on Fianna Fáil's misfortunes just as his predecessor, Alan Dukes, had been in 1990. Michael Noonan now succeeded Bruton, but was immediately snookered by some timely leaks about alleged links between businessman Denis O'Brien and Fine Gael.

With Fine Gael on the back foot, more bad news for Fianna Fáil was absorbed and digested comfortably by the party. Junior Agriculture Minister Ned O'Keeffe was forced to resign on a technicality when he had failed to disclose to the Dáil a potential conflict of interest during a vote on measures to deal with the bovine spongiform encephalopathy (BSE) crisis. The issue related to his ownership of a bone-meal plant on his Co. Cork farm. When the Opposition parties and the media refused to let go of the controversy, O'Keeffe was pressured into resignation by the party leadership.

Another difficulty for the party was the outcome of a libel action taken by Mayo TD Beverley Cooper-Flynn against RTE. The TD, who had worked as an executive with NIB Bank before entering the Dáil, was embroiled in a controversy which developed following disclosures on RTE about the bank's offshore investment scheme in the Isle of Man. RTE reporter Charlie Bird reported that the TD had encouraged some bank customers to evade tax and she took an action for defamation. After the longest and most costly libel action in the history of the state, a jury found against the TD on 3 April. The political fall-out was immediate and the Taoiseach was put under pressure in the Dáil, with the Opposition suggesting that if he failed to take action against the TD it meant that he condoned tax evasion. The upshot was that Cooper-Flynn was expelled from the parliamentary party after putting up a strong rearguard action.

At the Flood and Moriarty tribunals there was also further excitement. The investigation into the awarding of the first independent radio licence to Century Radio brought a new cast of characters into the witness box. Impresario Oliver Barry, whose company had been awarded the licence, was asked to account for his £35,000 donation to Ray Burke back in 1989. James Stafford, another backer of the venture, claimed that Haughey's Government press secretary, P.J. Mara, was paid money by Century Radio.

As for Ray Burke himself, a more worrying development was that he was dramatically forced to alter his evidence about the circumstances in which he had received a substantial amount of money from the builders Brennan and McGowan. There was a long association between Burke and the two builders, who had also been friends of his father's. In the 1970s there were persistent rumours that Brennan and McGowan had built Burke's house in Swords at no cost to Burke, and this was finally confirmed at the Flood tribunal in 2001. During their initial evidence to the tribunal, in 2000, the two builders claimed that they raised money for Burke's political campaigns at fund-raising events in England during the 1980s and the ex-Minister told a bewildering tale of transporting huge amounts of cash between bank accounts in Ireland, England and the Channel Islands.

Tribunal investigators came up with a different story and in May 2001 Burke had changed his position, claiming that he had suffered a 'failure of recollection' with regard to key events. It emerged that Burke had gone to Jersey in the early 1980s and set up an account in the name of Caviar Ltd. In 1984 and 1985 a sum of £110,000 was paid into Caviar's account from another Channel Islands-registered company, owned by Brennan and McGowan along with estate agent John Finnegan. At least £60,000 of this money was linked to a property deal in Sandyford in Co. Dublin, which was supported by Burke.[14]

As more information about Burke's murky dealings emerged at the Flood tribunal, the Moriarty tribunal began the process of reading Haughey's final days of evidence into the record. This evidence had been given in private in the early months of 2001 because of Haughey's deteriorating health due to prostate cancer. This evidence produced no significant new information, but Haughey did take serious issue with the interpretation which had been put on some of the disclosures about his use of the Fianna Fáil party leader's account. In particular, he defended his actions in setting up a fund for Brian Lenihan's liver transplant operation. 'I think it is absolutely preposterous that this whole genuine charitable effort on my part should now, 20 years or so later, be sought to be turned against me in a most cruel fashion ... The fact is that I, to save my friend's life, took the initiative, instituted the raising of funds, all of which funds were spent in his best interests and I did not, and couldn't and wouldn't divert one penny of those funds to any other purpose.'[15]

Haughey, though, was clearly a far cry from the domineering figure of old. At one stage he told tribunal lawyers: 'I am increasingly forgetful and I say with absolute sincerity I am mentally and physically incapable of dealing in any satisfactory way with the vast amount of documentation that I'm expected to do. I look forward to the period immediately ahead greatly perturbed.'[16]

In political terms the remarkable thing was not the continuing and humiliating revelations about Haughey and Burke, but the fact that their disgrace had no discernible impact on the party they dominated for so long or on their protégé, Bertie Ahern. It seemed that the public was punch-drunk with tribunal revelations and wished to consign the events to the past. Opinion polls showed Fianna Fáil holding solid and, if anything, gaining ground in the final days of May.

However, just when politicians of all parties had agreed that the tribunals were not going to be a factor in electoral politics, the public delivered a stinging rebuke to the entire political establishment by voting No to the referendum on the Nice Treaty on 7 June 2001. All the major parties backed the treaty to facilitate the enlargement of the EU, but the rejection was particularly damaging for the Government who advocated a Yes vote. Ahern and his ministers waged a dismal campaign, totally lacking in conviction. This was hardly surprising as a number of ministers had expressed veiled anti-EU sentiments over the previous 12 months and Minister for Finance Charlie McCreevy had engaged in loud bickering with the Commission in Brussels over the thrust of his tax-cutting budgets. Against that background, most Fianna Fáil ministers and TDs simply opted out of the campaign and many of the party's supporters voted No. The admission by junior Agriculture Minister Éamon Ó Cuiv, on the day of the count, that he had voted No pointed up the shambles that had been the Government campaign. The confusion at the heart of the Government about Ireland's place in Europe was exposed at the subsequent EU summit in Gothenburg a week after the referendum. Ahern and his Foreign Minister, Brian Cowen, tried to reassure other EU leaders and calm things down, only to have their efforts nullified by McCreevy who declared deliberately that the No vote was 'a remarkably healthy development.'[17]

The Nice debacle was followed later that month by a crushing by-election defeat for Fianna Fáil in Tipperary South, exactly 12 months after its previous defeat in the constituency. This time Senator Tom Hayes of Fine Gael romped home at the top of the poll and Fianna Fáil candidate Michael Maguire was forced into third place on the final count. The result marked the sixth by-election loss in a row for Fianna Fáil during the lifetime of the Ahern government and led to a serious reassessment about the real indicator of Fianna Fáil's electoral position: was it the consistently healthy opinion poll ratings or the disastrous by-election results?

Just to make things worse, the peace process, to which the government had devoted so much time and effort for four years, lurched into another crisis at this juncture. The relationship which Ahern had cultivated with Sinn Féin since taking over the Fianna Fáil leadership at the end of 1994 failed to produce the decisive move from the republican movement in relation to putting IRA weapons beyond use. The issue had been kicked to touch again and again, but the moment of truth could not be postponed indefinitely and matters came to a head on 1 July 2001 when David Trimble resigned as Northern First Minister because of the IRA failure to meet its obligations on decommissioning. To add to Fianna Fáil's woes, Sinn Féin appeared to be making significant inroads in the Republic, having advanced their position significantly in the Westminster elections in May 2001.

In late July Liam Lawlor was hauled back before the High Court for again failing to cooperate fully with the Flood tribunal. While he had provided more than 25,000 documents since his initial week in Mountjoy, the tribunal still believed he was withholding vital material. Mr Justice Smyth ordered the TD back to jail for another seven days, saying, 'The rot has got to stop.' The judge added that telling the whole truth was 'not an optional extra' and giving evidence under oath was 'not one of the performing arts'. The supreme court subsequently gave Lawlor a stay of execution but the long drawn-out saga put another dent in the credibility of Irish politics.

The combination of setbacks suffered by Fianna Fáil in the summer of 2001 raised questions about whether the party's luck was finally running out. Various straws in the wind, but particularly the successive by-election losses, capped by the Nice referendum defeat, indicated that the voters were growing increasingly disillusioned with their political leaders. One worrying aspect of the rejection of the Nice Treaty was that a great many people appeared to be losing faith in the entire political system. The scandals uncovered by the tribunals may not have inflicted as much damage on Fianna Fáil as might have been expected, but they eroded the authority of the political establishment. The winners in the Nice referendum were Sinn Féin, the Greens, various left-wing groups and conservative Catholics like Dana Rosemary Scallon, all of whom had urged a No vote. The result raised serious questions about the future shape of Irish politics and the country's status as a progressive, outward-looking member of the EU. The collapse of authority arising from the disgraceful behaviour of some leading politicians could ultimately have profound consequences for Irish democracy.

CONCLUSION

FIANNA FÁIL HAS CONFOUNDED IT CRITICS TIME AND AGAIN by its ability to retain its status as the dominant political party in the country despite all the traumas, divisions and corruption of the past 30 years. The party did not disintegrate like the Italian Christian Democrats or even suffer the electoral reversals endured by the British Conservatives or the French Socialists, who were sharply punished by voters for their excesses during long periods in office. Yet there were signs, as the first year of the new millennium progressed and the flood of revelations about sleaze and corruption continued unabated, that the patience of the Irish electorate was beginning to wear thin.

For the first time since he took over as leader in 1994 serious questions were raised about whether Bertie Ahern was capable of leading the party out of the morass into which Haughey had dragged it. Ahern has inextricable links to the Haughey era and was The Boss's anointed successor. Events of the past came back with depressing regularity to haunt him during his first years in office and Fianna Fáil TDs began to wonder if there would ever be an end to it. Some even began to have doubts about whether Ahern's style as the supreme pragmatist was appropriate to the position they found themselves in and they began to hanker after the principles and sense of honour that had inspired the party's founders. The problem is that Fianna Fáil's defining characteristic in recent decades has been its pragmatism; the party's strength and its weakness has been that it has simply adopted whatever policies suited it at a particular time. Bruce Arnold summed it up the position on the day of Fianna Fáil's first Árd Fheis of the new millennium. 'By not standing for anything very much, they manage to stand for everything. That is the abiding strength of the Fianna Fáil party. And it is more openly true today, under the leadership of Bertie Ahern, than in the past.'[1]

That pragmatic approach has dictated party policy even on such a core value as the aspiration to a united Ireland. Ultimately, Albert Reynolds and Bertie Ahern made the breakthrough in the peace process by jettisoning the approach of their predecessor, Charles Haughey, and accepting that the border would remain as long as the people of Northern

Ireland wanted it. Their real achievement was to bring Sinn Féin along with them to the same conclusion.

The party's economic policy has been more openly pragmatic and has varied with the conditions and, more importantly, with the political imperatives of the day. From the 1930s to the 1960s Fianna Fáil espoused the values of those living on the land. From the 1960s it became the party of industrialisation, winning support from urban workers and public servants. For most of the 1970s and 1980s the party was for massive exchequer spending and state intervention but, after 1987, it adopted the fiscal rectitude espoused by Fine Gael, as much because it needed Fine Gael acquiescence to remain in office as because it was the right thing to do. In the 1980s and early 1990s the party was totally opposed to privatisation because of its close links with the trade union movement and because it was in coalition with Labour from 1992 to 1994. In the late 1990s, however, when in coalition with the free market PDs, the party espoused wholesale tax cuts and privatisation.

The pragmatic approach to policy was even more starkly illustrated in the context of legislation on social issues. In the 1970s Fianna Fáil was against contraception, but for it in the 1980s. In the 1980s it was against divorce, but for it in the 1990s. In the 1980s it was against abortion in any circumstances, but became a little more flexible about it in the 1990s while still retaining links with the Pro-Life movement. In short, the party followed the voters rather than led them and by doing so managed to avoid alienating any significant segment of the electorate.

It is the near total absence of fixed principles in modern Fianna Fáil which has made the cult of leadership so important in the party. Loyalty to the leader has always been the supreme virtue in Fianna Fáil while disloyalty has been the biggest sin. It was the cult of uncritical loyalty which allowed Haughey to dominate the party so easily during his term in office. The same cult allowed respective leaders to write and rewrite the history of the party to suit their purposes with Stalinist indifference to the facts. When Haughey was leader, Jack Lynch was virtually written out of the party's history. Árd Fheis speeches paid florid tribute to de Valera and even more to Lemass, but Lynch was barely mentioned. Neither was he invited to attend Árd Fheiseanna as befitted his status as former leader, although it is doubtful, in any case, if he would have desired to go. It was not until Reynolds took over in 1992 that Lynch's 13 years as leader were suddenly remembered and he was invited back to the annual jamboree.

The same process in reverse has occurred since the accession of Ahern. In his early years as leader Ahern paid tribute to Haughey, but as the former leader's disgrace became greater the references to him diminished. By the time of the 2000 Árd Fheis, held a few months after the death of Lynch, history had been rewritten again. Lynch was now elevated into the pantheon of Fianna Fail heroes while Haughey barely rated a mention, and neither, for that matter, did Reynolds. Such writing of figures in and out of the party history is done without a blush. There was indignation in Fianna Fáil when the founder of the Progressive Democrats, and by common consent the best Taoiseach the country never had, Des O'Malley, who had been driven out of the party by Haughey, was invited by Máirín Lynch to deliver the oration at Lynch's graveside in December 1999. It was a commentary on what Lynch felt about the party which had turned its back on him and treated him with such scant respect.

In his graveside oration, O'Malley said: 'When a great statesman passes away, it is traditional to ask what political legacy he has left behind him. The Lynch legacy is manifold but, if you want to know his most important legacy, I would say: look around you. For the safe existence of this democratic State in which we live today is very much Jack Lynch's political legacy. Thirty years ago as a nation, we were confronted with a stark choice. We could have caved in to sinister elements and put our country at mortal risk. Jack Lynch chose not to. When he came to the crossroads of history 30 years ago he knew which turn to take. Confronted with some of the most difficult decisions to face any Taoiseach of the modern era, he took determined and resolute action to defend democracy and to uphold the rule of law. Upon such foundations are freedom and prosperity built. Had this country taken the wrong turn 30 years ago, I fear to think what might have befallen us. We didn't and for that alone Jack Lynch deserves his place in history.'[2]

O'Malley's oration was an unambiguous attack on those in Fianna Fáil who had worked so hard to undermine Lynch. Yet, despite the insult, the leadership of Fianna Fáil, including some of the very people who had worked to undermine Lynch in 1979, had no problem about appropriating his memory for the party's benefit at the Árd Fheis of 2000. It is that pragmatic ruthlessness which has made the party such a powerful force. 'We also remember this year the late Jack Lynch, a leader whose integrity and innate decency will always be deeply treasured,' Bertie Ahern told the Árd Fheis, following a filmed tribute to the former leader.[3]

Because it has held office for so long, Fianna Fáil has been able to entrench itself at every level of Irish society. Its extensive use of patronage has enabled the party to reward party supporters and to establish a network of influence at all levels. Tom Kettle's famous remark that when in office the Liberals forget their principles and the Tories remember their friends could easily be adapted by substituting Fianna Fáil for the Tories. The party has been in a position to appoint successive generations of judges, senior civil servants, semi-state bosses, and a wide range of other public officials. Many of these posts have nominally been removed forom political control in recent years, but the government almost always gets the man or woman it wants and, as Fianna Fáil is very rarely out of office, it calls most of the shots. The appointment of Hugh O'Flaherty was very much part of this pattern of the party looking after its own regardless of the consequences. Liz O'Donnell summed up the appointment as "misplaced political patronage."

The unbalanced nature of Irish democracy has fostered the culture of patronage in politics. This is not unique to Ireland or Fianna Fail. The Italian Christian Democrats, who were in power virtually uninterrupted for half a century, eventually collapsed under the weight of their own corruption. Rampant sleaze developed during the 16-year rule of the Conservative Party in Britain and the 14-year reign of President Mitterrand in France. The similarly long reign of the German Christian Democrats encouraged law-breaking by politicians to raise funds illegally. In the north of England and Scotland, Labour-dominated local authorities have equally succumbed to the virus. The common denominator in all cases was that parties held power without interruption for far too long. A healthy democracy requires regular changes of government and that has simply not happened in Ireland. In 1989 Fianna Fáil made a forced transition from single-party government to being the senior partner in coalition administrations, but it retained its position as the dominant party. In the 69 years since 1932 the party has held office for over 50. In the democratic world only the Mexican Institutional Revolutionary Party (PRI) has governed for longer and it is no accident that that country became a by-word for patronage and corruption. In July 2000 the 71 years of continuous rule by the PRI in Mexico was brought to an end with the election of President Vincente Fox who, incidentally, traces his ancestry to Ireland.

Fianna Fáil's problem in 2001 is that pragmatism has been at the core of the party's attitude for so long that it has difficulty formulating anything but a short-term response to the revelations about the culture of corruption which has flourished under Haughey. The party leader, Bertie Ahern, personifies the strength and weakness of making pragmatism the ultimate political principle. On the one hand, his popularity ratings, as measured by opinion polls, have remained at extraordinary heights because he always seeks to agree with the public mood. He famously even said that he agreed with the public for disagreeing with his government's decision to appoint Hugh O'Flaherty to the European Investment Bank.[4] The downside of this approach is that Fianna Fáil has been unable to come to terms with the sense of shock felt by a considerable number of people in Irish society at the revelations about the vast scale of the corruption which permeated public life during the Haughey years. 'The party has learned to regard scandals as passing storms. Though full of noise and wind they leave the essential landscape unaltered. The media whip up outrage, the public gets swept along and sometimes someone has to resign. But when it all blows over nothing matters except bottom-line economics,' wrote Fintan O'Toole.[5]

It is arguable that Haughey was as much a symptom as a cause of what went wrong with Fianna Fáil, although his unique blend of intelligence, charisma, greed and unscrupulousness brought the party, and the country, to its current state. The great Victorian writer, Anthony Trollope, summed up the effect on society of corruption at the top of the political and business world: 'A certain class of dishonesty, dishonesty magnificent in its proportions and climbing into high places has become at the same time so rampant and so splendid that there seems to be reason for fearing that men and women will be taught to feel that dishonesty, if it can become splendid, will cease to become abominable. If dishonesty can live in a gorgeous palace with pictures on all its walls and gems in all its cupboards, with marble and ivory in all its corners, and can give Apician dinners, and get into Parliament and deal in millions, then dishonesty is not disgraceful and the man dishonest after such a fashion is not a low scoundrel.'[6]

In Ireland in the 1970s, 1980s and 1990s there were enough people around who shared the view that dishonesty on a vast scale was something to be admired. It was only after Haughey retired that the public learned about his offshore accounts and the handouts involving millions of pounds from a gallery of leading Irish business figures. In a sad and ignominious end to his career, the details of Haughey's financial affairs were still being disentangled by the Moriarty tribunal in the autumn of 2001. Yet, despite his final disgrace, there is no getting away from the fact that for three decades Haughey represented a significant segment of the Irish electorate which was not particularly worried about how he behaved, and he certainly touched a chord with the Fianna Fáil faithful that Lynch never reached. His traditional nationalism, his anti-British rhetoric, his flight from economic reality all appealed to something deep in the Fianna Fáil psyche. The party is now paying a price for its long love affair with Haughey. The next few years in Irish politics will establish how heavy that price will ultimately be.

FOOTNOTES

ABBREVIATIONS: DD Dail Debates; MA Military Archives; NA National Archives;
NLI National Library of Ireland;

CHAPTER 1

1 Walsh, Dick, *The Party* (1986) p.11
2 op. cit. p.12
3 Moynihan, Maurice, ed. *The Speeches and Statements of Eamon de Valera* (1980) p.145
4 Coogan, Tim Pat, *De Valera* (1993) p.387
5 Longford and O'Neill, *Eamon de Valera* (1970) p.246
6 Collins, Stephen, The Cosgrave Legacy (1996) p.56
7 Lee, Joe, *Ireland 1912-1984* (1989) p.151
8 O'Clery, Conor, *Phrases Make History Here* (1986) p.88
9 *What Fianna Fáil Stands For* (1926)
10 Dwyer, T Ryle, in *Irish Examiner*, 8 March, 2000
11 Collins, p.52
12 Lee p.177
13 Moynihan p.224
14 Boland, John, interview with John Kelly (1990)
15 Moynihan p.466
16 Fianna Fáil and the IRA (1972) NLI (Ir 300 P26)
17 Lee p.514
18 Gallagher and Hannon, ed. *Taking the Long View* (1996) p.12
19 Whitaker Papers, UCD A P175

CHAPTER 2

1 Patrick Hillery interview with author (2000)
2 Walsh p.26
3 *Magill*, June, 1980 p48
4 O'Brien and Dudley Edwards ed. *Conor Cruise O'Brien Introduces Ireland* (1969)
5 Bobby Molloy interview with author (2000)
6 ibid.
7 *Magill*, November 1979 p.37
8 Jack Lynch interview with author (1986)
9 *Magill*, November, 1979 p.36
10 ibid. p.38
11 ibid. p.40
12 ibid.
13 ibid. p.41
14 ibid. p.42
15 *Business and Finance*, August, 1965
16 *Magill*, December, 1979
17 Hillery interview
18 Molloy interview
19 Hillery interview
20 *Magill*, p.42

21 Horgan, John, *Sean Lemass* (1997) p.336
22 Molloy interview
23 ibid.
24 Horgan p.337

CHAPTER 3

1 *Magill*, December, 1979
2 Padraig Faulkner interview with author (2000)
3 *Irish Times*, 25 October, 1999
4 Info from Paddy Creamer, former Limerick hurler
5 Dwyer, T Ryle, *Fallen Idol* (1997) p.32
6 Manning, Maurice, *James Dillon* (1999) p.390
7 Hillery interview
8 *Fianna Fáil and the IRA* (1973) NLI (Ir 320 P 109) p.8
9 Boland, Kevin, *Up Dev* (1977) p.11
10 Arnold, Bruce, *Haughey: His Life and Unlucky Deeds* (1994) p.12
11 Collins p.14
12 *Irish Press*, 16 May, 1986
13 Hillery interview
14 Whitaker Papers UCDA P175
15 Private source
16 Dwyer p.34
17 *Irish Press* 20 June, 1969

CHAPTER 4

1 Letter from private source, October, 1999
2 N.A. 2000/6/658
3 Boland p.11
4 Arnold p.73
5 Boland pp. 42/43
6 N.A. 2000/6/658
7 *Irish Times* 25 October, 1999
8 N.A. 2000/6/658
9 *FF and the IRA* p.14
10 N.A. 2000/6/657
11 Hillery interview
12 N.A. 2000/6/658 and *Irish Press* 14 August, 1969
13 Hillery interview
14 N.A. 2000/6/658
15 Whitaker Papers, UCDA P175
16 Boland p.12
17 Faulkner interview
18 N.A. 2000/6/461
19 N. A. 2000/6/658
20 Hillery interview
21 Lawlor interview with author

CHAPTER 5
1 Faulkner interview
2 Boland p.13
3 ibid. p.14
4 Hillery interview
5 *Sunday Times*, 24 August, 1969
6 Faulkner interview
7 Private source
8 *FF and the IRA* p.55
9 ibid. p.17
10 Hillery interview
11 *Irish Press* 20 August, 1969
12 NA 2000/6/658
13 Peter Berry Diaries, 20 August, 1969, published in *Magill*, June 1980
14 ibid.

CHAPTER 6
1 *FF and the IRA* p.17
2 ibid. p.37
3 ibid. p.39
4 Kelly, James, *The Thimble Riggers* (1999) p. 31
5 ibid. p. 31
6 Berry Diaries, 15 Sept, 1969
7 *Sunday Independent*, 2 January, 2000
8 NA 2000/6/660
9 Hillery interview
10 Faulkner interview
11 Berry Dairies, 5 October, 1969
12 ibid. 4 October, 1969
13 FF and the IRA pp. 33/34
14 Private source.
15 *Private Eye*, 12 September, 1969
16 *Sunday Independent*, 2 January, 2000
17 Whitaker Papers, UCDA P175
18 Hillery interview
19 NA 2000/6/658
20 *Irish Press*, 9 December, 1969
21 Berry Diaries, 29 December, 1969
22 FF and the IRA p.52
23 Boland p.33
24 FF and the IRA p.50
25 Boland p.35
26 Arnold p.84
27 Boland p.72
28 MA File 2, 2001
29 MA File 2
30 *Paddy Bogside*, Paddy Doherty (2001), pp219-226
31 MA File 2
32 MA File 2
33 NA Department of Justice
34 Berry Diaries, 7 October, 1969
35 *Hibernia*, 17 April, 1970
36 FF and the IRA p.56

37 DD 6 July, 2001
38 Berry Diaries, 13 April, 1970
39 Martin O'Donoghue interview with author (2000)
40 Berry Diaries, 17 April, 1970

CHAPTER 7
1 Berry Diaries, 29 April, 1970
2 ibid. 30 April
3 Aiken Papers, UCDA 2341
4 Kelly pp.49/51
5 Berry Diaries, 4 May, 1970
6 Private source
7 Dáil Debates, 5 May, 1970, col. 519
8 Jim Dooge interview with author (1996)
9 *Irish Times*, 30 April, 1998
10 Private source
11 Collins p.103
12 Hillery interview
13 Collins p.106
14 Hillery interview
15 Walsh p.120
16 Hillery interview
17 DD 6 May, 1970 cols. 641/643
18 ibid. cols. 643/645
19 ibid. col.659
20 ibid. 752
21 ibid. 870
22 *Magill*, May, 1980 p.52
23 *Irish Press* 23 and 24 October, 1970
24 Arnold p.82
25 DD, 3 November, 1970, col. 464
26 *Irish Times*, 30 April, 1998
27 Hillery interview
28 Faulkner interview
29 Gallagher and Hannon ed. P.90
30 AG's report on the arms trial, 2001, p.17
31 DD 6 July, 2001

CHAPTER 8
1 Senator James Gibbons interview with author (2000)
2 Arnold p.107
3 FitzGerald, Garret, *All In A Life* pp.96/97 (1991)
4 O'Donoghue interview
5 Collins, Stephen, *The Haughey File* (1992) p.22
6 Mansergh, Martin ed. *The Spirit of the Nation: The Speeches of Charles J. Haughey* (1986) pp.155/156
7 Walsh p.129
8 Arnold p.112
9 Collins, *The Cosgrave Legacy*, p.115
10 ibid. 126
11 Aiken Papers, UCDA 2341

12 ibid. 2339 (II)
13 ibid. 2340 (I)
14 ibid. 2341
15 ibid. 2338 (I)
16 Collins, *The Cosgrave Legacy* p.132

CHAPTER 9
1 FitzGerald p.204
2 Walsh p.137
3 Dwyer p.61
4 Arnold p.137
5 Private source
7 Arnold p.137
7 *Irish Press*, 27 May, 1986
8 Collins, *The Haughey File*, p.25

CHAPTER 10
1 *Irish Press*, 16 May, 1986
2 Collins, *The Haughey File* p.25
3 Arnold pp.148/149
4 Collins p.28
5 Walsh p.140
6 Mairin Quill interview with author (2000)
7 Collins p.28
8 ibid. p.29
9 Walsh p.141
10 Collins p.31
11 ibid. p.32
12 Molloy interview
13 FitzGerald p.339
14 DD, 11 December, 1979, cols. 1327/1328
15 Molloy interview
16 O'Donoghue interview

CHAPTER 11
1 *Sunday Tribune*, 26 September, 1999
2 McDonald, Frank, *The Destruction of Dublin* (1985) p.263
3 Report of the McCracken Tribunal (1997) p.48
4 ibid. p.57
5 *Irish Times*, 17 February, 1999
6 *Evening Press,* 28 January and 1 February, 1983
7 McDonald pp.265/271
8 *Irish Times*, 30 January, 1999
9 *Sunday Times*, 16 May, 1999
10 Private source.

CHAPTER 12
1 O'Donoghue interview
2 Collins pp.34/36
3 *Irish Press*, 22 December, 1979
4 FitzGerald p.342
5 Collins p.40

6 ibid.
7 Whitaker, Ken, *Interests* (1983) p.11
8 *Irish Press*, 18 February, 1980
9 ibid. 9 December, 1980
10 Mansergh ed. P.446
11 ibid. p.519
12 Lenihan, Brian, *For the Record* (1991) pp.16/24

CHAPTER 13
1 *Irish Independent*, 24 February, 1982
2 Collins pp.56/57
3 *Irish Press*, 7 October, 1982
4 *Irish Independent*, 7 October, 1982
5 Joyce and Murtagh, *The Boss* (1983) pp.11/13
6 *Irish Press*, 27 January, 1983
7 Collins p.64
8 *Irish Press*, 28 January, 1983
9 Smith, Raymond, *The Survivor* (1983) p.90
10 *Irish Press*, 10 February, 1982
11 Joyce and Murtagh p.344

CHAPTER 14
1 Molloy interview
2 DD 30 June, 1983, col 979
3 ibid. Col 981
4 FitzGerald p.480
5 Arnold p.221
6 Walsh, Dick, *Des O'Malley* (1986) p.84
7 Mansergh ed. p.913
8 DD 20 February, 1985 col.285
9 *Irish Press*, 29 October, 1985
11 Hussey, Gemma, *Cabinet Diaries* (1990) p.184

CHAPTER 15
1 Mansergh ed. p.1112
2 Collins, p.94
3 *Irish Press*, 23 May, 1987

CHAPTER 16
1 MacSharry, O'Malley, White, *The Making of the Celtic Tiger* (2000) pp.317/323
2 Mansergh ed. p.822
3 *Sunday Press*, 22 November, 1987
4 *Government Procedure Instructions*, 4th Edition (1983)
5 *Irish Press*, 19 June, 1989
6 *Sunday Press*, 5 March, 1989
7 Collins p.146
8 *Irish Press*, 10 March, 1989
9 DD 10 May, 1989 col.2045

CHAPTER 17
1 DD, 1 July, 1998, cols. 1018/1019
2 Collins p.156
3 DD 12 July, 1989, cols. 129, 153

CHAPTER 18
1 *Irish Times*, 26 October, 1990
2 Collins p.182
3 ibid. p.188
4 DD 31 October, 1990, cols 585/586

CHAPTER 19
1 *Sunday Press*, 2 December, 1990
2 ibid. 16 December, 1990
3 ibid. 29 September, 1991
5 *Sunday Tribune*, 20 October, 1991
6 *Irish Press*, 8 November, 1991

CHAPTER 20
1 *Irish Press*, 22 January, 1992
2 ibid. 23 January, 1992
3 Whelan and Masterson, *Bertie Ahern: Taoiseach and Peacemaker* (1998) p.89
4 DD 11 February, 1992, cols. 510/513

CHAPTER 21
1 Duignan, Sean, *One Spin on the Merry-Go-Round* (1995) p.4
2 ibid. p.4
3 Whelan and Masterson p.37
4 ibid. p.95
5 *Sunday Press*, 11 February, 1992
6 ibid.
7 Ryan, Tim, *The Longford Leader* (1994) p.160
8 Whelan and Masterson p.97
9 *Sunday Press*, 11 February, 1992
10 Duignan p.7

CHAPTER 22
1 Duignan p.20
2 ibid. p.40
3 ibid. p.33
4 Major, John, *An autobiography* (1999) p.440
5 ibid.
6 Duignan p.32
7 ibid. p.33
8 ibid. p. 49
9 DD 5 November, 1992 col.2320
10 *Sunday Press*, 22 November, 1992
11 Duignan p.59
12 *Irish Press*, 21 November, 1992

CHAPTER 23
1 Duignan p.70
2 *Sunday Press*, 6 December, 1992
3 Lenihan p.220

4 Collins, Stephen, *Spring and the Labour Story* (1993) p.194
5 ibid. p.195
6 Duignan p.75
7 Finlay, Fergus, *Snakes and Ladders* (1998) p.140
8 Collins p.194
9 Duignan p.85

CHAPTER 24
1 Major pp.447/448
2 ibid. p.448
3 Finlay p.195
4 Major p.450
5 Finlay p.202
6 Major p.252
7 Finlay p.158
8 Duignan p.86
9 Finlay p.264
10 ibid. p.172

CHAPTER 25
1 DD 23 March, 1994, col. 1113
2 Duignan p.112
3 Finlay p.231
4 Duignan pp.113/114
5 ibid. p.114
6 ibid.
7 Finlay p.237
8 DD 31 August, 1994, col. 17
9 ibid. 1 September, 1994, col. 190
10 ibid. col. 224
11 ibid. col. 270

CHAPTER 26
1 Finlay p.241
2 ibid. p.246
3 Duignan p.116
4 ibid. p.132
5 *Sunday Press*, 20 October, 1994
6 Duignan p.134
7 Finlay p.251
8 Duignan p.154
9 Finlay p.264
10 ibid. P.256

CHAPTER 27
1 Duignan p.156
2 *Report of Select Committee on Legislation and Security*, 20 December, 1994, cols. 249/347
3 Duignan p.157
4 DD 15 November, 1994, col 18
5 ibid. cols. 28/29
7 Duignan p.157
8 *Report on Select Committee, 12 January*, 1995, cols. 653/654
9 Duignan p.160
10 *Report on Select Committee*, 20 December, 1994, col. 254
11 ibid. 12 January, 1995, col. 656
12 Finlay p.260
13 *Report on Select Committee*, 5 January, 1995 col.151 and 10 January col.298
14 Duignan p.162
15 DD 16 November, 1994, cols.318/319
16 ibid. col. 357
17 ibid. 17 November cols. 474/484
18 *Sunday Press*, 20 November, 1994

CHAPTER 28
1 *Irish Times*, 18 November, 1994
2 Whelan and Masterson p.50
3 Finlay p.270
4 Whelan and Masterson p.139
5 ibid. p.132

CHAPTER 29
1 *Irish Independent*, 30 November, 1996
2 *Sunday Tribune*, 8 December, 1996
3 *McCracken Report* pp.43/47
5 *Irish Independent*, 4 June, 1999
6 *Irish Times*, 24 May, 1997
7 ibid. 21 July, 1997
8 DD 10 September, 1999, col. 617
9 *McCracken Report* p.106
10 ibid. p.108
11 ibid. p.51

CHAPTER 30
1 *Sunday Tribune*, 21 September, 1997
2 McCarthy, Justine, *Mary McAleese: The Outsider* (1999) p.164
3 ibid. p.171
4 *Sunday Tribune*, 21 September, 1997
5 McCarthy p.181

6 *Sunday Tribune*, 21 September, 1997
7 McCarthy p.184

CHAPTER 31
1 DD 10 September, 1997 cols. 616/638
2 ibid. cols. 675/677
3 *Irish Times*, 4 October, 1997
4 *Magill*, June 1998
5 DD 1 July, 1998 col. 1091
6 ibid. 16 December, 1998 col. 1116
7 *Sunday Independent*, 24 January, 1999
8 DD 27 January, 1999 cols. 45/82
9 *Sunday Tribune*, 2 May, 1999
10 DD 10 February, 1999, cols. 386/390
11 *Irish Times*, 17 February, 1999
12 *Irish times*, 6 March, 1999
13 *Sunday Times*, 16,23,30 May, 1999
14 *Irish Times*, 16 October, 1999

CHAPTER 32
1 *Irish Independent*, 25 May, 2000-07-2000
2 *Irish Times*, 20 April, 2000
3 ibid. 25 April, 2000
4 Statement by Moriarty tribunal, 24 May, 2000
5 *Irish Times*, 14 June, 2000
6 DD 21 June, 2000 col. 1100
7 *Irish Independent*, 27 May, 2000
8 *Irish Times*, 27 June, 2000
9 *Sunday Tribune*, 2 July, 2000
10 *Irish Times*, 1 July, 2000
11 Statement by Moriarty tribunal, 12 DD 30 June, 2000 col.1315
12 DD 30 June, 2000
13 *Irish Times*, 16 January, 2001
14 *Irish Times*, 16, 17, 18 May, 2001
15 *Irish Times*, 24 May, 2001
16 *Irish Times*, 23 May 2001
17 *Irish Times*, 16 June, 2001

CONCLUSION
1 *Irish Independent*, 4 March, 2000
2 *Irish Times*, 25 October, 1999
3 ibid. 6 March, 2000
4 ibid. 17 June, 2000
5 ibid. 1 July, 2000
6 Trollope, Anthony, *An Autobiography*, (1883) p.324

Index

- Haughey, relationship with, 114;
proposes Haughey for leader
(1979), 119
- telephone tapping controversy,
153, 154-155, 156
Magill magazine, 137, 148, 324
Magner, Pat, 254, 287, 299
Maguire, Conor, 270
Mahony, Denis, 127
Major, John, 245, 260, 295, 309
- and peace process: meeting with
Haughey (1991), 260; negotiations
with Reynolds, 262-263; Downing
Street Declaration (1993), 263;
IRA ceasefire (1994), 274
Malone, Bernie, 267
Malone, Joe, 327
Mansergh, Martin, 91, 162-163, 253,
259, 281, 285
- and presidential election contest
(1997), 314, 316
Mansergh, Nicholas, 162
Mara, P.J., 97, 106, 154, 182,
183-184, 190, 206, 208, 210, 215,
216, 217, 219, 221, 226, 295, 297,
315, 339
- career, 160-161; appointed FF
press officer (1984), 161
- director of elections (1997 campaign), 305-306
- Haughey's eyes and ears, 162
- personality, 161, 162
- relaxed style, 161-162
Martin, Micheál, 301, 307, 331
- Minister for Education (1997-),
308
Mater Hospital (Dublin), 236, 297
Meany, Tom, 112
meat-processing industry. See Beef
industry; Beef tribunal
media. see also RTE and individual
newspapers
- Ahern, relations with, 237
- Haughey, relations with, 40-41,
106, 149, 159-160, 215, 222;
FitzGerald's 'flawed pedigree'
speech (1979), 120
- Reynolds, relations with, 235-236,
243
Merchant Banking Ltd., 129
Mexican Institutional Revolutionary
Party, 346
Mills, Michael, 46, 82, 89, 90
Mitchell, George, 324

Mitchell, Jim, 95, 269, 339
Mitterand, President, 346
Molloy, Bobby, 85, 99, 167, 187,
196, 197, 199, 200, 219, 220, 229
- Colley, views on, 30, 158
- dropped from cabinet by
Haughey, 134
- and FF leadership contests: 1966,
30, 36-37; 1979, 118, 119, 121
- joins Progressive Democrats, 169,
170
Morgan, Donagh, 240
Moriarty, Michael (High Court
judge), 322
Moriarty tribunal, 128, 129, 131,
132, 193, 236, 322, 327-329,
339-341, 347
- Ahern's evidence to, 193, 328,
336-337
- Haughey payments and lifestyle,
327-328, 332
- Kavanagh payment issue, 335-336
Morrison, Bruce, 273
Moylan, Sean, 22, 33
Mulhern, John, 187
Murphy, Brian, 205
Murphy, Joseph, Jr, 308
Murphy, Ned, 81
Murphy, Paul, 289
Murray, Frank, 270, 272, 285
Murray, John, 195
Murtagh, Peter, 151

Nally, Derek, 323
Nally, Dermot, 138
National Archives, 59, 70, 91
national debt, 139, 145, 171
National Irish Bank, 326-327, 339
National Lottery, 172
national pay agreements
- Programme for Economic and
Social Progress (PESP), 216
- Programme for National Recov-
ery, 179-180
nationalism. See Irish nationalism
Nazi war effort
- republican support for, 20
NCB Stockbrokers, 181, 218
Neeson, Eoin, 82, 137
New Ireland Assurance Company,
62
New Ireland Forum (1983-84),
159-160, 175, 314
Ní Cheallaigh, Máire, 101

Nice Treaty referendum, 341-342
98FM, 239
Nolan, M.J., 211, 218
non-jury courts, 99
Noonan, Michael (Fianna Fail TD),
197
Noonan, Michael (Fine Gael TD),
153, 176, 182, 188, 228, 339
Noraid, 142
North-South relations, 22-23
Northern Ireland, 7, 8, 254. See also
Northern 'Troubles'; Partition;
Peace process
- Anglo-Irish Agreement (1985),
143, 167-168, 173
- Boundary Commission report, 14
- civil rights campaign, 41, 42, 44
- discrimination, 42
- Fianna Fáil policies, 7, 14, 20, 22,
41-44, 344; De Valera, 7, 14, 20,
22; Lemass, 8, 22-23, 41-42;
Lynch, 42, 47, 48-93. See also
Arms crisis (1970); 1975 policy
document, 107-108; Haughey's
views, 42-44, 48, 68, 97-98,
107-108, 109, 142, 160, 167, 173,
182, 260, 344. See also under
Haughey, Charles
- Lemass-O'Neill meetings, 22-23
- peace process. See Peace process
- territorial claim (Article 2 of Irish
Constitution), 23, 324
- united Ireland, aspirations for. See
United Ireland
Northern 'Troubles', 7, 41
- 1956-62 IRA border campaign, 23,
29, 41-42, 44
- 1969-70 crisis, 41-44, 47-61;
Derry riots (1969), 47, 48, 50;
Whitaker's views, 43-44, 52-53,
67, 68; Lynch's television address
(August 1969), 48-50; Irish
demands for UN intervention, 50,
51, 52, 54; British Army intervention, 51-52; Republic's aid fund for
victims, 55-61, 94-95; arms importation conspiracy, 8, 9, 39, 58-93,
94, 106. See also Arms crisis; IRA
resumption of violence (1969), 60;
Lynch's Tralee speech (September
1969), 67-68
- 1971-91: internment, 97, 98; Sunningdale Agreement, 107; murder
of British Ambassador, 108;